Capitalism
and
Equality
in the
Third World

MODERN CAPITALISM
Volume II

Capitalism and Equality in the Third World

Edited by

Peter L. Berger

**INSTITUTE FOR
EDUCATIONAL AFFAIRS**

Hamilton Press

LANHAM • NEW YORK • LONDON

Copyright © 1987 by

Hamilton Press

4720 Boston Way
Lanham, MD 20706

3 Henrietta Street
London WC2E 8LU England

Printed in the United States of America

British Cataloging in Publication Information Available

Library of Congress Cataloging in Publication Data

Capitalism and equality in the Third World.

Bibliography: p.
Contents:　　—v. 2. Modern capitalism.
1. Capitalism—Developing countries.　2. Equality—
Developing countries.　3. Income distribution—
Developing countries.　4. Developing countries—Economic
conditions.　I. Berger, Peter L.
HB501.C24234　1987　　　330.12'2　　86-24749
ISBN 0-8191-5574-8 (v. 2 : alk. paper)
ISBN 0-8191-5575-6 (pbk. : v. 2 : alk. paper)

Co-published by arrangement with the
Institute for Educational Affairs

All Hamilton Press books are produced on acid-free
paper which exceeds the minimum standards set by the National
Historical Publication and Records Commission.

CONTENTS

(VOL. II)

Introduction: Betting on Capitalism

Peter L. Berger

MODERN CAPITALISM was made in Europe. It decisively shaped European societies and their offspring in other parts of the world, such as North America. Thus there is some justification for the fact that "Western" and "capitalist" are cognate terms for many people today. Yet any discussion of capitalism, in any of its aspects, that limits itself to Western societies has only limited intellectual weight. There is, of course, the massive fact that a substantial portion of mankind now lives under regimes that call themselves socialist; whatever that term means, it certainly means that these are not capitalist societies, and that negative quality constitutes an important aspect of their legitimacy. Comparison between contemporary socialist and capitalist societies must be an important analytic task, especially in Europe, where the two types of societies confront each other in stages of economic development that make such comparison meaningful (it makes sense to compare the two Germanies; it makes little sense to compare Denmark and Albania). But the discussion of contemporary capitalism must also take due cognizance of the large number of countries now conveniently if ambiguously subsumed under the category "Third World".

This is so, no matter whether the discussion is with reference to the Marxist or neo-Marxist theories about this group of countries or whether the discussion follows a different logic. Ever since

1

Lenin and Rosa Luxemburg, the idea that the prosperity and even survival of the advanced capitalist societies depends upon the exploitation of what was then called the colonies has been a mainstay of Marxist theory. Today it is of high political significance far beyond the Marxist camp, properly speaking. In various reincarnations (such as "dependency theory" and "world-system theory") it not only dominates large areas of Western academia, but it has become an important source of legitimacy for Third World regimes, many of which can only be called Marxist or socialist by stretching these terms to the utmost. However, even if one wishes to discuss capitalism without reference to this particular theoretical syndrome, the Third World—empirically, the poorer countries of Asia, Africa and Latin America—is of very great importance. The reason for this is simple. These countries constitute a gigantic laboratory, in which different "models" of capitalist and non-capitalist development have been engineered ever since the breakup of the old colonial empires in the wake of World War II. They thus invite, even necessitate, comparison.

The focus of the present project is an investigation into the relationship of capitalism and equality—or, to use less ideologically charged terms, into the equity consequences of capitalism. The preceding volume in this series dealt with the case of America—certainly the biggest and arguably the most important case of a capitalist society. As was to be expected, the findings of this investigation were complex and not readily squeezed into the simple formulas of political advocacy. Yet the overall conclusion that most readers are likely to arrive at is that the equity effects of American capitalism are high, regardless of whether one compares present day American society with its own past or with other comparable societies (such as the more redistributionist societies of Western Europe). Even this conclusion, though, does not imply that the American "model" can be exported to any other place in the world or, if it can be exported, that it will produce the same equity effects. After all, the history of the United States is unusual. Capitalism is but one of its many ingredients. Other ingredients may be just as important or more important in having led to these effects—the democratic institutions derived from England, the Puritan religious and moral heritage, the values and sensibilities of an immigrant society, and so on. In sum, concluding that American capitalism has strongly egalitarian features in no way prejudges the question of how capitalism relates to equality elsewhere.

James O'Leary's chapter discusses the manner in which Marxist-Leninist theory, mostly in considerably vulgarized form, has become a worldwide ideology. Whatever its intellectual merits, it serves as a useful foil for an objective analysis of capitalist development. It is, of course, virulently anti-capitalist, but it is perfectly appropriate to take its major propositions and look upon them as empirical hypotheses to be supported or disproved by the available evidence. O'Leary is interested in one aspect of this ideology, namely its function in legitimating various Third World regimes and their policies. The ideology is highly visible on the international scene today, especially within the United Nations system, where Third World governments have been pushing an agenda of "North/South dialogue" or "global negotiations," a process supposed to lead to a "New International Economic Order." The root proposition here, of course, is that the present international economic order is unjust in that it is based on exploitation. Obviously this proposition, if accepted as empirically and morally valid, legitimates a miscellany of economic demands made by Third World governments on Western governments and on international economic institutions. The same ideology, however, serves domestic legitimating functions as well. Whatever idealistic visions of the future may be projected, socialist as against capitalist development policies mean a stronger role for government in the economy today. Many if not most Third World regimes today are highly statist, and those who administer these regimes stand to gain from any development strategy that emphasizes the paramount role of the state. Thus anticapitalism has a very direct (and, alas, vulgar) political function.

It would be a fundamental error, nevertheless, if one allowed an understanding of this ideological functionality to divert one from taking seriously the criticisms that have been leveled against capitalism in the Third World. To say that a proposition serves an ideological function is not *ipso facto* to say that it is false. For example, the proposition that bypass surgery prolongs the life of cardiac patients is clearly functional in enhancing the income and the status of heart surgeons; it does not follow from this that the proposition is empirically invalid. The most important proposition of what may loosely be called the new Third World ideology is that capitalist development is bad for its putative beneficiaries, or at least for most of them (the ideology allows for what neo-Marxists call a *comprador* class, an indigenous bourgeoisie that serves as agent for imperialist interests and that shares in the exploitation of its compatriots). "Bad" here implies, above all, distributionist factors. Thus it is proposed that capitalist development in the Third World fails to raise the living standards of the masses and that it accentuates gross inequalities in these societies.

In sum, the proposition is that capitalist development fails on the grounds of its equity effects.

This proposition should be accepted in the sense that it be converted into a master hypothesis. At that point, of course, it ceases to be a dogma and becomes an empirically testable hypothesis. This was precisely the methodological assumption of the present project. All the chapters in this volume, then, may be taken as explorations of this master hypothesis. One may, if one wishes, go one step further. Liberation theologians have been proclaiming the so-called "preferential option for the poor." Stripped of neo-Marxist esotericisms, what this means is that the condition of the poor should be the basic moral criterion for evaluating any society or social strategy. This is a morally plausible suggestion. After all, it was Dr. Samuel Johnson (hardly a proponent of liberation theology) who proposed that the condition of the poor was the prime test of civilization. One may agree, thus relating the methodological issue and the moral one.

This is why Nick Eberstadt's chapter is of great importance for the exploration of the aforementioned master hypothesis. He is interested in material standards of living, especially those of the poor. He asks how capitalism measures up by this criterion, especially as compared to the communist societies which claim superiority in this regard (a claim frequently conceded even by those who criticize communist regimes for other reasons, such as violations of human rights and political liberties). Eberstadt is a very careful social scientist; he is nervous about the definition of terms and even more nervous about the reliability of the data that are commonly cited in all the comparisons. Precisely because of this caution, his findings are highly instructive.

As a demographer, Eberstadt's focus is on what he calls the "physiology" of poverty rather than on economic measures by themselves. The wisdom of such a procedure becomes evident when one reflects that, for example (and what an example), a decline in mortality shows up as a negative factor in statistics on income distribution; conversely, high mortality (which, of course, wipes out especially the children of the poor) can end up as a statistically positive indicator of more equitable income distribution. Facets of this "physiology" are demographic trends, nutrition (where he makes a useful distinction between chronic and acute hunger), literacy, the status of women (an important factor in terms of poverty—groups in which half the population are prevented from productive contributions greatly diminish their chances of development), and material or social inequality. Put simply, what this "physiological" approach does is to draw attention to the actual lives of human beings rather than to dwell on what may be called the macro-abstractions.

Eberstadt's findings are not dramatic. In all the areas enumerated above, he concludes that the data do not support the notion that communist regimes have accelerated the decrease in these inequalities. What they have done is to politicize them. Put simply, whereas before there were inequalities of class, there now are inequalities of political status. This does not mean that there has been no progress toward equity in at least some communist societies (one curious case of relative success, which particularly interests Eberstadt, is North Korea). Indeed, given the tremendous power of modern technology in improving human life, it would be very surprising indeed if there were no progress at all even in societies whose development strategies are counterproductive; thus the deterioration of agricultural productivity in most communist societies constitutes a remarkable political "achievement." Nevertheless, Eberstadt's cautiously formulated findings are startling in their implications. For example (again, an example of profound significance), he does not deny that communist Cuba has reduced certain inequities and has improved the "physiological" condition of the poor. He adds, though, that Cuba's scores on the above indicators in, say, 1980 could have been predicted in 1960 (that is, *before* the communist takeover) by extrapolating from the data of 1950. This does no more, but also no less, than liquidate the favored legitimation of the Castro regime; in other words, the improvements in the condition of the poor could have been had, given continued technological progress, under *any* political system that was not downright mad, and that means that it could have taken place without the totalitarian terror imposed on the Cuban people by the communist regime. Put differently, Eberstadt unmasks a favored legitimation of communism as a fallacy of *post hoc propter hoc*. Positively, he concludes that market forces are most likely to pull people out of poverty in the long run.

Gustav Papanek also concentrates on the effects of different development strategies on the poor, though, as an economist, he does concern himself with income distribution. Unlike Eberstadt, though, he excludes communist countries from his purview, limiting himself to differences between non-communist countries. It should be noted that Papanek is critical of the so-called "Kuznets thesis," to which most of his fellow economists continue to give credence—namely, the thesis that capitalist development (and possibly socialist development as well) promotes high growth at the cost of rising inequality in income distribution, though the latter will tend to level off at a later stage in development. Papanek believes that, by introducing variables that Simon Kuznets did not consider, a somewhat different picture emerges.

Papanek sees a certain amount of conflict between growth and equality, but only slight evidence that development strategies relying on the market increase such conflict. In other words, whatever may be the driving force of the "Kuznets effect," it is unlikely to be capitalism. Therefore, there is little support for the idea that government intervention is needed to lessen income inequalities in the early stages of development. Positively, income distribution appears to be more equal with widespread education, with deconcentration in the ownership of assets (especially land), and in countries that are not heavily reliant on primary exports. Although he does not spell out policy prescriptions in any detail, it seems to follow that government policies designed to reduce income inequalities in the early stages of development, rather than directly fostering redistributionist schemes, would be well advised to push education (or, if one prefers, the development of human resources), land reform and, insofar as feasible, a variegated export strategy. Papanek also believes that income earned from unskilled labor is a very important factor in development—thus adding a "value-free" economic motive to the moral value of the "preferential options for the poor."

Papanek distinguishes between three existing development models, to which he adds a fourth, which is the one he would recommend in most cases. The first is capitalist or market-oriented; the second is also market-oriented, but with government intervention to bring about redistributionist effects; the third is "populist," with substantial government ownership. (One should note that outright socialist models are excluded from this list; it is safe to assume that the criticisms leveled by Papanek against the third model would apply to these *a fortiori*.) The comments made by Papanek on these three existing strategies are of very great interest. The first, he believes, releases forces that make for higher *absolute* incomes for unskilled labor; that is, the economic condition of the poor improves even if there is little change in the *distribution* of income; in the long run, however, there will be a tendency toward equality. The second model seeks to improve the situation of workers by raising their wages and to stimulate investment by holding down capital costs; the (of course unintended) consequence of these policies is to slow growth and to worsen income distribution; one basic reason for this is that the demand for unskilled labor is depressed. The third model is even more distortive, further lowering the demand for unskilled labor; despite the populist claim to represent the poor, these policies are effectively anti-poor.

It is very instructive that Papanek is anything but an apologist for capitalism. Indeed, his recommended strategy is not the first of the above three models, but a fourth synthetic one (which, he acknowledges, rarely exists today). He calls this a strategy of "capitalist production, socialist consumption." Its key ingredient would be government subsidization of *unskilled* labor (thus reversing the usual planning priorities), either directly or indirectly via cheaper food, health services, education and training. He also recommends taxes on the consumption of the rich, and *not* on their income. One may or may not find these recommendations plausible. What is to be observed, though, is that among *existing* development models in the non-communist Third World it is the capitalist model that Papanek finds to be most conducive to the well-being of the poor. One might also observe that the sum total of his recommendations constitute, *au fond*, a modification of this capitalist model by means of highly targeted welfare-state policies, which can only be called "socialist" by stretching that term rather strenuously.

The chapter by Laura Nash and Alan Kantrow is as cautious as Eberstadt's. Multinational corporations have been major villains in Third World ideology. Some of the charges leveled against them are not relevant to the equality/equity focus of the present inquiry. Thus multinationals have been attacked for allegedly fostering dependency, for political interference and for practising corruption (not to mention the issue of putatively nefarious cultural influences). Nash and Kantrow do not deal with these charges. Instead, they focus on the single question of whether multinationals foster inequality. Perhaps the most important contribution of their chapter is that it allows one to see multinationals as a variegated phenomenon rather than as the monolith of neo-Marxist demonology. Thus the authors distinguish between multinationals involved in Third World countries for export and others involved in serving local markets.

It is fair to say that Nash and Kantrow find themselves unable to make general statements about the equity effects of multinationals operating in Third World countries. They should not be faulted for that. These effects are extraordinarily difficult to measure; most of the assertions about these effects, on either side of the argument, are doctrinaire rather than empirically supported. What they do show, by looking at specific cases, is that multinationals have positive equity effects in certain places. These effects are achieved via the emergence of local support structures and other secondary economic benefits. Cases discussed are those of Corning in Indonesia, Unilever in Africa and Philip Morris in Brazil. For example, in the last of these cases one finds the following economic benefits to the host country (all of them with positive equity effects)—retail outlets, agricultural equipment stores, brick making, timber growing, transportation services, extension services, servicing of motor vehicles, subsidiary tobacco treatment, accommodations for tobacco buyers, and the design and fabrication of processing equipment. It is reasonable to assume that, in those sectors of Brazil in which Philip Morris has generated these economic activities, the condition of the poor involved in these activities will have improved. What is more, none of these effects are visible if one simply applies the criterion of "export of profits," which criterion is uniformly favored by radical critics as the single most important measure of "exploitation".

Do multinationals foster inequality in Third World countries? Nash and Kantrow do not allow us to answer this question definitively one way or the other. They do allow us to dismiss the blanket indictment of multinationals in terms of equity effects and they suggest empirical criteria by which, whenever such data become available, these effects can be assessed.

The chapter by Jason Brown is very much "on the ground" in its focus. It deals with an often neglected sector, that of small (often tiny) entrepreneurship in Third World cities. Neglected though it may be by both academics and planners, it is an important sector—and insofar as it is emphatically, indeed exuberantly, capitalist, it must figure in any assessment of capitalist development.

Data, as Brown concedes, are sparse and often impressionistic. All the same, one cannot ignore an activity that, Brown estimates, provides the principal income of between 20% and 50% of the urban labor force in Third World countries. Even the most casual observer notices the phenomenon—all the little stores, stalls, vending carts that clutter the streets and the sidewalks of cities. Brown (who has studied the phenomenon in several countries) notes cross-national similarities. There is the very dominant role of women. There is the preponderance of necessity over choice in motives. There are constraints to either the expansion and durability of these mini-enterprises, but there is also the impressive ability of people to change activities in the wake of a particular failure. There is government indifference and often (especially on the local level) exploitation by corrupt government officials; there is also the consideration that government indifference may be an asset.

Nevertheless, the story told by Brown is a dramatic one. Here is an increasingly important vehicle of the poor to improve their condition. Above all, it is a vehicle by which rural migrants (and especially women) are able to survive in the city, where their children can get a better education and thus improve *their* chances of mobility. Over and over again, in different countries, the education and mobility chances of children are given as the *raison d'être* of this type of economic activity. Beyond this, though, there is a more political function—incipient forms of organization to foster common interests and leading to new self-confidence.

One is impressed by the dynamism of the phenomenon. Some of this is, no doubt, due to the innate capacity of human beings to meet the challenge of adverse circumstance and to apply ingenuity to the task of improving the chances of their children. But some of it is clearly also due to the opportunities provided by a market economy, even at its lowest levels. It is noteworthy that even socialist regimes (such as that in China) have come to appreciate this fact. Socialist regimes, however, tend to want to limit entrepreneurship to precisely those lowest levels, which can also be described as "penny capitalism." Brown leaves us with the question of just what are the relations between this "penny capitalism" and the macro-entreprises discussed, say, by Nash and Kantrow. To what extent do the spinoff effects of large-scale capitalist enterprise stimulate these small-scale businesses? And conversely, to what extent do the latter provide an essential cultural "subsoil" for the development of a capitalist economy? If we knew more answers to these questions, we would also be in a position to assess more adequately the idea that mini-capitalism can creatively coexist with macro-socialism (an idea that Milton Friedman—in, of all places, a talk given in Peking—has recently described as playing with capitalism).

It is precisely these questions that Grace Goodell explores in her perspective of a broadly comparative anthropologist. Her paper too is very much "on the ground," taking a close look at the factor of grassroots organization in capitalist development. With considerable boldness, Goodell turns widely held notions on their head: it is not economic development that lays the groundwork for political participation, as is widely believed, but the sequence is the other way around.

Goodell explores the building blocks of participatory patterns, which later on become participatory institutions with enduring forms (in her formulation, "form follows function"). Such grassroots participation, she claims, is related to the necessary prerequisities of capitalist economies—economic rationality—

predictability, and "conditions conducive to bonding." She concedes that there can be initial spurts of development *without* such patterns, as in all centralized, from-the-top-down strategies of development (capitalist as well as socialist). Later on, however, such patterns are essential for *continuing* efforts, even in the face of (inevitable) disappointments. The grassroots participatory patterns build institutions of accountability and discipline. This building process takes time. It is all the more important that it be in place in the early stages of development; later on, as initial successes are (invariably) followed by periods of frustration, it will probably be too late. In Goodell's analysis, Iran under the Shah's regime is an important and instructive case of from-the-top-down development lacking the necessary socio-cultural "subsoil." Japan is an equally instructive counter-example of development building on such pre-existing patterns of participation.

Goodell's argument should not be confused with an argument for formal political democracy. There can be no doubt that Goodell is in favor of political democracy; indeed, she holds no brief whatever for so-called "development dictatorships." But, as with capitalism, political democracy too requires a socio-cultural "subsoil," or it will be an empty form. In this connection she contrasts India and Taiwan—the former, according to her, having formal political democracy without the underlying participatory structures, the latter still lacking the macro- institutions of democracy but possessing the underlying structures that are capable of evolving toward real democracy. One need not agree with all of Goodell's specific judgments (for example, many analysts of India would reject her view of it) in order to be persuaded by her insistence on the importance of grassroots participation.

Goodell is convinced of the merits of capitalism in improving the condition of the poor; for her, socialism is but one variant of the futile notion that development can be centralized and operated by the state (for the same reason, incidentally, she is critical of multinational corporations and of governments relying on them for development). Her interest is in clarifying the social and cultural conditions that favor capitalist development. The implications of her findings are gradualist.

The case of agriculture in India, analyzed in Myron Weiner's chapter, is of particular interest within the context of our master hypothesis. The Indian economy in its industrial and commercial sectors has been heavily statist; indeed, this statism has been cited by many observers as one of the causes of India's economic difficulties. Agriculture, on the other hand, has been very much capitalist in character. It has also had some remarkable achievements.

Thus agricultural productivity per acre *doubled* from 1950 to 1980, by which date India was self-sufficient in food and was moving toward food exports. That is success by any standard, and the facts are not in question. What has been questioned is the "on the ground" effects of this growth. Specifically, has this growth increased or decreased inequality in the countryside? Has it improved the condition of the rural poor? And does it have the capacity to provide continuing growth, or is it a short spurt to be followed by regression? (The last question is particularly stimulated by the fact that one of the important growth factors has been technological—the so-called "green revolution.") Not surprisingly, critics from the left have proposed that the Indian "agricultural miracle" has benefited the few at the expense of the many, having increased inequality and left poverty untouched if not worsened, and that in any case it will not last.

Weiner carefully examines these propositions. His conclusions are cautious but unambiguous. There is no evidence that the proportion of landless peasants has increased; in most of the country, the number of small holdings has increased (in view of India's population growth, of course, this does not mean that the absolute number of landless people has not increased; it may have). There is no evidence of either an increase or a decrease in the proportional incidence of rural poverty (again leaving aside the question of absolute numbers); there has been growth in the real wages of agricultural workers. There is evidence (from the Punjab, where agricultural growth has been most impressive) that small farms increased productivity almost as much as bigger farms. There is also evidence (again from the Punjab) of improvements in food consumption, clothing, medical care and housing for the poor. This evidence (at least for that region) indicates that the agricultural growth stimulated the entire economy; thus there has been considerable growth in *urban* employment.

Weiner is careful to say that there is no "hidden hand" that guarantees that capitalist agriculture must necessarily improve the condition of the poor. But neither is there evidence that capitalist agriculture must do the opposite. His conclusion is more positive: capitalist agriculture, at least as it has developed in India, increases the chances of improving the condition of both rural and urban poor people. In this connection one ought to keep in mind the immense problems of development in India; Weiner's argument then obtains a certain weight *a fortiori* if one considers capitalist agriculture in a broader cross-national perspective.

The case of Taiwan, analyzed by John Fei and Gustav Ranis, is of very great significance for our master hypothesis. A key ingre-

dient of the theories proposing that capitalism fosters inequality
has been the notion of a tradeoff between growth and equality
under capitalist conditions—high growth, yes; but at the price of
rising inequality. In a manner not necessarily antagonistic to capitalism as such, the same notion, of course, is suggested by the
"Kuznets thesis" (though that thesis predicts more egalitarian
effects in the long run). Taiwan, along with some other capitalist
societies in East Asia, challenges this tradeoff notion.

Taiwan has had remarkable growth, which continues to date.
Between 1952 and 1980, its average growth rate was 6%. At the
same time, Taiwan has radically improved the condition of its
poor and it has a highly egalitarian income distribution. To put
this in comparative perspective, Fei and Ranis point out that in
1960 in both Taiwan and Colombia the income share of the
bottom 20% of households was 5%; by 1970, it had risen to 8.8%
in Taiwan and fallen to 3.2% in Colombia. It is comparisons such
as this one that have led analysts to speak of an "East Asian model"
in sharp distinction to a "Latin American model." (It may be
observed in passing that it is precisely for this reason that Marxist
and neo-Marxist interpretations carry more persuasiveness in
Latin America than elsewhere in the Third World.)

The obvious question is how Taiwan (along with other East
Asian societies, such as South Korea) has managed to bring off
this "anti-Kuznets" trick. Fei and Ranis seek to answer the question
qua economists. They point out that an industrial export-oriented
development strategy was adopted in the 1950's after intensive
debates; that is, this development did not "just happen," but was
the result of conscious political decisions. The course was chosen
because Taiwan found itself in a situation of low natural resources
and what the authors call "high human resources." Factors tending toward equity, according to the authors, include a consistent
government policy favoring market forces, the rapid absorption
of unskilled labor into all sectors of the economy (here they echo
Papanek's insistence on the importance of this factor), the spatial
decentralization of industrial expansion (spread over the island
rather than concentrated in the Taipei area), and, last but not
least, the improvement of agricultural incomes (in both absolute
and relative terms) during the 1950's and 1960's in the wake of a
comprehensive land reform.

Fei and Ranis make only passing reference to possible cultural
factors in all of this. They are economists and they should not be
faulted for not straying into other disciplines' preserves. But it is
quite clear that their phrase "high human resources" is much too
vague to serve any explanatory purpose. Taiwan, after all, is

populated by Chinese, and it is to Chinese social and cultural patterns that one must look to put content into this phrase. It is here that Grace Goodell's perspective is of paramount importance. The question of cultural influences on East Asian development generally (beginning with Japan) is much discussed today. However one will eventually want to answer it, exploration of the question is very necessary to round out the economic picture drawn by Fei and Ranis.

The question is taken up in Brian and Rachel Griffiths' discussion of the variables of success and failure in development. Like the other authors in this volume, they readily count equity (in the sense of increasing prosperity reaching all people in a society) as one of the key criteria of success. They have no hesitation in being definite about the economic and political variables; these add up, in essence, to pro-capitalist policies. They are more hesitant in terms of the cultural variables, but their chapter clarifies the sort of questions one ought to ask in this area, and that in itself is a very helpful step.

The Griffiths' comparison is between the West and East Asia on one hand and Africa on the other. They argue that the cultural (and especially the religious) traditions of the former two regions foster individuality and personal responsibility, an acceptance of nonegalitarian outcomes of economic effort, and rational attitudes toward the physical world and toward gaining control over human life. By contrast, they argue, African culture fosters contrary orientations. One is entitled to be skeptical about the details of this argument. For example, can it be said that East Asian culture fosters individuality? For another example, if African culture has the overall qualities assigned to it by the Griffiths, how is one to explain the economic success of groups such as the Ibo? Nevertheless, one will have to take seriously the Griffithses' conclusion that "if we are seriously concerned with development, there is simply no way in which all cultures can be given equal protection and promotion." It will also be well to keep in mind, though, that cultures are not worthy of "protection and promotion" only, or even primarily, in terms of their being conducive to economic development (a point with which the Griffithses certainly agree). There are profound human values, elsewhere as well as in Africa, that do not contribute even one iota to the gross national product. But where the Griffithses must be taken seriously is in their suggestion that those who adhere to economically counter-productive cultural values should be conscious of the tradeoff for which they are opting.

John O'Sullivan also deals with the crucial question of how to

explain economic success, but he also asks what one can do to
foster it. His explanation, very much as the Griffithses', is in terms
of a mix of socio-cultural characteristics and government policies;
success, where it occurs, is the result of an interaction between
these two sets of factors. O'Sullivan's invidious comparison is not
with Africa, but with Latin America. Contrary to the North American stereotype, he emphasizes that what is *not* a factor is an
aversion to hard work; Latin Americans work very hard indeed.
The question rather is the goals and the means of work. O'Sullivan cites such alleged negative characteristics as a reluctance to
work for others, a reluctance to incite envy, an unwillingness to do
low-status work even if it is profitable, suspicion of economic
partners outside the family, and an aversion to taking risks once a
modest fortune has been achieved. *Mutatis mutandis,* one may have
here the same skeptical thoughts one had with the Griffiths' broad
generalizations about African culture. But be this as it may, there
is nothing much that policy-makers can do about culture, any-
where in the world. In terms of what *can* be done, O'Sullivan too
would place his bets on a market system and on government
policies that encourage it. He understands the political difficulties
of such policies in many Third World countries. For this reason,
his recommended approach is gradualist, going from one small
step to another. Three policy areas that he mentions favorably
(also in terms of the donors of development aid) are free trade
zones, entrepreneurial education and assistance to the small-busi-
ness sector.

The volume can be seen as a far-flung exploration of one single
master hypothesis, which was taken over from the critics of capitalism (though, in taking it over, it was converted from an ideological doctrine to a testable hypothesis). This master hypothesis
is that capitalist development fosters inequality. Coupling this
hypothesis with the moral demand that the success of any development model should be assessed in terms of its effects on the
condition of the poor, the critics of capitalism have asserted that
capitalism either does not alleviate or even worsens ("immise-
rates," in Marxist language) the poverty of the lower classes in
Third World societies, and that this is the principal reason why it is
morally unacceptable. Again, most of the authors in the volume
have, explicitly or implicitly, accepted this moral assumption. In
the nature of the case, no reader of the volume will be able to
conclude, definitely and with no residue of doubt, that the master
hypothesis has been disproved. The Third World is vast and
variegated, and the variables to be analyzed are immensely complex. Yet it is fair to say that the evidence gathered here lends very

little support indeed to the master hypothesis. Rather, it tends in the opposite direction—toward the proposition that capitalist development generates powerful equalizing forces, and that it tends to do so more reliably and more humanely than its empirically socialist or statist competitors. If this is so, however, the moral equation changes greatly—and (this is very important) it changes even if one concedes, as one must, that all the data are not yet in. In moral terms, one may quite simply put it this way: *given the evidence thus far, the burden of proof is on the side of the critics of capitalism.* Again in moral terms, this burden should be especially troublesome to those who advocate a "preferential option for the poor."

As one looks at the Third World today, one gets the impression that, as it were, word of all this is getting around. In Asia, the monumental disappointment of the Maoist experiment has deeply impressed many who had been hopefully watching it. In Africa, the less monumental but in some ways more instructive failure of Tanzanian socialism has also been seen as a lesson. In Latin America, there has been a comparable loss of illusions about Cuba. The positive counter-examples are not yet too many, and they tend to cluster in East Asia (in itself a fascinating fact inviting exploration), but they too have made an impression. Finally, as several of the chapters in this volume eloquently testify, there are positive experiences with capitalist development scattered throughout the Third World. It is fair to say that it is much easier to talk objectively about capitalism today in many Third World countries than it was even just a few years ago.

There are no certainties in the social sciences. There are only different degrees of probability. This, of course, presents the policymaker with a painful dilemma. The social scientist can always say, "more research is needed." The policy-maker has no such luxury. He must act under the pressures of the moment (these are urgent indeed in most of these countries) and on the basis of less than conclusive information. In other words, he must gamble. If there is one strong suggestion coming out of the present volume, it is that he will be well advised to bet on capitalism.

Third World Developmentalism

James O'Leary

A. Introduction

CAPITALISM HAS ENDURED from its inception fundamental criticism despite its unrivaled record of material achievement. Religious spokesmen denounced early commercial activities as usurious violation of the ethical codes of "just" price. Industrial capitalism invited the sustained criticism of the historians for its abusive disregard of the worker's welfare, its exploitation of the Dickensian cast of children, women and the infirm, and its flagrant befouling of city and countryside. Marxist theoreticians may adhere to the founder's gospel by lauding the progressive role of capitalists in dismantling the feudal straitjacket which retarded human progress. The Marxists also maintain, however, that the benevolent engine of progress must inevitably beggar its laborers and plunge its frenetic managers into conflict—perhaps global war. Even capitalism's staunchest supporters—Smith, Ricardo and Schumpeter—have pointed to the debilitating effects of the system upon its functionaries and warned of the fragility of capitalist institutions.

Until the post-World War II period, these criticisms remained primarily a debate among the Western intellectuals and the literati, with the isolated foil of Soviet "Socialism in One Country" as an example of benevolent collectivism in contrast to rapacious, depression-prone capitalism. In the West, widespread disaffection during the depression gave way to recovery. The global war effort shunted aside the question of Western capitalism's inevitable decline pending its victory over the fascist perversions of Nazism and Japanese militarism.

This global war effort would preserve the Western capitalist system from direct overwhelming threats and, simultaneously, would stimulate new forces which would ultimately corrode and threaten anew the institutions of Western bourgeois societies. Prosecution of the war in Southeast Europe, South and Southeast Asia, Africa and the Middle East involved cooperation of anti-colonial nationalists with the old colonialists to resist the Japanese and German advance, while the Axis powers proved adroit as well in organizing local nationalist groups to overthrow the Western colonialist yoke. The net result was a double blow to the old colonial system and the heady, emotional, frantic rush toward independence.

Decolonization had the practical effect of greatly multiplying the forces arrayed in opposition to Western-style capitalism. New elites, influenced by their indoctrination into socialism at the universities of the colonizing powers and by organized indoctrination from external communist sources, discovered in the cause of anti-capitalism the only cement which bound together the radically diverse new nations of the post-colonial international system. Virulent anti-capitalist voices within the Western liberal societies assisted this global rhetorical crusade in undermining support for capitalism both within and outside capitalist society.

A critical new element was added to the disaffected intellectuals' perennial distaste for bourgeois capitalism. Global institutions, dominated by disaffected Westernized and/or Communist elites, assumed the vanguard role in combating the doctrines and institutions of capitalism. As a result the anti-capitalist crusade became much more organized, assumed global proportions, consumed huge sums of capital (mostly subscribed by the targeted capitalist societies) and came to represent a virtual consensus of opinion among official spokesmen for the "developing areas." The United Nations system (principally the U.N. General Assembly's Group of 77 and specialized agencies such as UNCTAD, UNESCO and UNIDO) and related fora such as the Nonaligned Nations movement, the reports of the "Brandt Commission" and Jan Tinbergen's "Rio Report" *(Reshaping the International Order)* provided strong organizational support and intellectual respectability (in many circles) for this sustained attack upon capitalism. In the name of a "New International Economic Order" (NIEO) these forces have sought to dismantle the familiar liberal network of global private commercial activities and replace it with a system of tightly managed protectionist states, which in turn are subject to strong supranational planning and coercion.

While the New International Economic Order should not be interpreted as a monolithic program for reform, several common strands of thought appear throughout the NIEO literature. Most importantly, NIEO advocates dismiss, or at best, severely downplay the role of the individual in generating Third World economic activity. In contrast to the capitalist model which sees the individual as the major source of innovation in the production of wealth, the NIEO prototype views the individual as passive and incapable of responding rationally to change. This is especially true of individuals in the rural sector. Large-scale state intervention is viewed as the only means for effecting economic development. In the agricultural sector this implies a strong preference for collectivist schemes in which pricing, production and allocation decisions are made by a central authority.

The agricultural sector, however, is not viewed as a major engine of growth by NIEO proponents. Large-scale, centrally directed industrialization is considered the only means of achieving economic development. Individual entrepreneurship is viewed as antithetical to the creation of a socially just domestic economic order. Because the entrepreneur is working to promote his own welfare he cannot, according to the NIEO paradigm, also promote the welfare of society as a whole. While the activities of the private entrepreneur are exploitative, the activities of the "disinterested bureaucrat" are viewed as promoting social equity and development.

If the state alone can promote the "social good" then the resources to promote economic development must be placed in its hands. Accordingly, all natural resources must be controlled by the state and the activities of multinational corporations must be severely curtailed. The state is assigned the role of managing commodity flows and prices and allocating capital flows. Problems of absorptive capacity are ignored and large-scale state investment is considered the key to rapid development.

On the international side the NIEO calls for equally sweeping reforms. Trapped in a vicious cycle of poverty, the Third World can develop only if the old international economic system which rewarded the exploitative activities of Western industrialized states is replaced by a new centrally planned global system of economic reform. Since Third World poverty is the result of external, systemic factors, control of the global economy must be wrested from the Western entrepreneurs and placed in the hands of the same "disinterested bureaucrats" directing Third World domestic economic development. Again there is an unquestioned faith in the ability of such state bureaucrats to remold economic relations (through, e.g., massive transfers of wealth, commodity cartels and stabilization schemes and comprehensive trade preferences) in order to create a new "socially just" international economic system.

The Western response to this unbridled assault has been docile acceptance, silence or piecemeal criticism of specific components of the NIEO program.[1] There has to date been only passing acknowledgement that the NIEO represents a challenge to the fundamental tenets of Western industrial society. Indeed, the political and economic philosophy of the West has been most systematically castigated in those global and multilateral political institutions which were created by the West to aid and sustain the new post-colonial state.

The failure of the West to defend adequately its ideas and institutions against "Third World" development ideologies may be attributed to many causes. The socialist "march through the institutions," aided and abetted by a pacifist, preoccupied and visionless bourgeoisie, has progressed with alarming rapidity. Certainly any coherent response to the critics of capitalism must begin with a careful dissection of the most blatant errors of logic and a historical ignorance which suffuse the Third World program of reform. In any war of ideas, exposing the opponent's flaws and absurdities contributes immeasurably to the vitality of one's own defense and, it is hoped, the eventual shift to the offensive. The intellectual conviction that capitalism works tolerably well in delivering material goods efficiently and preserving a priceless measure of individual freedom and social equity has been lost. Despite the convincing refutation of the *intellectual* underpinnings of collectivist social planning by Hayek and others during the 20's and 30's, the political vitality of the anti-capitalist forces has strengthened. Ideological absurdities have gained worldwide respectability, and the cause of long-term Western and non-Western prosperity and security has suffered a severe setback.

B. The Fundamental Error of Third World Developmentalism: Neglect of the Human Factor

It is possible to identify diverse strands of Third World developmentalism. Some spokesmen have denounced the entire capitalist enterprise as rapacious and exploitative and urged global revolution to establish a more just social order. More moderate pragmatists have urged instead a more equitable distribution of the wealth generated by capitalism and a stronger dose of national and supra-national planning to correct the inequities associated with the free enterprise system. Among critics of the NIEO, the developed-country rejectionists view the NIEO as dogmatic anti-capitalism with which there can be no compromise, while more pragmatic liberals have found room for accommodation and negotiation.[2]

"Third World thought" about development is not monolithic. Indeed, the term "Third World" conveys a false sense of unity to what is in fact a widely diverse assortment of states. Nevertheless, there is a common and basic error which has pervaded the entire NIEO discussion: neglect of the *human* factor in economic development. One may read endlessly the analyses and programmatic declarations of the NIEO and find only passing reference to the role of *people*—their efforts, skills, achievements, drives, incentives, efficiency, and attitudes toward work. Precisely at a time when the critical role of "human capital" in economic growth is gaining unprecedented attention in Western economic science, non-Western development thought has constructed a vision of a new economic order which systematically ignores the human dimension.[3] The *intellectual* origins of this error can be traced in part to leftist ideological schemes which focus on macroeconomic global "dependency" and locate the cause of underdevelopment in external macroeconomic factors rather than in internal microeconomic behavior. The *political* origins of the neglect of the human factor are even more clear. To accept that human actors can respond rationally to incentives and improve their lot is to identify human choice as a major source of economic progress. Such a humanistic view of development can appear profoundly threatening to entrenched political elites. To acknowledge the crucial role of entrepreneurship is to raise the politically volatile issue of which type of social system best encourages such entrepreneurship. While entrepreneurship may—indeed *must*—arise in all economic systems, only liberal capitalism actually encourages, protects and nourishes it.

C. Themes of Third World Developmentalism

1. Human Agents Helpless to Improve Their Economic Condition

The ability of human beings to cope with change is perhaps the most basic dimension of development. Genuine economic development requires that traditional folkways adapt to the demands of commercial production and exchange. Yet it is precisely this most human aspect of the growth experience which is largely neglected in Third World developmentalism. Indeed, the *impossibility* of individuals acting rationally to improve their economic condition is an implicit article of this developmental faith.

Third World developmentalism has subscribed consistently to the doctrine that poverty involves a "vicious circle" of dependency.[4] In this view, poor people are trapped in a downward economic spiral which makes savings, investment and real growth impossible without massive external aid and vigorous state intervention to "break" the circle and pull the citizenry—by force, if necessary—into the twentieth century. The people must be constrained and directed toward their own good. State bureaucrats will necessarily have to curb consumption by private citizens in order to generate investment funds needed by the burgeoning state machinery. In this ironic "reverse paternalism" it is assumed that entrepreneurial success is beyond the capability of the poor. Despite abundant evidence that peasants are indeed capable of innovation and of rational response to economic incentives,[5] Third World development logic has denied that human agents are equipped to behave in such rational fashion. The "irrationalism" of the poor has been a recurring theme. Mired in backward traditions and hopelessly ignorant, the *rural* peasantry is particularly helpless in this view. Extensive state controls must wrench the peasantry from the stultifying grip of irrational traditions.

This denial of human capacity to act supports in turn a profoundly anti-rural bias in Third World development thinking. In this regard, industrialization is tantamount to economic progress and urbanization is considered a *sine qua non* of genuine development. Agriculture equals poverty.[6] Technological progress is assumed impossible in rural areas. Instead, improved technology and increasing urbanization are viewed as mutually compatible and reinforcing trends in developing areas. Such argumentation ignores the abundant evidence that even *minor* investments in small scale technological advances in the rural sectors bring tremendous spurts in productivity.[7] Third World developmentalism has embraced the fallacious reasoning of the "zero marginal productivity" thesis. Disguised unemployment in rural areas provides a rich pool of recruits for urban labor forces at *no cost* (beyond relocation expenses), since such labor yields *no marginal product* in the overcrowded backward agricultural areas. The failure of this theory to satisfy simple tests of logic and empirical evidence has not detracted from its appeal. The internal politics of most developing nations continues to provide greater access and favorable

treatment to powerful, organized and concentrated urban interests at the expense of the weak, unorganized and widely dispersed
farmers. Indeed, many radical critics of the left have indicted
Third World developmentalism as the ideological rationalization
of entrenched urban elites whose selfish aggrandizement comes at
the expense of the truly poor peasants. (Unfortunately, the solution of the radical left usually entails revolutionary bloodshed and
forced-draft agricultural collectivization.)

In short, "Third Worldism" persists in neglecting the "human
capital" dimension of economic development while mainstream
economic theory is now coming to grips with this most elementary
source of sustained material growth. Heavily influenced by socialist reasoning, U.N. generated studies and the rhetoric of dependency have failed to comprehend the critical role of
entitlements and consumption incentives in stimulating human
entrepreneurship and economic progress.

2. Third World "Reformism:" The Campaign Against the Entrepreneur

The Third World paradigm not only neglects the human dimension, but also largely defines development in terms of the
eradication of the entrepreneur. A large proportion of proposals
for "reform" of the global economy (the "New International Economic Order") are profoundly anti-entrepreneurial in spirit and
effect. The general attitude is accusatorial; entrepreneurial success invites suspicion, envy and often reprisal in the developing
world. Wealth earned through legitimate and risk-taking investment and hard work is often maligned as exploitative and subject
to punitive state confiscation.

The most pervasive example of officially sanctioned anti-entrepreneurial measures remains the government's manipulation of
price structures in ways which discourage the expansion of rural
agricultural production. In most developing nations the prices of
agricultural products are deliberately held down or subsidies are
paid to farmers in order to provide urban dwellers with cheaper
food. In some developing countries, state monopolies enjoy exclusive rights to purchase farm output at prices barely capable of
sustaining even subsistence standards of living. The impact of
such policies on social equity (i.e., on rural producers) is ignored.
That such policies increase emigration from farm to city is accept-

able, even desirable, in light of the presumed priority of urban industrial labor needs and the "zero marginal productivity" of rural workers. When the already meager earnings of the rural poor are in turn subject to taxation at high rates to subsidize urban-industrial projects, the plight of the rural dwellers becomes virtually unbearable. Such taxation further retards savings rates and capital formation among the peasants, providing superficial confirmation of the thesis that these poor people are incapable of rational behavior, investment and planning for the future. Given the high returns on even modest investment in agricultural improvements, the opportunity costs of such ill-conceived policies are enormous.

Officials of developing areas have displayed inordinate admiration for "bigness" at the expense of the small landholder. Again social equity arguments, focusing on the loss to the peasant, are ignored. Mainstream liberal economic arguments regarding "scale economies" have been used to justify suppression of rent, wholesale collectivization and coercive relocation schemes (such as the disastrous "ujamaa" of Julius Nyerere's Tanzania, underwritten in part by the World Bank). Marxist doctrine similarly buttresses the case for large-scale agriculture controlled by the state at the expense of the rural small-holder and entrepreneur.[8]

The condemnation of private enterprise as *ipso facto* exploitative is a recurrent theme of the NIEO. Contact between local private enterprise and foreign-owned multinational corporations (MNCs) is considered destructive. While legitimate complaints may be directed to these MNCs (i.e. that they crowd out local entrepreneurs in credit markets; that they may otherwise put local business at a competitive disadvantage), these are empirical questions to be resolved on a case-by-case basis. Instead, Third World developmentalism argues the need to substitute state-owned enterprises (SOEs) for foreign MNCs and local private enterprise.[9] Educational "reforms" frequently entail the elimination of programs conducive to developing entrepreneurial capacities. Instead, a pervasive egalitarianism prescribes reorienting universities and secondary schools toward social "reforms" which stress redistribution over production and incentives to produce. In implementing these educational "reforms" and fostering state-owned enterprises, bilateral and multilateral foreign assistance flows have been very important.

The major *positive* programs of global reform have focused upon "reforms" of international economic relations which are detrimental to individual human agents seeking to improve their economic situation. State bureaucrats and multilateral lending

agencies have not always focused on promoting the role of entrepreneurial individuals. For example, the Third World development paradigm emphasizes statist cartelization and *restrictions* on
production to buoy prices. Such cartel strategies ignore the effects
upon the excluded producer. The long-term negative impact
upon trading relationships, particularly the detrimental effects
upon a nation's reputation as a reliable trading partner, although
an elementary concern of the private businessman, is neglected or
rejected by the advocates of cartelization and "trade wars." The
neglect of elementary considerations of supply, demand and price
(such that an artificially high price encourages conservation, development of substitutes, and search for alternate supplies or
suppliers) is typical of statist bureaucracies. Grandiose proposals
for commodity price stabilization are focused upon problems of
short-term price fluctuations which are not significant factors in
the entrepreneur's long-term investment calculus. Such schemes
would substitute the state for private buyers and sellers in determining prices which both clear the markets and ensure a secular
increase in the returns earned by commodity producers (many of
which are developed industrialized states).[10] Such an objective is
contradictory on the face of it, even without appeal to the dismal
management record of most existing commodity buffer schemes.
Finally, many preferential trading arrangements, for which developing nations have argued so forcefully, have politicized the
international trading system. Periodic renegotiations inevitably
exacerbate political tensions and introduce uncertainties which
complicate entrepreneurial investment decisions. Evidence of significant positive economic benefits from preferential arrangements for developing areas is slight.[11] The prominence of trade
preferences in the NIEO demands indicates the distorted priorities of Third World development ideas in relation to true
domestic needs.

D. The State as the Major Engine of Development

While they frequently couch their demands in terms of the
urgency of meeting "basic human needs," Third World advocates
invariably prescribe solutions which enlarge the scope of bureaucratic state power at the expense of the needy. The NIEO is
about states' rights, not *human* rights. A logical corollary to the
determinism and pessimism about individuals is an unquestioning

faith in the powers of the state to organize and manage most productive activity. Despite abundant empirical evidence to the contrary, the superiority of centralized bureaucratic direction to decentralized individual initiative is a basic tenet of developmental dogmatics. Determinism fosters statism, and "development" itself is associated with the progressive accretion of state power both at home and in external commercial relations.[12]

The political utility of these notions for entrenched ruling elites is obvious. Such arguments bolster the claims of state economic managers for expanded powers over society despite a dismal, often catastrophic, record of mismanagement. Evidence of past failures only reinforces the claim that more power must be concentrated at the center to cope with increasing economic disarray. A related doctrine establishes that only increased powers of states over their foreign trade sectors can break the vicious circle of dependency fostered by more powerful advanced industrial states.

1. Increased State Control Over Natural Resources

The United Nations resolutions on the NIEO (and related documents such as the Brandt and RIO reports) call for increased state control over domestic natural resources as an obvious necessity. Indeed, a major allegation against the old colonial system is its deliberate failure to provide the successor regimes with control over the "national patrimony" of raw materials.

The alleged need for state control over natural resources derives in part from the threats of resource exhaustion and from "limits to growth" arguments. The serious conceptual and methodological weaknesses of neo-Malthusian models of resource exhaustion and "limits to growth" scenarios have been amply documented. Such models neglect the role of rising prices in discouraging consumption, encouraging conservation of scarce supplies and promoting exploration for new supplies or viable substitutes.

2. State-Owned Enterprise

The NIEO rhetoricians clearly favor state-owned enterprises (SOE's) over private capitalism, whether domestic or foreign. The litany of abuses by private foreign investors is all too familiar.[13] While certain MNC practices—transfer pricing, bribery, "crowding out" of local entrepreneurs—are legitimate cause for LDC grievance, there has been a great improvement in the relative bargaining power of the developing countries vis-a-vis the MNCs. The proliferation of highly competitive multinational corporations, including many with headquarters in LDCs, has resulted in an investor scramble to provide more favorable terms to potential host LDCs. While one may debate the long-term economic costs and benefits of so-called "performance requirements" insisted upon by hosts, there can be no doubt that such new stipulations enhance the host's ability to exercise leverage and extract perceived benefits from the MNCs.[14] The NIEO paradigm nevertheless continues to view the MNC as a predatory capitalist and an agent of underdevelopment. Nationalization and technology transfer rights are insisted upon[15] and state-owned enterprises are given clear priority over privately-held firms in the allocation of government incentives and foreign aid flows. The desperate need of LDCs for capital is to be met not by increased private capital flows but by increased bilateral and multilateral assistance flows to LDC governments. Evidence of harmonious and mutually beneficial LDC/MNC investment relations is suppressed. Familiar allegations which identify private market relations as *ipso facto* exploitative abound.

A related theme of Third World developmentalists is the consistent encouragement of state-owned cartels to control commodity markets of special interest. The obstacles to successful cartelization are well-known. The commodity must be one for which demand is relatively inelastic and substitutes are unavailable. There must be only a few producers who are capable of curtailing a significant percentage of total production and sustaining such cutbacks over a prolonged period. Political consensus among producers should be high. In the case of the developing countries, few commodities satisfy these requirements. The current dilemmas of the OPEC cartel graphically illustrate the difficulties of sustaining an oligopolistic pricing arrangement, even in so vital a resource as petroleum. Nevertheless, the political attractiveness of cartelization remains. Such strategies deliberately encourage expanded state power over critical resources and provide an external policy rationale for drastic increases in the domestic power of established governmental elites. The case for cartelization is, of course, reinforced by "Limits to Growth" arguments: given a presumption of disastrous resource depletion, production cutbacks managed by statist bureaucracies appear to be a reasonable response. Once the assumptions of the neo-Malthusians are refuted, the Third World prescription amounts to an ill-conceived program for the redistribution of existing wealth between the "haves" and "have nots." The prospects for mutually advantageous schemes to increase world production by means of cooperative arrangements between private investors and developing country entrepreneurs are largely ignored in such NIEO scenarios, despite abundant evidence that such cooperation is feasible and can be highly remunerative.

3. Capital Resources for the State

The literature and rhetoric of Third World developmentalism incorporates many themes of the neo-Keynesian development models. Regnant development models emphasize the critical role of large infusions of *capital* in the growth process. Large-scale inflows of capital—in many cases bilateral or multilateral aid flows—prudently managed and allocated by government planners are critical variables in the mainstream developmental paradigm adopted by the NIEO advocates. Such faith in the power of aggregate investment flows to spur development ignores evidence that capital flows *per se* do not guarantee growth.[16] The critical determinants of economic growth are those factors which govern the *uses* to which new capital infusions are put. Investments may be ill-conceived and contribute little or nothing to long-term development. The net costs of investment—both in terms of absolute costs and opportunity costs—may often far exceed the benefits gained.

Capital inflows may far exceed the capacities of the society to employ usefully new investment funds. While economists have long noted the importance of such "absorptive capacity," the concept has been dropped altogether from the Third World development paradigm. Instead, sheer aggregate increases in capital flows and technology transfers have been equated with improved growth prospects, regardless of whether such capital or technology is productively employed. The determinants of a society's "absorptive capacity" are precisely those aspects of "human capital"—entrepreneurial and managerial abilities, technical innovativeness, "prevailing work ethic"—which are systematically excluded from the Third World ideology. This unqualified endorsement of capital and technology transfers reinforces the equally unqualified preference for state planning. Whatever the nature of the development "problem" the solution amounts to ever-increasing transfers of real resources into the hands of government elites. The political attractiveness of such economic prescriptions far outweighs the extensive contrary evidence that sheer aggregate transfers may contribute little, or may even impede, sustained long-term economic growth.

4. Neglect of Small-Scale Prospects

The commitment to grandiose development projects requiring large-scale capital infusions has two principal domestic consequences. First, less glamorous projects demanding minimal new capital inflows receive far less attention than may be justified given the potential *returns* on such minimal investment. Second, the commitment to large state projects provides a strong rationale for regulating domestic consumption in order to expand domestic capital formation. Developing country elites wedded to industrialization as the *sine qua non* of progress have in most cases systematically neglected opportunities for improved agricultural production. Such improvements demand far less capital than the favored massive infrastructural and industrial projects. Small scale agricultural improvements—new seed varieties, improved cultivation techniques, small irrigation systems, improved marketing arrangements—have proven highly successful despite their unpretentious scale.[17] Admirable payoffs in terms of improved quality of life among the desperately poor and marginal rural dwellers have been realized. But while they improve social welfare, such simple projects yield no increase in state economic power. They may in fact *encourage* independent entrepreneurial initiatives inimical to the acceptance of state regulation. To the extent rural existence improves and farmers achieve some measure of economic autonomy beyond mere subsistence, centralized urban regimes may be less successful in exercising bureaucratic control. Large-scale agricultural relocation and collectivization schemes which expand direct state regulatory control and provide a simultaneous case for increased capital investment to be placed at the discretion of regnant elites—offer a far more attractive package suited to the political needs of developing country political elites.[18]

Large-scale industrial/urbanized development schemes, often complemented by agricultural collectivization projects, also provide a continuing justification for curbs on consumption by the public. Increasing the amount of discretionary funds available for allocation by ruling groups takes precedence over "wasteful" expenditures which might improve the quality of human life but which detract from resources available to the central government. When curbs on consumption are not voluntarily forthcoming, coercive state measures may be necessary.[19] Given the already low levels of consumption in developing nations such state-dictated "belt-tightening" is by no means a minor intrusion into daily life.

Demands for reductions in *domestic* consumption were (prior to the onset of the recent global recession) often accompanied by demands for cuts in consumption by the wealthy Northern populations. According to the prevalent Third World paradigm, Western living standards amounted to a scandalous and exploitative consumption surplus extracted from the poor nations by means of colonial and neo-colonial mechanisms. That such levels of consumption were directly related to Northern productive efficiency and provided essential incentives for increasing global output (and hence demand for Third World goods) remained unaddressed in the model. Western consumption levels instead represent a pernicious and wasteful lifestyle. Penetration of this lifestyle into Third World societies by means of an international "demonstration effect" was to be resisted by state coercion.

E. Supranational Planning

At first glance the repeated calls for global authorities to implement planning for development would seem to contradict the emphasis on enhancing the power of the independent sovereign LDCs. Many proponents of the Third World program have explicitly urged such world-embracing reform proposals as a tactic to weaken existing national elites.[20] In fact, however, calls for supranational planning reinforce increases in power for the "New Egalitarian" elites of the Third World. This is evident given several key components of the case for world planning.

1. Control of the Global Planning Process

It is clearly envisaged by Third World proponents of a centralized "global plan" that the plan will be the outcome of a process controlled from beginning to end by national representatives of the existing states. The NIEO is not, despite the popular and academic misperceptions in the West, a scheme for transcending the nation-state. Rather, the NIEO envisages wholesale transfer of both resources and decision-making powers away from the states of the "North" to the national elites of the states of the "South." The global plan is not a product of disinterested rational technocracy but rather the summation of the particular needs, demands and interests of regnant Third World elites. Precisely because no state is denied its particular "package" of demands, the North-South dialogue has lapsed into stalemate. Any concessions by the South might fatally unravel the package and provoke intra-Southern animosities. Such divisions would undermine the bargaining stance of the "Solid South" vis-a-vis the North. The history of the NIEO provides no evidence to support any type of "global planning" except a process which would be dominated by a weighted coalition of the existing states.[21] The envisioned "reform" of multilateral institutions—especially the International Monetary Fund and the World Bank—would transfer decision-making power from donor countries to the aid recipients.

Any alleged incompatibility between "global planning" and national sovereignty thus collapses once it is realized that the supranational planning envisaged by the Third World bears little resemblance to Western notions of rationalized, apolitical cost/benefit analysis. Instead, supranational planning as in the NIEO assumes increased decision-making power for the political representatives of the incumbent regimes.

Repeated calls for supranational solutions to Third World development problems have the added attraction of deflecting attention from the serious failures of the incumbent elites. Most formulations of the NIEO have contended forcefully that global ("macro-systemic") transformations must precede adjustments at the domestic ("micro-systemic") level. Global "dependency structures" allegedly condemn the developing countries to stagnation (and even annihilation) in the absence of massive resource transfers effected by global planning agencies. Perennial balance-of-payments deficits are inevitably attributed to global problems of sluggish demand rather than to long-established irresponsible *domestic* programs which retard growth and fuel inflation. The focus upon *global* problems in turn, yields proposals for global recovery via domestic reflation by the developed nations, regardless of the inflationary consequences of such "quick fix" solutions. In the most fundamental sense, emphasizing global and systemic causes of poverty permits the development problem to be cast in terms of macroeconomic aggregates such as the "widening gap," declining terms of trade, LDCs' declining share of world trade, and repatriated foreign investment earnings. As noted above, such aggregation deflects attention from the *human* dimensions of poverty, particularly rural poverty, and the need to address obstacles to micro-level improvements in productivity and standard of living. Such issues raise uncomfortable questions concerning national policies which destroy individual incentives and which are often blatantly confiscatory.

Finally, this enthusiastic embrace of supranational diagnosis and prescription represents the logical extreme of a development paradigm which aims at all costs to eliminate uncertainty and establish bureaucratic predictability and control. The sustaining passion of the bureaucrat is to eliminate uncertainty and to impose uniformity, standardization and "rationality." Because entrepreneurship is by definition the ability to exploit disequilibria and to profit from the absence of total conformity in expectations and tastes, the pursuit of bureaucratic predictability must, in the end, remove all possibilities for entrepreneurial self-improvement.[22] Given the threat which the widespread exercise of entrepreneurial talent would pose to the agents of state control, bureaucratic planning at the supranational level appears as a welcome supplement to domestic planning. The intellectual straitjacket of "The Plan" again appears to serve admirably the political purposes of controlling elites.

F. Cultural and Social Factors in Development

There is a pronounced schizophrenia evident in the dogmatics of Third World developmentalism. On the one hand, there is scant attention paid to the cultural, social, attitudinal and intellectual aspects of the development process. On the other hand, some proponents allege that, in light of the formidable obstacles of traditional folkways, only a complete transformation of human nature can ensure economic progress.

Such an apparent contradiction in fact makes sense from the perspective of the prevailing biases of the Third World paradigm. In seeking increased foreign assistance, state planners will naturally deemphasize those cultural and social obstacles to development which cannot be corrected by massive resource transfers. Thus, the NIEO demands ignore the abundant evidence in the

economic development literature of the inadequacy of even large
capital transfers to create *and sustain* a dynamic developing process. Because the NIEO amounts to a package of demands addressed to external sources of aid and trade and private
investment, it is not likely to raise uncomfortable questions concerning the adequacy of these measures.

When, on the other hand, Third World analysts turn to address
domestic elite groups and to prescribe appropriate national policies
for development, the emphasis shifts. Cultural and social reforms
to eradicate the semi-feudal backwardness of traditionalism necessarily entail massive interventionism by centralized "modernizing
elites." Nostrums which legitimize increased statism find a very
receptive welcome within the Third World. A recurring theme of
the planning advocates argues the indispensability of the "Plan" to
root out "primitive" and pre-modern attitudes, customs, institutions and practices which are allegedly incompatible with rational,
planned economic progress.

Thus, what at first glance appeared as a glaring inconsistency
within the developmentalist schools, alternately ignoring or plac-
ing at the center the problems of cultural and social dimensions of
growth, becomes, on further reflection, clear evidence of the
primarily political nature of this discourse. Such factors receive
attention when to do so will further the cause of increased national, governmental power over the poor. Where undue emphasis upon these internal factors might undercut the case for foreign
aid, preferences, and other varieties of North-South resource
transfers, they will disappear from the discussion.

Third World developmentalism can be aptly characterized as an
amalgamation of "disembodied" notions lacking any grounding in
the human, day-to-day realities of the poor. All manner of "resources" are viewed as essential save the most basic of all: productive human agents. Characteristics basic to economic progress—
enterprise, risk-taking, willingness to respond to perceived opportunities, foresight, willingness to work hard for deferred gratifica-
tion—are largely ignored. Instead, collectivist schemes prevail
which do not cultivate, and in fact systematically stifle, these salutary traits. Ethnic groups which have displayed economically productive behavior have been notoriously discriminated against by
ruling groups alarmed at the menacing prospect of independent
and autonomous citizens. Envious masses have willingly collabo-
rated against the Indians of Africa, the overseas Chinese, Jews
and other successful "out-groups." Societal enervation resulting
from the stimuli of Western ideas, especially commercial liberalism, foreign trade, and private foreign investment, goes un-

heeded in the litany of multinational corporate "abuses." The social and cultural factors which stimulate or impede economic prosperity are not seriously taken into account. Instead, Third Worldism eagerly proffers pseudo-sociological arguments to the effect that poverty breeds revolutionary violence, a not so veiled threat against any Western political interests which might challenge the redistributive schemes of the NIEO.[23]

G. The Trivialization of Human Rights

There can be no more convincing demonstration of the blatant neglect of the human dimensions of development than the outrageous trivialization of fundamental human rights perpetrated under United Nations auspices. In a negative sense this process includes the silence which envelops the United Nations in the face of the egregious violations of human rights routinely engaged in by its member states. Except for the ritualistic condemnations of pro-Western pariahs—Israel, South Africa, Taiwan—the human rights records of truly barbarous regimes enter hardly, if at all, into an agenda heavily stacked against the West.

The problem of *basic* human rights—the right to life, privacy, liberty under a framework of law, emigration, property and contract, protection against arbitrary arrest, proscription of torture—raises uncomfortable questions for a majority of Third World states. These fundamental rights have been obscured and trivialized by being lumped indiscriminately into a rights "package" which includes such ephemeral "economic and social rights" as the right to job security, disability benefits, training and paid holidays. Assurance of *basic* human liberties must take the form of proscriptions *against* arbitrary state actions—cruel punishment, detention without cause, torture, denial of rights to emigrate, controls over the information media. On the other hand, "economic and social rights" encompass a broad range of objectives obstensibly served by *expanded* governmental controls over private and public life. Indeed, the "right to development" itself is asserted in the NIEO as one demanding full implementation in order to improve the welfare of the existing Third World "nations"—"nations" in this context referring to established governments, not people.[24] Bloated bureaucracies expanded for the ostensible cause of furthering these human "rights to development" engage regularly in systematic brutality and rampant corruption. Incentives to engage in political manipulation expand geometrically with the growth of the public sector. The politicization of diverse aspects of daily life exacerbates internal tensions and directs attention away from productive enterprise and toward schemes to "beat the system" or manipulate it to one's own advantage.

Perhaps the clearest evidence of the trivializing scorn toward basic human rights typical of the United Nations development community is the grossly distorted nature of United Nations monitoring of human rights abuses. The droning about violations in Puerto Rico, South Africa, Chile, the Israeli-occupied territories, Rhodesia, and the Colonel's Greece betrays a moral myopia of serious dimensions. The brutality of Third World regimes which rely upon wholesale repression for their claim to power invites scarcely a ripple of protest from the self-proclaimed spokesmen of the "conscience of mankind." Socialist and communist variants of political servitude only rarely become targets of Third World criticism. What scope is left for *private* efforts at investigation and exposure of human rights violations may ultimately be neatly excised under the guise of the "New World Information Order," a globalized gag-rule which would insure the continuation of the politics of viciousness.

Conclusions: Toward a Humane Conception of Development

Third World developmentalism is by no means a homegrown product. In many respects the inhumane features of the NIEO rhetoric reflect a broader failing of contemporary economic and political thinking. The Fabian Socialist influences upon the NIEO have been noted prominently—and perhaps exaggeratedly.[25] To focus solely upon the neo-Marxist roots of the NIEO misses a more basic point, namely, that much of neoclassical economic theory encourages precisely the type of abstract, disembodied and anti-humanistic thinking evident in the NIEO program. Since the time of Adam Smith, economic science has tried to eliminate the purposeful human actor as a subject of investigation. The neo-Austrians have forcefully argued the bankruptcy of an "economics" which cannot take account of human action, effort and entrepreneurship in "real world" market processes and which instead expends enormous effort in elaborating rarefied models of equilibrium and perfect information. Similarly, "human capital" theorists have tried to reorient economic theory away from bloodless neo-Keynesian aggregate "growth models" and toward an exploration of how individuals respond to incentives and learn new behavior patterns to cope with disequilibria and change.[26] Nevertheless, mainstream neo-Keynesian theories of economic development and macroeconomic modeling reinforce the prevailing tendency to conceptualize development in terms of capital infusions, planned and centralized macroeconomic management, industrialization, and foreign assistance to help bridge the widening gap. The paternalism and pessimism of much of the NIEO reflects a broader pessimism endemic to modern economic analysis. As Irving Kristol has noted of post-Smithian economic theory:

. . . the whole climate of economic discussion moved from a buoyant optimism to a quite chilling pessimism . . . so that by the mid-19th century, economics was generally perceived, by both economists and laymen alike, as that science which discovered the "iron laws" that ruled the economic universe . . . Economics, which had breathed an expansive spirit in *The Wealth of Nations,* now seemed eager to inform people that the economic universe was frigid, deterministic, indifferent to human aspirations.[27]

In short, economic science is undergoing a paradigmatic revolution, a shift "back to basics" which involves a rediscovery of the classical humanistic tradition that *people matter.* Conventional abstract macro- and micro-economic models have become increasingly subject to challenge as their productive powers have atrophied. As this process of intellectual rethinking proceeds, the dogmatics and posturing of the NIEO will appear in clearer relief as the epitome of all that was false in the old economics, projected to the final lengths of absurdity. The perversion of thought by partisan political interest is certainly not a recent phenomenon, but the proponents of United Nations developmentalism have provided an apt and chilling affirmation of this perennial and tragic failing.

NOTES

1. The prolonged negotiations and ultimate rejection of the outrageous draft of the Law of the Sea treaty is a case in point.
2. A useful overview of the various schools of thought is provided by Roger Hansen, *Beyond the North-South Stalemate* (New York: McGraw-Hill, 1979).

3. On "human capital" see Theodore Schultz, *Investing in People: The Economics of Population Quality* (Berkeley, California: University of California Press, 1981).

4. The widening gap is a recurring theme in the "Declaration and Program of Action on the Establishment of a New International Order" General Assembly, Resolutions 3201 (S-VI, 3202 (S-W) and 3281 (XXIX). Reprinted, slightly abridged in *Yearbook of the United Nations*, 1979, Volume 28, pp. 325–332.

5. The evidence has been effectively synthesized by P. T. Bauer and Theodore Schultz. See especially Bauer, *Dissent on Development* (Cambridge, Mass.: Harvard University Press, revised edition, 1976), Ch. 1 and passim; T. W. Schultz, *Transforming Traditional Agriculture* (New Haven, Conn.: Yale University Press, 1964) pp. 3–35; and T. W. Schultz, *Investing in People: The Economics of Population Quality*, op. cit., pp. 24–26, 46–52 and Ch. 7.

6. Jacob Viner has bemoaned the influence of Raul Prebisch whose early postwar studies for the United Nations dogmatically identified agriculture with poverty. See J. Viner, *International Trade and Economic Development* (London: Oxford University Press, 1953), pp. 43–44. See especially R. Prebisch, *The Economic Development of Latin America and its Principal Problems* (New York: United Nations, 1949).

7. Theodore Schultz has written extensively on the promise of agriculture as a relatively cheap engine of growth. See his *Transforming Traditional Agriculture*, Ch. 7.

8. Karl Marx argued forcefully the case for large scale agriculture; see David Mitrany, *Marx Against the Peasant* (London: Weidenfield and Nicolson, 1951); on the role of the World Bank see Bettina Hurni, *The Foreign Lending Programs of the World Bank.*

9. On the case for state-owned enterprise and the attack on the MNCs see especially United Nations, Commission on Transnational Corporations, *Transnational Corporations in World Development: A Reexamination* (New York: United Nations, 1978).

10. On the complexities and anti-entrepreneurial impact of such commodity pricing schemes, see P. T. Bauer and B. S. Tamey, *Markets, Market Control and Marketing Reform* (London: Weidenfield and Nicolson, 1968), passim.

11. Evidence for the American Generalized System of Preferences is provided in Tracy Murray, *Trade Preferences in Developing Countries* (New York: Wiley, 1977); also see UNCTAD "Review and Evaluation of the Generalized System of Preferences" 7D/232 (Geneva: January 9, 1979).

12. The litany of states rights is best exemplified in the U.N. General Assembly "Charter of Economic Rights and Duties of States" adopted December, 12 1974 as Resolution 3281 in the face of strong opposition from the developed countries.

13. A thorough recent overview may be found in C. Fred Bergsten, T. Horstand, T. Moran, *American Multinationals and American Interests* (Washington, D.C.: The Brookings Institution, 1978). Also see T. Biersteker, *Distortion or Development: Contending Perspectives on the Multinational Corporation* (Cambridge, Mass.: MIT Press, 1978).

14. For many examples of such new LDC/MNC arrangements, see Raymond Mikesell, *New Patterns of World Mineral Development* (Washington, D.C.: National Planning Association, 1979).

15. On nationalization, see The Declaration on the Establishment of a New International Economic Order, para. 4e; on technology transfer, see the "Programme of Action," Section IV.

16. Simon Kuznets has estimated that increases in capital and labor accounted

for less than ten percent of Western growth over the past two cen~
growth derives from the residual factor-human capital, technologica~
organizational skills, entrepreneurial innovation, etc. See his *Modern E~
Growth: Rate, Structure and Spread* (New Haven, Conn.: Yale University P~
1966).

17. Abundant evidence has been collated by T. Schultz, *Investing in People*, passim.

18. A similar argument alleges the need for a highly developed infrastructure of "social overhead capital" ports, roads, railroads, sophisticated communications networks, etc.—as an essential prerequisite for any developmental progress. Such arguments neglect substantial room for small-scale improvements but reinforce the alleged need for state planning and increased aid.

19. Perhaps the most influential treatise within the Third World developmental tradition has argued the case for compulsory curbs on consumption. See Gunnar Myrdal, *Asian Drama* (London: Penguin Books, 1968).

20. For example, see the "Lima Declaration" adopted at the Second General Conference of the U.N. Development Organization, March, 1975. Other examples include Gunnar Myrdal's scheme for "integrated national planning" leading to a massive transfer of resources to a United Nations entity; the current text of the United Nations "Law of the Sea" treaty; and several draft texts for the U.N.-supervised "Common Fund" for global commodity price "management." The term "World Development Authority" is that used by Mahbub ul-Haq, an advocate.

21. The text of the United Nations Treaty on the Law of the Seas provides the clearest evidence of the politicized nature of any global "plan" as envisaged by the New Egalitarians.

22. On the entrepreneur as that agent peculiarly gifted to exploit disequilibria and as the major engine of growth, see Israel Kirzner, *Competition and Entrepreneurship* (Chicago, Illinois: University of Chicago Press, 1973); *Perception, Opportunity and Profit* (Chicago, Illinois: University of Chicago Press, 1979).

23. The "Declaration on the Establishment of a New International Economic Order" is replete with veiled threats of revolutionary violence, cartelization and economic warfare waged by the South against the North. See for example paragraphs 2, 3, 4c, 4e, 4h and 4t.

24. At a 1980 seminar on the "right to development" sponsored by the United Nations Economic and Social Council, discussion arose as to whether the "nation," as the subject of the right to development, should be equated with the government and state or with individual persons and groups. The final report notes that "There was large agreement that both legally and practically, it is Governments which represent their peoples and nations and which should exercise the right to development, on behalf of their peoples." Seminar on the "Effects of the Existing International Economic Order on the Economies of the Developing Countries and the Obstacle that this Represents for the Implementation of Human Rights and Fundamental Freedoms," Geneva, Switzerland, 30 June–11 July, 1980 (ST/HR/Ser, A/8), para. 36, 115.

25. See especially Daniel Patrick Moynihan, "The United States in Opposition" *Commentary* (March, 1975); *A Dangerous Place* (New York: Berkley Books, 1980)

26. A clear statement of the neo-Austrian critique is Israel Kirzner *Competition and Entrepreneurship* (Chicago, Illinois: University of Chicago Press; 1973).

27. On "human capital" see Theodore Schultz, *Investing in People;* Irving Kristol, "Rationalism in Economics" in Irving Kristol and D. Bell, eds. *The Crisis in Economic Theory* (New York: Harper and Row, 1981), p. 208.

Progress Against Poverty in Communist and Non-Communist Countries in The Postwar Era

Nick Eberstadt

A RECENT CORPUS OF SCHOLARLY LITERATURE suggests that the process of modern economic growth in the less developed countries has brought little material gain to the disadvantaged strata of poor societies, and may actually have contributed to a decline in living standards for significant fractions of many national populations. This contention, of course, is not new, but power and urgency are lent to these studies because they harness detailed arrays of economic statistics to make their point.

The conclusions of a few of these studies may be used to represent the findings of the many. A volume prepared by the World Bank and the Institute for Development Studies comes to the estimate that over 700 million people in the non-Communist world subsisted on incomes of under $25 per person in the mid-1970s; it also divined a tendency in non-Communist countries for the income share of the poorest 40% of the population to shrink during the "early" stages of economic development—perhaps rapidly enough for the incomes of the poor to fall even as a nation's per capita income rose.[1] The International Labor Office,

in a sweeping report on rural conditions in Asia, concludes that
the incidence of poverty and landlessness has been increasing in
Bangladesh, Java, the Philippines, India, Pakistan and elsewhere;
the only country surveyed in which rural poverty was said to be
unambiguously abating was the People's Republic of China.[2] Sylvia Ann Hewlett's investigation of Brazil's postwar "economic miracle" leads her to talk of "growing poverty" and widespread
declines in living standards in coexistence with a dazzling record
of aggregate economic performance.[3] And Paul Bairoch, in an
attempt to recreate a comprehensive picture of economic change
for the less developed countries since the turn of the century,
produces numbers that indicate a negligible increase in per capita
income for most of the "Third World" between 1900 and 1960;
according to his charts, per capita food production may have
fallen in many regions of the world over much of this period.[4]

The implications of these studies are disturbing. From the
immediate humanitarian standpoint, they suggest that the current
material needs of the world's politically inarticulate masses are
being grossly underestimated by institutions and governments
which are supposed to help them. But these studies also necessarily raise questions about the political and economic arrangements under which most of humanity is living. If the non-
Communist countries of the poor regions may be referred to as
"capitalist" then "capitalism" would seem at best an unreliable
accomplice for any poor nation attempting to make its escape
from mass poverty.

As we shall see, the conceptual and statistical foundations for
this growing body of documents are rather flimsy. Despite more
than three decades of concerted international efforts to accelerate
the pace of material progress in the less developed nations, relatively little reliable and even less comprehensive data on the social
and economic conditions of the poor can be found for Africa,
most of Asia, and much of Latin America. By itself, this fact
speaks volumes. Such data as are available, however, paint a more
interesting and less hopeless picture than the monochrome
brought to mind by the notion of immiserating growth.

Before delving into these numbers, it is necessary to emphasize
that this chapter will explore the differences in patterns of poverty
not between "capitalist" and "non-capitalist" countries, but rather
between Communist and non-Communist countries. However
badly abused measures of poverty may sometimes be, they afford
in principle the possibility of meaningful standardization. Comparable precision is impossible in the use of the term "capitalism."

"Capitalism" is, first and foremost, a political word, and political language depends in part on ambiguity for its impact. Marxist-Leninist parties around the world claim proprietary rights in deciding what is "capitalist," and they use it to describe their adversaries of the moment. Given the premium that Leninist doctrine places on tactical maneuver and the number of years the world's many Marxist-Leninist parties have had to engage in vendettas, it should not be surprising that a great many things have been labelled as "capitalist" by Communist spokesmen—including the planning apparatus of the Soviet Union and the radicals who surrounded Mao during the Cultural Revolution. But it is not just Marxist-Leninists who have opted for an opportunistic interpretation of "capitalism." Many of the nationalist (and unmistakeably anti-Communist) leaders who have come to power in Asia and Africa since World War II have found it convenient to label their domestic enemies and international opponents as "capitalist," entirely irrespective of what their attitudes towards public finance or private entrepreneurship might actually be. In the nationalist lexicon, "capitalism" is a cognate for "colonialism"; it is a pejorative, and few political leaders in the new nations will allow it to be applied to themselves. Singapore may seem an exemplar of "capitalism" to its overseas admirers, but Lee Kuan Yew and his ruling People's Action Party have never accepted the intended compliment. From independence until 1974, the People's Action Party was a member of the Socialist International; though PAP has broken with the Socialist International, it still officially describes the Singapore system as "socialism that works."[5]

If "capitalism" has become a less precise term in recent decades, this is not solely the fault of politicians. With the rise of the modern state apparatus, the notion of "capitalism" has been made considerably more complex. Ever since Imperial Germany's successful experiments with protected and subsidized state-sponsored investments in the nineteenth century, modern governments have been gaining confidence in the idea that they can improve upon, or even substitute for, the functions of markets and businessmen. In time, it has become not just accepted, but expected that governments will protect their citizens against untoward results of "normal" market behavior, and pre-empt market decisions in the name of the greater national good.

World War II seems to have changed irrevocably the nature of the modern state (thus "capitalism") in both rich and poor regions. In the colonies, the shift from commercial to war-winning policies brought a sudden and new importance to government efforts to mobilize and augment national resources: significant fractions of the labor force were redeployed by decree; import-replacing industries were constructed at a forced pace; market-determined prices were suspended in many areas of the economy; and for the first time, the state targeted the accumulation of capital (principally for loan to the colonizing powers).[6] A new view of the state quickly took hold in the colonies: by 1944, the British Government paper *Planning Of Social And Economic Development In The Colonial Empire* was asserting that poor regions could not make full and effective use of their national resources without government supervision of the economic process.[7] The nationalist leaders who came to power in Asia and Africa after the war had no problem with this idea. They demanded strong, "nation-building" governments, and were supplied by the West with the intellectual justifications and the policy tools for the work. Raul Prebisch, Sir Andrew Cohen, and others were to make the case that poor societies could not count on "price signals" from domestic and international markets for reliable stimuli in their quest for economic development; at much the same time, new econometric techniques seemed to offer governments practical instruments for "scientific" management of the economy, and even for "fine-tuning" economic growth.[8]

In all less developed countries today, regardless of their professed ideologies, the state routinely undertakes activities which were earlier left to markets, businessmen, and entrepreneurs. This confounds easy definitions of "capitalism," even in the most unlikely places. In "laissez-faire" Hong Kong, about half of the city-state's stock of housing is "publicly" owned, and central authorities control a larger fraction of GNP than in the United States.[9] South Korea directs its economy through "Five Year Plans," and until very recently managed the allocation of the nation's finance capital through state agencies.[10] In Taiwan, government expenditures account for about a third of the nation's output (a higher fraction than in Sandinist Nicaragua!), and state-owned enterprises account for over a third of the country's annual accumulation of capital.[11] With the rise of the modern state apparatus, "capitalism" is becoming ever less suited to serve as a criterion for distinguishing national economies from one another. Increasingly it is governments rather than markets which take the lead in shaping economic life, and policies of political leaders rather than entrepreneurs which must ultimately be judged in assessments of national poverty.

Modern politics and the modern state have, however, created a class of governments which stand apart from all others; these are not ones which proclaim the virtues of "capitalism," but rather the ones which embrace the tenets of Marxism-Leninism. To no small degree, Communist leaders have set the terms of discourse on poverty in the modern world. They have also set a challenge for all non-Communist governments by asserting that their ambitions for transforming society and planning economic growth offer more to the poor than any alternative system of governance. It is both feasible and instructive to compare their progress against material poverty with the progress of these non-Communist nations whose social and economic systems they would see overhauled and replaced.

* * *

Over the past generation a rhetoric of commitment to improving the material condition of the world's poor has become a staple of political consumption in both rich and poor countries. In itself, this is hardly surprising: as much might have been expected at a time when literally dozens of new governments were attempting to establish and assert themselves over regions in which poor health and illiteracy prevailed, and when the conflict between Marxist-Leninist states and their "bourgeois" counterparts was finally assuming the dimensions of a global struggle for power. What is surprising is the stark contrast in the less developed countries between the nearly universal rhetoric of commitment to the poor and the prevailing lack of reliable, comprehensive, and sequential data that would be needed for any serious evaluation of either the plight of the poor or the effectiveness of interventions on their behalf.

For reasons that have yet to be explained, none of the major voices in today's "development dialogue" acknowledge the sorry state of current statistics on world poverty. Yet the problem is apparent. For many countries, numerical information concerning broad portions of the economy—much less the condition of the poor within these sectors—is simply unavailable. Those figures that can be found, moreover, are often of questionable meaning. It is not too much to say that the statistics most commonly used to map out poverty in the less developed countries are neither reliable in and of themselves, nor comparable among countries or over time.

Social and economic data for the less developed countries are compromised by three sorts of problems. The first are conceptual. Even under the best of circumstances, it is not nearly as easy to get a clear picture of patterns of poverty as is commonly imagined. Conventional analyses of poverty focus principally on per capita income: how it differs among groups, or changes over time. But determining per capita income is not a science; it is an art, necessarily requiring judgement and assumption. For this reason it is impossible to arrive at a single, precise conclusion about either differences in per capita income or changes in it over time for any active social system.

Constructing a per capita income index is, unavoidably, an excercise in rewriting history. It involves assigning constancy to a changing array of goods and services that households and nations produce or consume, and hypothesizing about the behavior of economic actors in environments to which they were never exposed. The difficulties of "holding prices constant" illustrate the problem. Many of the changes over time in household demand and the composition of national output are occasioned by shifts in prices. In holding prices constant, as any "deflated" index of economic activity must do, response is divorced from stimulus. This is not a trivial matter; substitution and information about changing scarcities are at the heart of the economic process. In redoing a price structure, one implicitly proposes an alternative course for local or international events. The results need not correspond to any recognizeable reality. Holding prices constant, for example, would make it seem that American families spent about 20% less on energy in 1982 than in 1972, and that Saudi Arabia had been running a sizeable balance-of-payments deficit with its trading partners between 1973 and 1985.

The conceptual problems incorporated into per capita index numbers go beyond the indelicacy of holding fixed those quantities whose function it is to vary. There is the question of comparing purchasing power in societies whose prices, and patterns of purchase, are significantly different. There is the question of imputing value to government services—many of which are public, precisely because it is thought that they cannot be properly evaluated by the marketplace. And there is the question of technical innovation. Many of the benefits of technical innovation accrue to those who do not pay for them. This poses a fundamental challenge to the measurement of purchasing power, for technical innovation is the basis of economic change in the modern world. It affects our lives quite literally. Advances in medicine and public health technology, for example, have altered the relationship between income and longevity: at any given level of per capita income (as conventionally measured) a society could expect to obtain substantially greater life expectancy today than in the 1930s.[12] This indisputable improvement in national well-being is only the most obvious of the sorts of changes in material conditions, brought on by technological breakthrough and innovation, that go unrecorded and unvalued in conventional tabulations of per capita income. In the less developed countries, where technical change can have a rapid and discontinuous impact on patterns of daily life and the economic routine, the biases introduced into calculations of per capita income can be especially acute.

Conceptual difficulties are compounded by technical ones. As a practical matter, there are very real limits to the abilities of governments to collect accurate information on the economies and societies under their supervision. Uncertainties in American statistics, which are widely regarded as exceptionally reliable, underscore the point: according to one study by the Joint Economic Committee of Congress, something like $200 billion in business activity may be missed each year by the Department of Commerce.[13] Many developed countries have been less successful in their attempts to measure economic activity. In Italy, for example, there are indications that a rapidly growing "underground" economy may account for as much as a third of the nation's overall economic growth during the late 1960s and early 1970s.[14] Under such circumstances, the correspondence between official economic statistics and the actual state of economic affairs is questionable. Yet Italy's ability to collect accurate statistics is considerably greater than that of the great majority of countries in Asia and the Caribbean and in all likelihood greater than that of any single nation in South America or Africa.

From the technical standpoint, the limits of accuracy for a nation's social and economic statistics are set by the policy concerns of its leaders, the sophistication and reach of its bureaucracies and institutions, the efficacy of its channels of social communication, the ability of the population to deal in, and with, numbers, and the complexity of the phenomenon to be measured. This augurs ill for measuring poverty. Poor people tend to be socially invisible; disproportionately illiterate and frequently beyond the fringes of the data-generating enclaves in their societies, they seldom leave strong statistical trails behind them. In poor societies the institutions which gather numbers are often weak or fragile and poor governments generally lack the ability (and sometimes even the inclination) to learn about material conditions in the countryside in any great detail. The People's Republic of China provides a case in point. Despite the presumable need for accurate numbers in a centrally planned economy, the State Statistical Bureau, which fell from grace in the aftermath of the Great Leap Forward, did its work with a staff which at one time consisted of only 14 persons.[15] As of 1983, it employed less than 200 technicians. How they are to provide accurate data on social and

economic conditions in a country of a billion people—in which
only ten years ago about a third of all communes had no regular
roads to link them to the outside world—has never been explained.[16]

As a general rule, it is easier for governments to measure
physical quantities than to estimate economic values. Counting
heads is less complicated than calculating national income. Even
so, the ability of even comparatively skilled governments from
among the less developed countries to measure population, or the
output of basic commodities, should not be exaggerated. The
reliability of demographic data from the less developed regions is
suggested by the fact that scholars and policymakers did not begin
to recognize that the world rate of population growth had peaked
until 1977; today it is believed that the showdown may have begun
in the early 1960s.[17] As for food production, even international
food trade statistics are beset by wide discrepancies suggesting
margins of error,[18] and these are the easiest data on food to
compile. To this day there are no reliable numbers for tuber and
root production in the less developed countries.[19] But cassava,
yams, sweet potatoes and potatoes are the principal source of
calories for literally hundreds of millions of people in Africa, Asia
and Latin America.

The third problem with social and economic statistics from the
less developed countries is that they are often distorted for political reasons. The trouble is inherent in the very nature of the
modern data-gathering process. Modern governments collect information to assist themselves in making policy. Yet as soon as
statistics are put to policy use, political incentives to manipulate
them arise. Clumsily politicized statistics are sometimes easy to
catch: one did not need special expertise, for example, to evaluate
Sukarno's claim that his government completely eliminated illiteracy in Indonesia during the course of the year 1964. A great
many less ambitious adjustments, however, never come to light.
The adulteration of national statistics seldom requires mass com-
plicity.[20] In most cases, the job can be done by a single hand in a
single government office. The poorer a society, the less developed
its statistical services, the easier it is for government officials to
change numbers without detection. Since the poor usually need
others to represent them, and generate little independent data on
their own conditions of life, statistics about poverty are particularly vulnerable to deliberate distortions. There is, unfortunately, no reason to expect countervailing pressures for
statistical adjustments to offset each other. The more likely out-

come would be for unpredictable but systematic waves of bias to pass through national accounts. There is no reason to expect these biases to be the same among countries or over time.

The problems with conventionally accepted economic statistics assert themselves in any attempt to assess poverty in the less developed countries. Per capita product and per capita income numbers are the mainstay of the literature on material progress and economic development, and are used without hesitation or qualification in both academic treatments and policy papers. Let us examine some of these for a moment. Table 1 presents estimates of per capita product for ten countries for 1970, based on two different approaches to the calculation. The first, in accordance with accepted practice, makes an estimate of national income in local currency, divides this by a population estimate, and converts the figure into dollars at the going exchange rate. The second attempts to equate per capita product in different countries on the basis of purchasing power rather than exchange rates: that is, it attempts to place an equivalent value on equivalent products in different societies. Neither procedure can be expected to yield a single, unassailable set of numbers; nevertheless, the differences between these two sets are striking. In the less developed countries, "purchasing power" estimates can be twice as high as those based on exchange rates; the different methods, moreover, alter not only the valuing, but the ranking of output among nations. By the conventional approach, Kenya seemed to produce 44% more per person than India in 1970; by the second approach, it actually seems to produce less.

The second approach may be an improvement on conventional estimate of output per person in the less developed countries, but it cannot provide reliable and consistent estimates. Tables 2 and 3 emphasize this. They compare "purchasing power" estimates of output per person in the less developed countries from two different teams: one sponsored by the World Bank, and the other by the U.S. State Department. Both teams produce estimates for the ten most populous non-Communist LDCs for 1977. Only three of these countries' estimates differ by less than 20%; four of them differ by more than 50%, and the estimates for Bangladesh differ by more than 100%. Both teams provide estimates of change in per capita product from 1950 to 1977. For those same ten countries, only four countries' growth rates differ by less than a fifth; three differ by more than half. For two dozen smaller poor countries, growth rates differed by less than a fifth in only five cases; they differed by more than half in twelve cases, and came out with opposite signs in three cases! National income, of course, is much easier to estimate than income distribution. The problems with income distribution figures can be illustrated with some examples from developed Western nations, presented in Table 4. Each one of these countries is better equipped to measure the income of its households than virtually any less developed society. Yet estimates of pretax earnings for the poorest 40% of households differ by almost a quarter in three Western nations, by nearly a third in a fourth, and by almost half in the fifth.

Despite very real advances in the statistical capabilities of most less developed countries over the past generation, the margins of error for figures most commonly used in describing national and global poverty are typically greater than the differences or changes which they presume to measure. The literature which uses these numbers without qualification cannot be expected to yield meaningful conclusions.

It is for this reason that many studies of international poverty cannot be taken seriously. The World Bank's calculation that 700 million people subsist on $25 per year, for example, is based on recombinations of largely meaningless numbers. On its very face, the calculation is evidently without meaning: it would have been impossible for one person, let alone for 700 million, to survive for a year on the equivalent in goods and services of what $25 could have bought in American society in the mid-1970s. In the same fashion, the ILO study of poverty in rural Asia multiplies questionable income distribution numbers against problematic per capita income estimates. Professor Bairoch's account of economic growth in the less developed countries is even less sensitive to the use of economic statistics: in many tables he offers indices or figures for encompassing area regions which were producing *no economic data at all* for some of the decades his survey covers. In these works and many others, students of world poverty may be said with some justice to be dignifying assumptions and prejudices with decimal points.

The false precision of so much of the work on world poverty does not stand the world's poor in good stead. In an age of powerful state apparatuses and activist social policy, the material well-being of the poor depends in no small degree on the result of government intervention. Misleading or systematically biased data, seemingly legitimized by econometric manipulations, can only misdirect government energy and frustrate the inefficient use of those limited resources devoted to the alleviation of poverty. False precision furthermore increases the likelihood of erratic swings in periodic assessments of various poverty problems, which may themselves ultimately interfere with the abilities of governments to attend to the needs of the poorest. Thus, the misuse of numbers on poverty may not only limit government performance: it may actually undermine support for the problem-solving activities of the state.

Although there is reason to worry about the quality of social and economic data for a great many nations, a concern for accuracy does not justify the rejection of *all* statistics on poverty as inadequate or misleading. Through judicious use of available information, it is possible to get a sense of not only gradations in poverty in the countries representing the bulk of the population of the less developed countries, but also some idea of the progress against material poverty that has been made under both Communist and non-Communist regimes since the end of the Second World War. In the final analysis, the choice of criteria in measuring progress against material poverty is arbitrary, for poverty is a complex phenomenon which cannot be completely described by any given set of measures. It is my own opinion, however, that we can come to a useful assessment of material poverty if we focus on five areas. These are: population, nutrition, literacy, the status of women, and material or social inequalities.

Population

Demographic figures—population totals, death rates, and birth rates—are essential in any quantitative assessment of poverty. Demographic estimates for the less developed countries are more accurate today than at any time in the past, but they are still surrounded by considerable margins of uncertainty. From the demographic standpoint, only a few countries remain *terra incognita*. Ethiopia, Laos, and a handful of African countries have not yet attempted a count of their people, but while material want may be severe in these countries, they are thought to represent less than one fiftieth of the population of the less developed countries.[21] More problematic is the expanse of *terra infirma* in Africa, Asia, and Latin America. Underregistration and misreporting are dangers in even the most careful censuses and surveys; the United States census in 1970, for example, is thought to have missed more than five million people, over two percent of the American public. Only some of the smaller and more prosperous LDCs—Taiwan, Chile, some of the Caribbean islands—meet Western standards of enumeration. In the rest, population counts and vital statistics must be treated as incomplete—although in varying degree. Among the non-Communist nations, there is sufficient demographic data for India, parts of East Asia, and much of Latin America to make a reconstruction of the postwar experience in which assumption is not the key variable. The same cannot yet be said for sub-Saharan Africa or most of the Middle East—a fact which may in itself tell us something about the condition of the poor in those regions.

In the Communist nations of Asia and Latin America, the politics of population counts seems to have a life of its own, conditioned by Lenin's dictum that statistics in a revolutionary society are not meant to serve scholarly purposes. North Korea, for reasons best known to itself, has never officially released any census results. China's 1953 census appears to have been conducted not only to gather numbers, but to symbolize the consolidation of power on the Mainland; the government's assertion that its enumeration missed only 0.02% of the population was a political, not a scientific, statement; China's 1982 census was linked to a campaign to limit family size to one child per couple; its results may have been affected by the linkage. In Vietnam, Hanoi's 1960 census preceded the collectivization of the countryside and the escalation of the war against South Vietnam; its 1974 census took stock of manpower just before the military offensives that were to topple the Saigon regime; its 1979 census is believed to have been conducted—among other reasons—to facilitate the transfer of millions of people from the North to the South, and from the South to inhospitable "New Economic Zones."[22] Broad-based incentives for misrepresentation may arise when census-taking becomes associated with the imposition of hardship in the public mind. In Cuba, as we shall see, vital statistics appear to be shaped by the regime's desire to make health levels seem high. Population numbers from these Marxist-Leninist nations can be used, but they must be used carefully.

Since poverty is a problem that affects people, it is necessary to know where the people most likely to be affected are, and in what numbers. More than 150 governments and political entities represent the approximately three and a half billion people of the less developed regions today, but nearly half of them are thought to live in two nations, China and India (See Table 5). Over half a billion more live in seven other countries: Indonesia, Brazil, Mexico, Vietnam, the Philippines, Thailand, and South Korea. If we add to these nine nations seven smaller ones—North Korea, Taiwan, Sri Lanka, Chile, Cuba, Costa Rice, and Jamaica—we make a set accounting for two-thirds or more of the population of the less

developed nations, containing every well-established independent
Marxist-Leninist government in the "Third World," affording
relatively reliable social statistics, and offering bases for comparison among nations with dramatically different political systems. The selection is arbitrary, but we are not likely to come
much closer to describing both global patterns of poverty and the
performance of Communist and non-Communist societies in a
single cut.

A first, broad indication of postwar changes in living standards
in the less developed countries comes from changes in population
growth rates. As is well known by now, the less developed regions
have all experienced a surge of population growth since the end
of the Second World War. The well-worn phrase "population
explosion" connotes the abruptness of these accelerations, and the
speed with which they spread to all non-European areas of the
world. The global dimensions of the change in population patterns cannot be measured with any great precision, but it is
thought that rates of natural increase were lower for the less
developed regions than the developed regions in the 1930s,
whereas they were two or three times as high by the early 1960s.[23]

At a time when governments are increasingly held responsible
for supplying services and sustenance for their subjects, "rapid"
population growth has come to be labeled a social problem by a
wide variety of officials and institutions. Some contemporary governments even argue that population growth intrinsically reduces
the living standards of any people experiencing it.[24] This is a
curious contention. Whatever population growth may mean for
tomorrow—and the future implications of population change are
much less clearly understood than most analyses suggest—it in-
contestably reflects a recent improvement in material conditions
for the less developed countries.

While there are many uncertainties about the population patterns of the poor regions, it can be safely stated that their rapid
postwar rates of population growth have been powered principally not by a rise in birth rates, but by significant and widespread declines in death rates. For people in high mortality
societies, a sustained drop in death rates is a very good thing.
Death rates are high in poor societies because children and bread-
winners perish from famines, epidemics, and other scourges that
do not endanger the lives of affluent peoples. Reduced death rates
are perhaps the nearest thing to a universally desired good, and
may provide the best single indicator of improvements in a people's material condition.

Ironically, conventional economic statistics treat mortality decline as an economic liability. As Lord Bauer has noted, measured per capita output falls with the death of a calf, but rises with the death of a child.[25] One attempt to treat improvements in mortality as a consumer good, relying heavily on assumptions, suggested that imputing value to mortality reduction might add a point to Taiwan's annual postwar growth rate, and might more than double Sri Lanka's annual increase in per capita product in the early post-war period.[26] While these computations are only illustrative, they indicate the sorts of differences which may exist between conventional measures of economic progress and actual changes in personal well-being when death rates are declining rapidly.

The clearest measure of the relationship between death and the individual is life expectancy, which is based on survival probabilities. Table 6 presents estimates of life expectancy at birth from about 1950 to around 1980 for the sixteen less developed countries we have selected. For those countries with reasonably reliable censuses and surveys, the rise in life expectancy over the past generation has been unambiguous; for some of them it has been quite dramatic. None have seen their lifespans increase by less than a decade. Most have made even more significant gains. In Brazil, where Professor Hewlett writes of "growing poverty," life expectancy has increased by nearly twenty years since World War II. In India, life expectancy has risen by over half since the early 1950s, and may have nearly doubled since the decade of Independence. If we remember that the countries in Table 6 represent over two thirds of the population of the less developed regions, the World Health Organization's suggestion that life expectancy may have risen in "developing regions" by fifty percent between the 1930s and the 1960s[28] may not sound exaggerated.

To be sure, "it is not yet possible to determine levels of mortality—much less trends— in sub-Saharan Africa with any degree of confidence," as a recent U.N. demographic study noted. Figures for much of the Muslim expanse from Casablanca to Dacca are also highly problematic. But for the regions of the poor world in which mortality estimates are more firmly rooted in the results of useable censuses and surveys, it appears that the gap in life expectancies separating those less developed countries from developed societies has been narrowing. Some of the more advanced LDCs, like Taiwan and Costa Rica, have managed to eliminate the gap completely; their peoples can now expect to live as long as citizens of countries in Western Europe. Where gaps persist, there has been progress in closing them. Mexico's life expectancy is currently about eight years lower than the United States', but in 1950 the difference between the two nations was about eighteen years. Indian lifespans today are on average twenty years shorter than those in the West. The gap speaks to the severity of poverty in India today; it should not make us forget, however, that there was a gap of over thirty years between India and the West in the early 1950s.

When life expectancies in poor and rich nations converge, it may be the case that life expectancies within the poor nation are converging as well: that is, that health improvements for the disadvantaged strata of society are outpacing those for the more privileged.[29] However, we do not have enough data to generalize about systematic differences in life expectancy within poor nations by income levels or education. On the other hand, differences in life expectancy between cities and countryside are so common in poor societies that they may almost be treated as a rule. In many poor societies, that difference is striking: in India people can expect to live nearly a decade longer in cities than in rural areas and in Indonesia, six years; in Brazil, lifespans are nearly thirty percent longer in the region of San Paulo and Rio de Janeiro than in the predominantly rural Northeast. Interestingly, there is no evidence that this difference is less pronounced in Communist societies: Chinese data provided to the World Bank suggest that lifespans may be more than a dozen years longer in Peking and Shanghai than in some of the less developed provinces,[31] while Cuba's gap between city and countryside does not seem to be noticeably lower than nearby Jamaica's. Regardless of a government's professed ideology, a poor society's cities are likely to be enclaves of life-extending comforts.[32]

With a general picture of postwar progress against mortality in the less developed countries in mind, we can try to compare the performance of Communist and non-Communist nations. In all Marxist-Leninist societies, "Liberation" has ushered in campaigns of disease programmatic augmentations of medical and public health services, and a radical redistribution of property in the name of the poor. Have these efforts brought Communist societies superior results in health improvement?

Comparisons of performance between Communist and non-Communist nations in the poor world are necessarily inexact. This is not only a question of statistical inexactitudes; but of the unavoidable difficulties in measuring countries with different cultures, histories and resources against one another. Nevertheless, if we move carefully we may get some idea of how well Communist states in the poor world have fared in comparison with their neighbors.

In Latin America, it is often claimed that Cuba has made unusual progress in health during the past twenty five years under Fidel Castro and his Communist Party of Cuba. Careful inspection of Cuba's health statistics would lead to a different conclusion. Cuba is the only nation in Latin America or the Caribbean whose registered rate of infant mortality did not decline during the 1960s. In fact, registered rates of infant mortality in Cuba appears to have *risen* by over 25% between 1960 and 1969. Cuba's rise in infant mortality may not be a statistical artifact. Pre-revolutionary Cuba's birth and death registration systems, while not complete, were reasonably good. Recently, Cuban demographers have suggested that infant mortality had been under-reported by 15% in the late 1950s;[33] this would not be enough to explain away a 25% rise in infant deaths. Cuba's statistics on communicable diseases, moreover, fall and rise over the 1960s in very much the same pattern as its infant mortality rates, peaking first in 1962, then again in 1969.[34] Both 1962 and 1969 are believed to have been years of setback for the Cuban domestic economy.

Statistics from Cuba's Ministry of Health suggest that a dramatic decline in infant mortality took place in the 1970s. According to these numbers, the rate of infant mortality would have dropped from over 40 per thousand in 1970 to about 19 per thousand in 1980—a figure not too different from the United States' in the mid-1970s. Salutory though these improvements appear, there is reason to doubt them. Approximately ninety percent of Cuba's drop in infant mortality during the 1970s took place in two years: 1972 and 1976. These were years in which the Cuban statistical system was overhauled.[35] Since 1972, Cuba's State Statistical Committee, as it is now known, has been relieved of its responsibility to collect numbers on infant mortality; these are now simply given to it by the Ministry of Health.[36] Independent verification of infant mortality rates could be had through "life tables," which calculate survivorship for all age groups, and thus demand internal consistency. Cuba did produce a "life table" in 1974, and it is seriously at variance with the Ministry of Health pronouncements on infant mortality. The Ministry of Health puts infant mortality in 1974 at 26; the "life table" put it at 46.[37] Ministry of Health statistics suggest that infant mortality fell by 35% between 1970 and 1974; by contrast, the "life tables" indicate that it *rose* by over fifteen percent!

Compared with other nations from Latin America and the Caribbean, Cuba's progress in health appears unexceptional, as can be seen from Tables 6 and 7. In the early 1950s, Cuba was probably the healthiest nation in the American tropics, enjoying both the highest life expectancy and the lowest infant mortality rate. Today this no longer seems so. Costa Rica now appears to lead Cuba in life expectancy, and several countries appear to have lower levels of infant mortality—including possibly Chile, where to the amazement of many observers the Pinochet regime not only continued but accelerated the reduction of infant mortality rates that had been taking place under President Allende.[38] In terms of improvements in life expectancy, Cuba has been outpaced by Chile and Costa Rica, and has just about held even with Jamaica. In all, the only country in the Western Hemisphere against which Cuba's record could be compared very favorably would seem to be Argentina. No one familiar with modern Argentine history could be heartened by such a comparison.

In Northeast Asia, the Korean peninsula is divided between a Communist and a non-Communist government. Information on mortality and health for South Korea is scarce, but available; by contrast, North Korea has attempted to seal its people off from the rest of the world, and releases only facts and assertions which are deemed to make the Democratic People's Republic of Korea seem to excel over the Republic of Korea. According to Japanese colonial records, mortality was about the same in both North and South Korea before World War II.[39] Today the situation is unclear. According to one set of U.N. projections, life expectancy and infanct mortality is the same in North and South Korea; according to another, whose derivation is not explained, life expectancy is now about three years higher in the South.[40] At this point (1983), the most that can be said is that there is no reason to presume that North Korea's performance in health has been any better than South Korea's.

In Southeast Asia, there are too few hard data about current health conditions in Vietnam to assess its record in detail. One set of United Nations estimates put life expectancy in Vietnam at 48 in the late 1970s—below India. By contrast, a World Bank mission visiting Vietnam in the late 1970s put life expectancy at 62— almost thirty percent higher. That figure is almost certainly too high: even Soviet researchers give a lower number. In the cautious formulation of one country study, Vietnam's life expectancy "would be" 59 years in 1980.[41] The conditional phraseology suggests that the authors might have deemed life expectancy to be quite a bit below that level at some earlier date. The United Nations' Population Division's most recent projection of life expectancy for Vietnam may be the best of the lot: it places expectation of life at birth in Vietnam in the late 1970s in the low fififtes.[42] By this conjectural estimate, health conditions in Vietnam might be slightly better than in India or Indonesia, but it would not be significantly better (see Tables 6 and 7). Health conditions would be much less favorable than in nearby Thailand, or the Philippines. From the limited demographic accounts of the French colonial period, it would seem that health conditions in Vietnam in the 1930s were not worse than in India (Indonesia would offer a better comparison, but its colonial demographic data are too sketchy).[43] In terms of performance over time, there is as yet little reason to believe that Vietnam has done better than either its neighbors or some other populous and poor Asian societies. Vietnam, it is true, has attempted to raise health standards against a background of continuing war, while its neighbors have had long stretches of military calm and domestic stability in which to do their work. In the modern world, however, life expectancies have typically risen rapidly in societies that were at war, so long as civil order was maintained. Moreover, it is not clear that Hanoi's more or less continuous engagements in military hostilities since 1945 have been unrelated to the policies of the national leadership. Until and unless Vietnam develops a "peacetime" track record and makes more information available to the outside world, it will be difficult to compare its performance in health against that of other countries.

China is not easily compared with other nations: two comparisons which suggest themselves, however, are with Taiwan, whose government also claims authority to guide the destiny of the Chinese people, and India, the world's second-largest poor country. China's demographic accounts are incomplete—as late as the mid-1970s less than a third of the nation's may have been registered[44]—and adjustments must flesh out the gaps. The best reconstructions of China's mortality numbers to date (1983) come from the U.S. Bureau of the Census and a collaboration between the World Bank and the National Academy of Sciences.[45] These figures are presented against India's and Taiwan's in Tables 6 and 7.

On the other hand, life expectancy in China today appears to be significantly lower than in Taiwan, and would also seem to be much lower than in Singapore, Hong Kong, Peninsular Malaya, and other regions for which we have data on the health of overseas Chinese.[46] On the other hand, Taiwan and these other regions had enjoyed civil order for many decades, and had benefited from the efforts of colonial powers to develop them. They began the 1950s with lifespans in the mid-to-upper fifties—not far short of Japan's at the time. China's life expectancy was probably something like twenty years lower. Furthermore, it is not reasonable to equate the job of improving the health of a few million people who are already comparatively well off with the task of dramatically raising the lifespans of a disease-ridden quarter of mankind.

Comparisons against India are no more satisfactory. There seems to be little doubt that lives are longer today in China than in India. But this does not mean that China's record in health is self-evidently superior to India's. Three things must be remembered. First, both China and India are enormous nations characterized by stark regional differences, and national averages ignore these. Liaoning province, with its Manchurian heritage and its comparatively developed industrial base, might look very good next to India's impoverished Gangeatic state of Bihar, but it is not clear that Tibet or Anwhei would come off so well against Kerala or the Punjab. Second, despite the turmoil and bloodshed of partition, India's transfer of power in the 1940s was comparatively orderly; by contrast, China suffered two decades of disruption of civic life, climaxed by a devastating foreign invasion and an even more destructive civil war in the years immediately preceeding its liberation. Life expectancy in China in the early 1950s was unnaturally low; *any* government which could bring peace and civil order might expect to reduce the nation's mortality level substantially, regardless of its health policies. Finally, the record looks very different for different decades. Whatever else may be said about independent India's policies, they have never led to a dramatic decline in the nation's health. This is not true in China. In the wake of the "Great Leap Forward"—a period now known as the "Three Lean Years"—China is believed to have endured the worst famine of the twentieth century. The loss of life during these years will never be known precisely, but recent estimates of "excess mortality" for the period center around twenty to thirty million people.[47] China's life expectancy may have fallen into the low twenties by 1960. By contrast, India's policy interventions in civic life have almost always stabilized or lowered death rates: effective relief work during the crisis of the mid-1960s, for example, prevented any measureable rise in mortality in the states where the harvest failed. If the poor in China have gained the most when life expectancy has been rising, they also surely suffered the worst when it was falling. There can be no easy assessment of a regime that has presided in the same generation over both dramatic improvements and deteriorations in the health of its citizens.

In short: the record of Marxist-Leninist regimes in reducing mortality does not seem to be demonstrably superior to that of non-Communist governments in the less developed regions. If the Communist societies of the Warsaw Pact offer the poorer

Marxist-Leninist states any glimpse of the future, moreover, their prospects for rapid and continuous improvements in health are problematic. The U.S. Census Bureau believes that life expectancy in the Soviet Union may have fallen by over three years since 1964;[48] male life expectancy was lower in Czechoslovakia in 1977 than in 1960, and seems to have fallen in Poland, Bulgaria and Hungary between the late 1960s and the late 1970s.[49]

We have looked at population levels and at mortality. One other type of demographic datum can inform us about living standards: this is fertility. The relationship between fertility and poverty, however, is complex. Low death rates may be desired universally, but there is no corresponding consensus about appropriate levels or directions for birth rates. Birth rates can fall with the onset of economic development or with the onset of famine; they can rise because of a change in tastes, a change in health, or a change in economic conditions. Patterns of fertility and family formation in the less developed regions are diverse. The difference between population policies in Communist and non-Communist countries in the less developed regions, however, are distinct, and bear directly on patterns of poverty.

In non-Communist societies, experiments in "population control"—that is, in pressuring parents to have less, or more, children than they would choose of their own free will—have been brief anomalies.[50] In some of the poor world's Marxist-Leninist societies, however, "population-control" policies are routinely undertaken in the name of the public good. These interventions have improved neither health nor long term prospects for reducing poverty.

In the People's Republic of China, for example, intense efforts have been directed at pushing birth rates down since the early 1970s. In recent years, the government has promoted the "norm" of the one-child family, and has used not only positive incentives but also financial penalties, intimidation, and at least some forcible coercion in its attempt to make parents accede to it.[51] According to the Chinese press, one of the immediate results of this campaign has been a rise in infanticide. Chinese parents are still said to prefer boys over girls; the "one child norm" has made this preference a deadly matter.[52] There is some evidence that the "one-child norm" is also imperiling the health of grown women, for women who violate the state's population quotas must also avoid the services of the health care authorities.[53] To the extent that China's "population-control" policies are effective, they expose many Chinese to unnecessary risk of poverty in the future. Social security arrangements in China are still largely provisional;

in the countryside, and possibly in the cities as well, the family may well remain the most reliable source of support in times of hardship or danger.[54] The Chinese government has a far from perfect record in disaster management; indeed, the government itself has been an agent of chaos on more than one occasion in the past generation. To pressure families into having fewer children than they think desirable is to attempt to override their efforts at insuring their futures. Over the long run, the Chinese government's politicization of fertility seems likely to undo some of its achievements in reducing mortality: the more effective its "population-control" policies prove to be, the more they can be expected to undo.

Nutrition

Hunger may be acutely felt by the poor but it is imperfectly measured by statisticians. The conventional tool for judging a nation's nutritional well-being is the "food balance sheet," which estimates average per capita availabilities. Even if such numbers could be computed accurately—and these are least accurate in precisely the societies where malnutrition is most severe—they would tell us less than we would like to know. An average tells us nothing about distribution. Even if we had precise information on the caloric intake of the poor, however, we would still know less than we should want to, for levels of food consumption by themselves tell us nothing about individual needs, which vary not only between people, but even for the same person at different points in the year.[55]

Despite the formidable difficulties in quantifying undernourishment, we can get some basic sense of trends in serious hunger over the past generation in Communist and non-Communist nations. In a poor society the best measure of the nutritional status of a population is its health. Significant improvements in health are impossible without a reduction in nutritional vulnerability for some large portion of society. Until a nation achieves the life expectancy of a developed society (today, this would mean one in the high 60s or low 70s), mortality decline can be expected to depend in part upon reducing hunger, although this contribution diminishes at higher general levels of health.[56] Table 6 has already presented information of changes in life expectancies for many less developed countries; in a broad sense, the revolution in life chances that it outlines can be seen as a revolution in nutritional well-being as well.

Another indicator of progress against serious hunger is the death rate of children of the ages one to four. Children are especially vulnerable to nutritional setback, since they need more energy and protein for their weight than do adults, and suffer more for being denied. Death rates for the 1–4s are thought to reflect serious hunger more accurately than infant mortality rates because children who survive their first year of life typically develop resistances or immunities to many of the specific hazards which make infant mortality rates vary between differing environments.[57]

For those countries with reliable data, reductions have been consequential. In Mexico, the Philippines, and Thailand, child death rates are approaching the range (2–3 per thousand) at which hunger no longer makes its measureable impact through mortality. While their child death rates remain high, India's and Indonesia's nevertheless appear to have dropped by more than half since the 1950s.

If child death rates prove to be a reasonable measure of serious hunger, it would seem that serious hunger is an especially pressing problem in black Africa and the "Muslim world" that extends from North Africa through Bangladesh. In Kenya—one of the very few countries below the Sahara with even one good census—child death rates are as high as India's; over most of the rest of the continent they must be considerably higher.[58] India's child death rates also appear to be lower than those in Algeria, Egypt, or Turkey;[59] whatever the reason may be, children in those countries (and presumably in other Muslim nations which cannot supply data) do not seem to get as much nutrition as one might well expect.

There is little reliable information on child death rates for poor Communist countries. Cuba offers the most, and it is inconsistent. The Ministry of Health currently claims that Cuba's child death rate is 1.1 per thousand—about the same as for the United States in the early 1960s. But it also states that child mortality has dropped by 61 percent since 1960. That would place Cuba's child death rate at under 3 per thousand in 1960—a rate low enough to imply that pre-revolutionary regimes, rather than the Castro government, should be credited with eliminating serious malnutrition in Cuba. Better figures come from Cuba's "life tables"; these suggest that child death rates were in the range of 8–9 per thousand in the 1950s, and around 2–3 per thousand in the 1970s. This would represent meaningful nutritional progress and would indicate that serious hunger no longer troubles Cuba. Yet Cuba's performance over the past two decades would seem to be no better than Jamaica's or Costa Rica's, and would seem to be rather less rapid than Chile's. Whatever else one may say about Cuba's social and economic policies, they do not appear to have given Cuba a special edge over its neighbors in relieving serious malnutrition.

China's present child death rate is currently about 8–9 per thousand, according to US Census Bureau analyses.[60] This would be considerably lower than India's. On the other hand, it would be much higher than Taiwan's, Singapore's, or any of the other predominantly Chinese territories in East Asia.

China's child death rates would also look to be higher than those of Mexico or the Philippines. China's child death rate would seem to be close to Brazil's, and if the comparison with Brazil is meaningful, one would expect that a stratum of Chinese society, and perhaps a number of backward regions, are not protected today against deadly hunger. News reports from China would seem to confirm this: in the late 1970s, an average of a province a year was reported in the carefully managed Chinese press to be beset by "food shortage."[61] The breadth of the current hunger problem is suggested by a 1979 Plenum document which asserted that 100 million Chinese had "too little to eat"[62]—although it is impossible to know precisely what this was to mean, or how it was determined.

There is no reliable estimate for child death rates in Vietnam: the World Bank offers a figure, but it does so by assigning Vietnam a life expectancy, and then estimating the child death rate which would be associated with it in a "model" population. The best indication of nutrition in contemporary Vietnam may come instead from a World Bank mission from 1979, which reported that by a number of measures, including grain and cooking oil availability, Vietnam appeared to have a level of per capita consumption roughly between India's and Bangladesh's. Under such conditions, child death rates might be significantly lower in Vietnam than in India but only if the rationing and public health systems worked very effectively, but a significant differential in child death rates might be too much to hope for.

Marxist-Leninist nations have attempted to attack hunger with social revolution, rationing, and an economic mechanism whereby food and other goods are priced by their "social value" rather than in response to scarcity. If the Marxist-Leninist strategies for alleviating hunger have not distinguished themselves as notably more effective than those of a diverse array of non-Communist nations, it must be because these policies have distinctive drawbacks of their own.

Some of these drawbacks are not hard to identify. However much success Marxist-Leninist governments may claim in distributing food evenly among their people, they have generally found food difficult to produce. Collectivization and pricing policies seem generally to have actually lowered the efficiency of farm production, and seem to have lowered per capita production of foodstuffs as well in more than one Communist society. Per capita production of most foodstuffs appears to be lower in Cuba in the early 1980s than in 1960, and despite the Cuban economy's continuing dependence upon sugar, per capita production of that commodity has been falling as well.[63] In China, to judge by the partial statistics of the late 1920s and the late 1970s, per capita grain availability after thirty years of Marxist-Leninist policies was no higher than it had been half a century earlier.[64] And in Vietnam, to judge by even spottier numbers on agriculture and population, per capita rice production may have fallen by forty percent between the mid-1930s and the late 1970s.[65]

Whereas Marxist-Leninist regimes have put stock in the ability of politically directed flows of food to reach the poor, they have often neglected the ways in which markets can help avert nutritional disasters. In most of the poor non-Communist world, the decline of famine has been not only a matter of rising average food availability, but of an increasing ability to move food to the regions in which it is needed. Modern China may have emphasized regional "foodgrain self-sufficiency" and promoted the ration system, but it has let its markets fall into disrepair. By 1978, according to official statistics, the trade in foodgrains between China's provinces was down to a few hundred thousand tons—less than one tenth of one percent of recorded national output.[66] China's prosperous provinces were in effect separated from its poor ones; the traffic in grains had become too meager to permit needy regions to draw on external resources in times of distress.

Finally, there appears to be a great risk in societies with strong governments and weak economies that hunger will be politicized. In a poor society with far-reaching government interventions in economy and society, and few checks on the use of power, the emergence or persistence of hunger can be a result of state actions, and may even serve the purposes of state.

After the revolution, expropriated classes in Communist societies are at risk of becoming a class of hereditary paupers, since it is within the powers of government to deny them work, rationed food, and other social guarantees. In the wake of collectivization in North Vietnam, for example, one government survey indicated that former landlords were more likely to have "too little to eat" than any other rural group.[67] Throughout Asia, studies have shown that the education, skills, and hence the productivity of landlords are above the rural average.[68] Even *without* land, former landlords might be expected to earn above average incomes in rural societies under competitive conditions. The fact that they were apparently the hungriest group in North Vietnam suggests that a political decision had been made to impair their ability to feed themselves.

Politicizing the economy raises the danger not only of deliberate and planned nutritional insults, but also of inadvertant ones. In China, for example, the modernization drive known as the "Great Leap Forward" seems to have caused the virtual collapse of the economy and the breakdown of the food system in the early 1960s. In the famines that engulfed the People's Republic, it now seems that tens of millions of people may have perished.[69] Greater numbers of people may die today in India than China from "chronic hunger" and hunger-related disease, but over the past generation dozens of times as many people have probably perished from *famine* in Communist China as in the Republic of India. Paradoxically, despite their higher current levels of health, a greater fraction of the Chinese than the Indian adult population may have suffered from serious shortages of food.

Literacy

Exceptional individuals can raise themselves from poverty without learning to read or write, but for a society as a whole, the escape from poverty is impossible when illiteracy is widespread. The spread of technical skills and the improvements in administration which are vital to material progress depend heavily upon the ability to communicate by the written word. Illiteracy exacts a heavy toll from people in a poor society. Illiterates are generally less adept at making use of productive knowledge; in every society where such studies have been made, illiterates can expect to earn less than people who can read and write. Illiterate parents are more likely to see their children succumb to sickness and die, and are themselves less likely to be able to protect themselves against adversity in times of hardship.[70]

For all its importance to modern life, literacy is not as easily measured as might first be presumed. Literacy statistics are often gathered in questionable ways. In some surveys, everyone who has not been to school is counted as illiterate, even though people in poor societies do learn to read and write outside the classroom. Other surveys simply ask the respondent whether he or she is literate; when illiteracy confers stigma, such questions do not lend themselves to honest answers. There are other, more fundamental problems which frustrate the measurement of literacy. Criteria for literacy may differ dramatically from one nation, region, or profession to the next, in accordance with the technical requirements of daily life. Within a few decades the quality of literacy in a society can change tremendously; such changes are seldom captured by measures of literacy, much less analyzed in detail.[71]

For our purposes, it may be best to get some sense of the changing incidence of *total illiteracy* in less developed countries, rather than to attempt to measure improvements in literacy. Total illiteracy is easier to define, more nearly constant across time and space, and more directly connected with an individual's chances of remaining trapped in poverty or plunging into destitution.

Sample surveys and censuses in the less developed countries use different definitions for illiteracy; nevertheless, as Table 9 indicates, they suggest that illiteracy rates have diminished markedly among adults in many parts of the poor world. Of the large poor nations, Indonesia's achievements appear to have been the most rapid and substantial; it has seemingly reduced the incidence of illiteracy among adults by over 60 points since the end of the Second World War. Such speedy progress against illiteracy, however, is exceptional. As a practical matter, the reduction of illiteracy necessarily means teaching new generations basic skills, and creating incentives and pressures for unlettered adults to adopt a literate lifestyle. As such, it is necessarily an historical process.

Over the past generation, Mexico and Brazil, which had measured rates of illiteracy of 40–50% in the early 1950s, have apparently cut their incidences of illiteracy by more than half; starting with similar rates, Thailand and the Philippines have apparently managed to reduce their incidences of illiteracy by more than two thirds. Not all countries seem to have fared so well. Four fifths of India's adults were said to be unable to read or write three decades ago; more than three fifths still seem unable to do so. In sub-Saharan Africa, the "Muslim expanse," and other poor non-Communist regions where statistics on poverty are less easy to come by, the best indications are that progress against illiteracy has been slow. (This should not be surprising: mass illiteracy almost dictates spotty social statistics.)

More than any other philosophy of government, Marxism-Leninism has placed a premium upon eradicating illiteracy. Every Marxist-Leninist party that has come to power has set mass literacy as an immediate goal, and has devoted considerable effort to achieving the end. Have Marxist-Leninist regimes in the poor world been especially successful in reducing illiteracy? Communist regimes in poor nations have not only launched ambitious anti-illiteracy drives, but have made bold claims of their results. Hanoi announced that it "basically" eliminated illiteracy in the North in 1958—four years after Dienbienphu. Castro celebrated the end of illiteracy in Cuba in 1962, at the finish of a schooling campaign that lasted only a year. North Korea claims to have totally eliminated illiteracy in the course of a few months in 1947 and 1948.

These claims are extreme, and cannot be taken seriously. The elimination of illiteracy is an historical process; there are limits to the extent that the process can be accelerated. Adult illiterates, accustomed as they are to a life in which the written word plays no role, are not easily trained to read and write; when they do manage to pick up basic skills under intense drilling, they typically prove unable to retain them unless they have constant reinforcement. In the rural areas of poor nations and in the daily routines of low-productivity work, such reinforcement is hard to provide. Yet adults made up half or more of the populations in all the poor nations in which Communist regimes have come to power.

For the most part, a government's hopes of reducing illiteracy rest on educating the young. For Communist and non-Communist nations, these efforts are best described by gross primary school enrollment ratios, which are presented in Table 10. These figures are neither as error-free nor as meaningful as one might like: enrollment ratios can be no more accurate than the population estimates that underlie them; older people as well as children may be in school when illiteracy is declining; and the varying quality of education among nations means that similar rates of gross enrollment may hide differences in dropout rates, grade repetition, and skill retention. Nevertheless, if we take these figures together with census and survey estimates, we can tell some things about illiteracy in Communist nations, and their neighbors.

Cuba's record on illiteracy is easiest to measure. The Communist Party of Cuba now claims that 44 percent of Cuba's adults were illiterate before the revolution.[72] Censuses from the early

1950s, however, indicate that the recorded figure was close to 23 percent. Today a wide range of institutions, including the World Bank and the CIA, put Cuba's current rate of illiteracy at 5 percent. These guesses are not based on a close reading of Cuban educational statistics. In the late 1970s, Cuba released a survey which put the rate of illiteracy *for adults between 15 and 45* at about 5 percent. Older people, schooled before the revolution, must have higher rates, and they comprise more than a fifth of the adult population. Cuba's actual rate of illiteracy is thus more likely to be on the order of 10 percent. If it were, Cuba's progress against illiteracy would be no better than Costa Rica's, Chile's or Jamaica's. Intriguing inconsistencies in Cuba's educational accounts, moreover, raise the question of whether it has done even that well. In 1977, for example, Cuban officials told a *New York Times* correspondent that the actual rate of rural illiteracy in Cuba was 22 percent[73]—indicating virtually no decline in illiteracy since Batista. Before recent revisions, UNESCO data indicated that Cuba did not achieve universal enrollment from children of primary school age until 1975; figures from the early 1970s suggested that in both its rates of dropouts and its distribution of students among grades, Cuba's more nearly resembled Gutamala's than that of any advanced Latin American society.[74]

For China the record is less certain. According to the State Statistical Bureau, China's gross primary enrollment ratio was about 20 percent in the early 1950s; in 1980 it was said to be over 120 percent, a level high enough to be consistent with near-universal education for grade-school age children. In the intervening years, the expansion of educational opportunity was not steady: it was disrupted not only in the aftermath of the "Great Leap Forward," but also in the ten years of "Cultural Revolution" in the decade before Mao's death. There can be no sure figure for the extent of illiteracy today, but China's Ministry of Education has reported to UNESCO that there were about 220 million illiterates on the Mainland in 1979—by their reckoning, about a third of the adult population.[75] Yet even this figure, which is considerably higher than others that the People's Republic has chosen to release, may put the best face on the current illiteracy problem. According to Soviet claims, over forty percent of the recruits in the People's Liberation Army could not read or write in the late 1970s.[76] In China as in other poor societies, the army is an elite institution.

If we can judge by surveys and censuses of earlier decades, China's incidence of illiteracy may have been on the order of five-sixths of the adult population at the turn of the century, and may

have been on the order of seventy or eighty percent in the
1930s.[77] Communist China would seem to have made substantial
strides in reducing illiteracy, but its record of performance would
depend largely on what it was compared against. China's results
look impressive next to India's. Held up to China, India cannot
take refuge in geographical diversity or immense size to excuse its
slow progress in reducing illiteracy. But China does not come off
so well against Indonesia, another populous and geographically
diverse Asian nation, and the Mainland also seems to suffer in
comparisons with Taiwan. Both comparisons, however, are complicated by historical questions. In Indonesia, the Dutch colonial
policy of keeping education from the natives may have created a
political commitment to schooling on the part of nationalist leaders, and a social hunger for it on the part of the populace, which
would not otherwise have existed. Taiwan, for its part, was a
Japanese colony for the first half of the century, and the Japanese
put great effort into teaching the Taiwanese to read and write.
Taiwan might more properly be judged against a single advanced
province in the People's Republic where Japanese colonialists had
also built schools, such as Kirin or Liaoning in Manchuria; as of
1985, such data are unavailable.

Japanese colonialists also built schools in Korea; there, however,
they insisted that instruction be in Japanese. As elsewhere in the
world, the marriage of nationalism and "own language literacy"
seems to have produced a tremendous impetus for literacy in
Korea; the governments of both North and South Korea seem to
have gone far towards satisfying it. Illiteracy may have been somewhat higher in the South, which was a land of farmers, than in the
North, which contained more of the peninsula's heavy industry
before partition. Today, to judge by gross primary school enrollment ratios, there may be a slightly lower incidence of illiteracy in
the South. If South Korea has outpaced the North, this could be
explained by differences in both the demand for education, and
the supply provided. In South Korea, the economic boom of the
1960s and 1970 not only made education lucrative, but provided
unusually effective "reinforcements" for late converts to literacy
through changes in patterns of daily life. In the North, the educational system may, to judge from the very limited evidence, have
hit the political equivalent of diminishing returns. Political indoctrination is judged to be at least as important as imparting basic
skills in North Korea; sixty to seventy percent of a university
student's time, regardless of his field, is said to be given over to
studying the thought of Kim Il-Sung.[78] In the final stages of

eliminating illiteracy, the borderline student's retention of skills is unlikely to be improved by this sort of regimen.

Although North Vietnam claimed to have "basically eliminated" illiteracy by 1958, it released figures to UNESCO indicating that 35 percent of its adults were illiterate in 1960. That estimate may have been too generous: it apparently counted everyone who had participated in a literacy campaign, and according to independent reports, these campaigns seldom actually taught peasants how to read and write anything but a few slogans.[79] Gross primary school enrollment ratios are high in "unified" Vietnam; complete enrollment of school-age children may be in the offing. Near-universal literacy, however, would appear to be a remote goal. According to Vietnamese officials, about a third of South Vietnam's adults were illiterates at the time of the Liberation; enrollment ratios from the 1960s suggest more people were going to school in the South than the North.[80]

In short, available information suggests Communist states in the poor world have not been more successful than non-Communist states in reducing illiteracy. Their failure to achieve distinction speaks to the nature of illiteracy. To eliminate illiteracy, there must be both a supply of education and a demand for it. If Communist states have pushed harder than others to provide a supply, they may also have been less successful than others in creating an environment in which people seek and retain basic educational skills.

Status Of Women

The character of poverty in every society is shaped by the condition of its women. In most poor societies, women seem more likely than men to suffer from material and social deprivation. Harsh and unequal treatment of women affects not only the extent and severity of poverty today, but the prospects for alleviating poverty in the future, for it is overwhelmingly women who are responsible for nourishing, educating, and protecting the health of the children of the earth.

Vital though it is to the well-being of society, the status of women is not easily measured in numbers. In the developed Western nations, where data on women come in relative abundance, it has proved surprisingly difficult to "quantify" the position of women in society: differentials between men and women in employment and earnings are not as readily explained as one might first suppose, and polls of attitudes and opinion turn out to be highly sensitive to the expectations and survey techniques of those who conduct them. In poor nations, where less reliable information is available, the problem is considerably greater. Obvious degradations of women often do not make their way into statistics. It is known, for example, that women are bought and sold as slaves in Mauritania;[81] some have said that as much as a quarter of the population of Mauritania is still enslaved, yet it is impossible to find hard data about this in any international compendium. While we can only begin to assess the special burdens on women in poor nations, telling hints can be taken from numbers on health, literacy, and education.

In every developed nation, women can expect to live significantly longer than men. There is reason to view this as a "natural" difference, since considerable evidence suggests that the female system is inherently sturdier and healthier than the male.[82] In some poor societies, however, the treatment of women of all ages is so harsh that this biological advantage is negated, and women's lifespans are reduced below men's. In the non-Communist world, there is a regional specificity to the societies in which women perish before men. As best can be measured, the terrain marks out a crescent on the globe, encompassing territories from Casablanca to Dacca, and sweeping into Africa. Most of these are Muslim societies: censuses and surveys have indicated that men live longer than women in Morocco, Jordan, Iran, Pakistan, and Bangladesh.[83] But Islam is not the only way of life that seems to push women's life expectancy below men's. Sri Lanka, which is Hindu and Buddhist, had higher death rates for women than men until the early 1960s; South Africa's Indian community, composed of Hindus as well as Muslims, has had longer life expectancies for men than women consistently; and in India itself, the gap between male and female life expectancies has actually widened since Independence.[84] While very little good data can be found on life expectancy in Africa, there are indications that women may die earlier than men in several sub-Saharan societies.[85] This crescent of abnormally high female mortality, for all the diversity within it, appears to have some characteristic problems with overall poverty. These are by and large the nations of the non-Communist world which have had greatest difficulty in producing statistics on the plight of the poor; they are also the ones which seem to have the least evidence of rapid progress against material poverty in the postwar period.

Illiteracy rates provide another glimpse of the condition of women in poor countries; differences between recorded rates for women and men for several nations can be seen in Table 11. In non-Communist Latin America and East Asia, the gap between women and men appears to be small, or getting smaller. By contrast, a serious gap seems to have persisted over several decades in India, and may well have widened. Limited data suggest that the illiteracy gap is unusually wide in some of the other countries in the "crescent" mentioned above; it may actually be widening in some of the nations in that region. Differences in the incidence of illiteracy in a society depend, among other factors, on differences in the opportunity to go to school. Table 12 shows recorded differences over the postwar period for male and female gross primary school enrollment ratios for a number of poor nations. The patterns are broadly consistent with differences in illiteracy rates; once again differences appear to be small or diminishing in non-Communist Latin America and East Asia, while they are substantial and have widened in India. Limited data suggest that the enrollment gap is high in other countries in the non-Communist "crescent," and may well have widened in some of them.[86]

Do women appear to be less disadvantaged in poor societies guided by Marxist-Leninist directorates? Hard data from these nations are limited, but they can help us answer the question.

The overwhelming majority of women in Communist societies live in the People's Republic of China. According to its 1953 census, Mainland China had sixteen and a half million more men than women. In its 1982 census, the government counted almost thirty one million more men than women. (The 1982 count also found more men than women in each of the three provinces for which it released preliminary results.) Under Liberation, China's ratio of men to women appears to have risen; this fact, taken together with the striking "excess" of men at younger ages, suggests that women may live under unusual mortality disadvantages in Communist China. Recently released Chinese data do not allay suspicion: they show reconstructed death rates for women to be significantly higher than for men in 1957.[87] China's apparent surfeit of female mortality in the 1950s might be ascribed to historical factors, or to some practices inherent to Chinese culture; the same, however, cannot be said for the apparent rise of female mortality in the 1980s.

There were, as of 1983, no data on differences in illiteracy rates between men and women in revolutionary China. Figures can be found, however, on differences in primary school enrollment rates (Table 12). In 1980, the recorded gap was higher than for any other nation in East Asia; the difference, in fact, appeared to be only somewhat lower than in India. China's gap in enrollments suggests not only that opportunities for education are still accorded first to boys, but that a sizeable discrepancy in the incidence of illiteracy may be found on the Mainland today. In all, available information does not preclude the possibilitythat China may be the world's second great "crescent" of disadvantage for women. To the extent that Communist programs have transformed society on the Mainland, the special disadvantages of women in modern China may have been created by policies of government.

Neither Vietnam nor North Korea have published data on male and female death rates, or on differentials in illiteracy. Both, however, give data on differentials in primary school enrollment ratios (Table 12). After China's, Vietnam's appears to be the highest in East Asia. North Korea's appears to be comparatively low, but it is higher than South Korea's.

In its latest life table, lifespans in Cuba were about three years longer for women than men. In Jamaica, Costa Rica, and Chile, the difference is greater (four to six years), but it may not reflect meaningfully on differences in women's status. Differences in literacy and enrollment were likewise insignificant. If Cuba has done no worse for its women than its neighbors by these rough indicators, it would also seem to have done no better.

As far as the status of women is concerned, the gap between rhetoric and results of the Marxist-Leninist governments in the poor world appears to be substantial. It is true that Marxist-Leninist regimes have always enacted laws prohibiting forced marriage and bride price, establishing minimum ages for marriage, and legalizing divorce in their early days of power. It is also true that they have made efforts to expand educational opportunities for women, and to increase the participation of women in the process of "socialist construction." But improving the status of women has never been a goal in and of itself for these regimes. It has always been seen as a means to an end: a way of augmenting "socialist" power, or stimulating economic growth. The Marxist-Leninist view of the "women's issue" has proved to be extremely flexible. Women may have been exhorted to take up "men's work" in North Vietnam during the height of the manpower shortage in the war against the South, but with "Unification" they were just as vocally encouraged to return to their more traditional occupations: raising crops and children.[88] In North Korea, Kim Il-sung has pointedly emphasized that the "women's question" is a technical, not a social, issue:[89] this would seem to imply that the status of women will be tailored to the needs of the economy. But for women, the needs of the economy extend further than for men.

From the standpoint of the "socialist" planner, women are not only potential producers of good, but of the labor force of the future. When Marxist-Leninist planners take an active interest in shaping the birth rate, they necessarily intervene in the condition of women. These interventions are not guaranteed to improve the health of women—nor are they necessarily intended to. For women, indeed, the double burden of work and family may dramatically increase the impact, and attendant risks of state intervention in personal life in the name of the planned society will be adverse.

Socio-Economic Inequality

Inequality in the less developed countries is discussed at some length in other chapters of this book. It will suffice here to emphasize some points about material and social inequality that are not incorporated into those treatments.

In poor societies, where absolute and relative inequality tend to be closely associated, inequality does not merely stigmatize: it can be a threat to health, or to life itself. There is, however, no single satisfactory standard for measuring "inequality," for the social and economic attributes of human beings can differ in a vast variety of ways. The most commonly used measure of economic inequality is dispersions in income distribution. As a tool for describing even economic inequality (let alone social inequalities), it is at best of limited use. Few affluent societies, to say nothing of poor ones, measure their incomes with enough accuracy to permit unassailable comparisons of distributions among countries or over time. This technical problem aside, there remain real questions about what sorts of incomes ought to be measured. Household size and household incomes tend to increase together, but seldom at the same pace; some of the "richest" households in less developed countries are composed of the "poorest" people if we measure per capita rather than household income, and one-person households with comparatively high per capita incomes can can be ranked as "poor" if compared against struggling families with several poorly paid wage-earners.[90] "Snapshots" of income differences in a society, moreover, can take no account of the extent to which seeming "inequality" is actually due to the transiences of the business cycle, the shape of a society's age pyramid, or differences in "lifetime" earning strategies (such as going to school or into debt early in life in the hope of making more money later on).[91] Finally, income distribution figures place no special value on preserving human life: if poor people survive, it will seem as if society is becoming more "unequal"; if they die off, income distribution will seem to "improve."

There are other ways to measure material inequalities. Some of the most basic material inequalities have been discussed earlier in this chapter: the inequality that separates people who can expect to live long and healthy lives from those who cannot; between people who are adequately and regularly fed, and those whose lives revolve around the threat of hunger; between people who can read and write, and those who have no opportunity to avail themselves of the advantages of literacy; and between men and women in those societies where to be born female is to be assured of needless physical hardship. As we have seen, the greatest of these inequalities, the inequality of death rates, has been narrowing between Western nations and those poor non-Communist nations for which we can obtain data; though considerable distances may separate the lifespans of the privileged from the poorer strata within these poor societies, moreover, there is some reason to suspect that these gaps are also diminishing in many cases. With respect to hunger, we have seen a dramatic diminution of death rates for the elements of society most vulnerable to nutritional insult, the weaning children, in all poor non-Communist nations for which we can find information; great portions of the poor non-Communist world, moreover, appear to have been freed from the threat of famine over the past generation. Rates of illiteracy, by the same token, are apparently declining in all poor, non-Communist countries for which such information can be obtained—although they seem to be dropping more surely and rapidly outside the "crescent of poverty" than within it. As for discrimination against women, we have seen that women are healthier than men in non-Communist Latin America and East Asia, where sex-based differences in literacy are either small or narrowing. Within the "crescent of poverty" it appears that women are at serious disadvantage in both health and education; in the few of these nations with relatively reliable social statistics, it appears that the wide material gaps between men and women are not narrowing with any speed, and may be widening in some cases.

The fact that all these basic material inequalities are in unambiguous decline in non-Communist Latin America and East Asia, and that many of them may be reducing within the "crescent of poverty" as well, does not square with the widespread perception among the world's well-to-do and well-informed that inequalities are on the rise throughout much of the poor, non-Communist world. This discrepancy may owe much to the fact that it is easier to take the pulse of educated elites than of the poor themselves in less developed countries. In many parts of Asia, Africa, and Latin America, there is good reason to expect the educated and the affluent to feel "deprived." In the years following World War II, independence and "nation-building" created extraordinary opportunities for a single generation of educated people in the "Third World".[92] These opportunities could not be replicated for subsequent generations of elites—political stability and expanding educational bases saw to that—so that any privileged group which set their expectations by the careers of their predecessors were almost certain, in total, to be disappointed.[93] Elites do much to shape and inform public opinion; it would be a mistake, however, for outside observers to take the status anxieties of the well-to-do as an unbiased reading on the hopes and fears, much less the material plight, of the poor.

One sort of inequality affecting rich and poor alike is measured not by material differences at any given moment, but by the degree to which a person can rise or fall in society according to his or her own actions and abilities. Statistics cannot measure this "dynamic" aspect of equality with any precision, but they can, within crude limits, trace the outlines of intergenerational social mobility: the likelihood that an individual will have a different social status from his or her parents. There are obvious difficulties in measuring "social status" (including the problem of choosing the points in the "life-cycle" that should be compared). Few studies of intergenerational social mobility, moreover, have been attempted in the less developed countries. Nevertheless, the findings of the few studies available are instructive. Some of these are presented in Table 13.

Brazil has the reputation of a highly inegalitarian society—which, by many criteria, it may well be. Even so, the results from this occupational status survey from the 1970s suggest that it is quite possible in Brazil to rise from the lowest social ranking to the top, and to fall from the highest social ranking down towards the bottom. By several statistical measures of dispersion, intergenerational mobility appears to be greater than in several Western societies, including the United States. This is partly due to Brazil's more rapid shifts in occupational structure over the past generation (at least, as sociologists designate these): with economic growth and the move from agriculture, "occupational status," as it is measured, tends to rise more rapidly in poor nations than developed ones. After discounting the shifts in occupational status born of changing job structures, there appears to be distinctly less pure (or "circulation") mobility in Brazilian society than in the West. But this varies markedly by region: in the Southeast, there may be more "circulation" mobility than in the West, while in the impoverished Northeast, there seems to be very much less. Greater social mobility is apparently associated with those processes which help alleviate material poverty overall, while lack of social mobility, which by itself tends to trap those already poor in society's lowest slots—may also be associated with a poor record in raising overall living standards.[94]

One might expect social mobility to be lowest in the poorest regions of the poorer non-Communist countries. Rural India and Bangladesh would seem fair candidates for the description; it is for this reason that the data on intergenerational landholdings from these nations are of interest. (Landholding may measure wealth and status better than occupation in a poor rural setting.) Though the six villages used for Table 13 are not necessarily representative of the tens of thousands of villages in India and Bangladesh, they conform to a pattern: in each, large fractions of families which today are "large" holders were landless a generation ago, and a large fraction of those who are landless today come from families with large holdings in the recent past. Life in these few villages may be characterized by poverty, but it would not seem to be characterized by the inequality that comes of inheriting one's economic position.

Marxist-Leninist leaders are sharply critical of the social and economic inequalities of "capitalist" society, and insist that Communist policy is successful in reducing such differences. Marxist-Leninists often justify far-reaching government interventions in economic or personal life by the quest for equality, but Marxist-Leninist governments have released very little of the sorts of hard data which would allow outsiders to judge the results of their exertions. We can attempt, however, to make an evaluation on the basis of the information that is in the public domain.

As we have already seen, there is little reason to conclude that Marxist-Leninist governments in the poorer regions of the world have distinctly better records than non-Communist governments in dealing with the great material inequalities associated with disease, hunger, illiteracy, or discrimination against women. Under Communism, moreover, the nature of both poverty and the inequalities based in it seems to take a forbidding turn: to a greater degree than in non-Communist nations, great material inequalities tend to be a result of direct government action. Under Marxist-Leninist governments, all areas of life are legitimate avenues for ambitious and forceful experimentation, and these experiments need not be evaluated on the basis of their likely or actual effects on any given group of individuals.

Under Marxist-Leninist regimes, daily life tends to become highly politicized: that is, one's welfare depends to a large degree on the choices that people within the party and the government make. (This is not to say that daily life may not be highly politicized in non-Communist states; the question is of likelihood and ofdegree.) With the politicization of daily life, social opportunity would seem likely to be politicized as well, and this would not augur well for "equality of opportunity." The more that particular persons can arbitrarily determine who will gain or lose in society, the more likely it will be that connections and background rather than effort and achievement will determine one's social and economic rewards.

After every successful Communist revolution of this century, there appears to have been a period of rapid upward mobility for designated "friends of the people." In the countryside, new opportunites for advancement would arise with the dispossession of landlords and rich peasants; in the cities, nationalization of industry and business would open slots for new managers; and over the entire society a "new class" would come into being, generally drawing its members up from below. But once the openings in the new order were filled, it seems as a rule to have been in the interest of emplaced cadres to use the power of their offices not only to maintain their own positions, but to confer benefit and opportunity upon allies, relatives, and friends.[96] With only limited officially sanctioned market forces to serve as a guide to merit, economic rewards and punishments in Marxist-Leninist societies need bear little correspondence to measureable performance. Thus, over time one might suspect that "pure" social mobility in Communist societies tends to diminish—other things being equal. With little in the way of market forces to stimulate social mobility, we might suspect that these functions would fall on successive political tremors or purges.

There are no data from poor Communist nations against which to test these speculations. Data are however available on the inheritance of "status" in Hungary, both before and since the Communist takeover.[97] In the 1930s, the chances of becoming a "white collar" worker were high only if one's father was "white collar." In the 1940s, the "inheritance index" dropped precipitously, and reached its nadir in the years immediately following the 1956 uprising. In the prolonged period of political calm under President Kadar, this "inheritance index" has risen steadily. If the trends of the 1960s have been continued through the 1970s, privileged work would now depend as much on who one's father was as it did before the revolution.

While there are no data on social mobility in the poor Marxist-Leninist countries, there are indications that Hungary's experience is not entirely unique. At the top, it is seen in North Korea, where the world's first Communist dynasty is apparently in the making, and tolerance to nepotism is said to be creeping downwards.[98] At the bottom, it is now seen in China, where Soviet commentators note that "over half the young people entering the labor force (today) step into the shoes of their fathers and mothers, irrespective of their education, training, propensities, or sex."[99] The costs of bringing social mobility to such systems can be high: Chinese officials now say that the Cultural Revolution—a time of rapid advance for many cadres now well placed in party and government—"affected" one hundred million people, and there are indications that a million or more of those "affected" may have perished in the process.[100]

Special privileges and preferential arrangements inevitably reduce "equality of opportunity." They may have other effects as well. To protect special privilege, it is necessary to erect barriers, and barriers against mobility can both preserve poverty and endanger society's most vulnerable elements.[101] If political barriers against social mobility have an unfavorable long-term effect on the alleviation of poverty, extended Communist rule would not appear to stand the poor in good stead.

Concluding Remarks

In concluding this chapter, it may be useful to emphasize some of the principal findings and themes in the previous pages.

First, for all the talk about the condition of the poor in the less developed countries, it is still quite difficult to assess their plight with any precision in most regions of the world. Lack of comprehensive and reliable information on the condition of the poor cannot hasten the reduction of poverty. In a meaningful sense, the prospects of the poor in any society may be judged by the volume of reliable data that is generated on them.

Second, the notion that economic change in the postwar era has not brought significant material benefit to the bulk of the populations in poor non-Communist countries appears to be a judgement, not a conclusion supported by meaningful evidence. In all regions in which reliable data could be found, poor non-Communist nations appear to have experienced substantial improvements in life expectancy and health, and substantial reductions in the incidence of hunger and illiteracy since the end of the Second World War. Conventional methods of measureing living standards may have led to a serious underestimate of the progress against material poverty in many non-Communist societies. By the same token, the severity of the most significant material inequalities in poor societies may be exaggerated in conventional accounts of national poverty, while progress in narrowing the most important differences between privileged people and the deparately poor may be systematically undertstated.

Third, despite the tangible evidence of substantial and by some measures rapid progress against material poverty in many poor non-Communist societies over the past few decades, there is a large region in which progress against poverty may have been less rapid and less certain. This "crescent of poverty" stretches from Casablanca to Dacca, and sweeps down to encompass most of sub-Saharan Africa. Countries in this "crescent of poverty" seem generally to share three characteristics: difficulty or virtual inability to track and assess the condition of their poor people; harsh patterns of discrimination against women; and halting improvements in education and literacy. These three characterstics may serve as indicators of a country's prospects for rapid alleviation of poverty.

Fourth, there is little reason to think that the performance of Marxist-Leninist governments in attending to the poor has been generally superior to that of the non-Communist governments against which they might most reasonably be compared. In some ways, the performance of Communist governments appears systematically inferior to those of non-Communist counterparts in Asia and Latin America. The Marxist-Leninist regimes contribution to the less-developed countries has not been to abolish poverty; it has been to *modernize* it. Traditionally, lack of social choice has been associated with a lack of goods; material goods without choice is a uniquely modern formulation of poverty.

Fifth, if the problem of "income equality" has been exaggerated by conventional analyses of poverty, the problem of "equality of

opportunity" and social mobility seems to have been largely ignored. Yet it seems that social mobility may directly affect the
chances of the poor of escaping from poverty. In the immediate
sense, restricted social mobility traps the poor in the lowest rungs
of society; in a "dynamic" sense, however, it may also reduce the
stimuli which make for sustained and equitable economic growth.
Social mobility appears to be more problematic in Communist
societies than in non-Communist societies, with predictable implications for the long-term welfare of the poor in each.

* * *

At the beginning of this chapter, I suggested that there was
more discussion and analysis of the term "capitalism" in the context of the less developed countries than is merited by either the
concept or circumstances. At the end of this chapter, I would like
to suggest that there has been very much less discussion and
analysis of "markets" in the context of the less developed countries
than has been merited by circumstances. While we have not discussed the mechanisms by which the non-Communist nations
have made their partial escapes from poverty in these pages, it is
apparent that markets have played a role in each of these. In
facilitating the reduction of poverty and the spread of prosperity,
markets appear to offer two signal advantages: they possess an
inherent ability to transmit information, and they inherently stimulate mobility.

It serves no purpose to idealize the workings of markets. The
growth of economics as a field of study is to some extent a testi-
mony that the failure of markets, or at least to their imperfections,
and the rise of modern government states more eloquently than
words the ability of other forces to improve upon, or even substitute for, many of the functions of markets. Yet as the performance of Marxist-Leninist regimes in the poor nations would seem
to indicate, there are limits to the extent to which politics can
substitute for the functions of markets *effectively,* and to the benefit of the poor. In both Communist and non-Communist nations,
the extent to which progress against material poverty can be
accelerated in the future—and there should be no doubt that
there is much room for improvement—will depend in no small
part upon understanding what markets and governments can and
cannot be made to do. The technological potential of our era is
apparent; the social potential is yet obscure, and will not be
revealed without careful and reasoned exploration of the realm
that borders both market and state.

TABLE 1
1970 Per Capita Product of Selected Nations, Computed by Different Methods
(As Percent of U.S. per Capita Product)

	Foreign Exchange	Purchasing Power	Difference (%)
Kenya	2.99	5.99	+100
India	2.07	6.00	+190
South Korea	3.86	10.00	+159
Philippines	5.39	10.20	+ 89
Colombia	7.24	16.30	+125
Malaysia	8.10	17.40	+115
Iran	8.37	18.60	+122
Hungary	21.60	41.60	+ 91
Italy	36.00	49.00	+ 39
Japan	39.80	58.20	+ 46

Source: Irving B. Kravis et al., *International Comparisons of Real Product and Purchasing Power,* Baltimore: Johns Hopkins Press (1978).

TABLE 2
Differences in Estimated Per Capita Product After Purchasing Power Adjustments for Various LDCs, 1977 (1980 Dollars)

Largest LDCs	Kravis Group	Block	Difference
India	658	450	46%
Indonesia	653	807	− 19%
Brazil	3345	2359	42%
Bangladesh	534	245	118%
Pakistan	880	472	86%
Nigeria	876	1000	− 12%
Mexico	2618	2309	13%
Philippines	1396	859	63%
Thailand	1166	833	40%
Turkey	2294	1442	59%

Two Dozen Poor LDCs	Kravis Group	Block	Difference
Benin	437	643	− 32%
Burundi	356	315	13%
C.A.R.	443	431	3%
Chad	454	209	117%
Ethiopia	345	287	20%
Gambia	526	537	− 2%
Guinea	409	425	− 4%
Lesotho	364	503	− 28%
Madagascar	558	750	− 26%
Malawi	454	399	14%
Mali	278	208	34%
Niger	524	306	71%
Rwanda	343	410	− 16%
Somalia	427	263	62%
Tanzania	548	434	26%
Togo	471	650	− 18%
Uganda	546	649	− 16%
Upper Volta	265	296	− 10%
Zaire	350	366	− 4%
Afghanistan	301	454	− 33%
Bangladesh	534	245	118%
Burma	420	365	15%
Nepal	428	264	62%
Haiti	535	567	− 6%

Sources: Calculated from Robert Summers, Irving B. Kravis, and Alan Heston, "International Comparison of Read Product and Its Composition: 1950–79," *Review of Income and Wealth* (March 1980), and Herbert Block, *The Planetary Product in 1980: A Creative Pause?*, Washington, D.C.: U.S. Department of State (1981).

TABLE 3
Differences for Estimates of Change in Per Capita Product for Various LDCs, 1950–77

Dozen Largest LDCs	Kravis Group	Block	High/Low
India	41	53	29%
Indonesia	88	540	514%
Brazil	202	214	6%
Bangladesh	4	14	250%
Pakistan	75	66	14%
Nigeria	143	219	53%
Mexico	112	97	15%
Philippines	143	122	17%
Thailand	101	139	38%
Turkey	179	139	29%

Two Dozen Poor LDCs	Kravis Group	Block	Difference	High/Low
Benin	4	8	4	100%
Burundi	− 51	− 12	39	325%
C.A.R.	− 20	− 1	19	1900%
Chad	− 13	− 44	− 31	238%
Ethiopia	57	89	32	50%
Gambia	40	58	18	45%
Guinea	− 1	− 10	− 9	200%
Lesotho	109	118	9	8%
Madagascar	− 7	− 8	− 1	14%
Malawi	99	107	8	8%
Mali	25	114	89	456%
Niger	58	21	− 37	176%
Rwanda	2	18	16	800%
Somalia	2	− 10	− 12	−500%
Tanzania	81	70	− 9	16%
Uganda	5	− 3	− 8	− 60%
Upper Volta	5	36	31	620%
Zaire	16	69	53	331%
Afghanistan	8	5	− 3	60%
Bangladesh	4	14	10	250%
Burma	94	80	− 14	18%
Nepal	16	32	16	100%
Haiti	4	− 0	− 4	−800%

Source: Calculated from Robert Summers, *et al.*, and Herbert Block, as cited in Table 2.

TABLE 4
Comparison of World Bank and OECD Estimates of Pretax Income Share
for Bottom 40% of Households of Selected Developed Nations

	World Bank	OECD	Δ%
Canada	20.0 (1970)	15.2 (1969)	−24
USA	19.7 (1970)	13.8 (1972)	−30
Sweden	14.0 (1963)	17.4 (1972)	+24
Netherlands	13.6 (1967)	16.8 (1967)	+24
France	9.5 (1962)	14.2 (1970)	+49

Source: Donald McGranahan, *International Comparability of Statistics on Income Distribution*, Geneva: UNRISD (1979).

TABLE 5
U.S. Census Bureau Population Estimates For
Selected Communist And Non-Communist LDCs, midyear 1980 (millions)

Country	Population
China	1,013
India	685
Indonesia	151
Brazil	122
Mexico	70
Vietnam	54
Philippines	49
Thailand	48
South Korea	40
North Korea	18
Taiwan	18
Sri Lanka	15
Chile	11
Cuba	10
Costa Rica	2
Jamaica	2
H. Total, 16 LDCs	2,308
B. Estimated Total, "Developing Countries	3,342
A/B	68%

Source: U.S. Bureau of the Census, *World Population 1983* (Washington, D.C.: U.S. Department of Commerce, 1983).

TABLE 6
Estimates Of Life Expectency For Selected Communist And Non-Communist LDCs, c. 1950–c. 1980

	1950	1960	1970	1980
1. Cuba	59 (1953)	64	70	70
2. Jamaica	56 (1950–52)	65	68	(69)
3. Costa Rica	56	62 (1962–64)	69 (1972–74)	72 (1978)
4. Chile	55 (1952–53)	57	62	(67)
5. Mexico	48	58	60	66
6. Brazil	48	55	57	64
7. China	(30–35)	(30–35)	(50–55)	(60–65)
8. India	32 (1951)	41 (1961)	46 (1961)	52 (1978)
9. Taiwan	59 (1952)	65	69	71
10. Vietnam*	(38)	(42)	(45)	(52)
11. Indonesia*	(38)	(42)	47	53
12. Sri Lanka	58 (1953)	62 (1962)	66 (1971)	67 (1981)
13. Thailand*	(47)*	(54)	58	61 (1975)
14. Philippines*	(46)*	(53)	58	61 (1974–75)
15. North Korea*			(63)*	
16. South Korea*	(47)	53 (1955–60)	63	65 (1978–79)

*—parenthetical figures are estimates for first half of the decade. Note: with exception of North Korea and Vietnam, all estimates based on or extrapolated from census and survey data. Parentheses indicate adjustment or extrapolation.

Sources:

Line   1: Column   1: Fernando Ganzalez, Q. and Jorge Debosa, "Cuba: Evaluacion y Ajuste del Censo de 1953 y las Estadisticas de Nacimientos y Defunciones entre 1943 y 1958," *CELADE* Series C × 124, June 1970;

                  Columns   2–4: United Nations, *Levels and Trends of Mortality Series 1950* (New York: United Nations, 1982).

Line   2: Columns   1–3: *Levels and Trends, op. cit.;*

                  Column   4: Inter-American Development Bank, *Economic And Social Progress In Latin America* (Washington, D.C. IABD, 1983).

Line   3: Columns   1–3: *Levels And Trends, op. cit.;*

                  Column   4: World Health Organization, *World Health Statistics 1981* (Geneva: WHO, 1982).

Line   4: Columns   1–3: *Levels And Trends, op. cit.;*

                  Column   4: *Economic and Social Progress, op. cit.*

Line   5: Columns   1–3: United Nations, *Demographic Yearbook,* various editions;

                  Column   4: *Economic And Social Progress, op. cit.*

Line   6: Columns   1–3: United Nations, *Demographic Yearbook,* various editions;

                  Column   4: World Bank demographic data sheets, unpublished.

Line   7: Columns   1–3: Based on Kenneth Hill, "China: An Evaluation of Demographic Trends 1950/82" (World Bank, unpublished paper, 1983);

                  Column   4: based on personal communication with Judith Banister, U.S. Bureau of the Census.

Line   8: Columns   1–3: *Levels and Trends, op. cit.;*

                  Column   4: Government of India, *Survey On Infant And Child Mortality, 1979: A Preliminary Report* (New Delhi: Office of Registrar Journal, India: 1980).

Line   9: Columns   1–4: *Republic of China Demographic Yearbook,* (Taipei: Executive Yiian), various volumes.

Line   10: United Nations, *Demographic Indicators of Countries: Estimates And Projections As Assessed In 1980* (New York: United Nations, 1982).

Line   11: Columns   1–2: *Demographic Indicators Of Countries, op. cit.;*

                  Column   3–4: World Bank demographic data sheets, unpublished.

Line   12: Columns   1–3: *Levels and Trends, op. cit.;*

                  Column   4: World Bank demographic data sheet, unpublished.

Line   13: Columns   1–2: *Demographic Indicators of Countries, op. cit.*

                  Columns   3–4: U.S. Bureau of the Census, *World Population,* (Washington, D.C.: Dept. of Commerce), various issues.

Line   14: Columns   1–2: *Demographic Indicators of Countries, op. cit.*

                  Columns   3–4: U.S. Bureau of the Census, *World Population* (Washington, D.C.: Dept. of Commerce), various issues.

Line   15: Column   4: United Nations, *Demographic Yearbook, 1981* (New York: United Nations, 1983).

Line   16: Column   1: *Demographic Indicators of Countries, op. cit.*

                  Columns   2–4: National Bureau of Statistics, *The Life Table of Korea (1978–79)* (Seoul: Economic Planning Board, July 1982).

TABLE 7
Estimates Of Infant Mortality For Communist And Non-Communist LDCs, c. 1950–c.1980 (rates in deaths per thousand births)

	1950	1960	1970	1980
1. Cuba	79 (1952–54)	66	38	46 (1974)
2. Jamaica	79 (1950–52)	56	35	22 (1976)
3. Costa Rica	97	87 (1962–64)	51 (1972–74)	19
4. Chile	120 (1952–53)	115	77	35
5. Mexico	113	78	71	61 (1977)
6. Brazil	136	107	89	81 (1926)
7. China	(225) (1954)	(330)	(109)	(71)
8. India	(190)*	(157)*	133*	129*
9. Taiwan	91	42	27	22
10. Vietnam	(180)*	(150)*	(140)*	(106)*
11. Indonesia	(166)*	(145)*	(112)*	(99)*
12. Sri Lanka	82	57	51	46
13. Thailand	(135)*	(97)*	(68)*	(59)*
14. Philippines	(132)*	(93)*	(65)*	(59)*
15. North Korea				
16. South Korea	(116)*	(71)*	50	36 (1978–79)

*See Sources

Note: Figures in parentheses come from adjusted estimates rather than directly from life tables or other in-country figures.

Sources:

Line	1:	Columns 2–4:	*Levels and Trends of Mortality Since 1950* (New York: United Nations, 1982).
Lines	2–6:	Columns 1–3:	S. Baum and E. E. Arricaga, "Levels, Trends, Differentials, and Causes of Infant Mortality and Early Childhood Mortality In Latin America," *World Health Statistics Quarterly* 1981.
		Column 4:	U.S. Bureau of the Census, *World Population 1979* (Washington: Department of Commerce, 1980).
Line	7:	Columns 1–3:	Kenneth Hill, "China: An Evaluation of Demographic Trends; 1950–1982", (World Bank: unpublished paper. June 1983);
		Column 4:	World Bank, *World Development Report 1983* (Washington: World Bank, 1983).
Line	9:	Columns 1–4:	*Social Welfare Indicators*, Republic of China, 1982 (Taipei: Manpower Planning Committee, Executive Yuan, 1982).
Line	12:	Columns 1–3:	*Statistical Pocketbook of Ceylon 1974* (Colombo: Department of Census And Statistics, 1974).
		Column 4:	*World Population 1979, op. cit.*
Line	17:	Column 3–4:	National Bureau of Statistics, *The Life Table of Korea 1978–79* (Economic Planning Board, July 1982).

All other Figures: United Nations Secretariat, "Infant Mortality: World Estimates and Projections, 1950–2025," *Population Bulletin of the United Nations #14, 1983*. These refer to the following years: for Column 1, 1950–1955; for Column 2, 1960–1965; for Column 3, 1970–1975; for Column 4, 1975–80.

TABLE 8
Estimated Rates Of Illiteracy For Communist And Non-Communist LDCs, c. 1950–c. 1980 (percentage of population over 15)

	1950	1960	1970	1980
1. Cuba	22 (1953)	(21) (1959)	13	(10) (1979)
2. Jamaica	23 (1953)	18	4	(10)
3. Costa Rica	21	16 (1963)	12 (1973)	(10) (1978)
4. Chile	20 (1952)	16	11	(6) (1979)
5. Mexico	43	35	26	17
6. Brazil	51	40	34	25
7. China	(70–80)?	(55–60)		34 (1979)
8. India	81 (1951)	76 (1961)	66 (1971)	64 (1981)
9. Taiwan	42 (1952)	27	15	10
10. Vietnam	(80 + ?)			(30 + ?)
11. Indonesia	(80 + ?)	61	43	28
12. Sri Lanka	32 (1953)	15 (1963)	22 (1971)	16 (1981)
13. Thailand	48 (1947)	32	21	(12)
14. Philippines	40 (1948)	25	17	(10)
15. North Korea	(50?)			(10?)
16. South Korea	(50?)	29	12	(6)

Note: Bold figures come from Census or sample survey results; parenthetical figures have undergone census—or survey—based adjustments; parenthetical figures with question marks are estimates not based on census or survey results.

Sources:
Line   1: Columns   1–3:   Carmelo Mesa-Lago, *The Economy of Socialist Cuba* (Albuquerque: University of New Mexico Press, 1981).

            Column   4:   calculated from Unesco, *Statistical Yearbook 1982* (Paris: Unesco, 1982).

TABLE 9
Estimated Gross Primary School Enrollment Ratios For Communist
and Non-Communist LDCs, 1950–1980 (Students Enrolled as a
Percent of Children of Primary School Age)

	1950	1960	1970	1980
1. Cuba	74	109	121	112 (1979)
2. Jamaica	110	92	119	99 (1979)
3. Costa Rica	78	96	110	107
4. Chile	93	109	107	117
5. Mexico	62	80	104	120
6. Brazil	68	72	84 (1971)	93 (1979)
7. China	21	58 (1958)	85	121
8. India	28	61	73	76
9. Taiwan	84	96	98	99
10. Vietnam	(12)	(46)	(110)	16
11. Indonesia	45	71	77	112
12. Sri Lanka	89	95	99	100
13. Thailand	76	83	83	96
14. Philippines	91	95	114	110
15. North Korea	(near 100?)			116 (1976)
16. South Korea	83	94	103	109

Notes: Figures for Taiwan refer to *net* primary enrollment; parenthetical figures for Vietnam refer to gross primary
school enrollment rates for Republic of Vietnam (South Vietnam).

Sources:

Line 1–8:   Unesco, *Statistical Yearbook 1982* (Paris: Unesco, 1982) and earlier years.
Line 9:   *Taiwan Statistical Data Book 1982* (Taipei: Executive Year, 1982.
Lines 10–14:   Unesco, *Statistical Yearbook, 1982, op. cit.* and earlier years.
Line 10:   Column   1:   Robert Scalapino and Chong-sik Lee, *Communism in Korea* (Berkeley: University
                                  of California Press, 1983).
               Column   4:   Unesco, *Statistical Yearbook 1982, op. cit.*
Line 16:   Unesco, *Statistical Yearbook 1982, op. cit.* and earlier issues.
Line   2: Columns   1–4: Unesco, *Statistical Yearbook,* various issues.
Line   3: Columns   1, 3: Unesco, *Statistical Yearbook 1976* (Paris: Unesco, 1977).
               Column   4:   Inter-American Development Bank, *Economic and Social Progress In Latin Amer-
                                  ica* (Washington: Intra-American Development Bank, 1981).
Line   4: Columns   1–3: Unesco, *Statistical Yearbook, 1976.*
               Column   4:   Intra-American Development Bank, *ibid.*
Line   5: Columns   1–4: Unesco, *Statistical Yearbook,* various issues.
Line   6: Column 1, 3, 4: Unesco, *Statistical Yearbook 1982.*
               Column   2:   *Brazil Series Estatisticas Retrospectives* (Rio de Janeiro: IBGE, 1977).
Line   7: Column   1:   estimate based upon Herbert Day Lawson, *Social Pathology In China* (Taipei:
                                  Ch'eng Wen Publishing Co., 1974).
               Column   2:   estimate based upon World Bank, *China: Socialist Economic Development* (Wash-
                                  ington: World Bank, 1981).
               Column   4:   Unesco, *Statistical Yearbook 1982.*
Line   8: Columns   1–3: Unesco, *Statistical Yearbook,* various issues.
               Column   4:   U.S. Bureau of the Census, *World Population: 1983* (Washington: Dept. of Com-
                                  merce, 1983).
Line   9: Columns   1–4: *Social Welfare Indicators Republic of China 1982* (Taipei: Executive Yuan, October,
                                  1982).

Line   10: Column   1, 4:   Estimated figures refer to population age six and older based upon Unesco, *Statistical Yearbook 1965* (Paris: Unesco, 1965) and Unesco, *Literacy In Asia: A Continuing Challenge* (Bangladesh: Unesco, 1978).

Line   11: Column   1:   estimate based on data in Unesco, *Literacy In Asia: A Concluding Challenge*.
         Columns   2, 3:   Unesco, *Statistical Yearbook*, various issues.
         Column   4:   U.S. Bureau of the Census, *World Population: 1983*.

Line   13: Columns   1–3:   Unesco, *Statistical Yearbook 1982*.
         Column   4:   estimated through cohort projection based on 1970 census data, and on primary school enrollment ratios, both taken from *Statistical Yearbook 1982*.

Line   14: Columns   1–3:   Unesco, *Statistical Yearbook 1982;*
         Column   4:   National Census and Statistics Office, "Projections of the Illiterate By Sex and Broad Age Group In the Philippines: 1970–2000," *Philippines Journal of Statistics*, V.28, #2, 1977.

Line   15: Column   1;   Based on Jon Halliday, "The North Korean Model: Gaps and Problems," *World Development* Sept./Oct. 1981.
         Column   4:   based on differential in primary school enrollment ratios between North and South Korea, 1976, as given in Unesco, *Statistical Yearbook 1982*.

Line   16: Column   1;   based on Paul Kuznets, *Economic Development and Structural Change In Korea* (New Haven: Yale University Press, 1977).
         Columns   2, 3:   Unesco, *Statistical Yearbook 1976*.
         Column   4:   Calculated from cohort projections from 1970 census and primary enrollment ratios, in *ibid*.

TABLE 10
ESTIMATED DIFFERENCE BETWEEN FEMALE AND MALE ILLITERACY RATES FOR COMMUNIST AND NON-COMMUNIST LDCs, c. 1950–c. 1980

(PERCENTAGE OF POPULATION OVER 15)

	1950	1960	1970	1980
1. Cuba	−4 (1953)			(1) (1979)
2. Jamaica	−6 (1953)	−6	−1	
3. Costa Rica	2	1	0	
4. Chile	3 (1952)	3 (1963)	2 (1973)	(1) (1979)
5. Mexico	7	10	8	4
6. Brazil	11	8	6	2
7. China				
8. India	21 (1951)	28 (1961)	29 (1971)	30 (1981)
9. Taiwan	28 (1952)	21	21	13
10. Vietnam				
11. Indonesia	(under 40?)	27	25	17
12. Sri Lanka	28 (1953)	18 (1963)	14 (1971)	8 (1981)
13. Thailand	33 (1947)	23	16	(12)
14. Philippines	8 (1948)	5	3	(2)
15. North Korea				
16. South Korea	(about 40?)	25	13	(7)

Sources:

Line   1:   Columns 1–3:   Carmelo Mesa-Lago, *The Economy of Socialist Cuba* (Albuquerque: University of New Mexico Press, 1981).
         Column   4:   calculated from Unesco, *Statistical Yearbook 1982* (Paris: Unesco, 1982).

TABLE 11
Differences Between Male and Female Gross Primary School
Enrollment Ratios for Communist and Non-Communist LDCs, 1950–c.
1980

	1950	1960	1970	1980
1. Cuba	−4	0	0	7
2. Jamaica	−6	−1	0	−2
3. Costa Rica		2	2	1
4. Chile	8	4	−1	2
5. Brazil	0	1	0	0
6. Mexico		5	5	7
7. China				22
8. Taiwan	5	1	0	0
9. India	28	40	34	39
10. Vietnam			16 (1975)	15 (1979)
11. Indonesia		28	10	15
12. Sri Lanka		10	10	6
13. Thailand	8	9	8	5
14. Philippines	6	5	2	3
15. North Korea				4
16. South Korea		10	1	2

Source: Calculated from sources in Table 10.

TABLE 12
Indications of Intergenerational Mobility
In Brazil, India and Bangladesh

Brazil

Father's Status	Individual's Status in 1973						Total
	1	2	3	4	5	6	100%
1. upper	**29.8**	22.5	27.1	12.5	5.0	3.1	100%
2. upper-middle	15.2	**28.7**	28.7	15.5	6.1	5.8	100%
3. middle-middle	8.6	14.3	**36.2**	18.9	10.5	11.5	100%
4. lower-middle	3.8	8.7	21.6	**46.3**	14.9	4.7	100%
5. upper-lower	3.2	7.4	20.7	35.4	**23.8**	9.5	100%
6. lower-lower	1.0	2.5	13.1	21.1	17.4	**44.9**	100%
Total	3.5%	6.3%	18.4%	23.8%	16.0%	32.0%	100%

(sample: 44, 307)

Bangladesh (Char Gopalpur)
Present Landholdings

Inheritance	Landless	Small	Medium	Large	
Landless	**13**	7	2	1	23
Small	11	**17**	1	2	31
Medium	6	3	**14**	8	31
Large	3	2	3	**21**	29
	33	29	20	32	114

India (pooled sample, 3 villages)

Inheritance	Present Holdings				
	Landless	Small	Medium	Large	
Landless	**17**	9	11	2	39
Small	2	**20**	4	1	27
Medium	0	0	**23**	4	27
Large	0	0	5	**21**	26
	19	29	43	28	119

Sources: Brazil: Jose Pastore, *Inequality and Social Mobility in Brazil* (Madison: University of Wisconsin Press, 1981).
Bangladesh and India: Mead Cain, "Risk and Insurance: Perspectives On Fertility and Inequality in Rural India and Bangladesh", (Population Council, Center for Policy Studies, Working Paper #67, April 1981).

NOTES

1. Hollois Chenery *et.al.*, *Redistribution With Growth* (New York: Oxford University Press, 1974).

2. International Labor Office, *Poverty And Landlessness In Rural Asia* (Geneva: ILO, 1977).

3. Sylvia Ann Hewlett, *The Cruel Dilemmas Of Development: Twentieth Century Bazil* (New York: Basic Books, 1980).

4. Paul Bairoch, *The Economic Development Of The Third World Since 1900* (Berkeley: University Of California Press, 1975).

5. C. V. Devan Nair, ed., *Socialism That Works . . . The Singapore Way* (Singapore: Federal Publications, 1976).

6. For a description of some of these changes, see Michael Crowder, *West Africa Under Colonial Rule* (Evanston: Northwest University Press, 1968), D. G. E. Hall, *A History Of Southeast Asia* (London: Macmillan, 1964), and K. Venkatagiri Gowda, *Fiscal Policy And Inflation In Postwar India, 1945–1954* (Mysore: Wesley Press, 1959).

7. Sir Frederick Pedler, "British Planning And Private Enterprise In Colonial Africa", in Peter Duignan and L. H. Gann, eds., *Colonialism In Africa, 1870–1960*, Volume 4, (New York: Cambridge University Press, 1975).

8. For a description of how these arguments affected Latin America—where poor nations had enjoyed formal independence since the nineteenth century—see Albert O. Hirschman, "Ideologies Of Economic Development In Latin America", in his volume *A Bias For Hope* (New Haven: Yale University Press, 1971).

9. Wall Street Journal, February 22, 1982.

10. David C. Cole and Yung Chul Park, *Financial Development In Korea, 1945–1978* (Cambridge: Harvard University Press, 1983).

11. *Statistical Yearbook Of The Republic Of China 1981* (Taipei: Directorate-General Of Budget, Accounting And Statistics, 1981).

12. Samuel H. Preston, "The Changing Relationship Of Health And Economic Development", in his *Mortality Patterns In National Populations* (New York: Academic Press, 1976).

13. See Vito Tanzi, ed., *The Underground Economy In The United States And Abroad* (Lexington: D. C. Heath, 1982) and US Congress Joint Economic Committee, "Maintaining The Quality Of Economic Data" (Washington: GPO, 1981).

14. Antonio Martino, "Measuring Italy's Underground Economy", *Policy Review,* Spring 1981.

15. S. Ivanov, "Politics And Statistics", in the Soviet journal *Far Eastern Affairs,* 3, 1982.

16. Eduard B. Vermeer, "Social Welfare Provisions And The Limits Of Inequality In Contemporary China", *Asian Survey,* September 1979.

17. On the difficulties with population numbers from less developed countries, see my articles in Nick Eberstadt, ed., *Fertility Decline In The Less Developed Countries* (New York: Praeger Publishers, 1981).

18. Leonardo Paulino and Shen Sheng Tseng, *A Comparative Study Of FAO And USDA Data On Production, Area, And Trade Of Major Food Staples* (Washington: International Food Policy Research Institute, 1980).

19. T. James Goering, "Tropical Root Crops And Rural Development", *World Bank Staff Working Paper #324, April 1979.

20. An exception was Nigeria's 1964 census, in which the population of the nation was apparently *overcounted* by a substantial margin. Tribal animosities

explain the anomaly: revenues and representation were to be awarded on the basis of the results.

21. See US Bureau of the Census, *World Population 1983* (Washington: Department of Commerce, 1983).

22. Background on the situation may be had from P. J. Honey, "Coolectivizing South Vietnamese Agriculture", *China NewsAnalysis*, March 30, 1979.

23. Simon Kuznets, *Modern Economic Growth* (New Haven: Yale University Press, 1966).

24. See, for example, *Population And Other Problems* (Peking: Peking Review, 1981).

25. P. T. Bauer, "The Population Explosion: Myths And Realities", in his *Equality, The Third World, And Economic Delusion* (Cambridge: Harvard University Press, 1981).

26. Dan Usher, "An Imputation Of The Value Of Increased Life Expectancy", in Milton Moss, ed., *Measuring Social And Economic Performance* (New York: Columbia University Press, 1973).

27. World Bank, *Health: Sector Policy Paper* (Washington: World Bank, 1980).

28. "Mortality Trends And Prospects", *WHO Chronicle*, 28, 1974.

29. United Nations, *Levels And Trends Of Mortality Since 1950* (New York: United Nations, 198?).

30. *Health: Sector Policy Paper, op.cit.;* Lee-jay Cho *et. al., Population Growth Of Indonesia* (Honolulu: University Of Hawaii Press, 1980); Brazil, *Series Estatisticas Retrospectiva 1977* (Rio de Janeiro: IBGE, 1977).

31. World Bank, *China: Socialist Economic Development* (Washington: World Bank, 1981).

32. For an elaboration of this argument, see Michael Lipton, *Why Poor People Stay Poor: Urban Bias In World Development* (Cambridge: Harvard University Press, 1977). Interestingly, the gap in lifespans between urban and rural people provides one of the stronger indications that life expectancy in sub-Saharan Africa and the Muslim expanse is still rising, for the population of the cities is believed to be rising much more rapidly than the population of the countryside in virtually all of these countries. See United Nations, *Patterns Of Urban And Rural Population Growth* (New York: United Nations, 1980).

33. Alfonso Farnos Morejon and Sonia Catasus Cervera, "La Mortalidad" in *La Poblacion de Cuba* (Havana: Centro de Estudios Demograficos, 1976).

34. Carmelo Mesa-Lago, *The Economy Of Socialist Cuba* (Albuquerque: University Of New Mexico Press, 1981).

35. Carmelo Mesa-Lago, "Cuban Statistics Revisited", *Cuban Studies/Estudios Cubanos* July 1979.

36. This is explained in *Anuario Estadistico de Cuba* 1979 (Havana: CEE, n.d.).

37. *Levels And Trends Of Mortality Sice 1950, op.cit.*

38. See Ministerio de Salud, *La Salud de Chile* (Santiago: 1981). Chile's reductions in infant mortality appear to be associated closely with two social programs: subsidized supplemental child feeding and children's health centers. Both have been substantially expanded since Allende's assassination.

39. Tai Hwan Kwon *et.al., The Population Of Korea* (Seoul: Seoul National University, 1975).

40. United Nations, *Demographic Yearbook 1981* (New York: United Nations, 1983). Although North Korea has claimed that it brought tuberculosis, trachoma, cholera, and the other communicable diseases so often associated with poverty under control shortly after the Korean Workers Party assumed power officially in 1948, the government's own administrative concerns seem to tell another story. In 1969 the Central Disease Prevention Office was made an autonomous

unit of the Ministry of Public Health, and a Hygenic Propaganda Office was established in each province. Nina Vreeland *et.al., Area Handbook For North Korea* (Washington: Government Printing Office, 1976).

41. A. S. Boronin and I. A. Ognetov, *Sotsalisticheskaya Respublika Vietnam* (Moscow: Indatel'stvo Politicheskoii Literaturi, 1983).

42. United Nations, *Demographic Indicators Of Countries: Estimates And Projections As Assessed In 1980* (New York: United Nations, 1982).

43. See Widjojo Nitisastro, *Population Trends In Indonesia* (Ithica: Cornell University Press, 1970), and Gerard Kherian, Le Problem Demographique En Indochine (Hanoi: Impremieres d'Extreme-Orient, 1937).

44. Judith Banister and Samuel Preston, "Mortality In China", *Population And Development Review,* March 1981.

45. Kenneth Hill, "China: An Evaluation Of Demographic Trends-1950/1982" (World Bank, unpublished, 1983) and Judith A. Banister, *The Population Of China* (Stanford University Press, forthcoming).

46. For data on overseas Chinese communities, see *Levels And Trends Of Mortality, op.cit.*

47. John S. Aird, "Reconstruction Of An Official Data Model Of The Chinese Population" (Bureau of the Census: unpublished paper, June 15, 1980) and Kenneth Hill *et.al.,* "Famine In China, 1959–61" (World Bank, unpublished paper, 1983).

48. Stephen Rapawy and Godfrey Baldwin, "Demographic Trends In The Soviet Union, 1950–2000" in *Soviet Economy In The 1980s: Problems And Prospects* (Washington: Government Printing Office, December 31, 1982).

49. Ansley J. Coale, "A Reassessment Of World Population Trends", *Population Bulletin Of The United Nations,* 14, 1982.

50. Among these, India's flirtation with involuntary sterilization during the period of "Emergency" rule in the mid-1970s figures prominently. Implications and repercussions have been analyzed in Myron Weiner, *India At The Polls* (Washington: American Enterprise Institute, 1978), and Marika Vicziany, "Coercion In A Soft State", *Pacific Affairs,* Fall and Winter 1982.

51. See John S. Aird's chapter in U.S. Congress, Joint Economic Committee, *Chinese Economy in the 1980's* (Washington, D.C., 1986).

52. Fang Shen, "Baby Girls On Chinese Mainland", *Issues And Studies* April 1983. According to this review and analysis, three million baby girls may have been killed or abandoned on the Mainland in the past two years.

53. Judith Banister, U.S. Bureau of the Census, personal communication.

54. On social security arrangements in rural China, see *Broken Earth: The Rural Chinese, op.cit.,* William L. Parrish and Martin K. Whyte, *Village And Family In Contemporary China,* (Chicago: University Of Chicago Press, 1978), and E. B. Vermeer, "Income Differentials In Rural China", China Quarterly March 1982.

54. For more details on the technical difficulties with quantifying hunger, see my article "Hunger And Ideology", *Commentary,* July 1981.

56. See *Mortality Patterns In National Populations, op.cit.,* on changing causes of death at different levels of life expectancy.

57. Donald McGranahan, *Improvement Of Information On The Conditions Of Children* (Geneva: UN Research Institute On Social Development, 1980).

58. *Levels And Trends, op.cit.* It is widely believed that per capita food consumption has declined in sub-Saharan Africa in the 1970s. It may have, but there is reason to question the data upon which such conclusions have been based. See Nick Eberstadt, "A Dissenting View Of The World Food Problem", *World Bank Agriculture Working Paper #73,* August 1983. There is reason to believe that the

incidence of serious malnutrition in the less developed countries is considerably lower than would be suggested either by the World Bank estimate that over one billion people in developing countries suffer "caloric deficits", or the World Bank suggestion that 800 million people suffer from "absolute poverty". See Thomas T. Poleman, "Quantifying The Nutrition Situation In Developing Countries" *Food Research Institute Studies*, 1, 1981.

59. *Levels And Trends, op.cit.*

60. *The Population Of China, op.cit.*

61. Miriam London and Ivan D. London, "Hunger In China: The 'Norm Of Truth' ", *Worldview*, March 1979.

62. Nicholas R. Lardy, *Agriculture In China* (New York: Cambridge University Press, forthcoming).

63. *The Economy Of Socialist Cuba, op.cit.*

64. *Agriculture In China, op.cit.* Grain consumption may have been made to rise in China's cities over the past generation, but without improvements in national foodgrain availability, these gains could only be had by making the country people get by on less. Nicholas R. Lardy, "Food Consumption In The People's Republic Of China", in Randolph Barker and Radha Sinha, eds., *The Chinese Agricultural Economy* (Boulder: Westview Press, 1982). By Lardy's computations, the gap in foodgrain consumption per capita between urban and rural people widened from 9% in 1956/57 to 35% in 1978; over the same period, average consumption in the countryside is said to have fallen by over 5%.

65. Calculated from *Le Problem Demographique, op.cit.*, Ng Shui Meng, "The Population Of Indochina: Some Preliminary Observations" (Singapore: Institute of Southeast Asian Studies, July 1974), *World Population 1983, op.cit.*, and US Department of Agriculture, *Asia, WAS Report*, 1983. Even if one takes as too bleak Douglas Pike's assessment that the Socialist Republic of Vietnam in the early 1980s could "not even meet the 1500 calories a day considered to be subsistence level" ("Vietnam In 1981: Biting The Bullet", *Asian Survey*, January 1982), and even if one discounts for the production in colonial times which went to export markets and land taxes, it nevertheless appears that both the quality and quantities of food in the peasant diet in Vietnam has deteriorated significantly since the 1930s.

66. Nicholas R. Lardy, "Prices, Markets, And The Chinese Peasant", *Economic Growth Center* Discussion Paper #428, December 1982. It was by relying upon markets, but supplementing the effective purchasing power of the poor, that India coped successfully with its prospective famine in the mid-1960s. See Alan Berg, "Famine Contained: Notes And Lessons From The Bihar Experience" *Brookings Institute Reprint Series* #211, 1971.

67. *Nhan Dan,* May 22, 1959; quoted in David W. P. Elliott, "Political Integration In North Vietnam: The Cooperativization Period", SEADAG Papers On Problems Of Development In Southeast Asia, Asia Society, May 1975.

68. Hans P. Binswanger and Mark R. Rosenzweig, eds., *Land Tenure, Contracts, And Entrepreneurial Arrangements In Asia* (Baltimore: Johns Hopkins University Press, 1984).

69. China is not the only Communist country in which agricultural experiments have brought on famine. The Soviet Union's experiences with collectivization in the 1930s are well known; in the Ukraine alone five million people may have perished from man-made famine. See Robert Conquest, *The Ukrainian Famine* (Cambridge: Ukrainian Research Institute, forthcoming). Vietnam may also have suffered famine with its first attempts at collectivization. See Gerard Tongas, *L'Enfer Communiste Au Nord-Vietnam* (Paris: Nouvelles Editions Debresse,

1960). Tonas, who taught school in Hanoi in the 1950s, writes that statistics were juggled to cover the actual shortfall that resulted from the new agrarian policies in 1958. He also writes that North Vietnam attempted to divert attention from its own problems by announcing an offer to donate rice to the hungry in *South Vietnam!*

70. Timothy King, ed., *Education And Income World Bank Staff Working Paper* #402, July 1980.

71. Data from Singapore suggest highlight the problem: in the early 1970s, 88% of the adult population was estimated to be newspaper readers, but only 74% were considered "literate" in government statistical accounts. For a discussion of the problems of evaluating literacy, see John Oxenham, *Literacy* (London: Routledge & Kegan Paul, 1980).

72. New York Times, December 18, 1977.

73. *Ibid.*

74. *UNESCO Statistical Yearbook 1975* (Paris: UNESCO, 1976).

75. *UNESCO Statistical Yearbook 1982* (Paris: UNESCO, 1982).

76. V. Semyonov, "China: Internal Political And Social Problems", *International Affairs*, 4, 1981.

77. Evelyn S. Rawski, *Education And Popular Literacy In Ch'ing China* (Ann Arbor: University of Michigan Press, 1979), and H. D. Lamson, *Social Pathology In China* (Taipei: Ch'eng-wen Publishing Co., 1974).

78. Andrew C. Nahm, *North Korea: Her Past, Reality, And Present* (Kalamazoo: Center for Korean Studies, 1978). For more information on education in North Korea, see B. C. Koh and C. I. Eugene Kim, eds, *Journey To North Korea* (Berkeley: Institute of East Asian Studies, 1983).

79. *L'Enfer Communiste Au Nord-Vietnam, op.cit.* See also his "Indoctrination Replaces Education" in P. J. Honey, ed., *North Vietnam Today* (New York: Praeger Publishers, 1962).

80. *UNESCO Statistical Yearbook,* various annual editions.

81. John Mercer, *Slavery for Mauritania Today* (Edinburgh: Human Rights Group, 1982).

82. See, for example, C. Wayne Bardin and James F. Catterall, "Testosterone: A Major Determinant Of Extragenital Sexual Dimorphism", *Science,* May 20, 1981.

83. *Levels And Trends, op.cit.; Demographic Yearbook 1981, op.cit.;* United Nations, *World Population Trends And Policies, Monitoring Report 1977* (New York: United Nations, 1979); United Nations, *World Population Trends And Policies, Monitoring Report 1979* (New York: United Nations, 1980).

84. *Levels And Trends, op.cit.; South African Statistics 1980* (Pretoria: Department of Statistics, 1980).

85. *Levels And Trends, op.cit.; Demographic Yearbook 1981, op.cit.*

86. See back issues of *UNESCO Statistical Yearbook* for estimates of these literacy and enrollment differentials.

87. Ling Ruizhu, "A Brief Account Of 30 Years' Mortality Of Chinese Population", *World Health Statistics Quarterly,* 2, 1981;

88. Jayne Werner, "Women, Socialism, And The Economy Of Wartime North Vietnam, 1960–1975", *Studies In Comparative Communism,* Summer/August 1981.

89. "The North Korean Enigma", *op.cit;* Mun Woong Lee, "Rural North Korea Under Communism: A Study Of Socio-Cultural Change", *Rice University Studies,* Winter 1976.

90. Gautam Datta and Jacob Meerman, "Household Income Or Household Income Per Capita In Welfare Comparisons", *World Bank Staff Working Paper* #378, March 1980; see also Michael W. Kusnic and Julie DaVanzo, "Who Are

The Poor In Malaysia? The Sensitivity Of Poverty Profiles To Definition Of Income", in Yoram Ben-Porath, ed., *Income Distribution And The Family* (New York: Population Council, 1982).

91. These problems and others are taken up in Alan Blinder, *Towards A Theory Of Income Distribution* (Cambridge: MIT Press, 1974).

92. On this score, see Clifford Geertz, "After The Revolution: The Fate Of The New Nation State", in his *The Interpretation Of Cultures: Selected Essays* (New York: Basic Books, 1973).

93. This is the "tunnel effect" that Albert Hirschman described in "Changing Tolerance For Inequality In Development", *Quarterly Journal Of Economics*, November 1973.

94. This discussion draws heavily on Jose Pastore, *Inequality And Social Mobility In Brazil* (Madison: University Of Wisconsin Press, 1982). Pastore notes that "circulation" mobility in Argentina has been measured as unusually low. This may have something to do with the nation's uncertain progress against poverty over the past two decades.

95. There is little information on income distribution in Marxist-Leninist societies as a whole, and still less for the poor ones. Even if such information were readily available, it would be considerably more difficult to evaluate than comparable data from poor non-Communist nations. In non-market economies, income need not measure either purchasing power or standards of living with any consistency. This point is made with some force for Soviet Central Asia in Nancy Lubin, *Labor And Nationality In Soviet Central Asia* (London: Macmillan, forthcoming).

96. In non-market economies, it often seems to be the case that "politically affluent" citizens not only have greater access to goods and services, but pay less for them. In Wuhan in recent years, it is said that an ordinary person paid 1.80 RMB per 1½ kilo for fish and waited three hours in line for it, while a party member paid 0.40 RMB and would not have to wait. (Stephen N. S. Cheung, "Will China Go 'Capitalist'?" *Hobart Paper* #94, 1982.) A more descriptive account of the economic priviledges which accompany political power in different Marxist-Leninist systems include Hedrick Smith, *The Russians* (New York: Quadrangle, 1975) and *Broken Earth, op cit.*

97. Albert A. Simkus, "Historical Changes In Occupational Inheritance Under Socialism: Hungary 1930–73", in Donald J. Treiman and Robert V. Robinson, eds., *Research In Social Stratification And Mobility: A Research Annual* (Greenwich: JAI Press, 1981).

98. See for example Tai Sung An, *North Korea In Transition: From Dictatorship To Dynasty* (Westport: Greenwodd Press, 1983).

98. Y. Kinovalov and S. Manazhev, "Social And Economic Contradictions in China", *Far Eastern Affairs*, 2, 1981.

100. See my "Introduction" in Iosef G. Dyadkin, *Unnatural Deaths In The USSR 1928–54* (New Brunswick: Transaction, 1983).

101. This may be seen, among other places, in China's rural regions. At the end of a careful article, Eduard Vermeer concludes that "the forced continuation of a premodern agrarian settlement pattern, together with a doubling of the rural population since the Second World War have driven an increasing number of the ill-favored villages to the limit of possibilities for economic survival". If his evaluation sounds alarming, it is not much different in tone or conclusion from what has appeared in the Chinese press at different intervals since 1979. E. B. Vermeer, "Income Differential In Rural China", *China Quarterly*, March 1982.

The Importance of Political Participation for Sustained Capitalist Development

Grace Goodell

> Custom should be followed only because it is custom, and not because it is reasonable or just. Otherwise they would follow it no longer, although it were custom; for they will only submit to reason or justice. Custom without this would pass for tyranny . . . It would therefore be right to obey laws and customs because they are laws; but we should know that there is neither truth nor justice to introduce into them, that we know nothing of these, and so much follow, what is accepted.
>
> Pascal *Pensees*.

Sustained Capitalist Development: Its Requirements[1]

THE PROBLEM FACING most of the Third World today is no longer how to launch development, but rather how to sustain it. Consider the colossal disappointments, after *150 years* of independence, of Brazil, Mexico, Uruguay, Colombia, Venezuela, Costa

Rica, Nicaragua, El Salvador, and Peru—and the debacle of Argentina![2] Recall the historic leadership which set Egypt, Thailand, and Turkey on their drives to modernization *fully a century ago:* now, nearly stagnant. Contrast the economic promise inherited from the colonial period and the determination and unbounded elan inspired by independence with today's languor in India, Kenya, and Malaysia, the listlessness of Zimbabwe, Indonesia, the Philippines, and north Africa: indeed, the failures of Ghana and Nigeria. The issue is no longer how to assure political stability— but even *with* stability, how to foster steady development whose gains will accrue and whose momentum can be sustained.

Like alchemists, Western and Third World planners and rulers have focused attention on the surface—the economic, the aggregate, and the statistically measured—before confirming the political and social foundations, the local, regional, and institutional structures. In their singular drive to attain the former, they have debilitated the latter which are the underpinnings for sustained development. Hence the repeated failures, forever buying more time. In some cases, we may well ask whether the damage of short-term but ill-founded brilliance has not been irreparable.

This essay argues that without vigorous political participation within leading fields of interaction and then increasingly more and more arenas at every social level, a society cannot sustain capitalist economic development. In Part I we review the basic building blocks of society to understand the decisive fields of social activity; these lie *between* the micro- and macro-levels which economists study. We go on to explain the connection between participation on the one hand, structured within fields of interaction and between them, and on the other hand the three principal requisites of capitalist economics: rationality,[3] predictability, and bonding. In Part II we examine how and why capitalist development must be firmly rooted in the broad base of society to sustain the momentum that may be gained during the initial period of expansion. Sociopolitical participation must open the way for the increasing economic participation which capitalism requires. How this evolved in England and in Western Europe in general, and what its consequences were in the shaping of British and European societies, are contrasted with the main patterns of development in the Third World today.

The Underpinnings of Sustained Investment in the West

As Table One indicates, many of the basic norms, skills, institutions, and rules for a free market economy were firmly rooted in

England *two hundred years ago* (and on the continent soon after)—
well before the Industrial Revolution—but are nowhere yet to be
seen in most Third World countries. Yet in many Third World
societies every level, including the peasantry, could mobilize capital for a surge in investment like that of early industrial Europe,
the United States, and Japan.[4] The potential is there—or under
the bed, or in Swiss banks. Some of the conditions enabling the
rational allocation of these resources have begun to appear, but
the underlying requirements for their *commitment* to the public
endeavor are absent, especially predictability and bonding (upon
which, ultimately, rational allocation depends). Table One summarizes these fundamental requirements at the national level, but
they apply as well to the regional and local levels. Economic
development theory today places high priority on the software—
roads, elite investment in industry, etc.—and no priority at all on
the bedrock hardware: the predictability which rational allocation
and sustained investment require.

Although Table One summarizes these *pre*conditions which
were in place before free-market development gained momentum in the West, it in fact represents the *culmination* of a
centuries-long process. During the long "Middle Ages" in Europe,
thousands of medieval manors, guilds, free towns, church bodies,
and geographical regions succeeded in establishing themselves as
self-directed mini-societies fenced off from arbitrary interference. Within these highly participatory modules the means for
expressing and resolving conflict, especially between different
social strata, had gradually evolved (for instance, peasant strikes
were often successful). The lower orders, frequently incorporat-
ing themselves—for example, in communes—learned to hold authorities to impersonal contract, the beginning of predictability
and bonding. Thus, over the centuries these separate political
modules or mini-societies consolidated *first,* firmly implanting the
norms of predictability, rationality, and bonding in the population
at large and developing institutions for participatory local governance. *Then,* once these achievements were firm at the micro level
and in the middle ranges of society—and only then—could they
converge in the singular task of reining in the King at the top. An
almost identical process took place in Japan.[7] In Table One we see
the British results: centralized spending, war-making, law-mak-
ing, taxation, and regulation had all been brought under the stern
monitoring of participatory bodies by 1750, and the population
had acquired the means to hold other engines of development
accountable as well, such as scientists and the coordinating agencies of the civil service.

In sharp contrast, the Third World has put the cart before the horse. In India and many other nations, the entire country participates in formal, macro-level elections with formal political parties, while virtually no decentralized field of interaction in the whole society can claim predictability, from the poorest village to the circles of industrial giants. Without local predictability, how can there be rational allocation or bonding? Indeed, despite the trappings of democratic participation, most Third World societies have far less leverage against centralized arbitrariness at every level than did European peasants of the Middle Ages.

Thus, the English, French, and American revolutions and the revisions they brought about in government only crystallized in institutional form what people "on the ground" had already been doing and taking for granted for a long time. Admittedly, the twin problems of the free movement of productive resources, and the confidence and trust necessary to bond them together, were not solved once and for all in 1688, 1789, or by *any* historical event. Largely peaceful mini-revolutions have continued to be necessary, often for newcomers to gain entry to the market. But the ground rules that would enable sustained investment of all resources had been established a century before the Industrial Revolution. More importantly, society's *tool kit* for political participation and accountability had become widely accessible, even to peasants, workers, and the landless. We are told today that this is a bourgeois amenity which comes *after* development: its harvest, not its seedbed.

Santa Dalena

Convinced that we must look at the *inside*, not just the *top*, of society to examine its actual fabric, let us glance at a case drawn from the contemporary Third World. In the village of Santa Dalena in the Philippines, two Tagalog farmers started raising chickens. They had to build larger cages when they added a few more, requiring neighbors' skills to expand construction; while working on the coops one neighbor tried to rig up a watering device. As the poultry prospered, the landlord forbade what was going on so the farmers hid the chickens in the very back of their yards.

Soon the villagers needed regular transportation to bring feed twice a week: this prompted the cousin of the rural bus driver to try to sell their eggs in *his* provincial town, which had a larger market. But to justify the townsman's provision of feed and regular marketing, many more facilities were needed to raise hens, so other neighbors got into the act. In making more coops, the carpenters decided to improve their watering-rig invention and construct a few first-class ones to sell elsewhere; these sold well, requiring landless laborers to help make even more. Then the landless laborers' wives took over collecting the eggs, which gave one of them the idea to make better boxes and streamline the packing. Meanwhile, several new farmers just starting with hens searched for a better breed, spurring village-wide demands for veterinary services from the government, and loans, and electricity at last for the carpenters' equipment and for better brooders, and a decent road during rainy season, and finally assistance in organizing a cooperative. Before it would provide that, the government sent inspectors swarming in to condemn the coops as unhealthy, the feed storage facilities, the bookkeeping, the carpenters' home-made electrical wiring, the feathers everywhere, the middlemen deals, the manure disposal, the pesos kept under the bed, and the absence of refrigeration, minimum wages, labeling and grading of eggs, drivers' licenses, vitamins in the hen feed, respect for bureaucrats, even the absence of kids from school! The landlord said, "I told you so!" But by that time, the villagers of Santa Dalena were strong enough to serve as watchdogs over what they had started for themselves. After all, by then they had a vigorous cooperative in all but name, while the cooperative which the government had organized years before by starting with the name had never gotten farther than that.

In five years, Santa Dalena hardly launched a backward-linking-forward-linking steel industry. But its little happening of hens and eggs and boxes and coops with watering rigs is far closer to Europe's Industrial Revolution than is the steel industry the Filipino planners and the Japanese launched in those same years, and far closer to the prerequisites for sustained capitalist development.

With this juxtaposition in mind, of England on the brink of the Industrial Revolution and of Santa Dalena in the Philippines, let us turn to the basic theoretical concepts this paper finds useful in analyzing the underpinnings necessary for sustained development.

1. Fields of Interaction

Santa Dalena throws light on the dynamics that probably lay behind and eventually culminated in Table One's foundations for sustained economic development. Neither macro nor micro studies have proven reliable in describing conditions propitious for economic "development" because in fact an individual's or any social unit's most frequent and important actions take place within the routine *fields of interaction* of which he or it is a part: not the aggregate and not the firm, the prevalent units of analysis. In our brief sketch we have focused on one field of interaction in Santa Dalena, comprising the hen farmers, carpenters, landless laborers, and in time their provincial-level middlemen with transportation, feed and marketing services. In the sequence "once a day X goes to M's house to collect eggs and put them in F's boxes," a little field of interaction with X, M, and F is being knit together. Fields of interaction spring forth out of repeated dealings between people, and their regularity and intensity can be charted by actual observations.

The field of interaction is the real locus of initiative and risk-taking, saving and investment, habits of work or laziness, decisions to link with another for any common endeavor—and certainly the locus of predictablity, mobility, optimism, and incentive. Our present concepts and instruments would never have detected that an inconspicuous field of interaction among cottagers and craftsmen in the British Midlands was coalescing into something as momentous as the Industrial Revolution, just as Japanese development still comes as a surprise to us because our crude implements did not pick it up until it had become an *aggregate* phenomenon after World War II, when it was full-blown. Conversely, on the basis of aggregate evidence many economists trumpeted the success of Iran under the late Shah, the macro indices of prosperity belying the debility of that society's constituent fields of interaction.

Repetition and intensity of interaction create a field's "culture," which enables those interacting with one another more or less to predict the field's parameters. This "culture" of a field is *generated by* and thus expresses the actual patterns of behavior which give rise to it; then it in turn regularizes behaviors within the field and systematizes their interrelationship through coordination and governance.[8] For example, the Santa Dalena poultry farmers very quickly evolved the rule that you leave eggs at four houses which are the bus pick-up points, and if you don't get yours there in time no one else is liable. The pattern became an actual rule and the rule regularized new farmers' behavior, where they would leave *their* eggs. In the repetition of these behaviors over a long enough time lay the seeds of later formal arrangements and formal governance. Form follows function.

As the intensitiy or volume of interaction increases over a long enough time and participants develop their procedures for regulating their internal and external common affairs, the field becomes a system. Within this field you know how to get around. This becomes part of your familiar baggage, including broad policy outlines and range of choices, rules, and, in time, a "tool kit" of channels, skills and perhaps specific institutions you can use for starting new things or for linking with others in the field. Many of these channels, though, are not formal ones.

2. Predictability and Participation

Economic development requires increasing rationality or precision in the allocation of productive resources.[9] If factors of production are to seek out their most exact productive use on their own (capitalism) they need conditions of ample mobility such as those mentioned in Table One. But except in desperation—and then not rationally—people are unlikely to venture their resources beyond their existing situation (whose risks are at least known) and certainly are unlikely to commit themselves to *new combinations,* unless two other conditions are met: predictability and the security of bonding. Inasmuch as economic development entails an increasing division of labor, it *depends on* an ever wider and firmer guarantee of bonding, which assures resources a safe linking with their economic complements and enables accumulation through time. Of these three requisites for capitalist development—rationality, predictability, and bonding—predictability is the foundation, because just as there can be no rational allocation without it, neither can there be bonding.

Let us return to our unit of analysis, the locus of all critical economic decisions—the field of interaction. We have seen that in an economic system based on the participants' initiatives, predictability has to be defined from *their* point of view, with reference to the fields of interaction they create out of their day-to-day transactions. By the end of even the first year of Santa Dalena's events, hundreds of people knew when to predict the bus' arrival, how much a dozen eggs would bring, what opportunities landless laborers could expect, which carpenter was the most reliable for repairing watering taps, whose hens would probably take ill in the rain, etc. But in addition, outsiders had begun to deal with the network as though it were—for their purposes—a single and predictable entity: for instance, merchants, by contacting the driver, could count on a certain number of eggs to be delivered, or a certain amount of feed or medication to be purchased. The optimal conditions for predictability and bonding were developing both within the field and for outsiders. Yet these conditions did not spring forth overnight, and the government's imposing what was clearly more predictable and reasonable to *it*, would have jeopardized the stable underpinnings of Santa Dalena's momentum.

Santa Dalena illustrates, too, how the definition and continual redefinition of reasonableness are hammered out through day-to-day interaction: for instance, when some of the landless laborers' wives asked to take home a few eggs and old coops that were being thrown away, to raise hens themselves, several farmers objected strenuously; but the pattern got started. In a rapidly changing field, participants are constantly initiating new ventures, testing them out, finding them permissible, and then repeating them often enough, with sufficient intensity, to establish them as routine. If someone objects to a behavior, the whistle may be blown, it may be brought to "law" (formal or informal) and perhaps stopped. That defines a limit. But those new behaviors which become repeated and repeated eventually "feed back" into the field's cultural repertoire and its established tool kit as being "routine." This is how fields incorporate change. The *feedback makers* program and continually reprogram the system: law is being created by the participants themselves allowing what they think is reasonable to become routinized.

The most destructive force in any form of economic development is arbitrariness. Psychologists have shown how unpredictability makes a person feel helpless, and this sense of having no control naturally extinguishes initiative.[10] Because of relative scale and complexity, sociopolitical and economic arbitrariness is much easier to curb *within fields of interaction* than within a vast aggregation; on the other hand, once the conditions, expectations and institutions assuring relative predictability are established in one or several leading fields of interaction, they may enjoy a spread effect into adjacent fields.

If it is those who are active within a field of interaction who determine what is reasonable, hence determine law, these people themselves assure predictability in two main ways: by providing *feedback* which defines the norm (often simply by no one objecting to new behavior), and by serving as *watchdogs* against the arbitrariness of coordinating or governing mechanisms. These two services define "participation" as it is used in this paper: playing a role in the polity's *policymaking* (within one's field of interaction, etc.), not simply providing labor for building roads, obediently attending meetings, etc. In the European Middle Ages, long before the lower orders of society had gained any direct role in government, they demanded and insisted upon one thing from the lords, and through the lords, from the King: they granted him the prerogative to make any laws he wanted, but they required him to bind himself to his own law. To hold the ruler to steady course was the first and maybe greatest achievement of Western law. Even before "justice," the lower orders first had to establish themselves as watchdogs over the very *stability* of law. Few Third World countries have come as far yet, as had European medieval society at that point.

Thus there is no way in which the predictability of a field's culture and tool kit can be imposed on it in order to make it a system. The participants' own purposes must constitute the standard: *not* what seems reasonable, predictable or trustworthy to the rulers or planners or lawyers or economists, with their aggregate data and models. How can rulers or planners ever serve as watchdogs to keep the system—indeed, to keep themselves or The Plan—on course? Nor can a shared culture and its tool kit for predictabililty be brought forth by law. To the contrary, it is the job of jurists to "find the law" in the judgments and habits of people's everyday behavior.

3. Coordination and Governance

In relatively small or long-established fields of interaction the "feedback makers" can program their coordinational mechanisms informally and interpersonally, as we have seen in Santa Dalena. But as a field expands or as frequent interaction merges it with other fields, more sophisticated means of assuring rationality, predictabililty, and bonding are needed.

In the first place, as a field expands, participants must evolve the cultural requisites and tool kit which enable rational allocation and secure bonding beyond informal or personal acquaintance and which enable one to predict strangers' key behavior. Many Third World countries—in Latin America, for instance—have failed to make this "quantum leap" to impersonal predictability and trust.

Secondly, as fields of interaction grow more complex, governance tends to become entrusted to particular leaders and institutions, eventually to formal ones. These lengthen an individual's arm, enabling him to launch larger undertakings, to bond more easily with others, and to project feedback into society beyond his singular means. An effective leader or institution gives him a higher soap box in Hyde Park. The advantage of institutions that are permanent is that they can be ready-at-hand (still, in some societies informal fields of interaction can incorporate themselves quickly when necessary). It is almost solely through large groups or institutions that participants can check the state's systemic arbitrariness.

Such representational participation through leaders and institutions must be *structured* (though not necessarily formally); otherwise would-be participants are simply numbers in an aggregate. In Santa Dalena the bus driver served as such a representative of the villagers' egg-and-coop field of interaction, to the larger field of provincial merchants, and they in turn had their associations and leaders through whom they participated in the general civic life of the province and in Manila's fields of wholesale and retail interaction. Although the means for structuring participation in viable organizational forms (of all sorts, not just economic corporations) are central to capitalist economic development, not all societies have the same skill for creating them. Certain economists think institutions are simply "induced" when needed, but if this were true the poor would have the most effective organizations! To the contrary, the conditions and aptitudes favorable to building lasting institutions vary considerably from one culture to the next. All of these intermediate mechanisms for extending beyond one's immediate fields of interaction require time, trust, and exceptional momentum to establish. Centralized governments actively discourage their formation. Furthermore, if they are allowed to fall into disuse they will not be at hand when needed. Even a socialist government in Spain finds it difficult to re-establish labor unions after decades of Franco's rule.[11]

Thirdly, when fields of interaction become large or composite, they attempt to insure rationality, predictability, and secure bonding through formal—or "enacted"—law. Formal law almost invariably threatens spontaneity, flexibility, and clarity—hence rationality—and it may erode social cohesion—hence, secure bonding. Not surprisingly, although businessmen subscribe to formal law at great expense, numerous studies attest that they actually use these channels very little.[12] If formal law is not restricted to a very narrow sphere, and even then not monitored closely by the participants themselves, it starts proclaiming as "reasonable" things which are not at all, and forbidding behavior which those which a particular field consider perfectly routine. When that happens, one needs a specialist to decode it, rather than being able to rely for predictability on one's common sense norms and experiences.

The late Shah of Iran made elaborate laws about what was and was not permissible or reasonable, most of which had little to do with people's own systems of testing and screening out behavior.[13] In time, the Shah's formal law became detached from the real social law, and the discrepancy between the two became institutionalized. Many observers think that formal law's gaining the upper hand over social law signals incipient sterility.[14] Of course, even when formal law does reflect real behavior and norms, it can never be taken as a complete repository of them. To the contrary, it usually deals with the exotic and highly particular, before behavior becomes "routine."

Thus, when the coordinating mechanism of a field or of society in general starts *commanding* rather than *coordinating,* and upward feedback loses its effective leverage, then predictability is gone. To avoid this it is essential that fields of interaction consolidate as smaller units first and then link into larger organizational forms slowly, so that they and the intermediate structures they build upward into are strong enough to resist centralized power. This building-up gradually, confirming each unit and step before expanding further, entails a particular *process* and not just an organizational form. We consider this process below, called piecemeal change.

4. Cohesiveness

The greater the autonomy a field of interaction enjoys, the more cohesive it tends to become and the greater its predictability to its members and to others. But many fields of interaction are so loosely-knit that they cannot be called "systems" at all, and they offer little predictability. Interaction within them may be sporadic or of frequent but trivial concern, or may take place between temporary participants that move in and out again without strong ties, intense or sustained purpose. Many of these fields are the products of colonialism or a highly centralized thrust to "modernize" which destroyed formerly cohesive sociopolitical units that stood in their way. Through innumerable forms of divide-and-rule, premature concentration of power at any level (by indigenous governance, not only by foreigners) retards society's or a given field's organizational and bonding capacities. Thus without direct observation from *inside,* we cannot assume that a field of interaction *exists at all* or that simply because it bears a formal name, it has a clear-cut, integrated—much less, autonomous and predictable—character. Many Third World villages, political parties and peasant cooperatives, and unions and professional bodies formed by the state have virtually no common interaction which holds them together, existing as "fields" only on government lists and beneath state-appointed headmen.

Like cohesiveness, conflict cannot be appraised from the outside. Anthropologists have long argued that many types of conflict express and foster social cohesion, even between opponents. When in this analysis we discuss how social law is shaped by participants' interaction, we by no means suggest that this is always accomplished *harmoniously* (although it is also not true that in most cultures might equals right in such matters).

5. Tinkering or Piecemeal Change

Economic development requires efficient allocation along an ever-expanding production-possibility curve within, especially, the leading fields of interaction. When someone expands the known possibilities through a venture, that in turn affects others' perceptions, resources, and risks within that field.[15] The glimpse into this piecemeal process which Santa Dalena offers us suggests the Industrial Revolution in its progression of risk, initiative, bonding, and new openings within relatively predictable but continually changing fields. Someone sees an opportunity for initiative; further tinkering requires resources someone else has, or exposes a new imbalance that needs innovation; success frequently calls for joining together with others on a larger scale.[16] This type of action and counteraction takes place at all levels of society, though never uniformly. In the process, the units involved become firmly linked in a veritable *system* bound by mutual accountability. The economic literature is replete with spectacular investment "linkages" whose scale and sensation tempt planners to mastermind and control such chains themselves. Believing that development is about things rather than social processes, they impose their elite logic on piecemeal change, destroying predictability from the participants' perspective . . . indeed, destroying real participation, since only obeying others' orders is not participation.

A major virtue of piecemeal change for the purposes of economic development is that it is parsimonious, giving as much freedom of action and responsibility as possible to those closest to the problem, who have the most experience in that environment and can react the fastest. At the same time it fosters continual fine-tuning. In the public sector, too, piecemeal change reserves society's limited "overhead" funds until they are needed. For years the government had been offering Santa Dalena farmers training in tractor maintenance for which they had no use, but now what they really needed and couldn't get were carpentry and para-veterinary skills. No one could have anticipated this in advance.

Partly because of piecemeal change, not even in highly integrated societies do all fields share across the board the same norms or channels for feedback and bonding. In the European Middle Ages, merchant law had its own principles, rules, officials, and courts as did Church law, feudal and manorial law, each separate municipality, and so on. Even in our relatively homogenous society, different fields of interaction have distinct, often contrasting codes and standard operations for behavior which can in no way be reduced to uniform legal or management principles. Familiarity with a field is so important for operating effectively that people entering new fields are apt to move first towards those contiguous to the ones they already know; from that base they learn about the next field along, sequentially. For these reasons, norms, expectations, rules and a tool kit for interaction most accurately reflect real behavior when they are established by participation on a *field-to-field* basis. People within a given field are by far the best ones to safeguard *their* field's predictability.

Another result of piecemeal change is that fields within society develop, consolidate, and even disband at different rates. Thus it is by no means necessary that all fields provide feedback upward into the governing mechanism in equal measure. Being closely in step with the *overall* culture is far more important to some than to others; in return, every field need not be equally subject to central directives. Indeed, since there are *liabilities* in being a coordinated part of the system, many fields enjoy greater prosperity free from the regulations, competition, and higher costs of full integration, as Santa Dalena realized. This allows them to develop greater autonomy and then to strengthen their own institutions and integrating mechanisms internally before being subject to governance by a larger system.

Because of its scale and gradualness, piecemeal change encourages grassroots experimentation; it develops creativity, independence, and the confidence in risk-taking over a broad scale at all levels of society. Furthermore, piecemeal development gives people time to test and change their leaders, and to learn how to maintain their institutions over a long time. Finally, such incremental change recognizes the ecological advantages of a diversity of solutions. The predictability, rationality, and bonding of piecemeal change and their important effects upon the fundamental habits and institutions of a society are well exemplified by the widespread participation in investment, technology development, management, and (soon afterwards) in public policy itself during the early centuries of England's Industrial Revolution. (See Table Two.)

In short, no one in Santa Dalena began by saying, "What this place needs is an egg cooperative—here is how egg cooperatives should be set up." No agency came in with a big loan, a thousand chicks, and thirty ready-made UNICEF hen coops. Rather, through trial and error, need, initiative, convenience, and local effort the villagers went through the process of consolidating their own field of interaction for their own self-defined purposes, which is precisely what gave them their elan and expertise and enabled them to fend off the landlord's and bureaucrats' efforts to stop them. Throughout history autocrats and their technocrat henchmen continue to advance powerful economic arguments for imposing short-term "efficiency" which blocks these local foundations for long-term predictability, rationality, and bonding.

II. The Decisive Early Stage of Capitalist Development

We have seen that the primary loci of that predictability which is necessary for a society to sustain initiative, rationality, and bonding over a long period of time are the fields of interaction intermediate between the individual and the aggregate; furthermore, that such predictability can only spring from the social law which participants in any given field are continually making and redefining as they initiate their actions and counteractions. Participatory norms, skills, and institutions assure predictability within a field as well as for outsiders who deal with it, while keeping the overarching governing mechanism on a predictable course through feedback as well as through watchdog checks against arbitrariness.

If a field or society is to retain these fundamental requisites for sustained development, it must experience change incrementally, piecemeal, initiated primarily from within rather than imposed whole-hog from without. The absolute speed of change is not the issue, but it should be no faster than the leading participants' or fields' abilities to expand as internally-coherent systems. That is, no overall coordinating mechanism should become more powerful than the structured political capacities of the critical fields it governs. In such conditions, *scale* (the intermediateness of the leading fields of interaction) corresponds to *pace* (the piecemeal process of change) and both of these, to the responsiveness of *coordination* (the vigor of feedback upwards and of watchdog constraints). Now let us consider how these principles apply to the early stages of capitalist development.

The Trickle-up Effect

The engine of sustained capitalist development is the creative vacuum, as we have seen in Santa Dalena. It is well documented that propitious conditions can bring forth the ample savings, entrepreneurial and managerial abilities, and hard work which are latent in every developing society's villages and provinces, not only among its national elites. During free-for-all periods of rapid expansion, the creative vacuum is vast. Much more so in many Third World countries today than in the West during the eighteenth century, the sky is the limit for investment opportunities at every level of society. And, indeed, many Third World societies have begun to enjoy such an initial period of rapid expansion (or did some decades ago): Brazil, South Korea, Thailand, Mexico, and Ivory Coast, to mention a few of them.

When such a burst of expansion is under way, little attention is paid to its foundations. Today, all concern is focused on the macroeconomists' measures of health. But, in fact, expansion in the West and in Japan depended upon the leading fields of initiative and investment continually tapping a broader and broader base. To specialize, diversify, and expand, units must farm out more work to subsidiaries, must have other units to link with, and must draw upon an expanding pool of labor and management skills, of domestic savings and investment capital, of new ideas and initiative, a broader base of confidence, discipline and motivation. In the European Industrial Revolution, workers themselves and lower level managers often started these complementary firms; savings from every level of *domestic* society supported expansion.[17] The innovators and investors who launched each new break-through phase have been "new men, devoid of privilege or social standing, who carried on a struggle against the privileges of older established interests."[18] Frequently the smaller fields of interaction, such as the provinces, tested the new arrangements before they were adopted by the mainstream. In sustained development resources do not trickle down, but *up:* though growth is necessarily extroverted, every society must ultimately rely on this fundamental base of itself.

Initiative must spark this trickling up, not acquiescence to some sort of "pull." For initiative-making to become the norm across a wider and wider base, the conditions for rationality, predictability, and bonding, which we have hitherto described as requisites for the creative majority in the *leading* fields of interaction, have to fan out into more and more fields, so that these will not only render up their resources, but do so deliberately, creatively, with energy and a relatively long-term commitment. That means new fields must have all along been evolving into mini-systems characterized by internal participation and participation in the overall coordinating mechanisms which govern them. (For remember, predictability is measured from *the participants'* point of view, not ours or the governor's.)

Let us return to the proportions of scale, pace, and intensity of coordination, and to their corollary: that important changes must not run ahead of participants' growing integrity as political units. In the actual development process the whole aggregate "sky" need not open *at once;* if so, only the few strong and ready will grab the lion's share (precisely what happens in World Bank projects). To the contrary, since neither the mobility which rational allocation calls for nor the trust which bonding must have, can ever be imposed by fiat, only a participatory—and hence, piecemeal—process can develop these requisites.

Competition

During rapid expansion there is, initially at least, ample room at every level for all the creative majority's initiatives and investments without anyone having voluntarily to enter a highly competitive field of interaction. Of course, as such "pioneers" stake out claims for themselves in their respective fields, they establish the political complements necessary to protect and develop these territories as exclusively theirs. This happens at every level of society among private as well as *bureaucratic* entrepreneurs. But sooner or later, the trickle-up momentum begins to pose competition to the early settlers, who respond, quite naturally, by trying to secure their domains more firmly (by dealing more and more selectively only with friends and kin; by seeking strong, autocratic leaders, etc.).

The law of participation and predictability is in jeopardy. However, at this stage most theories and models of development are so busy raising GNP that they cast not a glance at these underpinnings. The extraordinary difficulties of later having to back up and rebuild confidence eroded by cynicism, regenerate local predictability from scratch, or reconstruct corporate groups that have disintegrated through ennui, are hardly the concern of those whose singular focus is on immediate aggregate growth. Only when stagnation eventually sets in will people wonder what is then missing which the previous years should have put in place: Argentina, Lebanon even before its recent troubles, India, Mexico, Nigeria, Egypt, and the Philippines are only a few of the many such cases.

For sustained development, capitalism *must* submit itself to the continual pressure for greater efficiency. The permissiveness of the initial period of expansion inevitably ends, whether because of external conditions (such as recession, prolonged drought, unfavorable changes in certain partner-countries, etc.) or *internal* mechanisms (as scarcity of capital, cheap labor or skilled workers; "second-generation" problems of maintenance and fine-tuning; overconfident expansion; failure to keep up with changes in the market and in technology; slack management and the inability to tighten discipline, etc.). Pervasive slack must be taken up by greater precision and discipline in reducing marginal costs. The elites may have run out of ideas or, more frequently, of drive; they may have run out of capital because they spent their profits on themselves rather than plowing them back into development; the general population may not have developed the habits and institutions for saving. A common cause for such a slow-down is the continued reliance on personalism to determine criticial resource allocations, when personalistic claims increasingly conflict with economic rationality and the free entrance of new initiatives. Now more than ever competition is salutary, the opportunity and incentive for all comers to enter any market and compete there freely. Needless to say, those who "govern" at every level are loathe to encourage this in their own spheres.

In the development of modern Europe, the United States, and Japan an increasingly larger proportion of the population insisted upon competing in the rapidly developing sectors of the economy. Their struggle to open up channels and to keep them open had to be sustained for many generations at virtually every level until mobility became institutionalized: guilds had to be pried open, licenses challenged, prerequisites abolished, educational restrictions dismantled, one by one, again and again, piecemeal but in the long run systemically, often hatcheting away at the same restriction repeatedly. The process continues today as many obstacles still remain. But the challenge itself is now accepted as reasonable, and in the West and Japan the skills and institutions for upward feedback have become routinized.

Similarly, the public sector must be challenged continually to keep it on course. Corruption and declining morale, once idiosyncratic and localized, become general. Bureaucracy and formal law become increasingly slower and more costly as they suffer debilitating factionalism and pettiness, often the price of having come to power without contest. The allocation of public funds must be tied more closely to the efforts and claims of those who need them, and not simply to bureaucratic largesse. "Oiling the wheel that squeaks" reinforces the principle of piecemeal efficiency and strengthens the political fiber and participation of society's intermediate-level organizations. In short, the processes of upward feedback and watchdog accountability are equally crucial for sustaining development in the *public* sector. Thus both the trickle-up process and competition—in short, access to the creative vacuum—renew society's productive forces and its coordinating mechanisms.

The Decisive First Phase

This sequence of initial expansion followed by increasing competition and a subsequent critical period when "belt-tightening" is necessary occur often in history, within particular fields of interaction as well as in society as a whole, and at every social level. The decisive phase of the sequence is the *first* period during the process of expansion. If in this phase numerous fields of interaction at every level of society congeal into social units with political integrity, and if the norms, skills and institutions assuring predictability are established as we have outlined, then the tighter discipline of subsequent stress will strengthen a country's development potential. If, however, these foundations are not laid, then it may be impossible to do so later on when competition and contraction are most needed.

Eventually, without these underpinnings, the initial expansion will lead to involution. There is but a limited number of trustworthy combinations available to someone who can rely only on kin or close friends; yet as society becomes more complex, development requires that each unit be able to reach further and further afield to allocate resources in the most rational way and to bond with the optimal economic complements. Thus the domain of general social predictability must continually expand, predictability rooted in *interaction* not personal ties. If society's energies and leading fields which have gained momentum cannot expand or deepen their base of reliable operations, they turn inward upon themselves, careful to remain within their personalistic module (which is not to be confused with decentralization). All bonding becomes endogamous. Cronyism governs economic rationality. The only other alternative for such energies is to seek impersonal links in an external environment which does assure impersonal predictability—investment in America or the proverbial Swiss bank. Nowhere is such involution more dramatically exemplified than in the People's Republic of China.

In this manner the drive for expansion and innovation has broken down prematurely in many Third World countries *before* society's main resources have been roughly rearranged in industrial configurations. In the process of growth indispensable stages have been skipped, and yet society has become dependent upon the mechanical churning set on its surface as an illusion of a new order. How can such a society now unwind this churning and retrace its steps to put in place what finally at this late date appears indispensable for rationality, impersonal predictability, and bonding? (The solution is not revolution, because revolution does not build durable participatory structures in a society which had none when the revolution began.)

Table Two contrasts the processes which launched this decisive early phase of expansion in England and in Europe with their equivalents in the Third World today. Whatever fundamental habits and expectations, institutions, and law become routinized in the population as a whole and especially in its relations to authority during this more fluid phase will to a great extent shape all subsequent configurations and ways of doing things, largely determining whether development can be sustained throughout the years, indeed the centuries, to come. Because of the very nature of culture, basic cultural forms at this level *persist* beneath seemingly radical surface changes (often in what appear to be very perverse ways). Later on, planners cannot simply decide that now is the time to establish broad-based predictability and so flip on the switch for participation.

Such forms are created through the *processes* of interaction; they are not brought about by the accoutrements of modernism. Third World planners, economists, and elites in general assume that if they can just get the same *things* the developed countries have, or even the right numbers, along with these *in the same package* they will also get the institutions and underlying norms which brought them into being in the first place in Europe and Japan. Along with factories one will automatically get law, along with a civil service one will get accountable civil servants, along with highways and banks one will get economically rational mobility and entrepreneurial trust, etc. But function does not automatically follow form. Thus Table Two emphasizes not the forms themselves, but how the way development is brought about affects those in its vortex and on its sidelines.

The most striking sociological aspect of England's burst of investment reviewed in Table Two is that through the duration of more than a century and a half this radical new mode of production, industrialization, was evolved by tens of thousands of tiny, decentralized units of production bonding with each other in long chains over considerable distances; because each was highly specialized and evolved pragmatically, it was dependent upon its partners through complementarity and thus in turn easily held accountable. For instance, special harness tabs cut out in certain households were sent to others who made the straps, and after them to others who only fitted the buckle, and others, and others, until an assembled harness emerged. In myriad diverse types of combination, each enterprise carrying out its little project, homes across the landscape and deep into the countryside created vast regional production systems—cohesive and vertically penetrating—through their own linked schedules and arrangements. Of course, the putting-out entrepreneurs organized these networks, but they themselves were highly decentralized and included many subcontractors and sub-subcontractors who were artisan/peasants themselves.

In time, these cottagers and artisans converged into factories (quite literally "converged," each bringing with him his own means of production and his own management: each rented his own separate floor space in the building, paid for his own power, even hired his own assistants and determined his own workload pace, etc.). Consolidation under one "governance" was extremely gradual.[26]

The piecemeal yet structured character of Europe's social organization throughout the initial burst of investment gave its various units exceptional flexibility. Their concreteness of purpose and their scale enabled people at every level in the system to hold others responsible in simple, explicit, measurable terms. Such fields of interaction extended horizontally as well as vertically since production units often grew by amalgamation. Thus it was here at the grassroots that the early channels for business and finance were hammered out; it was these mini-entrepreneurs who invested (along with the petite bourgeoisie) in the early enterprises, and who became investors and larger entrepreneurs, while others of them eventually created the trade unions. Society's *base* was the springboard of development. The criteria for predictability, bonding and "the bottom line" were generated internally, not by the state, and were rooted in highly participatory and pragmatic economic exchange, not the personalism or "law" of distant elites. Well into the nineteenth century the lowest rungs of workers in these capitalist industries maintained one foot in the agricultural economy, which gave them strong leverage against their industrial employers. Industry sought labor, not vice versa.

It is true that through time the putting-out entrepreneurs gained a stronger and stronger hand over the small producers. But even then, well up to the nineteenth century, the latter retained final control over production (for example, quality control, promptness and seasonal variation in the allocation of labor, misappropriation of raw material into the black market, etc.) and hence retained bargaining leverage over the entrepreneurs.[27] Indeed, the decentralized social structure of feudalism and manoral life, with its concomitant norms and skills of contractual bargaining, can be seen to underlie Europe's social organization throughout this initial burst of investment and expansion. "The rural petty-producers were conscious of the importance of being organized in groups, for they tenaciously held on to the remains of guild and corporative rights—as far as they existed in the countryside. They also repeatedly attempted to form new guilds . . . [When] this resistance was unsuccessful, the workers turned toward fighting for their wages and working conditions within the framework of the new form of industrial organization. And strikes assumed a prominent place in the new struggle."[28]

In England this decentralized, piecemeal, gradually additive, and highly participatory form of capitalist production flourished for *two hundred years* before factories came to dominate industry, allowing these values and norms, political and economic skills and new institutional channels plenty of time to take hold through repeated patterns of behavior. On the continent and in Japan the process was essentially the same.

It is not surprising, then, that in England as early as 1825, long before most workers had become dependent upon wages for their livelihood, they had succeeded in having repealed those laws forbidding them from organizing. Immediately unions emerged. Within five years, although well over half the industrial labor force worked at home and thus was extremely difficult to organize, a national labor union had been established; in the Midlands, potters industry-wide won pay raises as hefty as 25 percent in a single strike.[29] The culture and skills of political participation through structured organization and bargaining, of interdependence and mutual accountability, became "internalized" by society at large through centuries of practice during this formative phase of early capitalist development, enabling the sustained rationality, predictability, and bonding we still see today. But it was these rugged *dynamics,* not factories and laws from on high, which constituted this foundation.

The same piecemeal character of England's period of intense investment was found in the public sector, again in contrast to the Third World today. Villages, regions, or private groups initiated their own schools, roads, irrigation systems, etc.; locals supported their own hospitals, welfare programs, and scientific societies—in some instances up to now. Only gradually and by *local* demand did the state begin to supplement these efforts with its own assistance. In many cases control still remains in local hands. Besides this being more efficient and assuring local monitoring of the state's efforts, the principal gain of such a state-local relationship was the development of these separate fields' own integrity at the grassroots and their capacity to make demands for social overhead according to their respective needs.

Notice that as workers' organizations appeared they were formed first according to region and industry—and so were the entrepreneurs'. Civic organizations followed the same pattern. Such field-by-field consolidation need not obstruct the integration of state-level society, but because of the invariable tendency to divide and rule, the latter cannot *precede* the former. After all, what more cohesive yet highly complex societies can one find than England, France, and Japan, national societies which grew out of ruggedly decentralized initiatives and groupings (not out of such "integrating" forces as ethnic homogenization or television satellites).

In summary, Table Two calls attention to the importance of the *fabric* of society, the day-to-day and routine, for sustained development. Economists have sought the impetus for development in the usually exceptional individual: the Henry Fords. But the increased volume of exchanges of every type, the knitting together of fields of interaction, of a common texture, must precede Schumpeter's entrepreneur.

Secondly, Table Two emphasizes the importance of corporate *groups* in the capitalist development process. Growth is achieved as much by joining units together, as it is by accumulation. Entrepreneurial individualism is in vogue today as an affirmation of the capitalist dynamic, as though producers' efforts to combine for greater strength—small producers, especially—somehow intrinsically smack of "socialism." There is no evidence whatsoever in the determinative stages of early European and American development, and certainly none *at all* in Japan, that going it alone is a key to capitalist success.

Thirdly, we see now that the corporate groups which continue to play such a crucial role in Western and Japanese development are both economic incorporations and political ones. The former are widely acknowledged as a central feature of capitalist development, but it was the latter that made economic incorporation possible. Having reviewed these organizations at the base, we return to Table One's reminder that long before the Industrial Revolution, the emerging middle class had assured society a strong curb on the willfulness of centralized power at the top. What a contrast to the Third World today!

Finally, Table Two emphasizes that the initial impetus to Western development came not from London and Paris, but from the thousands of small towns which sprang up in *"the periphery"* during the late Middle Ages and which provided capitalism's sustaining drive. Toynbee has documented how rare it is that people in any heartland initiate a burst of exceptional creativity and investment. In terms of this paper the heartland is not just a place, the capital city, but all fields of activity which the center no longer "coordinates" but now *commands*. (For example, the processing of wool— England's *heartland* industry—became mechanized much more slowly than cotton.) Thus the heartland often embraces older fields of interaction which seek the center's protection from competition; fields which have come to be dominated by formal law, thereby growing rigid and losing their predictability; fields in which the initial vigor of participatory feedback has become stultified by bureaucratic governance. In contrast, it should not surprise us that those areas of society maintaining their intermediate structures against the center's domination should offer innovators, long-term investors and the producers themselves the firmest conditions for rationality and bonding—hence a more ambitious workforce, a more pervasive expectation of accountability, stronger and more determined institutions to resist arbitrariness, greater self-reliance and responsibility, a longer time-horizon. In Western and Japanese capitalism, it is here that one finds the gathering points of broad-based savings and initiative sustained through generations. The periphery is not just a place with more "elbow room," but a cultural environment, a "mind set," and a set of institutions which holds its own governance in tension off against the center.[30]

Conclusion

We have argued here that only through participation which is structured and rooted in actual behavior (not just voting, etc.) can society acquire and maintain the requisites for sustained capitalist development: predictability, rationality, and bonding. Capitalism requires continued vital input from the broad base of society, but this will not be forthcoming without the firm conditions of predictability as defined from the point of view of the would-be initiators, investors, inventors, or workers themselves. The norms, skills, and institutions for such participation evolved gradually during the centuries leading up to the Industrial Revolution in the West and Japan. In the process of their evolution the speed and level of political development among the participants in society kept pace with and was not overcome by the parallel development of overall coordinating mechanisms at the center. The governance of these central coordinating mechanisms became embodied in law, a law which reflected rather than sought to command the norms and patterns of social interaction.[31]

In contrasting these requisites for long-term predictability with the way Third World societies are attempting to industralize today, we find little evidence that the foundations are being laid there for sustained capitalist development. To the contrary. In most Third World countries corporate groups throughout society are deliberately being fragmented and middle-range institutions eroded; the base of society, its bedrock, has no responsible role at all to play in development; the lower orders have no leverage whatsoever over their governors' or employers' accountability (except through self-defeating riots). Indeed, the elites of the centralized state can more easily be checked in their excesses by bankers in Washington, than internally by the social systems they are meant to coordinate. The supreme value placed on economic measures of development encourages and justifies this radical misdirection.

TABLE 1
THE UNDERPINNINGS OF SUSTAINED CAPITALIST DEVELOPMENT BEFORE THE INITIAL INVESTMENT EXPANSION

England 1750	*Third World 1983*
I. INVESTMENT CAPITAL	
1. *Traditional upper class* has shifted from "status" investment, now actively investing in industry (due to the increasing security and predictability of investments other than land)	beginning
2. *Vigorous investment by other classes* (locally/regionally), non-traditional "upstarts" among leading entrepreneurs[1]	in some societies
3. *Village integration* into provincial non-agricultural production; strong small-farmer investment in agriculture[2]	rare
II. THE PROCESS OF CAPITALIST INVESTMENT	
(A) ECONOMIC RATIONALITY/FREE FLOW OF RESOURCES	
1. *No systemic social barriers to entrepreneurial competition*[3]	beginning
2. *Channels at all social levels for investment in capital formation*, in which the saver and investor are differentiated[4]	extremely weak
3. *Peasant mobility*[5]	increasing though with notable barriers re. caste, tribe
4. National *transportation network*[6]	rapidly improving
5. *Free press, information flow*	nonexistent
B) PREDICTABILITY, ACCOUNTABILITY, AND BONDING	
1. *Arbitrary power of ruler checked by regularly elected assembly*[7]	virtually non existent
2. *Expanding central bureaucracy curbed, tax revolt, local autonomy restored*[8]	non existent
3. *National economic policies stabilized* by being removed from autocratic control[9]	virtually non existent
4. Sound commercial law, effective channels for *impersonal* links[10]	on paper but not generally operative
5. Institutions for challenging *scientists, inventors* to serve society's needs dominate scientific research[11]	non existent
6. *Civil service accountable to citizenry*[12]	non existent
7. *Military spending subject to citizens'* (Parliament's) control[13]	non existent

NOTES TO TABLE ONE:

(1) Shopkeepers, artisans, inn-keepers, farmers; Arkwright was a barber, died with a knighthood, worth £1 million; in France the Peugeots were millers and inn-keepers before establishing a fortune in textiles and much later in motor cars.

(2) Arthur Young and Adam Smith extolled the yeoman farmer's commitment and persistence in investing in higher agricultural productivity, but the early domestic system with its relatively cheap and widely-available implements enabled village craftsmen and farmers to invest in local industrial production as well. Land reform encourages small-farmer investment in Third World agriculture and often clears space for villagers to enter other entrepreneurial niches, at the local level.

(3) In many Third World societies minority ethnic groups are restricted in their scope of dealings, or tribal or caste distinctions prevent free competition.

(4) Government-organized rural savings cooperatives are not generally viable. In contrast, by C18 the "general public" in England was accustomed to banking. See footnote 5.

(5) In France the serfs were not freed until the end of the century but had considerable mobility. In many Third World societies lower classes enjoy virtually no mobility.

(6) Often opposed by the landed class; not begun seriously until after the Revolution in England, under Parliament's direction.

(7) Most entrepreneurs were not themselves active in Parliamentary politics in England at this period, but sought to affect trade, taxation, government procurement of industrial products (armaments, etc.), labor legislation, credit and finance through their spokesmen. This of course strengthened the development of *representational* politics, enabled entrepreneurs to belong to more than one interest group, and led away from personalistic allegiances.

(8) The century and a half ending in 1700 saw an unprecedented rise in bureaucratic power throughout Europe, the percentage of the population employed in a centralized bureaucracy quadrupling. Everywhere taxes soared (in France in one twelve-year period

they tripled), and central government penetrated innumerable new areas of local and regional life. Not until the upheaval of 1640–60 and the lesser eruptions which followed, in England, and later still on the Continent, was local self-direction re-established at least in major policy domains, including the courts, certain critical areas of economic regulation, poverty and welfare administration, etc. See footnote 6.

(9) In 1694 the Bank of England was established under Parliamentary control, the Chancellor of the Exchequer placed under Parliament soon thereafter. Parliament from then on controlled customs, the issuing of monopolies and subsidies, interest rates of the Bank of England (strongly affecting general public interest rates), and price regulations. The government could no longer repudiate its debts.

(10) Although formally in place and seemingly operative in some Third World countries, still highly subject to manipulation and bribes at all levels. Certainly *impersonal* bonding among capitalists at all levels still relatively rare.

(11) eg, Royal Society debates, effective public lobbies holding scientists and inventors accountable, science funding private hence strictly supervised, laymen's science publications flourished, etc.

(12) By the early eighteenth century the Offices of Trade and Customs of the Admiralty and of the Treasury had been brought under Parliament's—no longer the King's—control; salaries replaced fees, perquisites and "commissions"; entrance examinations had been introduced; and the sons of squires had widespread access to bureaucratic positions, based on talent with meritocratic promotions. Cromwell's army, in fact, had abolished automatic commissions for peers, had instituted appointment on the basis of merit regardless of sectarian or ethnic affiliation.

(13) The public had begun to perceive that war, which diverts resources to non-productive ends, had primarily become a vehicle for political centralization.

TABLE 2
THE *PROCESSES* OF THE PERIOD OF RAPID EXPANSION

ENGLAND/EUROPE *1750–1900*	*THE THIRD WORLD[1]* *1945–PRESENT*
I. *PIECEMEAL, GRADUAL*	**I.** *WHOLE-HOG SUDDEN*
—*technology generated incrementally*, in small inventions, tinkering,[2] often by employees themselves.	—*technology imported from developed countries ready-made*: incremental growth paced by piecemeal invention impossible, technology capital-intensive so does not conform to factor availabilities.
—production grew through highly flexible, *patch-work organization* of putting-out system: machines in cottages, contractors at local and provincial levels. Factories emerged very late.[3]	—organization of production leaps right into *fixed, large-scale packages* except in select artisan/workshop fields, by-passing cottage involvement, small, independent subcontractors or middle-sized intermediaries.
—*finance piecemeal*: most enterprises began as family firms of middle class; entrepreneurs (often workers) sought finance incrementally; financial combinations ad hoc, varied extensively, institutions invented as needed.	—*finance complex, frequently large-scale*, whole plants often launched from the outset; family firms rare; forms of finance and combination imported rather than evolved; limited scope for broad-based participation in expansion, hence less incentive to save and invest.
—process of *growth* gradual and springing from *local, grass roots accumulation, involvement*: plowing profits back from small base or consolidation of small units; penny-pinching accountability.	—process of growth determined by size of imported models, technology; directed by *professional* expertise: dependent on *large-scale* credit from *distant* banks, government, foreign creditors; management by professionals means far less scope for local, private involvement, stockholder accountability.
—geographically dispersed: began in provinces wherever resources dictated location;[4] a single firm commonly extended from urban hub out to smallest cottage.	—*geographic concentration*: extreme polarization of rural-urban investment/development between provinces and capital city; local comparative advantages hardly recognized.
—*worker independence*: workers often highly skilled in initial stages, inventive; enclosure movement caused labor shortages;[5] still in 1890 most workers could fall back on agricultural livelihood hence had bargaining leverage with entrepreneur.	—*workers undifferentiated, with no alternative employment*, little leverage: moreover, industrial relations highly complex from the outset, determined by State paternalism not by worker organization and demands; challenge of worker-organizing extremely difficult.
—"*social overhead*" *piecemeal*, gradual; roads, schools, Civil Service provisions (inspections, regulations, etc.) brought forward bit by bit when demanded: *local, private initiatives* provided most services for over a century before national government assumed responsibilities, by then strictly subject to local review.	—"*social overhead*" also *whole-hog, national-level* from the outset, not directly determined by society's needs and certainly *not by local efforts or leverage*: nation-wide literacy campaign, nation-wide primary school system, etc. not generated incrementally, internally nor piece-meal; private sector, local initiatives by-passed for aggregate, state-planned services.

NOTES:

(1) Some Third World countries could hardly be considered to have embarked on this phase yet, such as certain ones in Africa.

(2) Power machinery was not widespread in England until 1870, well over a century after Kay's flying shuttle and other important inventions were common in cottage industry.

(3) Early factory workers coming together in a single building continued to manage their little enterprises individually—hiring, renting, contracting out and assembling as needs required. Their system of production was additive to the extreme, taking decades to evolve organizational uniformity. See footnote 19.

(4) At a mine, at a mill, in small "free" towns where guilds not dominant, in rural valleys where dispersion of cottages prompted centralized production, etc.

(5) See Landes, footnote 20.

124

TABLE 2: II

ENGLAND/EUROPE 1750–1900	THE THIRD WORLD 1945–PRESENT
II. *PRAGMATIC:* NEEDS DICTATE INVESTMENT, MANAGEMENT	II. *PERMISSIVE:* POLITICS AND TECHNOLOGICAL SMORGASBORD DEFINE THE MAIN PARAMETERS
—*entrepreneurial and managerial decisions* (technology development, finance, production, organizational forms, expansion, location, etc.) primarily determined by *the market:*	—*entrepreneurial, managerial decisions* far more subject to *political considerations,* which govern virtually every aspect of investment, production and marketing:
a) in those spheres mainly influenced by politics, *local and occupational fields* of interaction often determinative	a) *national-level politics* decisive, decentralized; political arenas irrelevant.
b) public skills, channels of the population at large well-developed for *generalizing* the application of law	b) pervasive government regulation usually *particularistic and discretionary,* not clearly circumscribed by law; bureaucratic law dictated not generalized to population at large.
—*capitalist accounting* requires society to yield to its demands for *mobility of factors* (including entrepreneurial talent and even plant location); investment of landed classes in industry a pragmatic move away from status investment: social mobility based on pragmatic criteria.	—*mobility of factors* largely determined by *personal contacts* (even mobility of labor) and status, partly due to enormous scale differential at outset and to lack of firm legal underpinnings, predictability. Because of enormous disparity in power and resources, traditional social system able to resist demands of meritocracy.
—*keen competition* due to broad base of entrepreneurial endeavor, principal financing by owner/managers, and technology conducive to incremental improvements; hence	—single firms able to *monopolize* main fields, due to size, scale, range of existing technology and credit institutions, sophistication of technology and finance, importance of politics, etc.; hence:
a) *worker feedback* and expertise decisive, artisan workers not interchangeable.	a) *employee initiative of minimal potential contribution*
b) *maintenance* critical: from the outset of production, oiling the wheel that squeaks.	b) *maintenance not considered critical* from outset because slower depreciation of sophisticated equipment, and monopoly, government protection, loose accountability, etc.
c) *technological up-dating* possible on firm by firm basis, constantly required.	c) *professionalized, proportionally much more expensive research and development,* especially vis-a-vis developed-country technological changes, so workers and individual firm can participate very little
d) institutionalized priority for *efficiency.*	d) institutionalized priority for political and wheeler-dealer *contacts*
—*risk-taking routinized* as the operational norm, due to incremental trial-and-error problem solving, wide competition, scale:	—allocation, production through *government collaboration shields from risk,* discourages trial-and-error correction, does not require close capital account-

125

ing: investment based on import substitution or "finishing touches" is less risky; *social/political parameters* rather than risk-taking in the market build *less confidence* in pragmatic decision-making, place higher priority on personal networks, short-term status. Since government determines a firm's or industry's future risks are personalistic rather than economic.

—*personalism* strong in decision-making, not transcended, due to primacy of socio-political considerations, hence:

a) reluctance to share control of enterprise outside of family, or to decentralize authority; family size, members, determine size, direction of firm's expansion;

b) "bottom line" easily over-ruled by personal demands;

c) wages and salaries affected by personalism not by strict capitalist accounting;

d) the people who know people get ahead; cynicism and opportunism

—*"social overhead"* infrastructure determined *not by need but by aggregate Plan* and by *international* welfare, theories, programs, publicity, pressure and *uniform, national coverage* regardless of need or demand; structured local, regional or sectoral political leverage does not affect allocation of social overhead directly. Furthermore, social overhead packaged entirely by respective national ministries, no local or institutional initiative or fine-tuning.[2]

a) *rational accounting, impersonal management* necessary for risk-taking; strong sense of the bottom line.

b) risk-taking requires *planning ahead.*

c) risk-taking builds *confidence* in meeting objective market, production demands.

—partnership, promotion, bonding on the basis of *merit*, not personal ties[1], hence:

a) managerial experience and opportunities diffuse; management disaggregated from personalities, becomes a science;

b) clear-cut and impersonal criteria emerge for allocational decisions; since these are empirical workers, stockholders, the public can hold management accountable; participation in production process diffuse;

c) remuneration tied more closely to performance;

d) scope for upward and downward mobility appears very early, hence some evidence (though select) to justify ambition, collaboration, longer time horizon.

—*"social overhead"* infrastructure also established in response to need or organized demand, (ie, hard lobbying by would-be beneficiaries), often after having been *evolved locally:* for instance, extraordinary variety of school systems, curricula, teachers' training, etc. in nineteenth century; combinations of different sizes, on different principles numerous; public/private mix freely resorted to for *pragmatic solution* to needs.

NOTES:

(1) Frequent examples of partners, even family partners, fired for inefficiency. See footnote 21.

(2) For example, when a village receives a school, everything is pre-determined: its architecture and building materials, size, class size, curriculum, teacher preparation and supervision, regulations governing teaching, etc.—disregarding local needs or preferences.

TABLE 2: III

ENGLAND/EUROPE 1750–1900	THE THIRD WORLD 1945–PRESENT
III. INTERNALLY-GENERATED BY INITIATIVES, RESPONSIBILITY OF BROAD POPULAR BASE	III. EXTERNALLY-DERIVED; LOCAL RESOURCES, INITIATIVE, DIRECTION SUPERFLUOUS
—Agricultural investment established the normative and institutional precedents for all subsequent development, founded on recognition that *at the base of society lay its greatest resource potentials*; elites and the base itself had vigorously invested in this level. • the base taken seriously as the springboard for development.	—Agricultural investment in *the broad base* of yeomen/tenants and their holdings *by-passed* entirely as a foundation for later accumulation or for human resources potential, hence: •from the outset the base given no serious part to play in development
—*finance for development of early industries provided by broad base of* artisans, cottage craftsmen, laborers, part-time farmers as well as merchants, millers, innkeepers, etc. *who risked own savings, initiated inventions, direction* for period of rapid expansion; also participated vigorously; hence:	—Period of rapid expansion to a large extent *externally financed*, technology lifted from Japan and West, the products themselves externally given; yeoman farmers irrelevant; even elites rarely participate through personal risk but largely with loans from government, often by investing funds accrued through non-productive means; invariably secure with savings, investments abroad before assuming domestic risks, Hence,
a) delayed gratification; b) knitting together through organic development, trust, predictability rooted in participation and enhanced by it; popular sense of English (French, German) "nation" long before nationalism; c) low toleration for arbitrariness: arbitrary rulers beheaded, deposed, (see Table 1)	a) instant gratification more pronounced; b) "mechanical" cohesion rather than organic: neither the purpose, the forms nor (to a large extent) the means of social cohesion evolved in the process of development; c) high toleration for arbitrariness, because leading investors, managers, decision-makers cushioned by foreign savings, personalism, status; even bad rulers assured foreign asylum.
—*complementarity* of many small, highly specialized producers *compulsory* in the piecemeal development of early Industrial Revolution.	—*local, domestic complementarity optional* because complementarity available internationally, and because technological complexity prevents spontaneous complementarity; hence, less pressure to develop domestic channels or domestic guarantees for secure impersonal bonding.
—*the provinces are the engine of economic development*: rich proliferation of vital industries and whole leading fields of interaction in the provinces and at village level, for: a) exploitation of *raw materials* (iron, clay for pottery, alkali, etc. for chemical industries);	—*provinces by-passed* because a) *raw materials* processed in urban centers for economies there; in any event, the period of rapid expansion is based more on import substitution or finishing industries not dependent on provincial comparative advantages;

b) cheap power (coal, water power, etc.);

c) cottage-based labor, (industry went to labor);

d) advantages of provincial flexibility (eg, to avoid regulations such as guild restrictions which persisted in established centers);

e) locational preferences of provincial inventors/entrepreneurs.

Hence, many growth poles.

—relationships to international economy complementary to but not determinative of domestic development.

—competition/efficiency an internal motor

—"Tool Kit" for socio-economic interaction evolved in development process:

• institutions, (banks, transportation networks, educational establishments, factories themselves, Civil Service corporations, etc.) called forth through the productive process: hence those that evolve are necessary, functional, congealing out of repeated behavior.

• legal system grew organically out of abuses, claims, new perceptions of change[3], vigorous yeomen demands, conscious sense of "rights" within politically-viable local units. Due to this organic process, relatively slow, vigorous and opposing interest groups, local/provincial organizations could establish themselves, as well as norms, skills of integrating feedback into coordinational mechanism. No rules until called for.

—"social overhead" and Civil Service grew out of internal efforts (often carried on for centuries by locals/private agencies first) and out of internal demands/regulations on government. Hence, accountability/norms of efficiency locally-defined; concrete purpose

—robust local/interest-group initiatives.

b) power brought to factories, not vice-versa;

c) labor brought to factories, not vice-versa;

d) provinces controlled by central government, so not allowed to offer special incentives (free zones controlled by central government);

e) all entrepreneurs want to live in the capital city; industry does not need local inventors.

Hence, all development springs from and serves the national capital.

—international economy (foreign exchange rates, etc.) decisive in determining domestic development: enormous disparities of scale, etc.

—the motor is external: imitation, catching-up with others

—almost the entire "tool kit" derived:

• institutions imported, indigenous institutions deliberately destroyed[1] hence institutions superimposed without accountability[2], without lower orders knowing how to use them.

• legal systems also imported

a) often long before awareness of the respective offenses which laws claim to correct;

b) imported whole-hog partly to help central government destroy competing indigenous authorities and systems, politically-viable local units;

c) rather inan formal law being the last stage in society's integration of behaviorial change it now anticipates behavior, pre-empting the feedback, deliberation and formalizing processes within society, making participants institutions superfluous. Watchdogging formal law is impossible because law is derived from abroad and is the exclusive domain of professional elites.

—prepackaged services, civil service bureaucracies, imitative of Western models, most of the government exists to perform "services" or solve problems which the citizenry never knew they needed.[4] Real problems often not seriously tackled by government because no mechanisms for demand-making and accountability.[5]

—paternalism.

NOTES

(1) Such as tribal structures and boundaries, village militias, communal irrigation systems, with the exception of such institutions as India's caste system or Muslim courts, etc.

(2) For instance, Lions Clubs which perform no "services," government farmers' cooperatives which serve no function, Parliaments that are powerless, national parks open only to tourists, unions which cannot strike, newspapers which cannot report, taxation without taxpayer leverage, etc.

(3) Though admittedly, often at a slow pace, such as the Poor Laws and their abolition, Factory Laws, etc.

(4) For instance, aeronautical controls, statistical bureaux, most regulating and inspecting services (seed testing, water testing, student identification systems, etc.) Foreign Service, etc.

(5) For instance, malnutrition, soil classification for fertilizer application, inflation, health services for the poor, claims against the government, etc.

TABLE 2: IV

ENGLAND/EUROPE 1750–1900	THE THIRD WORLD 1945–PRESENT
IV. THE STATE TRIES TO KEEP UP WITH CHANGES INITIATED IN SOCIETY	**IV. SOCIETY MUST KEEP UP WITH CHANGES ORDERED BY THE STATE**
—Industrial Revolution in England born in *anti-government era*; 1640–1789 stripped autocrat, bureaucracy of powers, subjected them to control of assembly: taxation, economic policies, army, Civil Service, etc. Municipal corporations OUTSIDE CENTRAL JURISDICTION were the political units of development. (These followed a century later in France.)	—Third World development born under *unprecedented state power,*[1] the Leninist state the political model of development, even to Western planners.
—*citizen-leverage high* because government depended on taxes and fighting men.	—*citizen leverage nil* because the state derives revenues from other sources, taxes not crucial, and no need for broadly-based popular army.
—*fiscal and monetary policy neutral*	—*rapid development a national political imperative*, hence the State frequently and arbitrarily manipulates fiscal and monetary policy (exports, import duties, interest rates, etc.). See footnote 22.
—when government attempts to "direct" development it is *unsuccessful*, as Colbert.	—*The Plan legitimized* in a relative *vacuum* of countervailing initiatives.
—the period of rapid expansion *caused mass consumerism* rather than being driven by it.[2]	—twentieth-century *mass consumerism a major driving aim* of development[3].
—*no time frame*. The future is open-ended, to be created.	—time frame usually the *life-time of the ruler*, or the Party's expected span of unchallenged rule: half a century at the most. The future is given, only to be implemented.
—the development process with all its antagonisms *gave muscle to the level of sociopolitical organization between the individual and the state*; the state mistrusted.	—the development process with its command center at the top must *obliterate middle-level institutions* that might challenge the State; Myrdal's levelling force of nation-building is the ideal, endorsed by Western Nobel-prize experts.
—politics, *political controversy* considered an art and service, attracted *broad-based participation* (publications, meetings, etc.) and illustrious statesmen.	—political controversy criticized as *disloyalty*, obstructionist, self-serving (especially in the popular mind); attracts little vital interest,[4] mainly extremely petty, insecure, plodding figures. If the state is mistrusted, the population still looks at it as their only hope; but even middle class feels *government is beyond their reach.*
—*business not the responsibility* of the State, not even in Japan; often the State a dependency of business.[5]	—*government directs* investment, finance, import/export, labor, etc. Business and industry are dependencies of the state.

130

a) state regulation evolved *piecemeal*, through controversy; need for regulation sparked many middle-range institutions to combat government/business alliance and to force the state to "coordinate" relatively equal contenders.

b) *labor organized effectively* with considerable speed (in England, and even faster on the Continent,[7] where the manorial villein well accustomed to strikes went straight into factory trade unions.) See footnote 23.

—"social overhead" services demanded and hence *monitored by the public.*

—*the state and its mechanisms forced to adapt* to provinces, interest groups, changing fields of interaction, new needs and forms created through interaction: government at the beck-and-call of society in development process.

a) regulation derived from developed countries and imposed without controversy, *pre-empting the need for popular political organization*; government and law do not serve as coordinating mechanisms but as the dominant protagonists.

b) *labor unions prohibited* or government-controlled, hence often highly erratic, irresponsible.[6]

—in exactly the reverse dynamic, one of the state's major efforts is *to persuade people to use* the social overhead it forces upon them.[8]

—according to national policy people and their behavioral diversity *must adapt to the state.* This norm and process must be institutionalized socially and internalized individually. The society is at the beck-and-call of the state in the development process.

NOTES

(1) While it is true that in England especially the Tudors actively interfered in economic life, especially with respect to international trade, yet at the same time many medieval restrictions were being removed freeing small businesses, guilds, etc. In quite the opposite dynamic Third World societies, politically fragmented under colonial rule, have subsequently been subjected to radical centralization: a combination of technocracy, military power, propagandistic degradation of tribes and local structures, the nationalism of opportunists, etc. Such onslaught against decentralized direction has nothing to do with technical causes like illiteracy but rather with the power of the State.

(2) Early mass consumerism comprised the popularization of buttons, improved pottery, plumbing, etc.

(3) This is mainly due to the state's over-development of social facilities beyond their immediate need, but also due to nationalism, the international involvement of all nations in the Second World War, etc.

(4) With a few exceptions, like Sri Lanka.

(5) State supervision retarded industrial growth in France and Germany, and is increasingly challenged in Japan. See footnote 24.

(6) Such institutions cannot simply be turned-on when desired. In contrast to England as early as 1825, most Third World countries with a much higher percentage of total workers in factory conditions and completely dependent on factory wages, still deprive workers of the right to organize.

(7) For example, as early as 1825, when most industrial work was still done by people who had agricultural resources to fall back on, the Anti-Combination Law forbidding unions had been repealed. It did not take labor 20 years of organizing—under more difficult conditions than today—to win the Ten Hours Bill, which was rapidly followed by a long series of reforms. See footnote 25.

(8) For instance, agricultural extension, health care, schools, population control, malaria control, etc.

131

NOTES

1. I would like to thank my colleagues in the seminar as well as Harold Berman, John Powelson and Bostan Zupancic for their very helpful criticisms of earlier drafts of this paper. In this essay I am deeply indebted to Conrad Arensberg for the corpus of his work and teaching.

2. Which by 1930, equalled Canada in leading the world's exports in grain and in attracting massive European investment; like Canada, too, it boasted a low population density, very few indigeneous peoples of contrasting tribal cultures, and an influx of hard-working European immigrants.

3. We use the term rationality in Weber's sense, to refer to the *economic* calculation of the capitalist.

4. See, for instance: Dale Adams, "Mobilizing Rural Household Savings Through Rural Financial Markets," *Economic Development and Cultural Change* 26 (1978); John Gurley and Edward Shaw, "Financial Intermediaries and the Saving-Investment Process," *Journal of Finance* 2 (1956); R. McKinnon, *Money, Capital and Economic Development* (Washington, D.C.: The Brookings Institution, 1973); H. Patrick, "Financial Development and Economic Growth in Under-developed Countries," *Economic Development and Cultural Change* 14 (1966); E. Shaw, *Financial Deepening in Economic Development* (New York: Oxford University Press, 1973); G. Singh, T. Gupta, and B. Singh, "Pattern of Voluntary Savings in India," *Savings and Development* 2 (1978), pp. 224–234; J. D. Von Pischke, "Towards an Operational Approach to Savings for Rural Development," *Savings and Development* 2 (1978), pp. 43–57; U Tun Wai, *Financial Intermediaries and National Savings in Developing Countries* (New York: Praeger, 1972).

5. D. Landes, "Technological Change and Industrial Development—Europe 1750–1914," in *Cambridge Economic History of Europe*, Vol. VI, Part I, edited by Habakkuk and Postam (Cambridge: Cambridge University Press, 1965), p. 307.

6. Theodore Rabb, *The Struggle for Stability in Early Modern Europe* (New York: Oxford University Press, 1975), pp. 61ff.

7. G. Goodell, "From Status to Contract: the Significance of Agrarian Relations of Production in the West, Japan and 'Asiatic' Persia," *European Journal of Sociology* XXI (1980), pp. 285–325.

8. C. M. Arensberg, "Culture as Behavior: Structure and Emergence," *Annual Review of Anthropology* I (1972), p. 20.

9. M. Weber, "The Social Psychology of the World Religions," in *From Max Weber*, edited by Gerth and Mills (New York: Oxford University Press, 1946), p. 293.

10. See Seligman, *Helplessness* (San Francisco: W. H. Freeman & Co., 1975), p. 36.

11. Robert Fishman, "The Labor Movement in Transition to Spanish Democracy" (Seminar at Harvard University, February 1982).

12. Stewart Macaulay, "Non-Contractual Relations in Business," *American Sociological Review* 28 (1963), p. 55.

13. See Goodell, *The Elementary Structures of Political Life*, (Ph.D. Dissertation, Columbia University, 1978), pp. 363ff.

14. See F. C. Savigny, *Of the Vocation of Our Age for Legislation and Jurisprudence*, translated by A. Hayward (London: Littlewood and Co., 1881).

15. W. Loehr and J. Powelson, *The Economics of Development and Distribution* (New York: Harcourt, Brace and Jovanovitch, 1981), pp. 360ff.

16. See A. Hirschman, *Strategy of Economic Development* (New Haven: Yale University Press, 1959).

17. G. C. Allen, *The Industrial Development of Birmingham* (London: G. Allen, 1929), pp. 137, 158, 171, 240.

128. M. Dobb, *Studies in the Development of Capitalism* (London: Routledge and Kegan Paul, 1946), p. 22.

19. *Ibid.*, pp. 265ff.

20. Landes, *op cit.*, p. 302.

21. *Ibid.*, pp. 304–5.

22. J. Powelson, "Population Growth and Unemployment in Africa," *Cultures et Developpement* (Louvain: Université Catholique, 1978), p. 6.

23. Landes, *op cit.*, p. 344.

24. *Ibid.*, p. 372

25. Mitigating against the early and quite efficacious vitality of the labor movement in the eighteenth century and first half of the nineteenth were many factors. These included the political system's unresponsiveness to the lower orders' demands, but also:

a) the putting-out system which dispersed labor in distant, isolated places, and left workers unfamiliar with commonly-experienced complaints;

b) the vast immigration of Irish workers at the peak of the period, to regions of heaviest industrialization; these workers did not bring with them the British farming population's staunch organizational skills and experience, and as foreigners they were much more easily intimidated;

c) the century-long persistence of paternalistic measures such as the Poor Laws, etc.;

d) the generally *high* wages (which in fact served as a stimulus for the invention of machinery).

Yet despite these obstacles, by 1860 unions had become very powerful. See Landes, *op cit.*, p. 344; and Allen, *op. cit.*, pp. 170–1, 206ff.

26. See Dobb, *op cit.*, p. 265ff.

27. J. Schlumbohm, "Relations of Production," in Kriedte *et al.*, *Industrialization Before Industrialization* (Cambridge, England: Cambridge University Press, 1982), pp. 108–136.

28. *Op. cit.*, p. 106.

29. Allen, *op cit.*, pp. 206ff.

30. This should explain why the current political science concept of "corporatism," by which the State coopts intermediate structures into its orbit, cannot in the long term provide the requisite underpinnings of development. The State cannot carry out its mandate to "coordinate," as referee, if it is also a major player. Though technocrats despise it, the *tension* between center and periphery is essential.

31. The important role of religion, law, and of participating checks and balances against centralized power is dramatically documented in Harold Berman's new volume, *Law and Revolution: The Formation of the Western Legal Tradition* (Cambridge: Harvard University Press, 1983).

Multinational Corporations and Economic Development

Laura L. Nash and Alan M.Kantrow

IN RECENT YEARS, few issues having to do with the economic development of Third World nations have touched so raw a nerve or generated so heated a response as the role—and responsibilities—of MNCs. Substantial international businesses (relative to the GNPs of the participating nations) are, of course, nothing new. Nor, for that matter, is substantial direct foreign investment. What has changed since World War II, however, is the sheer magnitude of the institutional units involved, the complexity of their operations, the emphatically multinational character of their financing, and the degree to which decisions once left to the "invisible hand" of market forces have increasingly fallen under what Alfred Chandler has called the "visible hand" of management. [See Tables I & II]. In other words, and especially against the backdrop of limited government bureaucracies in developing nations, the post-war era has witnessed a radical shift in the scale of MNC activities. Like nothing before them, they dwarf the local institutions of business and government.

A century ago in the rough and tumble days of American capitalism, the great railroads, not yet fettered by the apparatus of regulation, also provoked a visceral reaction. To the nations's wheat farmers, the railroad was, in one celebrated account, "the galloping monster, the terror of steel and steam, with its single eye, Cyclopean, red, shooting from horizon to horizon . . . the symbol of a vast power, huge, terrible, flinging the echo of its thunder over all the reaches of the valley, leaving blood and destruction in its path; the leviathan, with tentacles of steel clutching into the soil, the soulless Force, the iron-hearted Power, the monster, the Colossus, the Octopus." To some constituencies in the Third World today and, in particular, to their most ideologically strident apologists, the MNC is but the octopus reborn, its rapacious tentacles grasping everything in sight.

The litany of outraged grievance has become familiar. Inevitably one hears about the checkered history of United Fruit or the machinations of I.T.T. in Allende's Chile. It is not enough, to be sure, to dismiss these accusations by cynically arguing that, even if true, they represent a level of behavior perfectly in keeping with the international dealings of most governments. But it is also not enough to let such excesses define the terms in which MNC involvements in the Third World are generally understood or analyzed. Too much is at stake—in financial investment, in economic health, and in the promise of a better life for the citizens of developing and developed countries alike—for so important a discussion to become the prisoner of ideologues on either side. Now, more than ever, we require a way of thinking about MNCs that is adequate to the facts, not to the exigencies of polemical debate.

All too often, for example, as Raymond Vernon points out, the effort to understand MNC involvements in the Third World gets unfortunately caught up in the discussion of a different, albeit related, issue: the "dependency" of the world's poorer countries. Dependency, in Vernon's lexicon, "includes the idea of an unbalanced relation between nation states and an unbalanced relation between classes, and it lays the causes of imbalance on the processes of international capitalism." Thus, according to this view, MNCs, as instruments of dependency, help to perpetuate a situation in which:

there may be growth of output in the dependent country, but it is likely to be growth of the wrong products. There may be growth of income, but for those that need the income least. There may be growth even in political power, but for purposes that serve no useful social end. Accordingly, those who stress the problems of dependency generally assume that under the existing system of relations between rich and poor countries, the gains to the poor countries are not so great as to preclude radical experiments with other forms of relationship. The assumption is that if Indonesia sharply curtailed the operations of Japanese firms in its territory, if the Ivory Coast impeded the entry of French firms, or if

Brazil restrained the activity of U.S. firms, this would probably be a good thing for the poorer country.

The concept of interdependence, on the other hand, tends to emphasize a somewhat different set of problems. To an increasing extent, the economic, political, and social lives of nations have become intermeshed. Nations draw more heavily on one another for the sources of their material and intellectual growth. This may seem a good thing at times from the viewpoint of the poor country. But the result is that when any big country sneezes, all the other countries catch cold.

> [Vernon, "Multinational Enterprises in Developing Countries: Issues in Dependency and Interdependence" in David E. Apter and Louis Wolf Goodman (eds.), *The Multinational Corporation and Social Change*, Praeger (1976), pp. 40–41.]

Both dependency and interdependence have their vocal supporters as well as their equally vocal critics, but all these interested parties argue from too narrow a conceptual base. As Vernon sees clearly, they talk as if "nation states [were] the only significant actors . . . [and do not give] much weight to the distinctive motivations and resources of multinational enterprises themselves." That is, they regard MNCs as stalking horses for national policy or as proxies for governmental action and attribute to them the purposes and the power of central policymakers. Nowhere in the equation is there room for a dispassionate assessment of what MNCs are actually trying to do or of the means actually at their disposal to accomplish their ends. Damned or celebrated as instruments of international realpolitik, MNCs do not lead a self-directed existence. Or so this view of things would have it.

But this view is mistaken and, worse, mischievous. It imputes to MNCs a measure of power they do not possess while seriously misconstruing the nature of the power they actually have. It denies them in practice an independence of action they do enjoy while ignoring the real constraints under which they operate. It criticizes purpose without understanding it and, in doing so, foresakes the opportunity to balance the true skills and resources of MNCs with the particular needs of local societies and cultures. In short, it indiscriminately tars 20th-century MNCs with the brush of mid 19th-century capitalism.

Now, we do not for a moment underestimate the generic ticklishness of the situation in which the government leaders, bureaucrats, and professional elites of developing countries often find themselves. But we also recognize that the straitened terms of discussion intended for local consumption have a troubling way of clouding judgments, confusing negotiations, and undermining legitimate interests. Nor do we underestimate the irresistibility of those forces that lead MNC executives, when driven to operate in the arena of public opinion, to try to mould that opinion in a manner favorable to their own interests. But here, too, we recognize that short-term victories in the marketplace of ideas do not necessarily guarantee the persistence over time of sensible and mutually beneficial arrangements. If there is to be a healthy role for multinational enterprise in the development of Third World economies (and we think there is), it can emerge only from an unprejudiced effort to understand both the interests and the limitations of MNCs and host governments alike.

Still, when the focus of attention shifts away from the dependency agrument to the concrete behavior of MNCs, knee-jerk criticism rages unabated. One representative summary of the criticism runs as follows:

It is alleged, for instance, that MNCs use their considerable market power to make excessive profits; that they avoid local taxation by manipulating import/export prices (especially where intra-company transactions are involved) . . .; that they produce goods suitable for the elite and are in this respect irrelevant to the needs of the masses; that they worsen inflation by putting heavy pressure on limited local supplies of certain material inputs and grades of labour; they destroy, through intense competition, long established local craft or workshop industry—and the traditional way of life that went with it; that they erode local sovereignty; and finally—but very significantly—that they frequently *install the "wrong" technology* . . . [Forsyth, in Malcolm Crawford and James Poole (eds.), *Ten Years of Multinational Business*, Ballinger (1982), p. 22.]

Though extensive, this list does not begin to exhaust the angry charges often leveled against specific MNC managers or against multinational enterprises in general. Investment and facilities decisions are made without regard to the economic or employment needs of host countries and are, moreover, often used to play one off against another. Indeed, the constant threat to move capital or production elsewhere or even to source from a variety of suppliers is both a shrewd and cruel bargaining ploy used to keep local governments and labor in line. Even when investment does take place, the majority of financing usually comes from the capital markets of the host country, which crowds out local borrowers, and the majority of profits are usually repatriated, which plays havoc with the host country's capital flows. Worse still, with so much capital at their disposal in so many countries, MNCs are inevitably currency speculators on a massive scale, which deranges whatever minimal stability remains in local economies. Thus, shielded from true competition by their monopolistic or, at worst, oligopolistic position, these international behemoths do not provide a sheltering environment within which local industry can flourish but, rather, make a specialty of driving that industry to the wall. And should anything or anyone threaten these sweetheart arrangements, MNCs will buy them off if possible, corrupt them if necessary.

But this is not all. By turning previously un- or under-developed economies not only into a valuable source of raw materials but also, more importantly, into a production base for export, MNCs inevitably draw away from their self-contained lives and into urban or factory-associated areas an endless horde of ill-trained people looking for work. This "magnet" effect disrupts traditional social and economic patterns and, inevitably, overloads the limited abilities of Third World governments to care for their people. In other words, by pulling marginal populations rudely into the global economy, MNCs create a massive and virtually insoluble welfare problem. These people cannot return home to their farms or villages; there are not enough jobs to employ them all, and their needs far outdistance the capacity of local services. In the name of profit and efficiency, multinational enterprise callously disrupts the fragile social order on which developing economies rest. If MNCs do anything good, it is interred, we are to suppose, with their bones.

Now, in point of fact, the evidence for such charges as these is anything but clear cut. Take, for example, even so apparently straightforward a matter as the alleged tendency of MNCs to bring into developing nations a level of production technology altogether at odds with indigenous labor skills or employment needs. Most often, the proxy for this misdeed is taken to be the relative capital-intensity of the technology imported (a measure of investment in plant and equipment per worker), Third World nations being thought better suited to production systems that are relatively labor-intensive.

In Kenya, however, as one study reports, "it was typically a subsidiary of a foreign firm which carried out labour-intensive adaptations and was more willing to use older equipment." [cited in Crawford and Poole, *op. cit.*, p. 25]. In Ghana, a detailed study of nine industries showed the foreign participants in five to be less labor-intensive—but in four to be equally or more labor intensive—than were local companies. [ibid., pp. 25–6]. And as Ray Vernon observes, "a number of studies indicate a disposition for multinational enterprises to pay higher wages and provide better working conditions than their local counterparts." [Vernon, p. 46; also, see Table III].

What are we to make, therefore, of this conflicting and inconclusive body of data? If nothing else it should drive home with some force the simple realization that categorical damnations or defenses of MNC activities are worthless. Talking about them as if they comprised a single, undifferentiated monolith—a single giant enterprise with one-dimensional motives and unchanging habits of behavior—is to talk nonsense. Treating the various national situations in which they operate and the several industries in which they take part as if such local detail paled in importance when held up against some fictional regularity of MNC activity is to build castles in the air.

There is, for example, an important and regular difference between those MNC involvements in the Third World geared to exporting and those geared to serving local markets. Not suprisingly, export-oriented activities rely substantially less on locally-raised capital than do local-market activities—a commonsense finding that runs directly counter to the familiar charge that all MNC operations in developing countries so distort indigenous capital markets that local enterprises are necessarily starved for capital. Why, after all, should export-oriented MNCs dip into host country funds when they must be concerned to hedge assets whose returns follow closely exchange rates for the local currency? [see: A. C. Shapiro, "Exchange Rate Changes, Inflation and the Value of the Multinational Corporation," *Journal of Finance,* 30 (May, 1965), pp. 485–502].

The best recent summary of economic literature on MNC performance in developing countries (Richard E. Caves, *Multinational Enterprise and Economic Analysis,* Cambridge University Press, 1982) judiciously balances the available evidence in the light of this variety of modes of participation and of strategic aims. Even so, the picture that emerges gives the lie to the more strident and one-dimensional attacks on the effects of MNC involvement. As Caves notes, "Although MNCs tend to be found in concentrated sectors, they do not enjoy universal advantages over native entrepreneurs, nor do they always claim commanding market shares. National enterprises in the more advanced LDCs may do more R&D (if they do any at all), and native entrepreneurs who cannot compete successfully in sectors where MNCs are advantaged do flourish in other sectors." In other words, if unhealthy or exploitative arrangements can be found, they are by no means inevitable, nor are they the rule.

A United Nations report on transnational corporations (*Transnational Corporations in World Development*, Third Survey, 1983) confirms this balanced view:

Developing countries, especially the newly industrializing countries, achieved a strong performance in exports of manufactured goods in the 1970s an achievement which greatly contributed to their high rates of industrial growth. Transnational corporations participated actively in this process in most of the newly industrializing countries, and play a leading role in at least two of them. However, in most of the newly industrializing countries domestic enterprises contributed materially to the growth of manufactured exports, and, in some countries, export-led industrialization has been largely achieved by national firms. In most countries for which evidence is available, transnational corporations do not seem to have a higher propensity to export than domestic enterprises within the same industry, while their import propensities are usually higher than those of their local counterparts.

What we must look at, then, if we are to get a fair sense of the facts is, not surprisingly, what MNCs actually do in this or that particular context. Nowhere is this modest, though often ignored, caution more applicable than when trying to determine the merits of arguments that charge MNCs with either neglecting or retarding the equitable distribution of the benefits that follow on economic development. In coming to a fair judgment on such sensitive issues as these, a rich appreciation of context is indispensable. We think here of the relevant context in two senses: first, the larger historical backdrop against which alone we can see clearly the nature of current MNC activity and, second, the strategic purposes that MNCs are trying to accomplish by their varying involvements in developing countries. Without an appreciation for the kind of institutional creature an MNC is or for the ends it serves, we cannot hope to make meaningful sense out of the complex patterns of its activity.

Consider, then, the simple fact that MNCs represent not the first but only the most recent form of direct foreign business involvement. The European-based charter companies that first came to prominence during the 17th century as agents of a colonialist economic structure were, in David Apter's estimation, agents of a "rough and ready method of reducing risk for foreign enterprise while bringing to bear appropriate commercial techniques. . ." During the 19th and early 20th centuries, they were largely replaced by the appearance of giant international cartels, which carved up the internal markets of developing nations among themselves and which represented, more often than not, the interests of national policy among the larger powers.

The MNC, by contrast, is a third stage of development, distinguished from the charter company and the cartel, and by far the most far-reaching in its effects. Whereas the two older forms of enterprise brought only certain constituencies within host countries into their orbit—fostering the development, say, of an active class of entrepreneurially-minded middle-men—the MNC, with what Apter calls its "exceptional capacity to re-create or reproduce networks in a novel environment, tends to establish the conditions for [its] own functioning. The result is a network suitable for [its] prosperity locking a host country into a complex international system of reinforcing social institutions: financial, educational, sociological. The dynamism of the MNC enables it to be an agenda-setting instrumentality."

This requires a word of explanation. So intermeshed are the operations of an MNC with multinational production planning and capital flows, so needful is it of specialized skills and expertise, that it inevitably generates its own web of institutional support. Unlike the more limited effects of charter companies or cartels, which require but an operational foothold in a host country, MNCs both need and create their own indigenous support systems. Like the bottom layer of cannonballs stacked on a courthouse lawn, the organizational logic of MNCs gives shape and structure to—that is, sets the agenda for—follow-on arrangements.

Keep in mind, however, that the precise extent of this "structuring" influence will vary from situation to situation, largely as a function of the state of development in the host country. When these countries are in the early stages of modernization, the institutional networks stimulated by MNCs will be restricted to identifiable "enclaves" with little connection to the rest of the local society or economy. When they are further advanced, the networks may well spread to whole classes or sectors but not to others. When they are fully developed, the networks will be so widely integrated with other institutional structures that they will be virtually invisible.

On balance, of course, through these phases of modernization the thrust of MNC influence is to create within ever expanding concentric circles a universe of professional talent and institutional capacity linked, even if at some remove, to such universes elsewhere. No matter how complex, the operations located in any one country are almost never entirely free-standing—that is, without intimate connections to production, marketing, and credit arrangements beyond its borders. At the same time, however, host governments have increasingly attempted to take upon themselves (partly in response to these changed social realities) the active management of policies in which, as Vernon notes, "they had not [previously] been involved: to replace their imports of manufactured goods with local production; to expand exports; to upgrade the capabilities of the labor force; to increase government revenues; and so on." In other words, as MNCs have gradually expanded the range and scope of local influence and international linkage—often, we should note, not only with the permission but also at the request of local governments—those same governments have progressively felt the need to enlarge the domain of their own control. It is at the intersection of these two broad historical developments that issues of equity begin to come into focus.

The criticisms of multinational activity which are based on the asssumption that multinationals are an undifferentiated species of public enemy #1 allow for a shotgun blast of blame which is neither supportable by logic, experience, nor even political ideology. Unilever is not the same as IBM, and both are worlds apart from Levi Strauss & Co., yet all are multinationals. To allow one marketing policy of, say, a Nestlé to symbolize all multinational activity is to chastise the operations of other international businesses whose place of origin, economic goals, and ideological bias are hardly the same as that of the Swiss.

Thus in order to explore the various charges of exploitation and inequity which are claimed against this spectre called the multinational, it first requires fleshing out the illusory being and identifying its various parts. For without drawing clear distinctions between the differing strategies and institutional structures of the multinationals, it is impossible to assess the effect which they have on the equally varied national contexts in which they operate. Among other things, distinctions form themselves around markets, product, technological requirements, mode of production, financing, competitive situation, corporate goals, and business mix. Each area has a host of contrasting examples and each example does not automatically imply the same accompanying policy in other functional areas of the same firm.

Take, for example, the vastly different international marketing strategies which are seen in multinational companies. One familiar approach is to regard developing countries as a dumping ground for products which have become outmoded in the West. To use Ray Vernon's now classic formulation, products reach a "mature" stage of their life cycle wherein little more can be done to increase their home market or profitability. With research complete and the production process refined and in place, any further increase in volume of production exacts only an incremental cost. By the time this stage of the product life-cycle is complete, however, the home market may be nearly saturated or even declining as another revolutionary process or substitute product begins to replace the old. Under the dynamics of a highly industrialized and competitive marketplace, it is thus difficult indeed for a company to reap the final effortless rewards of a mature product.

At this point a multinational frequently has available the opportunity to "dump" its outmoded product in a developing country where the market is in fact still quite new—or even as yet nonexistent. It may even make sense to ship the older machinery used in the production process to the Third World country where product X is being marketed: labor is cheaper, transportation costs and export-import quotas are nearly eliminated, competition is mild, and the U.S. plant is given space in which to locate a new production process.

In sharp contrast to this attempt to take advantage of an incremental market is the "global" market strategy, wherein the multinational seeks to market roughly the same product simultaneously in its home market and around the world. The chief economic rationale for this approach is that it allows the production process to be standardized, thereby achieving economies of scale which contribute to a reduction of costs. Parts can be produced in several areas around the world close to their source of raw material or in a cheaper labor market, after which they can be shipped to any of several countries for final assembly. It is largely (though not exclusively) through the global market approach that the Japanese can produce a small-size car for $1500 less—even after import tariffs and transportation costs—than the American automobile companies.

When viewed unadorned by strategic or environmental logic other than their approaches to an international market, both the incremental and global strategies have been vulnerable to charges of exploitation, primarily for the very thing which polarizes them so, namely their treatment of market demand. The global strategy seeks to homogenize demand in order to standardize production. In some African states for example, the first TV now bought is a modern color model produced worldwide by Philips. To some this

rapid introduction of highly advanced technology (both in product and production process) is an imperialistic undermining of
traditional cultural patterns in TWCs that is also exclusionary to
the local potential labor force and so revolutionary in change that
its social effects are disastrous. The global market, then sym-
bolizes insensitivity to local market requirements, which are instead subordinated to the economic gains inherent in imposing
Western tastes on the rest of the world. Moreover, in that the
global market often gains economic advantage by having a global
production process, it adds to the charge of cultural imperialism
the unfair exploitation of cheap labor sources and raw materials.

On the other hand, no better are the incrementalists, for they
too are charged with exploitation—as the term "dumping" implies. Here the assumption is again that Western taste is being
imposed: markets for outmoded products are being "created" in
TWCs in order to squeeze that last dollar out of old equipment
and past research efforts. In short, the sins of the fathers are
visited on other peoples' offspring.

In each case, although the strategies and final products are
vastly different, the underlying opportunity for exploitation is
provided by the modern corporation's ability to manipulate markets, to create demand. This is a power patently demonstrable in
the variety of superfluous or redundant products which are sold
here and abroad, but persistently exclusive with regards to its
potential and limits, as companies which have tried to harness it
indiscriminately in the past have discovered. Thus "market creation" is an easily believed but hardly understood phenomenon. As
such, it can be applied without discrimination to multinational
activity in developing countries whenever there is a wide enough
gap between Western and non-Western custom: in other words, if
a product is newly marketed in a TWC and brings its consumers
closer to Westernization, then the market is understood to have
been unjustifiably "created," hence exploitative. These disadvantaged people neither needed nor could they afford to spend their
limited cash on such foreign items.

Even if we could accept as true an argument as openly imperialistic as this—who, after all, has the right to assume for individuals what they do or do not "need," what they should or should not
value?—and as anti-Western as this—for is not part of the objection clearly to Western goods in general out of a preference for a
simpler, "natural" lifestyle?—it would be wrong to judge multinational marketing strategies as exploitative out of hand. For in
certain contexts, several factors of the formula carry the potential

to serve locally perceived needs rather than to exploit the less advantaged.

The first such factor is appropriateness. How appropriate is the product to the existing conditions of the TWC? Here appropriateness must be addressed in terms of cultural disparity, relative accessibility, and potential to injure. These aspects can be summarized in three basic questions, although their implications are many:

1. Is the product painfully at odds with its new environment to the degree that its introduction is tantamount to cultural blasphemy?

2. Does the product require a much greater proportion of disposable income vis-a-vis fundamental costs of food and shelter than in the West?

3. Will the product cause physical injury or significant damage to the environment, and is it most likely to be used improperly in a less-regulated or less-literate society?

If the answer to any or all of these questions is yes, then clearly the appropriateness of the product comes into question, for in each case the product carries with it the potential for serious injury, and thus may depend on the exploitation of local ignorance for its success. To the degree that all development implies *some* cultural disparity, the multinational from western nations is ever vulnerable to the possibility that its marketing and production strategies in TWCs are exploitative. And while appropriateness provides a reference point for determining the *likelihood* that a certain strategy will involve the exploitation of a people's ignorance or desperation for employment, there is no automatic formula which can be applied to multinationals to predict which strategies will be exploitative and which will not take unfair advantage of the conditions inherent in existing inequalities of development between the two countries.

Nor is the responsibility for exploitation clearly assignable, even when it occurs in the eyes of some. Cultural and economic appropriateness carries a confusion of obligations. For example, a product may by its very ultra-Western style be all the more attractive to a developing nation, and thereby provide a means for *self*-exploitation which requires little advertising or promotion on the corporation's part. To take two extreme examples, the initial success in introducing, say, makeup in China or hair straightener in Nigeria may cause a multinational quite naturally to assume that if a product is that desirable and does no physical injury, the company is immune from charges of falsely creating a market. The ideological affront of such visible disruptions to perceived social norms, however, may draw fire on a political front. Appropriateness, then, becomes quite difficult to test for, and the multinational may be introducing an inappropriate product or process unwittingly. There are after all, few governments in developed or developing countries that are capable of monitoring or predicting the degree to which its people desire to change, what the effects of change will be, or the degree to which Western taste is imposed or embraced. Without such foresight and feedback, it is difficult to assign responsibility for exploitation to the multinationals alone. It may even be that cultural exploitation has in practical terms become less of an issue for MNC projects. In one impressive survey of 124 MNCs, who together represented projects in developing countries in every part of the world, 102 cases of conflicts with the host countries were reported but only two were centered on the basic beliefs and value systems of the society. The rest of the conflicts were more organizational in nature and tended to focus on violations of the perceived contract at a company or industry level (especially with regard to equity holding and market power) or concerned operational issues such as labor and supplier relations. [Anant R. Negandhi, B.R. Baliga, *Tables Are Turning: German and Japanese Multinational Companies in the United States* (Oelgeschlager, Gunn & Hain, Publishers, Inc., Cambridge, MA 1981), p. 67.]

At the same time, when social and cultural conflicts did occur, they tended to be of extreme intensity and involve the MNC in a broader range of disputes than simply the immediate operational or market issue. What we are here suggesting, then, is that while market appropriateness is a very real issue for the MNC, it cannot be resolved by an indiscriminate understanding of basic market approaches. How the global and incremental market approaches will ultimately impact the LDC hangs on a whole network of strategic and operational forces. Market strategy and production policies will depend on a variety of conditions within the host country and variety of goals specific to each multinational company. As Reuber points out, these goals will never be one dimensional . [Grant L. Reuber, *Private Foreign Investment in Development* (Oxford 1973) pp. 117f.] Rather, the MNC will invest in a developing country for a variety of reasons—market growth, defense of existing market against other exporters, product differentiation and exploitation of R&D strength—and no one of these factors will tend to be of overriding importance. Each of these factors will in turn have varying and interdependent effects on the economic and social health of the developing country. Market exploitation, then, is no more generic than strategy itself, which depends on an assessment of the environment for which it is formulated to determine ultimate appropriateness.

In addition to being impossible to generalize the exploitativeness of a particular market strategy, it is unreasonable to characterize MNC activity in a developing country exclusively by its approach to market. As remarked earlier, a whole range of structures and policies will support the decision to produce and/or market a product in an LDC, and only a consideration of the entire range of these factors provides access to an informative view of what the proper role of the MNC might be.

No fools to the business process, most developing nations are now quite aware of this range of business activities and negotiate accordingly on everything from equity ownership to equity employment. Most MNC firms now bear nearly all the cost of training local employees. While many host countries insist that international firms set up some R&D locally as a condition entry, especially when the MNC strategy is ultimately geared to local markets. Interestingly enough, American multinationals frequently incur the worst press on their attitude to such issues while having the best record in terms of compliance. In the Negandhi study, for example, host countries frequently complained that American executives were the most obstructive in their resistance to government policies on such things as equity employment. If Americans did not like the law, they insisted that it be clarified or changed. At the same time, they had a much higher compliance rate on such issues as equity employment at the managerial level than did their European and Japanese counterparts [see Table 4].

In short, a shimmering veil of rhetoric and negotiating postures has more than obscured the very real problems of interdependency between nations and within the functional areas of international firms vis-à-vis development goals in LDCs. Several examples of basic multinational strategies will illustrate just how glib indiscriminate charges of multinational exploitation against LDCs can be. Examples of each of the basic multinational strategies will illustrate just how glib the indiscriminate charges of multinational exploitation against TWCs can be.

The Global Market Strategy. In Iran, for example, the revolutionary Westernization of Teheran, which brought with it tremendous injury to the environment and to the cultural strengths of its people, was encouraged by the government of the Shah and confirmed by the thousands who poured into the city to participate as best they could in the effects of such development. To whom, then, would the European multinational automobile maker refer in deciding the appropriateness of its strategy to introduce a relatively low cost, smaller sized automobile whose parts could be mass-produced for a world market and imported to Iran for final local assembly? On the one hand, the car was embraced as the first means of access to a status item which was otherwise completely inaccessible to the lower middle class, for most of the automobiles were mid- to large-sized imported items carrying up to 800% tariffs, and hence available only to government officials or to the private upper class. On the other hand, Teheran traffic patterns were a disaster, small cars and motor bikes were frequently seen on the sidewalks along the clogged thoroughfares, and the smell of exhaust towards evening was choking. The national assembly plant, however, had no trouble attracting workers, and the government refused to sponsor a public airing of the effects of carbon monoxide on health.

All of these conditions helped underscore the obvious economic disparities and environmental and cultural upheaval which some of the Shah's development programs brought to Iran. But was the responsibility for the inappropriate aspects of mass marketing a small sized automobile that of the multinationals? Here the global production strategy carried the seeds of both equalizing the disparity between the developed and underdeveloped countries and of aggravating the cultural shock which accompanies the rapid emergence of a "recently poor" class that suddenly found the status items of the Westernized upper class available on a mass scale.

Mass marketing and homogenization of demand, then, promised to make cars available to the lower middle class for the first time, and in this the strategy had the potential to reduce one inequality between Iran's upper class elites and the rest of the country. However, the extreme economic disparity between classes—for there was in fact almost no middle class to purchase this item—and the social disparities between a mass automobile transit system and Teheran's street and sewer systems (which made immediate road expansion impossible within the city) argue for an inappropriateness in the product which borders on the exploitative. The same ambiguities applied to the car maker's global production strategy. By locating part of the production process in Europe, it was possible for the company to locate the less sophisticated assembly operations locally—thereby creating a labor intensive production facility which improved the economic condition of a few lucky Iranian workers but also drew more people out of the impoverished countryside to the already over-crowded capital.

What cannot be argued, however, is that the global strategy of the multinational automobile manufacturers is thus endemically inequitable on some absolute scale of utopian effort for world-wide equality. For while the mass marketing of smaller auto-mobiles may have been inappropriate to Iran's urgent need for controlled expansion in Teheran, it is this same strategy—aided by the increase in oil prices—which has effected the switch in Amer-ican buying patterns away from oversized family tanks to cars whose fuel consumption and steel usage begins to fall in line with the rest of the world. It is this same global strategy to produce a small-sized "world car" that has made automobile transit accessible for the first time to those in a host of developing countries who are outside the privileged world of government limousines. Clearly, then, it is the developmental context and specific product, not the generic global strategy which determines the exploita-tiveness of the multinationals who adopt such an approach to their international business in TWCs.

The Incremental Market. If the globe strategy carries the potential both to injure or improve standards of living by reason of its very homogenization of product, so, too, the incremental market ap-proach has the power to exploit TWCs as a dumping ground for inappropriate and outmoded products, or to effect the develop-ment of markets which prove to be beneficial to both the multina-tional corporation and the developing nation. Once again, corporate context and national conditions are so varied that the likely outcome of this basic multinational strategy cannot be gen-eralized. Without commonly agreed-upon criteria for equitable development, it is very hard indeed to determine whether such multinational activity is producing a flower or a weed.

Before jumping to a conclusive verdict on MNC marketing policies in this or any other paper, it is first necessary to dissect and examine the many procedures and structures which an incre-mental marketing strategy may introduce. Here an extended ex-ample of one company's efforts in Indonesia offers a basis for evaluating the potential relative equity of another fairly common multinational strategy.

In 1979 Corning Glass Works prepared to launch its first major operation in a developing country, the establishment of a $26 million joint venture in Indonesia to produce a specialty dinner-ware. [Data is drawn from A. Mahine, *Corning Glass Works*, Har-vard Business School Case #9-381-119, 1981, Rev. 7/82.] The international operations at Corning had played an important strategic role for the company since the mid-1960s, when the new chairman, Amory Houghton, Jr., had first targeted major world markets as a desirable area for further growth. Up until that time Corning had concentrated on developing the U.S. market, and had limited its foreign marketing primarily to exporting goods manufactured in the U.S. By 1978 the international division was contributing 25% of the corporation's total sales revenues. At that time the company's international efforts were concentrated in Europe, which contributed 87% of its international sales revenue (1978 total international sales: $314 million).

But the few limited investments which Corning had made in developing countries, such as Argentina, Korea, and India, indicated to the company that developing countries offered market opportunities which were compatible with its overall growth goals, hence an External Business Development Group (EBDG) was set up within the International Division to explore new business opportunities in developing countries. EBDG's mission was to compose strategies for pursuing these markets, and to establish beachheads from which to participate further in the country's growth. Unlike many U.S. multinationals, whose time frame for a given project in a developing country is generally shorter than for their European counterparts, Corning was planning on a long-term continuing investment in developing countries.

The EBDG began its strategic formulation not by running off an inventory of "dumpable" items and likely targets, but rather by a sensitive consideration of the income level, stage of economic and technological development, and government attitudes toward development in a variety of TWCs. For Corning the introduction of a product whose price and production requirements would be an easy complement to existing national conditions was a necessary fundamental of setting up a strategy that made business sense. For the country in question, it was also a strategy which was likely to be the least disruptive to its social and economic structure.

Thus, when an Indonesian entrepreneur approached Corning about arranging a licensing agreement to produce *Corelle*, one of the company's most technologically advanced glass-ceramic dinnerware products, the company rejected the proposal as being inappropriate to the Indonesian market in both its high-tech production process and the relatively high-priced market niche. Nor did the company wish simply to arrange a licensing agreement for a proprietary technology. Out of this request, however, emerged a growing interest at Corning in the Indonesian tableware market. Two executives with former experience in developing countries and with Corning operations in India and Taiwan were recruited to conduct an extensive study of Indonesia's market and the opportunities which it presented to Corning's international division. They found Indonesia a promising place indeed, for despite the relatively low per capita income ($228, which was about a third of that in South Korea), dinnerware represented a $60 million industry. These porcelain, glass, and metal items were an integral part of the country's hospitality customs, and even the poorer rural households averaged 70 pieces of dinnerware. Much of that was imported, primarily from the People's Republic of China (70% of Indonesia's dinnerware market in 1978), and was second-quality porcelain. Only 7% of the dinnerware was made locally. What was imported was in theory subject to a high tariff which on average amounted to an 800% *ad valorem* rate, but in practice there was widespread tariff avoidance—one expert estimated that over 50% of all imports entered the country via some illegal channel.

On Corning's assessment, the Indonesian dinner market was thus large enough to support a local large-scale manufacturing operation. To the EBDG, the most appropriate product seemed to be a borosilicate opal glassware which Corning had developed in the 1940s and which had recently been phased out of the United States. Opalware was, however, of demonstrably higher quality and durability than the second-grade porcelain ware which currently dominated the Indonesian market. Corning proposed to set the wholesale price of this opalware midway between that of Chinese porcelain and local porcelain.

The company called on another of its TWC operations, Rigolleay, S.A. in Argentina, to provide the technical assistance and lay-out information for setting up production in Indonesia. A Corning project manager and a company engineer would oversee the establishment of the plant and early operations, but all other sales, financial, and administrative positions would be staffed by Indonesians. Indo-American Industries (IAI), as the project was called, would require skilled and semi-skilled workers, whose average wage rate would be approximately 25% of a leading local glass producer's. A total of 267 workers would be employed, 65 of whom would be in administrative and managerial positions.

Corning projected that by the fifth year of operation, P. T. Indo-American Industries would reap an after-tax profit of approximately $7 million on $17 million in sales. Its own equity position would be 40% of total shares, a local glassworks company headed by an Indonesian of Chinese descent would own 31% of IAI, and the remaining 9% would be assumed by the International Finance Corporation (IFC), which was a subsidiary of the World Bank. IFC had a well-established policy of selling its shares to domestic purchasers to broaden local ownership and Corning estimated that such a sale would probably occur about six years after initial plant start-up. (For full statement of IFC policy see Appendix A.)

Once the international division had received the go-ahead from Corning to pursue the Indonesian project, implementation of the plan required a long series of negotiations with the Indonesian government over equity-ownership. Colonialistic fantasies aside, it has no longer been possible by the 1970s for western MNCs to make unfettered forays into foreign markets and labor forces. The Indonesian government had already established restrictions on its dinnerware industry which included 100% Indonesian ownership of local concerns. Corning relied to a large degree on the head of P. T. Indonesian Glass Group to act as its liaison with that government in its attempts to have the ownership requirement altered.

Corning's efforts to tailor its product to the existing dinnerware market conditions appeared potentially beneficial enough to the Indonesian government that it eventually waived its equity requirements and approved the joint venture. IAI would make available to the consumer a highly regarded line of items which would be offered at competitive prices. The production process utilized a local labor force but also introduced a specialty glass manufacturing process which accelerated the local industry's development several stages. The foreign exchange advantages were obvious. In short, the standard of economic and cultural appropriateness which was posed earlier in this piece clearly operated to advantage in Corning's advocacy of its Indonesian strategy, and eased the fears of cultural and economic displacement which understandably accompany MNC transfer of outmoded technology abroad. This happy accomodation of Indonesia's existing values and Corning's strategic goals was effected in large part through the extensive mutual participation at the planning stage of the local Indonesian glassworks firm, the national government, and experienced Corning executives.

In the Corning example, entry into a developing country market entailed the use of pre-existant products and the transfer of production processes which were for all practical purposes obsolete in the West. Not all MNC projects make use of old technology. One outstanding example would be Unilever's recent entry into the laundry products market in Nigeria, where the very special circumstances of clothes washing methods—mainly cold streams and rivers—rendered Unilever's conventional powdered detergents useless. The only product then available was bar soap. By utilizing an R&D center in India (itself a product of local government conditions for operating a foreign project), the company was able to develop a cold water detergent which could be manufactured in bar form, a process which employed the very latest chemical and production technologies.

Corning's development of a highly innovative product technology is splendid illustration of how far MNCs can and have departed from the old "dumping" strategy, but what of the overall economic benefit of such activities to the LDCs? The record is mixed, as other essays in this book attest, but there are clearly signs that MNC activities have in some cases sparked a very strong emergence of local support structures and other secondary economic benefits [see Table V], but again, the individual conditions of MNC activity are not easily generalized—even within a given industry.

International tobacco operations, for example, which have been dominated by seven multinationals since the 1950s, have quite extensive projects throughout the developing world, but the economic effects of these activities have been quite varied. An extensive study by the Economist Intelligence Unit Ltd. in 1980 revealed that the industry's effect on local development varied extensively in proportion to its ultimate use, overall percentage of the nation's agricultural activity, and reallocation of tax revenues. ["Leaf Tobacco: Its Contribution to the Economic and Social Development of the Third World," The EIUL, London, 1980].

In the Santa Cruz area of Brazil the economic "spinoffs" from tobacco growing were considerable, and ancillary economic activities included:

1. retail outlets for consumer durables purchased by farmers, instructors and processing plant employees;
2. agricultural equipment stores;
3. brick making (for barn construction);
4. timber growing (for fueling barn operation);
5. transportation of tobacco and agricultural inputs;
6. extension services;
7. motor vehicle servicing facilities; for trucks, for instructors' Volkswagens, Jeeps or motorcycles, for farmers' cars and tractors, etc.;
8. tobacco grading, redrying, threshing, etc. plants and associated infrastructure and employee provisions;
9. accommodation for international tobacco buyers;
10. the design and fabrication of processing equipment to point of consumption/export transport and associated infrastructure.

These, in turn, generated medical services, legal services, a newspaper and radio station, and rural electrification.

In Nigeria, however, the secondary economic effects were much more limited. The Shinkafe-Sabon Birni district of Sokoto State in the extreme northwest of Nigeria was chosen for the study, although tobacco was grown in widely spread areas throughout the country. As in Brazil, rural/urban migration was a major problem for Nigeria. Sokoto is hot and harsh; seven months of the year it suffers a drought. The Hausa population there was primarily engaged in subsistence agriculture and were only partially cash-oriented. Those who grew tobacco had access to the only good soil in the region near tributaries of the Rima River, and the air-cured tobacco which they produced was low in yield (700 kg per hectare with potential of 1,000 kg). Few were willing to adopt the extra agronomic practices which would increase yield, but by regulating tobacco sales the farmers were able to obtain cash even during the dry season, and were associated with the highest social and economic class in the area. Despite an undersupply of leaf, prices were low and tobacco was not attracting further interest. In some instances following the development of tobacco cultivation, farmers were stimulated to produce food crops for cash sale and if tobacco prices remained the same, some food crops might even be more rewarding to the farmers.

EIU's report summarized tobacco growing in the Third World as follows:

There is no evidence of deliberate manipulation of development to suit the companies' own ends at the expense of the host territory or country. . . . The impression gained is one of the companies undertaking a purely commercial activity with only limited awareness of its overall development consequences (broader socioeconomic matters only require consideration to maximize the cost effectiveness of the operation): as a matter of sound business principle, a company will endeavor to pay the grower the perceived minimum consistent with maintaining adequate and continuing supplies of leaf and provide the perceived minimum assistance to achieve this end. In order to accomplish this, of course, the companies must offer the farmer a satisfactory return for tobacco in comparison with other possible alternative crops. (p. 9)

Perhaps the most significant observation we can make about Corning's experience in Indonesia, Unilever's in Africa, or Philip Morris's in Brazil is that these are increasingly representative of MNC involvements in the Third World. They are not, to be sure, a fair index of what happens in all cases—nor, for that matter, of the attitudes of all multinational managers or host government officials. Nonetheless, they do stand as a reasonable proxy for a related series of developments now underway around the globe: ever more balanced compromises between MNC purposes and host government interests. In other words, we can see in the Corning example one possible way among many to achieve a fairer and more equitable structure for foreign direct investment.

Third World governments are not, it turns out, without substantial power to influence the allowable terms of MNC activity. They can, for example, set clear limits to the companies' exercise of strategic policies. As one MNC manager put it in relation to European operations, "On any significant decision such as plant construction, plant closing, or reallocation of production, we take a first cut at an economically optimal solution; then we amend this economic solution to fit with the demands of governments and to our top management in the United States." [Cited in Dox and Prahalad, *Harvard Business Review*, March–April, 1980, p. 150.] So, too, with operations in developing countries, where host governments are generally well aware of their power to negotiate beneficial conditions for the establishment of MNC operations in their countries, and now have had sufficient experience at doing so. It has become a standard part of the strategic process for an MNC to consider host country customs and development plans before formulating a plan to market or operate in an underdeveloped nation.

When, for example, the government of India began to make clear during the 1970s the full measure of its exactions of those MNCs doing business in India, some managements—those of IBM and Coca Cola, to take two well-known cases—refused to bow to the pressure and discontinued activities there. Others—a subsidiary of Union Carbide, for one—had a strong enough endowment of needed technical capabilities (here, in carbon products and agricultural chemicals) that they could face down government demands with impunity. Still others, wishing not to leave and not strong enough to survive a contest of wills, gave ground and adapted to what was required of them. Put simply, both MNCs and host governments have powerful negotiating arguments and authority to put into the balance against each other. Out of such open-ended processes of bargaining, as in any market transactions where the information available to both parties becomes progressively more accurate, the course of action ultimately agreed on more and more takes on the aspect of equity—that is, it increasingly reflects the true mix of needs and interests, rights and obligations.

This, of course, is not to absolve some companies and managers of their persistent ham-fisted selfishness. It is, rather, to under-score two quite simple points: first, the conditions which in the past made for the unfettered exercise of that selfishness are rapidly disappearing; and second, both managers and government officials are coming to understand that so potentially fruit-ful—as well as divisive—a relationship must be entered into only with the greatest care, the most painstaking definition of accept-able types of involvement and of timing for moving from one form of involvement to another, and the most realistic assessment of precisely where such a relationship might fit into the global plans of the MNC and the domestic plans of the host government. Experience shows that it is far too easy to blame a gradually discovered lack of "fit" on evil intentions, criminal incompetence, or worse. After the fact, the sheer complexity of ends rarely proves a satisfactory explanation of difficulties in the eyes of an ideologically hostile public here and abroad.

APPENDIX
International Finance Corporation's Statement of Policy

Objectives

The purpose of the Corporation is to further economic de-velopment by encouraging the growth of productive private enterprise in member countries, particularly in the less developed areas, thus supplementing the activities of the International Bank for Reconstruction and Development. . . . In carrying out this purpose, the Corporation shall:

i. in association with private investors, assist in financing the establishment, improvement and expansion of productive pri-vate enterprises which would contribute to the development of its member countries by making investments, without guar-antee of repayment by the member government concerned, in cases where sufficient private capital is not available on reason-able terms;

ii. seek to bring together investment opportunities, domestic and foreign private capital, and experienced management; and

iii. seek to stimulate, and to help create conditions conducive to, the flow of private capital, domestic and foreign, into productive investment in member countries.

Operations

IFC's objectives are achieved by way of the following:

1. Equity investments and debt financing of new ventures or expansion projects in association with domestic private, public, and/or foreign investors.
2. Project promotion through the identification of investment opportunities, private capital, and management.
3. Assistance to establish, finance, and improve development finance companies, capital market institutions, and other intermediaries which help develop the private sector by mobilizing domestic capital or raising funds abroad.
4. Promotion in the capital exporting countries of an interest in investments in enterprises located in the developing countries.
5. Advice and counsel to member countries on policies that will create a climate conducive to the growth of private investment.

Through these activities IFC offers local and foreign entrepreneurs, corporate sponsors, technical partners, and investors advice on financial, political, legal, and technical matters as well as other aspects related to private enterprise in developing countries. To accomplish this IFC can draw on its own resources as well as the World Bank's experience, plus its contacts with financial institutions, business concerns, economic development agencies, and governmental organizations.

Policies

IFC adapts itself to a varied and changing environment by maintaining flexible policies. Although philosophical or organizational guidelines are seen as subordinated to its need to be effective as a development institution and an investment banker, certain basic policies have evolved.

The project should benefit the economy of the host country. Examples might include the balance of payments effect through foreign exchange savings or earnings; the employment, national income, or growth effects through increased employment or the higher productivity of capital or labor; the effect on the economic structure through the supply of needed goods and services; the transfer of technology; and/or the development of natural resources.

It should have the prospect of earning a profit. This requires that there exists a market for the company's products or services, the management is capable and experienced, the technology is appropriate, and the financial plan is realistic.

IFC never invests alone and will not be the majority shareholder. It is normally required that the sponsors have a substantial shareholding in the project and that other sources of private capital not be available on reasonable terms as IFC expects to supplement private capital not to compete with it. This does not imply that IFC acts only as a lender of last resort, as such a policy would make it difficult for the Corporation to play a lead role in complicated ventures or to fulfill its "umbrella" function. (IFC provides a "seal of approval" to prospective investors since it is felt that IFC participation is the result of a rigorous evaluation of the project.) Provisions for immediate or eventual local equity participation are also necessary. IFC's policy of selling its shares to domestic purchasers helps increase local ownership.

IFC will not invest if appropriate conditions for the repatriation of its investment and earnings do not exist. Nor will IFC make an investment if the host country objects. Participation in projects which include a substantial government interest can be undertaken in countries with scarce private capital.

Within this context, IFC's total commitment, in debt plus equity, is usually above U.S. $1 million, under 50 percent of project costs, and limited to under 25 percent of equity capital. Exposure in any single project is usually limited to 10 percent of IFC's equity, or currently about U.S. $18 million. (Smaller objects which are of an uneconomic size for IFC can be referred to local development finance companies.) The form and terms of an investment depend on the circumstances of each case. Normally, the package includes either equity investments, in local currency, and/or loans, denominated in U.S. dollars or other convertible currencies, if appropriate, for a term of seven to twelve years at fixed interest rates with a grace period, equal semi-annual repayments, and a commitment fee on the undisbursed balance. The only requirement for the use of these funds is that they be spent in one of the 124 member countries of the World Bank Group in Switzerland.

IFC does not take part in the management of the enterprises, it assists and exercises its voting rights as a shareholder only in exceptional cases. Continuing interest in the projects in which it invests is maintained through field visits, periodic consultations with management, and regular audited financial statements. Ongoing support is reflected in the fact that IFC has made second, or third, commitments to more than 55 of the 225 enterprises it has financed.

TABLE I
FLOWS OF FOREIGN DIRECT INVESTMENT FROM DEVELOPED MARKET ECONOMIES TO DEVELOPING COUNTRIES BY MAJOR HOME COUNTRY, 1970–1980
(Millions of dollars)

Country	1970	1971	1972	1973	1974	1975	1976	1977	1978	1979	1980	1981
Australia	106.2	48.0	101.7	104.0	117.1	48.3	74.7	84.3	68.1	112.8	136.4	—
Austria	4.6	–0.1	4.2	4.7	8.3	6.8	32.9	18.4	19.9	12.9	20.0	31.5
Belgium	45.7	28.5	57.7	48.3	49.5	68.8	235.8	69.5	137.8	253.8	198.2	123.1
Canada	64.2	76.0	176.0	125.0	193.0	300.0	430.0	390.0	558.0	–100.0	400.0	700.0
Denmark	8.4	24.7	9.5	16.1	26.3	30.4	30.0	—	76.5	65.6	79.3	66.0
Finland	0.8	0.8	0.7	0.1	0.3	2.6	.5	2.0	6.1	15.4	26.5	17.4
France	235.2	170.4	230.6	287.1	239.4	274.2	245.5	264.7	413.4	681.2	899.5	1,137.0
Germany, Fed. Rep. of	317.5	358.1	601.2	786.6	701.3	815.9	765.4	846.0	1,025.1	817.7	1,578.9	1,351.8
Italy	123.4	213.7	280.1	245.6	99.9	150.1	212.9	162.2	71.1	454.9	316.0	131.8
Japan	261.5	222.4	204.0	1,301.1	705.4	222.7	1,084.2	724.4	1,318.3	690.6	906.0	2,426.1
Netherlands	183.2	130.2	321.3	88.5	241.9	228.5	244.7	485.7	443.5	167.4	135.3	353.9
New Zealand	—	—	–1.9	0.9	3.3	0.8	0.6	9.3	10.5	7.1	23.5	15.4
Norway	18.9	10.6	6.8	14.4	14.9	16.8	42.7	15.7	30.2	7.8	9.0	8.2
Sweden	36.5	40.1	41.9	21.9	49.0	82.2	125.0	126.3	115.0	127.4	90.1	85.5
Switzerland	55.4	65.7	73.1	80.5	128.0	208.2	226.1	211.3	174.1	415.9	352.8	340.0
United Kingdom	340.6	233.2	390.7	698.8	718.7	796.5	986.3	1,178.2	820.0	1,028.7	1,231.0	1,216.8
United States	1,888.0	2,010.0	1,976.0	2,887.0	3,788.0	7,241.0	3,119.0	4,866.0	5,619.0	7,986.0	3,367.0	6,475.0
Total	3,690.1	3,632.3	4,473.6	6,710.6	7,084.3	10,493.8	7,856.3	9,454.0	10,906.6	12,745.2	9,769.5	14,479.5

Source: Organization for Economic Co-operation and Development, *Development Co-operation,* (Paris), various issues.

TRANSNATIONAL CORPORATIONS IN WORLD DEVELOPMENT (1983)

160

TABLE II
IMPORTANCE OF FOREIGN DIRECT INVESTMENT TO INDIVIDUAL DEVELOPING COUNTRIES, 1978–1980
(Millions of dollars)

Country	GNP per capita, 1979 ($1)	Gross national product, 1979	Stock of foreign direct investment end-1978	Domestic investment	Flows from OECD countries — Foreign direct investment	Flows from OECD countries — Bank loans	All resources	Foreign direct investment	Bank loans	Foreign direct investment as percentage of GNP	Foreign direct investment as percentage of domestic investment
	(1)	(2)	(3)	(4)	(5)	(6)	(7)	(5)/(7)	(6)/(7)	(5)/(2)	(5)/(4)
Latin America											
Antigua	1,150	90	—	—	0.6	—	5	12.3	—	.70	—
Argentina	2,210	60,310	3,340	21,069	637.4	2,214.7	1,969	32.4	112.5	1.06	3.0
Bahamas	2,770	650	2,060	—	435.6	15.7	476	91.5	3.3	67.02	—
Barbados	2,680	660	180	155.7	6.5	—	27	24.6	—	.99	4.2
Belize	980	140	75	—	—	—	19	-0.2	—	-0.02	—
Bolivia	550	2,960	140	1,101.0	-0.2	63.7	273	-0.1	23.3	-0.01	—
Brazil	1,770	206,600	13,520	66,202	1,385.9	3,018.3	4,775	29.0	63.2	.67	2.1
Chile	1,890	20,660	1,440	3,237.3	85.5	1,087.3	273	31.4	399.0	.41	2.6
Colombia	1,060	27,790	1,510	6,539.3	96.6	217.7	557	17.4	39.1	.35	1.5
Costa Rica	1,630	3,530	290	1,022.7	12.4	76.3	125	10.0	61.2	.35	1.2
Cuba	1,410	8,550	—	—	—	22.3	95	—	23.6	—	—
Dominican Rep.	1,030	5,410	390	1,333.7	0.1	27.7	106	0.1	26.0	.10	0.4
Ecuador	1,110	8,980	660	2,462.0	9.0	379.7	412	2.2	92.2	.17	0.7
El Salvador	640	2,800	150	658.7	4.9	5.7	105	4.7	5.4	.05	—
Grenada	650	70	—	—	—	—	3	1.1	—	—	—
Guatemala	1,010	6,890	290	1,282.0	2.3	14.3	147	1.6	9.7	.03	0.2

161

TABLE II (continued)

IMPORTANCE OF FOREIGN DIRECT INVESTMENT TO INDIVIDUAL DEVELOPING COUNTRIES, 1978–1980

(Millions of dollars)

Country	GNP per capita, 1979 ($1)	Gross national product, 1979	Stock of foreign direct investment end-1978	Domestic investment	Flows from OECD countries			Foreign direct investment	Bank loans	Foreign direct investment as percentage of GNP	Foreign direct investment as percentage of domestic investment
					Foreign direct investment	Bank loans	All re-sources				
(1)	(2)		(3)	(4)	(5)	(6)	(7)	(5)/(7)	(6)/(7)	(5)/(2)	(5)/(4)
Guyana	630	500	230	133.7	0.6	5.0	48	1.3	10.5	.12	0.4
Haiti	230	1,150	80	227.0	1.5	3.0	115	1.3	2.6	.13	0.7
Honduras	520	1,870	270	600.0	0.8	20.7	156	0.5	13.3	.04	0.1
Jamaica	1,110	2,400	900	422.0	−21.1	28.7	141	−14.9	20.3	−0.88	−5.0
Mexico	1,880	122,920	6,000	36,129	1,186.3	3,231.3	3,442	34.5	93.9	.97	3.3
Nicaragua	610	1,570	90	193.3	0.3	6.7	139	0.2	4.8	.02	.1
Panama	1,550	2,770	3,140	797.3	350.6	1.3	668	52.5	0.2	12.66	44.0
Paraguay	1,140	3,400	110	983.7	3.9	42.7	79	4.9	54.3	.11	.4
Peru	850	14,520	2,150	2,227.3	164.4	−76.0	624	26.4	−12.2	1.13	7.4
St. Vincent and the Grenadines	480	50	—	—	—	—	7	—	—	—	—
Suriname	2,480	910	420	214.7	0.5	—	80	0.6	—	.05	0.2
Trinidad and Tobago	3,910	4,500	1,300	1,251.7	22.8	77.7	82	27.8	94.4	.51	1.8
Uruguay	2,500	7,250	330	1,313.7	4.0	46.0	52	7.6	87.9	.06	0.3
Venezuela	3,440	49,680	3,620	15,881.0	145.0	0.0	1,087	13.3	0.0	0.29	0.9

Africa

Country											
Algeria	1,770	32,360	385	17,278	13.6	850.7	2,308	.6	36.9	.04	0.1
Angola	430	2,970	100	280.0	13.8	-1.3	117	11.8	-1.1	.46	4.9
Benin	270	940	34	205.7	0.7	2.7	186	0.4	1.4	.07	0.3
Botswana	780	610	57	372.7	1.9	-3.0	72	2.6	-4.2	.31	0.5
Burundi	190	760	26	104.0	1.7	1.7	96	1.8	1.7	.23	1.7
Cape Verde	260	80	—	16.0	—	—	44	—	—	—	—
Central African Republic	280	620	70	104.3	2.2	-6.3	93	2.3	-6.8	.35	2.1
Chad	120	500	26	124.7	0.2	-0.3	82	0.3	-0.4	.05	0.2
Comoros	260	90	—	27.7	0.6	—	25	2.6	—	.70	2.3
Congo	670	1,010	170	234.7	-0.1	-0.3	84	-0.2	-0.4	-0.01	-0.1
Djibouti	460	150	10	—	0.1	—	88	0.2	—	.09	—
Egypt	500	19,570	245	7,065.3	29.8	27.7	2,391	1.2	1.2	.15	0.4
Equatorial Guinea	390	130	20	5.7	—	—	4	—	—	—	—
Ethiopia	120	3,810	100	399.3	0.3	3.3	187	0.2	1.8	.01	0.1
Gabon	3,420	2,210	780	996.0	18.0	7.0	6	313.4	122.1	.81	1.8
Gambia	220	130	15	104.7	1.0	2.3	54	1.9	4.3	.79	1.0
Ghana	400	4,470	280	1,274.3	0.5	1.3	202	0.2	.7	.01	—
Guinea	270	1,430	200	226.3	0.2	—	110	0.2	—	.02	0.1
Guinea-Bissau	170	130	—	20.0	—	—	59	—	—	—	—
Ivory Coast	1,070	8,810	530	3,032.0	8.9	141.0	696	1.3	20.3	.10	0.3
Kenya	390	5,940	520	1,479.0	45.8	142.0	549	8.3	25.9	.77	3.1
Lesotho	370	480	4	95.3	—	—	68	—	—	—	—
Liberia	520	940	1,230	362.7	85.9	93.7	493	17.4	19.0	9.14	23.7
Libyan Arab Jamahiriya	8,480	24,280	660	6,167.0	199.4	—	910	21.9	—	.82	3.2
Madagascar	330	2,760	190	627.3	-0.3	11.7	245	-0.1	4.8	-0.01	—
Malawi	220	1,260	100	373.3	-2.9	31.3	170	-1.7	18.4	-0.23	-0.8
Mali	180	1,240	10	180.7	-0.4	—	213	-0.2	—	-0.03	-0.2

TABLE II (continued)
IMPORTANCE OF FOREIGN DIRECT INVESTMENT TO INDIVIDUAL DEVELOPING COUNTRIES, 1978–1980
(Millions of dollars)

Country	GNP per capita, 1979 ($1) (1)	Gross national product, 1979 (2)	Stock of foreign direct investment end-1978 (3)	Domestic investment (4)	Flows from OECD countries			Foreign direct investment (5)/(7)	Bank loans (6)/(7)	Foreign direct investment as percentage of GNP (5)/(2)	Foreign direct investment as percentage of domestic investment (5)/(4)
					Foreign direct investment (5)	Bank loans (6)	All resources (7)				
Mauritania	300	480	25	187.0	-4.9	-2.7	175	-2.8	-1.5	-1.01	-2.6
Mauritius	1,080	1,010	24	357.3	7.5	—	59	12.8	—	.75	2.1
Morocco	780	15,250	350	3,768.3	13.9	182.3	1,103	1.3	16.5	.09	0.4
Mozambique	250	2,550	100	247.0	2.9	.7	201	1.5	0.3	.12	1.2
Niger	300	1,530	100	230.3	7.9	29.7	246	3.2	12.0	.52	3.4
Nigeria	910	75,130	1,130	23,394	107.2	623.0	808	13.3	77.1	.14	0.5
Rwanda	190	930	25	183.0	—	1.0	143	—	0.7	—	—
Senegal	450	2,510	340	443.3	0.4	-4.3	366	0.1	-1.2	.02	0.1
Seychelles	1,580	100	12	—	2.4	—	27	9.1	—	2.43	—
Sierra Leone	250	860	82	161.7	3.0	.3	68	4.5	.5	.35	1.9
Somalia	140	600	100	253.7	—	-2.0	336	—	-0.6	-0.01	—
Sudan	450	8,060	60	1,617.7	4.1	10.0	641	.6	1.6	.05	0.3
Swaziland	650	350	50	187.3	4.9	6.0	68	7.2	8.9	1.39	2.6
Togo	400	970	100	489.0	-0.5	24.7	220	-0.2	11.2	-0.05	-0.1
Tunisia	1,160	7,200	280	2,166.3	18.8	85.3	430	4.4	19.9	.26	0.9
Uganda	290	3,710	10	617.3	2.7	2.7	17	15.2	15.2	.07	0.4
United Rep. of Cameroon	590	4,890	370	1,328.0	25.0	10.7	557	4.5	1.9	.51	1.9

United Rep. of Tanzania	250	4,430	170	1,006.3	6.2	25.7	700	.9	3.7	.14	0.6
Upper Volta	180	1,000	20	262.0	-0.1	-1.3	201	—	-0.7	-0.01	—
Zaire	210	5,750	1,250	1,253.3	117.1	2.7	738	15.9	0.4	2.04	9.3
Zambia	540	3,000	330	658.7	34.5	-5.3	361	9.6	-1.5	1.15	5.2
Zimbabwe	550	3,940	400	627.3	53.9	1.3	84	64.2	1.6	1.37	8.6
West Asia											
Bahrain	5,150	2,030	210	—	3.6	—	153	2.4	—	.18	—
Democratic Yemen	370	690	150	—	0.2	—	138	0.1	—	.02	—
Iraq	2,710	34,180	—	10,758	1.1	-26.0	172	0.7	-15.1	—	—
Israel	4,230	15,980	1,000	—	8.4	101.3	1,451	0.6	7.0	.05	—
Jordan	1,200	2,680	70	904.0	2.2	20.7	1,167	0.2	1.8	.08	0.2
Kuwait	20,520	26,250	180	3,220.3	1.0	—	81	1.2	—	—	—
Lebanon	1,740	5,370	100	—	-3.6	-3.0	275	-1.3	-1.1	-0.07	—
Oman	3,530	3,060	50	—	3.0	—	176	1.7	—	.10	—
Qatar	20,020	4,500	150	—	8.1	—	76	10.6	—	.18	—
Saudi Arabia	9,960	85,690	250	24,791	59.3	—	327	18.2	—	.07	0.2
Syrian Arab Republic	1,170	10,070	70	2,700.3	—	-3.7	1,297	—	-0.3	—	—
Turkey	1,380	61,020	450	12,700	-0.4	473.3	1,695	—	27.9	—	—
United Arab Emirates	23,410	19,500	190	—	67.1	—	341	19.7	—	.34	—
Yemen	420	2,420	—	—	0.6	5.3	378	0.2	1.4	.02	—
South Asia											
Afghanistan	170	4,600	20	443.7	3.4	0.3	86	3.9	0.4	.07	0.8
Bangladesh	110	9,910	80	1,725.0	2.7	-0.3	1,149	0.2	—	.03	0.2
Bhutan	80	100	—	—	—	—	6	—	—	—	—

TABLE II (continued)

IMPORTANCE OF FOREIGN DIRECT INVESTMENT TO INDIVIDUAL DEVELOPING COUNTRIES, 1978–1980

(Millions of dollars)

Country (1)	GNP per capita, 1979 ($) (1)	Gross national product, 1979 (2)	Stock of foreign direct investment end-1978 (3)	Domestic investment (4)	Foreign direct investment (5)	Bank loans (6)	All resources (7)	Foreign direct investment (5)/(7)	Bank loans (6)/(7)	Foreign direct investment as percentage of GNP (5)/(2)	Foreign direct investment as percentage of domestic investment (5)/(4)
India	210	135,790	2,500	31,638	48.6	10.7	1,698	2.9	0.6	.04	0.2
Iran	2,030	8,243	1,000	13,736	384.8	160.0	1,138	33.8	14.1	4.67	2.8
Maldives	220	30	—	—	0.6	—	13	4.5	—	1.89	—
Nepal	130	1,840	10	238.0	0.3	—	127	0.3	—	.02	0.1
Pakistan	270	21,170	790	4,076.7	13.9	42.7	911	1.5	4.7	.07	0.3
Sri Lanka	230	3,310	70	967.0	6.8	6.0	371	1.8	1.6	.20	0.7
South-east Asia and Oceania											
Burma	150	5,020	65	855.7	0.1	20.3	426	—	4.8	—	—
Democratic Kampuchea	80	660	—	—	—	—	130	0.3	—	.05	—
Fiji	1,650	1,020	220	—	12.4	9.7	61	20.5	15.9	1.22	—
Indonesia	370	52,930	5,760	12,231	111.7	56.3	1,212	9.2	4.6	.21	0.9
Malaysia	1,450	19,030	2,880	5,186.0	104.5	113.7	515	20.3	22.1	.55	2.0
Nauru	4,540	30	—	—	—	—	2	—	—	—	—
Papua New Guinea	760	2,230	860	551.7	30.9	9.3	353	8.8	2.6	1.39	5.6

Philippines	640	30,100	1,820	8,932.3	200.4	475.7	1,061	18.9	44.8	.67	2.2
Republic of Korea	1,510	56,970	1,500	17,849	−28.6	831.3	1,311	−2.2	63.4	−0.05	−0.2
Singapore	3,770	8,890	1,700	3,810.7	383.9	107.0	521	73.6	20.5	4.32	10.1
Thailand	600	27,070	445	7,858.0	98.1	283.3	901	10.9	31.5	.36	1.2
Tonga	470	50	—	—	—	—	17	0.2	—	.07	—
Vanuatu	520	60	40	—	4.2	—	36	11.4	—	6.94	—
Socialist Asia											
China	260	250	—	770	—	7.9	—	151	5.2	—	—
Vietnam	170	5,720	—	—	—	38.0	369	—	10.3	—	—
Europe											
Cyprus	3,170	1,960	90	647.7	1.6	54.0	54	2.9	100.4	0.08	0.2
Malta	2,790	950	120	221.7	19.6	—	40	49.0	—	2.06	8.8
Yugoslavia	2,370	52,410	170	—	22.1	1,019.3	1,203	1.8	84.7	.04	—

Sources: GNP and GNP *per capita:* World Bank, *World Bank Atlas 1981* (Washington, D.C.); Domestic investment: United Nations Department of International Economic and Social Affairs; Foreign direct investment and other flows: Organisation for Economic Co-operation and Development, *Geographical Distribution of Financial Flows to Developing Countries, 1977–1981* (Paris, 1982) and Organisation for Economic Co-operation and Development, *Development Co-operation: 1980 Review* (Paris, 1982), Table IX-4.

TABLE 3
WAGE POLICIES FOLLOWED IN SAMPLE PROJECTS*
(Number of projects)

		Management and professional workers			Blue-collar workers		
		Below going rates	Going rates	Above going rates	Below going rates	Going rates	Above going rates
A. Home Country of Investor							
Europe	(32)	1	15	16 (33)	0	10	23
North America	(24)	1	16	7 (26)	0	23	3
Japan	(15)	3	6	6 (15)	2	7	6
B. Type of Investment							
Export-oriented	(22)	1	15	6 (25)	1	18	6
Market-development	(31)	2	15	14 (31)	0	16	15
Government-initiated	(18)	2	7	9 (18)	1	6	11
C. Host-country Area							
Latin America	(25)	1	15	9 (25)	0	14	11
Far East	(19)	2	13	4 (19)	1	14	4
India	(12)	0	2	10 (12)	0	2	10
Other	(15)	2	7	6 (18)	1	10	7
D. Total	(71)	5	37	29 (74)	2	40	32

*Figures in parentheses indicate the number of projects in the sample.

Grant L. Reuber, *Private Foreign Investment in Development* (Oxford, 1973), p. 176.

TABLE 4
EXTENT OF LOCALIZATION OF TOP-LEVEL MANAGEMENT BY MNCs

Localization of Top-Level Management	MNC Ownership		
	U.S. (N = 44) N/%	European (N = 33) N/%	Japanese (N = 19) N/%
100	12/27.3	3/9.1	0/0
75–99	14/31.8	13/39.4	0/0
51–74	7/15.9	4/12.1	2/10.5
1–50	10/22.7	8/24.2	2/10.5
0	1/2.3	5/15.2	15/78.9

Source: Author interviews.

Chi Square = 53.03.

D.F. = 8

Level of Significance = 0.01.

Anant R. Nehandhi, B.R. Baliga, *Tables Are Turning: German and Japanese Multinational Companies in the United States* (Oelgeschlager, Gunn & Hain, Publishers, Inc., Cambridge, MA 1981) p. 84.

TABLE 5
EMERGENCE OF LOCAL SUPPLIERS, LOCAL DISTRIBUTORS, AND SALES ORGANIZATIONS AS A CONSEQUENCE OF SAMPLE PROJECTS

		Local suppliers				Local distributors and sales organizations		
		None	Some	Number of suppliers (mean)[a]		None	Some	Number of organizations (mean)
		(number of projects)				(number of projects)		
A. *Home Country of Investor*[b]								
Europe	(33)	18	15	47	(33)	19	14	11
North America	(22)	16	6	6	(20)	18	2	7
Japan	(18)	15	3	3	(18)	8	10	8
B. *Type of Investment*[b]								
Export-oriented	(24)	21	3	9	(23)	14	9	2
Market-development	(30)	17	13	11	(29)	19	10	10
Government-initiated	(19)	11	8	55	(19)	12	7	14
C. *Host-country area*[b]								
Latin America	(27)	18	9	29	(26)	18	8	6
India	(12)	5	7	120	(12)	6	6	5
Far East	(18)	15	3	35	(18)	13	5	11
Other	(16)	11	5	21	(15)	8	7	11
D. *Total*	(73)	49	24	30	(71)	45	26	9

[a] Mean of those projects giving rise to 'some'.
[b] Figures in parentheses indicate number of projects in sample.
Source: Reuber, page 157.

170

The Role of Small-Scale Business

Jason Brown

Introduction

Horatio Alger in a Conical Hat

THERE IS A MAJOR TRANSFORMATION taking place in the Third World today. Its scope and potential implications are only beginning to be perceived. It involves the movement of large numbers of people away from a way of life dominated by subsistance agriculture and into a market economy in which small-scale business is the principle source of both income and employment.

This develpment pattern was not predicted by scholars and is in most cases not what the people involved would have desired, if given a choice. Yet it is having significant impacts on social, cultural and economic patterns.

Let us briefly meet a few prototypical people caught up in this change. Neelam Sharma began selling vegetables in the local market town in North India with her cousin 12 years ago. She was forced to seek work because her husband's job as a farm laborer was too intermittent to support her growing family. Now she has her own stall, offering a variety of fruits and vegetables. The

$2.00 a day she earns is the principle source of income for her family of eight.

Jose Rodriquez began as a worker in a tannery in a small town near Mexico City at the age of 14. The death of his father led to the loss of the small family farm, forcing him, his brothers and sisters to seek other employment. Now, after 20 years of hard work, he has his own business making shoes for the local market. He brings home an average of $3.50 a day to support his family of 10.

Nene Dagotho left his village in Kenya when he was 16 because there were too many children to be supported by the small piece of land owned by the family. After a series of jobs as a laborer, he now, at the age of 32, has his own tailoring stall. His income of $1.00 a day was sufficient for him to arrange a recent marriage with a girl from his village.

Lilia Reyes followed her husband to a large city in the Philippines. Her husband's job as a construction laborer, though intermittent, produced more income than he could obtain on his family farm. Six years ago, she began to make inexpensive toys for a larger buyer because her husband was injured and could no longer work. Now she employs 30 people, including her six children when they are not in school. She sells the plastic purses she makes, earning an average of $6.00 a day.

Surprising Transformation

As little as 20 years ago, business activity such as that described above was held in complete disrepute by people in almost all traditional agricultural cultures throughout the Third World. Business activity was the domain of "foreigners" in most cultures, such as the Chinese in Southeast Asia, the Indians in East Africa, and the Lebanese in West Africa.

Given the traditional antipathy, the change in only two generations surprises many observers. Even more surprising is the large proportion of women among the ranks of these fledgling business people.

This new class of entrepreneurs is remarkably similar, whether found in Cairo, Jakarta, Lima or Harlem. They demonstrate the same task orientation, hard work and willingness to take calculated risks.

What has led to the emergence of these small business people and what will be the impact of their growing numbers? Will the experience in business, when combined with the broadened outlook, improved education and increased income, lead them to become a force of change? Will the economic and political systems of countries find it necessary to adapt to their increasing presence? Will small business activity support greater economic, social and political equity in countries as a whole? And will small business serve as a vehicle for improved income distribution?

The Momentum for Change

Traditional System

Traditional living patterns in most Third World countries were dominated by agriculture. Prior to World War II, the vast majority of people in these countries were living on farms. Cities were few and their populations small. People tended to produce sufficient crops to support themselves and their family and to provide a margin of safety in case of crop failure. Transactions were typically on a non-cash basis. Dependent on the country, its climate and soil conditions and the manner of land ownership, farmers could be heavily in debt. Tradition played a dominant role in daily life. Education, though desired, was not accessible to most farm families beyond the primary level. Meaningful political participation was almost totally absent.

Population Growth Leads to Off-Farm Employment

Conditions have changed dramatically in most Third World countries over the past 40 years. Two factors have played a critical role in these changes. One has been rapid population growth. Despite substantial increases in farm productivity, arable land is not sufficient in many countries to support the rapidly growing population. The result is that an expanding number of farm families must seek at least a portion of their total income in off-farm activity. This can consist of work as laborers, or increasingly, can involve one or more members of the family establishing their own business.

The extent of off-farm employment is difficult to assess. Available statistics are scattered and in most cases, not current. A recent World Bank paper estimates that in Asia and parts of Africa, agriculture is providing the principle source of employment for less than two-thirds of the additional workers who have remained in the rural labor force.[1] This paper estimates the rural non-farm workforce as high as 61% in certain areas of Nigeria, 23.2% in the state of Sinaba, Mexico and 20.4% in a ten-village sample in Thailand. It observes that, "For most of the 15 developing countries where recent statistics are available . . . the percentage of the rural labor force primarily engaged in non-farm work is between 20% and 30%." These should be taken as minimal estimates, "since they exclude small, local towns, where much rural off-farm labor is concentrated." In the few cases where statistics include these towns, the percentage of non-farm employment rises to between 30% and 40%.[2]

Expansion of Markets and Resulting Urbanization

The other key factor contributing to change has been the rapid expansion of national and international market economies. This has, in turn, generated other changes. Government and government-generated jobs have expanded dramatically. Urbanization has progressed at a geometric rate, to provide the specialization required to respond to the needs of a more sophisticated political and economic system, and as a consequence of population pressure.

As a result of these factors, a gradual restructuring of demand has occurred. Non-farm, increasingly urbanized workers often make more than their farm-based cousins, luring others into the sector. As the sector grows and its members become more specialized, they generate new demands for goods and services.

As the non-farm employment sector has grown, particularly in the last 20 years, those within it have increasingly established their own small businesses, for a variety of reasons. Growth of formal employment opportunities has been much slower than growth of the "informal" sector labor supply. For some years, government and government-generated jobs absorbed substantial numbers of new job seekers. However, expansion of government employment leveled off in the mid-seventies and this sector no longer absorbs an increased percentage of the excess labor force. It was the great hope of the 1950s and 1960s that large-scale industry would absorb a large percentage of available labor. This dream never materialized and in many countries, the proportion of the labor force engaged in industry is actually falling.[3]

Demand created by the small but growing middle class and agriculture is largely being met by imports from industrialized countries and the modest domestic industrialized sector. The demands generated by the growing small enterprise sector, however, are of a type which is most easily met by this sector itself. Since income in the sector is relatively low, but numbers are large, low quality items can be produced in hundreds or thousands of small units and quickly sold for very narrow margins. This method of production lends itself to the shifting needs and incomes of the sector and largely defies competition from large-scale capital-intensive production.

These small, largely family-based enterprises are in keeping with the employment needs of those in the sector. Entry into the sector is relatively easy, with minimal capital, education or experience required. It allows for intermittent work as a farm or industrial laborer when this work is available. It is particularly well-suited for women who, by working out of their homes, can continue to care for their children while operating a business. As a result, although statistical evidence across cultures is not available, personal observation suggests that the majority of new small business proprietors in the Third World are women.

The net result of these many factors is that new small business formation in the burgeoning small enterprise sector seems to be proceeding at a rapid rate. It would appear to be occurring most often among the poorest people, who have few alternatives.[4]

Characteristics of the Sector

Definition

Definition and measurement of this sector pose severe problems. Over the past 10 years, there has been a proliferation of terms used to describe the phenomenon, including self-employment, small-scale entrepreneurship, micro enterprise, informal or non-formal enterprise and non-farm employment. Some of these terms include other categories of employment, as for instance, in India, where the "unorganized sector" includes day laborers. There is, at present, no agreed definition. There is no agreement on the amount of capital involved, number of employees, or any other criteria.

The most widely used definition of what they term the "informal sector" is that of the International Labor Organization. They define it in terms of its characteristics as follows:[5]

- Ease of entry;
- Reliance on indigenous resources;
- Family ownership;
- Small scale of operation;
- Use of labor intensive and adapted technology;
- Use of skills acquired outside of formal schooling; and
- Dependence on unregulated and competitive markets.

A recent study conducted with funding from the U.S. Agency for International Development added to this list:[6]

- Small scale (normally under $25 in initial capitalization);
- Often linked to the formal sector (from which they acquire materials and to which they market products);
- Localized (responds to immediate area market);
- Modest sales (typically less than $10/day);
- Low profits (typically less than $1/day); and
- Flexible (adapting daily to new market conditions).

Although it can lead to confusion, for the purpose of this paper, I will refer to these characteristics as applying to "small-scale business."

Size of Sector

Statistics on the sector are difficult to obtain and generally unreliable. Until recently, there was practically no interest in the sector and therefore, almost no effort to measure it. Available data tends to have been collected for other reasons. Studies of existing data or efforts to collect new data have to date been largely restricted to single towns or regions, with little national level or cross-national comparison. Because the people in the sector are "unorganized" and poor, very mobile and very suspicious, data gathered about them especially in regard to financial matters, is very unreliable.

Given the lack of data, few reliable estimates exist as to the size of the sector. The most substantial measurement efforts have been undertaken by Michigan State University, with funding from USAID, for four countries. The International Labor Organization has also conducted studies of six large cities around the world. In addition, individual studies have been conducted by researchers on Senegal, Mexico City, Manila and several other locations. The consensus of these studies seems to be that on the average, between 20 and 50% of the more urbanized workforce finds a principle source of their income in small-scale business. In some countries and cities, small-scale businesss provides a principle source of income for as much as 90% of the work force.[7]

Patterns of Entrepreneurship

The Hard Hand of Necessity

Scattered interviews world-wide suggest that few people initially enter upon a business activity by choice. It is only the hard hand of necessity that impels them in this direction.

As population pressures have increased, off-farm employment has become essential. Families typically seek every alternative before entering business. The first choice is government employment. Most children enter secondary schools with this as their primary objective. A second choice is large-scale business. A third choice is employment in a smaller business or work as a day laborer. Only when every other alternative has been exhausted will business be considered as "employment of last resort."

Symptomatic of the attitude was an interview with a man in a Manila slum. He was working with his wife and children in production of simple toys for the local market. However, when asked about his employment situation, he referred to himself as a "temporarily unemployed laborer," rather than accept his role as a member of a family business.

Interestingly, women typically have less problem with shifting employment patterns toward business in response to economic necessity. As a result, in many Asian, African and Latin American cultures, women tend to make the first steps into business, often gradually pulling the men with them. Women often seem better able than men to assess realistically the risks involved in a business and have more staying power. Although these findings are impressionistic, women seem more likely than men to succeed in business.

Certain initial approaches to business are particularly common: a younger wife or teenage son or daughter opens a small stall on family property abutting a roadway; a son or daughter seeks "seasonal" employment in a small town, working with village, tribe, caste or clan members; a son is "apprenticed" to a craft or tradesman; a child may leave home to "seek his fortune," either with encouragement, tacit approval or as a runaway from mistreatment or family misfortune; a child may be sold into servitude (as a laborer or prostitute). Over time, these activities may lead to increasing business activity.

Initial business operation is most commonly closely connected with village life, and may include the selling of vegetables, blacksmithing, or money-lending to neighbors. As business expertise increases, product sales expand first to staple goods and then to a more diversified range of products. The blacksmith may make parts for rototillers or decorative ironwork for homes. The money lender might move into rice wholesaling.

Case Studies

From a variety of case studies around the world, three have been synthesized, which are considered relatively representative. These case studies help to throw light on the sector and its members. Although the particular businesses described are comparatively successful, as will be pointed out later, there are numerous constraints on the sector which can thwart business expansion at any time and which keep many businesses operated by the poor modest in size.

A Village Girl

A village girl, while in her early teens, is encouraged by her mother to supplement the meager income of their large family by growing and selling vegetables in the village market. With her mother's help, she learns quickly and begins to make a modest profit. Part of the profit is set aside by the mother and with it, the mother purchases two chicks for the girl to raise and sell.

Gradually, the girl takes full responsibility for the business and continues to increase vegetable and poultry activity using reinvested profits. She expands the business, preparing cooked foods for sale on the market day, after she has sold her vegetables and poultry.

As her savings expand, she rents a stall. Her younger brothers and sisters increasingly take over vegetable and poultry raising and cooking while she concentrates on sales. As sales expand, she buys more vegetables from her neighbors and begins to stock a small line of staple goods, such as sugar, candy, cigarettes, coffee, oil, etc. Through experience, she learns which products sell well and return the greatest profit. She expands staple goods, adding cloth and drops the cooked food.

She is able to take on one, two, and then three of her brothers and sisters as full-time employees. By the time she is 20, she has her own small wooden shop and is also engaged in wholesaling rice. She is considering taking over the shop next door to do tailoring, but first, she has to choose among numerous suitors.

The Peripatetic Boy

A teenage village boy with little education is encouraged by his father to join his third cousin, who is a construction worker in the city. Once there, the boy becomes a day laborer and begins the complex process of adjusting to city life. He quickly becomes aware of the not-so savory aspects of the city, but his cousin manages to keep him out of serious trouble.

Day labor is intermittent work and in between, at the urging of some friends, he begins selling magazines and newspapers to motorists. He finds he is good at this and that it is more regular and lucrative than work as a laborer. He decides to do it full time.

After two years, he visits a fellow immigrant from his village who makes small oil lamps for sale, mainly in rural areas. Because manufacturing carries more prestige than sales, he begins a one-year apprenticeship, followed by another as an employee. He then sets up his own business making lamps, but the quality is poor and the competition is stiff. He uses up all his savings and has to close.

He returns to his village, where he finds he has acquired enough skills to assist local craftsmen in the construction of a school and other buildings. After two years, he has saved enough to try the city again. He has found village wages too low for his new standards and village life too constraining.

He apprentices himself this time to another village migrant making bicycle baskets. After a period as an employee, he again sets up his business. Again he fails to meet quality standards. He repeats the same pattern of return to the village and then to the city. On his third try, he becomes an employee of a family relative who has a small retail shop. His talent for sales now comes to the fore and business expands rapidly. He gradually takes over and expands the shop. By the time he is 30, he can have his pick of brides from the village.

The Deserted Mother

After her husband leaves the village, there is no way a mother's poor family can support her and her four children. She moves to the city to live with her sister's family in one of the slums.

With no education and several pre-school aged children, there is little she can do away from the home. She begins sewing dresses for a neighbor who is a seamstress.

As her skill increases, she inquires of friends and learns there is a market for rag dolls. She begins making them and after some trial and error, is able to produce to the quality required for the local buyer.

Within two years, with the help of her daughters, she is making dolls and children's dresses on her own, selling to neighbors, small stores and a larger buyer. Three years later, she rents her own large building, where she lives and employs seven people beyond her children. Other women in the area follow her example and soon the area becomes known for production of modest quality children's clothing and rag dolls.

A large buyer comes in and helps upgrade the quality of the products for a national market. Because the mother is a better manager than others, over 100 women are working for her in five years.

PROBLEMS AND CONSTRAINTS

Typical Problems

Even for those few business people who manage, as in our case studies, to become relatively successful, the constraints on further development are large. The very factors which encourage the formation of new business also mitigate against their expansion and long-term viability. Most small-scale business provides very meager income for its owners, at least in the short run.

Because of the low skill and capital requirements, new businesses tend to form around successful existing ones, with little sense of the unique talents which may have led that business to succeed or of the ability of the market to absorb additional entrants. As a result, there is considerable movement from one business to another of those new to business activity.

Market conditions in the sector tend to shift very rapidly, partly due to the enormous flow of new people into and out of the sector. While the sector responds to macro economic conditions, it also has a dynamic of its own, which tends to have much more radical and rapid gyrations than the larger economy. Changes in the larger economy with respect to one segment of an industry, such as children's clothing, can have a dramatic impact on an entire slum area of a city. Because of these factors, businesses which are very profitable one month can turn completely sour the next, requiring rapid change of business operations for thousands of small producers.

These small businesses opeerate on razor-thin margins, for the most part. An increase by a penny a yard in cloth prices or a penny a pound for sugar, can make them unprofitable. Normally without significant savings, if they cannot sell a given volume each day, they cannot both eat and pay rent, school tuition and doctor bills.

Suppliers and buyers know this. Normally, because the small businessperson must buy and sell in small volumes, they pay the highest price for raw materials and get the lowest price for their products. Suppliers will often add a margin even to normally high prices, knowing the small businessperson has to have the material to produce for vital daily sales.

The small businessperson is often forced into debt to suppliers or buyers or to moneylenders. Interest rates on these small loans can reach 20% a day. Given these high rates and the low potential sales, it is often impossible for the small businessperson to escape from debt. They become, in effect, little more than the employees of their suppliers or buyers. These businesses are typically too small and lack the collateral to qualify for regular commercial credit.

If disaster strikes the family in the form of accident or illness, a small businessperson is typically in a very poor position to cope. A few doctor bills will usually be beyond the means of a family. Lack of adequate medical care frequently leads to aggravation of simple medical problems.

Even daily problems such as school fees and clothing can put a severe strain on family resources and drain capital needed to allow the business to grow. It is also not untypical, where a woman runs the business, for the husband to view the business income as his own property and to spend it on liquor or other women, irrespective of the needs of the business or the family.

Government policy toward this sector typically ranges from indifference to outright hostility. Some argue cogently that it has been governmental indifference which has been the single most critical factor in the rapid growth of the sector. Such policy level indifference, however, does not necessarily translate to the level of the petty bureaucrat. At this level, exploitation is the rule. The small businessperson is seen as fertile ground for augmenting meager government salaries. Policemen, health inspectors, licensing officials and firemen, all require heavy bribes to be kept away. Since the businesses are normally illegal from an official standpoint and they are small and unorganized, they have little defense. "Positive" governmental action usually takes the form of "slum clearance" or "street beautification" which can displace thousands of small businesses.

Once they reach a certain level, lack of business management and technical skills is a serious constraint. Technical skills, though expensive, can increasingly be obtained. Management training, keyed to this level of enterprise, is normally in short supply at any price. Simple problems, which could be solved through better bookkeeping, for instance, continue for years without being corrected.

Given these difficulties, that these businesses survive, multiply and sometimes prosper is a tribute to the human spirit and the will to survive. For many, the choice is either to make it in business or not to make it at all.

IMPACT OF GROWTH OF SMALL ENTERPRISE SECTOR

Typical Attitudinal Impacts

Small enterprise is increasingly coming to be used by the poor as the vehicle through which they hope to escape poverty and, inevitably, traditional village life.

Each step up the business ladder improves family income, while taking the family further away from the village. Small enterprise is basically a more urbanized activity. It both reinforces and is influenced by urban values. In scattered interviews, business people tend to place a high value on "being on one's own," particularly among women with few skills. There seems to be a sense that small business provides the person with an increased sense of mastery over their own fate. There is a surprisingly high value placed on encouraging one's children to enter business, rather than the professions, principally because of the sense of independence and mastery it offers.

Small business people clearly see their business as having the potential to provide them the economic and social mobility denied them in other ways. A surprisingly large proportion of business people view the long hours they work in a positive light. They view their role as sacrificing so that they can save and build a business which will enable them to provide educations for their children. Their view is that their children will be able to escape poverty, bringing the whole family with them.

Small business families seem to suffer more than their share of the social problems typical of urban slum living. Female headed families and businesses are common. Drinking problems are common among adult males. Children are often caught up in gang activity and petty crime. Among the very poor, prostitution is often the fate of teenage girls. A sense of disorientation is common.

It is women who are at the forefront of small business activity world-wide. Interviews suggest that through business, they obtain a sense of self worth and independence which might not otherwise be available to them. When these businesswomen have been organized by voluntary organizations in such countries as India and the Philippines, they have developed leadership and other skills of great value to their families and their communities. In the search for social and economic equity, it may well be these organized businesswomen who will be the impetus for change.

Institutional Impacts

To compensate for the village structure which would have provided a cushion for such problems, institutions emerge in urban slums. People from the same village live together and help each other in business if they can. Groups tend to form of people in the same kind of business, such as cooked-food vendors, or doll makers. These groups establish mutual support structures, which can include rudimentary insurance systems in case of illness, revolving loan funds and assistance in getting licenses. Sometimes these groups actively protest against governmental policies.

The Role of Government

As the sector has grown, existing institutions have had to gradually adjust to the presence of small-scale business. Many governments, having first unsuccessfully tried to regulate them out of existence, are not resigned to their inevitability and some, including those of India, the Philippines, and Jamaica, have even set up institutions, designed to assist them. Other countries are in the process of considering this option. Government programs to date are small and relatively ineffectual.

Government may continue to view the sector negatively in many cases, but political pressure will grow in at least some countries for positive action. India was one of the first countries with a sizable proportion of its population in the sector. As a result, government policy has increasingly recognized and provided support. Many of the resulting programs, it has been argued, have done more harm than good. However, on the whole, government support may have been helpful. As a result of government policy, institutional credit is available to amazingly small business. Certain products must be produced on a small-scale basis. Large business is required to obtain a proportion of their goods and services from small-scale business. Other countries, including Indonesia, the Philippines, Zimbabwe and El Salvador have attempted to set up positive programs.

The harassment by petty officials is, however, the most serious problem. It remains to be seen if anything can be done to substantially reduce this problem.

The Role of Private Voluntary Agencies

Private voluntary agencies have increasingly become a force in Third World countries. Their direct contacts with the poor led them to recognize before most others the importance of the small-scale business sector as a vehicle for improving the conditions of the poor. In many Third World countries, particularly in South and Southeast Asia and Latin America, voluntary organizations have been operating programs to assist this sector for ten or more years now and have gained considerable experience and sophistication. Their programs often provide credit, technical and managerial assistance and help organize a business group through which to protect and extend small business rights. These private agencies, though they are small and reach relatively few businesses, have been more responsible than anything else for highlighting the problems and needs of the sector and for experimentation essential to determine what could be done at the level of policy and program.

The role of private voluntary organizations in determining the future of the sector can be expected to increase, particularly in the very poorest countries. In countries such as Bangladesh, the role of these organizations is already overwhelming. Their links with international groups make them formidable. They will be building experimental programs all over the Third World. Increasingly, they will be putting pressure directly on governments for policy change. They are also in a position to influence bilateral donors, such as USAID, and multilateral donors such as the

United Nations and World Bank, for which they act as consultants. Donors, in turn, can place considerable pressure on Third World governments.

The Role of Financial Institutions

Banks and other financial institutions have increasingly had to respond to the sector. In some cases, as in India, it was the result of a government policy. In others, such as the Philippines, it was more a result of the growth of the sector and the desire of the financial institutions to reach new markets. Most of the smallest and poorest businesses continue to be denied credit. However, this is beginning to change. Banks have been surprised to discover that with some ingenuity, they can lend to this sector at an acceptable cost and even make a profit, if they can at the same time encourage savings from the same sector. After one bank in the Philippines experimented with this approach, other banks and finance companies quickly entered the market and there now appears to be stiff competition.

This trend will continue partly as a result of government pressure and government financing. Financial institutions are, however, by nature very conservative and it remains to be seen how quickly they will respond to pressures for change.[8]

The Role of Large-Scale Business

Larger business has had both a negative and a positive impact on the small business sector. It is all too common to hear the complaint of one small detergent manufacturer in Madras. He indicated that large manufacturers controlled the supply and price of raw materials, making it nearly impossible for him to operate. However, it is also true that larger companies can play a very healthy role. Many establish subcontracting relationships with thousands of small producers, providing them, in many cases, with raw materials, technical assistance, equipment and a steady market. These arrangements, of course, can be and often are, quite exploitative. However, in at least some cases, they are quite fair and provide the small businessperson with stability and support they would not otherwise have.

Government will put increasing pressure on big business to be more helpful. This may result in a loosening of constraints on raw material flows and may lead to improved and expanded sub-contracting opportunities. Big business is itself quite marginal, however, in many of these countries and the impact of any action it might take cannot be expected to be great.

Overall Impact on Equity and Income Distribution

Small-scale business is one of the few sectors which in most Third World countries is, for the most part, operating in response to free market forces. The sector has grown so rapidly and so far from public concern that in most cases, government policy and management have not caught up. As indicated earlier, although there is little data to support this contention, it may be the lack of intervention which is responsible for rapid growth in the sector.

Because of the lack of data, it is difficult to assess the impact of this rapid growth on equity and income distribution. It could be argued that because this is "employment of last resort," that without the sector, incomes of the growing numbers in the sector would be lower. However, it is not an easy point to prove. We already know that when people cannot find work in one sector, the alternative is seldom total unemployment. They find work elsewhere, even if more marginal in nature.

A concern of many economists is "redundancy" in the sector and the possibility that as a result, real income may be continually pressed downward. A related concern is, as indicated earlier, whether people who operate these small businesses have the opportunity to grow. It is difficult to assess the validity of these concerns. As indicated earlier, the sector is characterized by rapid movement from one activity to another. There are few measures of the extent to which this movement results in net improvement.

However, it is this observer's impression that there is less reason for concern about these problems than is sometimes argued. Observation by many of those working with this sector suggests that so-called "redundancy" results from looking at one point in time. In fact, over time the sector seems to have a remarkable capacity to generate *new* activity to respond to emerging demand.

The boy who was selling newspapers to motorists last year is now recycling motor oil. The woman who was making children's dresses is now making doll clothing for a large buyer. As new people move into the sector, people already there find new activities.

These new activities are *net additions* to employment. Net addition is possible for two reasons: 1) the small-scale business sector is growing rapidly and while they create new labor supply, they also add to demand—a demand which is typically met by others within the sector; and 2) because it is a source of cheap and unregulated supply (i.e. there are no hourly wage requirements as in large factories), the formal, large-scale sector increasingly views it as a source of supply, which provides a net addition to demand.

While the total effect of these factors has not been studied, it is this observer's opinion that the whole issue of redundancy, while important, is considerably overstated in practice and is a relatively short-term problem, sorted out by the marketplace.

Do significant numbers of businesses have the opportunity to grow and provide increased income for their owners and workers? Again, although supporting data is not available, it seems likely that small business is as likely to grow in Thailand as in the United States.

It needs to be remembered that small businesses in the U.S. fail at a high rate. But it should also be remembered that the profile of a successful U.S. small businessperson is generally one who has failed once or twice before. It should also be remembered that small business in the U.S. is: 1) the principle source of new jobs generated; 2) the principle source of value added; and 3) the principle avenue for rapid increases in income.

It must be remembered, therefore, that appearances are deceiving. Again, many economists who have assumed small business in the Third World will not be a source of increased income have looked at the static nature of income over a relatively short period of time. What appears to happen over the longer term is that there is a normal curve in which many people fail, perhaps several times. Others succeed dramatically. The majority range along a curve from declining to substantially increased real income, as one would expect. Those at the bottom often end up working for those who manage to succeed.

We do not know and will probably not know for some time the absolute proportions of those who increase their real income significantly. What is more important, however, is that we recognize that, as in the U.S., this is one of the few sectors which is relatively *dynamic* and to which access is still relatively free. The sector provides the *opportunity* for increased income for the very poor, with little or no education or other requirements.

Generally speaking, if they are initially poor and have no connections, those who succeed are those who work the hardest, are the best at accumulating and reinvesting savings, and who can learn to solve business management problems. Luck, of course, is also an important factor—being at the right place at the right time to take advantage of a new market or cheaper source of supply. However, as with business everywhere, of the many who will be potentially able to take advantage of a situation, only a few will do so effectively.

It is the nature of the small business sector to be continuously in flux, offering new opportunities in great frequency. Thus, the business which failed to take advantage of an opportunity this year may do so next week, next month or next year. It is this dynamic element, made possible by relative freedom to respond to market forces, which makes it possible for small business in the Third World to play the same significant role it has in the U.S. and elsewhere.

This has important implications for the equity issue. In the U.S., small business has traditionally served as a vehicle for increased self-respect and self-confidence. A typical attitude of a successful small business person in the U.S. is a sense of mastery over his immediate environment. He can make things happen and is proud of it. This sense of mastery is typically not present in a peasant culture. However, in interviews with successful third world business people, it is one of their most notable qualities. It often translates into efforts to improve their political or social situation through organization.

Although scattered interviews cannot be more than indicative, it does seem likely to this observer that small business will have a positive effect on self-image and the sense of ability to get things changed. This, in turn, is likely to lead increasingly to organized efforts to improve social, political and economic equity.

In summary, it is possible and indeed, very likely, that the rapid growth of the small business sector in the Third World over the last thirty years will have increasingly important impacts. This is particularly true if governments pursue their predominant policy of ignoring the sector. Likely impacts can be expected to be increases in real income for the very poor people entering the sector, thus improving income distribution and improved social, political and economic equity, as a result of the increased organized pressure placed on the society by the small business community.

REFERENCES

1. Dennis Anderson and Mark W. Leiserson, *Rural Enterprise and Nonfarm Employment, A World Bank Paper.* World Bank: Washington, D.C., Jan., 1978. p. 20.

2. *Ibid.,* p. 17.

3. Derek Byerlee and Carl K. Eicher, "Rural Employment, Migration and Economic Development: Theoretical Issues and Empirical Evidence from Africa." *Africa Rural Development Paper, No. 1.,* Dept. of Agricultural Economics; Michigan State Univ.: East Lansing, 1972, *passim* and Richard J. Barnet, "The World's Resources, Part 3: Human Energy." *The New Yorker,* Vol. 56, No. 7, April, 1980, pp. 46–115.

4. *Ibid.,* Barnet and John Friedman and Flora Sullivan, "The Absorption Labor in the Urban Economy," Unpublished Paper, 1980.

5. *Employment, Income and Equality: A Strategy for Increasing Productive Employment in Kenya.* International Labor Organization: Geneva, 1972. p. 6.

6. Jeffrey Ashe, Jason Brown, *et. al., The PISCES Study: Assisting the Smallest Economic Activities of the Urban Poor.* USAID: Washington, D.C., 1981.

7. *Ibid.,* p. 12.; Stephen Guisinger and Mohammed Irfan, "Pakistan's Informal Sector," *Journal of Development Studies,* Vol. 16, No. 4, July, 1980, pp. 412–26; Carl Liedholm and Enyinna Chuta, "The Economics of Rural and Urban Small-Scale Industries in Sierra Leone," *African Rural Economy Paper No. 14,* Department of Agricultural Economics, Michigan State University: East Lansing, 1976; Pieter van Dijk Meine, *Developing the Informal Sector in Senegal,* International Labor Organization, JASPA Team Report, Dakar, Senegal, December 10, 1976. Kaliman Schaefer, *Sao Paulo: Urban Development and Employment.* ILO: Geneva VIII, 1976; S. V. Sethuraman, "The Urban Informal Sector in Developing Countries," ILO: Geneva, 1981; Paulo Souza and Victor Tokman, "The Informal Urban Sector in Latin America," *International Labor Review,* Vol. 114, No. 3 Nov.–Dec., 1976, pp. 355–66.

8. The author is currently engaged in research funded by USAID on the experience of banking institutions throughout the Third World in lending to small-scale enterprise.

Capitalist Agriculture, Peasant Farming and Well-Being in Rural India

Myron Weiner

INDIA's AGRICULTURAL GROWTH of the past three decades has been heralded by some as an example of what can be done when modern agricultural technology is combined with the market incentives of capitalist agriculture. But, say the critics, India's experience demonstrates the defects of agrarian capitalism: it increases inequality in the countryside, decreases the well being of the rural poor, and is unable to provide for *continuous* agricultural growth.

There is now a raging debate among Indians over the dynamics of their peasant society—whether it is semi-feudal or capitalist, whether immiseration and inequality are growing, whether land reform is an essential condition for future agricultural growth, whether there are "contradictions" between exploited agricultural workers, tenants and the near landless and those who own land and provide credit, whether there are "contradictions" between the countryside and the city, and whether government should extract resources from the countryside to provide the capital for industrial growth. There are few policy issues that are not affected by these broader conceptual questions. How much grain, for example, should government procure for its reserves and for fair price ration shops and what should the procurement price be?

Should government subsidise fertilizers, seeds, and pesticides?
Should government provide credit and if so, should it make a
special effort to aid small farmers and tenants? Should farmers be
allowed to import tractors, harvestors and diesel pumps? Should
trade in food grains be controlled by private traders or by gover-
ment? Should government permit food exports? What, if anything, should the government do about the terms of trade
between the countryside and the city? How these questions are
answered in large measure depends upon whether one believes
that capitalist farmers, operating in an open market, will grow
rich at the expense of the rest of rural and urban India, or
whether capitalist farming can be both productive and beneficial
to ever larger numbers of people.

These issues are reminiscent of one of the greatest intellectual
debates of the twentieth century—the nature of peasant society in
Russia at the beginning of this century. Teodor Shanin writes:

"The conception of the basic dynamics of peasant society accepted by
Russian policy-makers and, indeed, by the majority of educated Russians
at the beginning of this century can be outlined in a few sentences. It was
believed that, in the process of inevitable economic advance, every
human society necessarily headed toward an increasing division of labor,
the establishment of market relations, the accumulation of capital, and
social diversification. It was also believed that these processes were centered in towns but inevitably spread into the countryside. Rich peasant
farms, which were larger and better equipped and had a higher capital/
worker ratio, found themselves in an advantagous position as far as the
optimal use of the factors of production and their further accumulation
were concerned. For precisely opposite reasons, poor peasant farms
were at a disadvantage in any attempt to improve their economic position. Continuing cumulation of economic advantages and disadvantages
led to a polarization of peasant society into rich farmers, who increasingly acquired the characteristics of capitalist entrepreneurs, and
poor farmers, who lost their farms and became landless wage labourers
in the employ of rich farmers, estate owners, or urban entrepreneurs.
Some of the typical characteristics of a traditional peasant family farm
could still be seen in the middle strata of the peasantry, but these would
disintegrate or change in the inevitable process of economic advance.
With them would disappear the survivals of the traditional peasant
society. A new social structure based on capitalist farming would finally
come to be established in the countryside."[1]

This picture, writes Shanin, became so much a part of the
prevailing ideology that it shaped the rural policies of Russia for a
quarter of a century. This image of immiseration leading to polar-

ization was the basis for Stolypin's policies from 1906 onward, Lenin's New Economic Policy (1921–28) and Stalin's policy of liquidating the kulaks and collectivizing the land.

No significant political group in India today openly advocates "liquidating" the "kulaks" or rich farmers or collectivizing the land, but the question of whether one should encourage the growth of capitalist agriculture has been and continues to be a central issue. One question is whether it can continue to provide increases in agricultural productivity. And the second is whether capitalist agriculture is or is not equitable, that is, how it affects the well-being of the landless, the near landless, small farmers and agricultural laborers.

To do full justice to these questions one needs to review a large and controversial literature, describe the significant variations from one region to another and from one crop to another, and explore the complex and contentious questions of what data are appropriate and reliable for assessing growth rates, regional variations, the relative contribution of small and large holdings to increased productivity and a host of related questions. In this brief essay I can only deal with two issues. One is whether on balance the evidence suggests that capitalist agriculture has improved well being in rural India, as well as increased productivity; and the second is the question of how Indian beliefs as to what the distributive effects are have shaped Indian agricultural policies. A central argument will be that the *belief* that capitalist agriculture will have inequitable effects has at times led to policies which slow the rate of agricultural growth and, thereby, in my judgment, slow the improvement in the well-being of the rural poor.

Agricultural Productivity in India: An Overview

The expansion of grain production in India is rightly considered one of the country's major accomplishments. Foodgrain production rose from 55 million tons in 1950–51 to 82 million tons in 1960–61, 108 million tons in the early seventies, and 150 million tons per year in the mid eighties. The growth rate compares favorably to that of other developing countries and is higher (though not on a per capita basis) than that achieved by Japan before World War II.

The growth rates were greatest in the 50s (49% in a decade) when the amount of arable land used for cultivating foodgrains increased from 97 to 115 million hectares. In the 1960s and 1970s, the annual increases in production were smaller (32% and 21% per decade respectively) but they reflected increasing *yields* on existing acreage. The largest increases were in wheat which rose from 6.8 million tons in 1950 to 35 million tons in 1978. Rice production increased from 22 million to 54 million tons. *From 1950 to 1980 productivity per acre doubled in a country whose agriculture had been more or less stagnant for the previous fifty years.* Without these increases in food production India would have had to import vast quantities of food simply to keep pace with population growth. Instead, by 1980 India was self-sufficient in foodgrains and was even exporting some of its production to pay back earlier loans. In 1979 India exported grains to the Soviet Union (1.5 million tons of wheat), Vietnam and Mauritius, and loaned grain (1.5 million tons of rice) to Bangladesh.

Though almost all states in India have registered some growth, the greatest increases in foodgrain production were in Punjab (8.1% per annum), Haryana (5.3%), Gujarat, (3.6%) and Rajasthan (3.0%) in the northwest and Karnataka (3.4%) in the south, compared with an average national growth rate of 2.8% per annum for 1960 to 1978.

Increases in productivity were made possible by extending the irrigation system, introducing high yielding variety (HYV) seeds, an expansion of rural credit and by price policies which increased the profitability of agriculture, thereby enabling and giving incentives to peasants to acquire new seeds, fertilizers, pesticides and water to expand production.

Increases in foodgrain production slowed in the 1970s and for the decade as a whole actually fell slightly below population growth. The failure of the monsoon in 1972 was a sharp blow to agriculture, although the decline in production was not as great as in the drought of 1965. Since a portion of agriculture is now price and input responsive, especially irrigated areas that produce for the market, the availability and price of fertilizers and diesel fuel readily affects productivity. A sharp increase in fertilizer prices and, in some years, actual shortages, may have limited agricultural growth in the 1970s. Differences in productivity as between wheat and rice has led some observers to conclude that the high yielding varieties of wheat have been more adaptive to Indian conditions than high yielding rice, that the limited availability of irrigation is a more serious constraint upon rice production, and that, for some years, there were greater price incentives for wheat than for rice.[2] As of the late seventies only about 25% of the land under cultivation in India was irrigated; the remainder was dependent upon rainfall. Moreover, some of the largest increases in rice production have taken place in the same areas as increases in wheat production, suggesting that whatever factors are conducive to growth in some regions (be they the availability and management of water, or land tenure systems, or the technology) benefits both wheat and rice production. Whether the growth in agricultural production, which has averaged 2.6% per year from 1949 to 1977, can be kept at this level for the remainder of the century depends to a considerable extent upon whether India can double the amount of land brought under irrigation, the price and availability of a variety of agricultural inputs, the effectiveness of agricultural research, the continued extension of credit, and a host of considerations specific to each region. In some regions land tenure systems may slow the pace of agricultural growth as well as accentuate inequalities in income distribution.

In the areas of comparatively high growth a central issue is whether the benefits have been widely shared. Some critics of the new agricultural growth strategy have suggested that growth has been at the expense of small peasant farmers losing their land to capitalist farmers, tenants losing their security, and agricultural laborers receiving lower wages. In short, the growth in productivity has resulted in greater immiseration on the part of large sections of India's rural population. Capitalist agriculture, according to this view, even as it increased productivity and enabled India to become self-sufficient, has led to a decrease in the well-being of a majority of the countryside.

At best, say the critics, the poor are marginally better off in some absolute sense, but their relative economic position has worsened; moreover, the number of poor, it is said, has grown and among the poor some are even absolutely worse off.

One scholar, Francine Frankel, assessing the distributive effects of the green revolution in high growth districts in the late 60s and early 70s, wrote that in Ludhiana district in the Punjab, "it is the bottom 20 percent of cultivators, with holding of less than 10 acres, who have fared worst as a result of the green revolution. These farmers may have been able to make some marginal gains in good weather years by applying small doses of chemical fertilizer to Mexican wheats, but, in general, they have not been able to sustain the indivisible inputs—tubewells and agricultural machinery—required for the efficient cultivation of the new varieties. Actually, there is some reason to believe that their position may have suffered an absolute deterioration as a result of the green revolution."[3] In Thanjavur in Tamil Nadu, another high growth district, she found that "it is in contrast to the large landowners that the landless workers have experienced the greatest relative decline in their economic position. In some cases, moreover, negative changes have added up to an absolute decline in the standard of living . . . payments for harvesting and even cash payments for day labor have remained stationary in the face of rising prices."[4] And in Burdwan district in West Bengal, employment has increased as a result of multiple cropping but "any additions tend to be cancelled out by rising costs of essential commodities."[5]

It is not always easy to distinguish betwen those scholars who argue the immiseration thesis, that is that there has been an *absolute* increase in poverty, and those who argue that *inequalities* are increasing, for sometimes scholars themselves do not make the distinction and some have shifted from one position to the other. Among those who have focused on the negative consequences of the green revolution are Pranab Bardhan, Keith Griffin, Asok Mitra, C. T. Kurien, Asok Rudra, T. Byers, B. Farmer, and Francine Frankel.

Other scholars argue that the introduction of the new agricultural technologies and policies to provide incentives has improved the well-being of small farmers and agricultural laborers, as well as the larger farmers, and that where poverty has increased it is primarily in areas where economic growth has not kept pace with population growth. This position is taken by Theodore Schultz, David Hopper, John Mellor, Raj Krishna, Inderjit Singh, S. Bhalla and Montek Ahluwalia. While these scholars generally support the new agricultural strategy and reject the immiseration thesis, they also recognize that larger farmers have often been better able than smaller farmers and tenants to gain access to agricultural inputs and that improvement in the well-being of the rural poor remains marginal at best. The debate involves more than an academic assessment of a particular strategy for agricultural development. The two sides have divergent views as to what policies should be pursued, and what strategies political parties should follow to support or undermine policies. The debate is perhaps the single most important controversial issue in India today. The position taken by policy makers will have a profound effect on India's future agricultural productivity, its politics, and the well-being of its vast rural population.

To a large extent the debate rests on the question of what the facts are concerning the distributive effects of capitalist agriculture. But there are also various conceptual and ideological questions involving the question of what constitutes "capitalist" agriculture.

Capitalist Agriculture: A Matter of Definition

Capitalism is a term ordinarily used to describe a particular kind of industrial system, but Marxists (and others) have used the word to describe agriculture as well. Marxists usually define capitalist farmers as having four characteristics: they produce for the market, employ wage labor, have mechanized their farms, and reinvest the surplus within their own farms. The capitalist farmer is distinguished from the peasant small holder who does not employ labor (he depends upon his own and family labor), is engaged in subsistence agriculture, and has too few resources to mechanize or reinvest. A fundamental consequence of capitalism in agriculture is a change in scale. Capitalist farming implies, at least from the Marxist perspective, large-scale production.

Marx and his followers argue that peasant farming is bound to be replaced by capitalist farming. Peasants might survive for a while through self-exploitation but in time the increased productivity and profitability of large-scale farming will force peasants off the land. Marx believed this process had taken place in Germany and elsewhere in Europe, and Marxists believe that the process is now taking place in the third world. Marx himself did not lament this development. To the contrary, he believed that large-scale capitalist farming was efficient, that the growth of large estates facilitated mechanization and that the proletarianization of agricultural labor was an important step toward a socialist revolution. A socialist state would nationalize land and peasants would become an agricultural proletariat. But in the meantime socialists cannot afford to alienate the peasantry. To win their support socialists should promise "land to the peasants." The small holder has to be politically separated from the capitalist farmers (or kulaks) just as the petty bourgeoisie has to be separated from the industrial capitalist class.

Critical to any Marxist conception is the distinction between the exploiting classes—landlords and rich peasants—and the exploited classes—the poor peasants and agricultural laborers. Capitalist farmers exploit wage laborers by appropriating a surplus. There is also an important distinction between "feudal" landlords and the rich "capitalists" peasants. Some Marxists point to contradictions between capitalist farmers and feudal landlords, while others maintain that the main class divisions are the agricultural laborers and small peasants against both.

The Marxist view in its varied forms has a powerful influence on contemporary scholarly analysis of India's agrarian system, shapes political perspectives and at various times has influenced

Indian policy makers. Many scholars, politicians, and policy makers who would not describe themselves as Marxists are nonetheless affected by a Marxist perspective on agriculture. Within this perspective there are of course many different views, so that characterizing the common view is not easy. But there is a shared perspective expressed in the pages of the professional economic journals in India, by economists within the government and by many Marxist-minded scholars abroad. These views—portions of which are shared by those who reject the Marxist paradigms—can be summarized as follows:

1. India's agrarian system is characterized by substantial inequalities in land ownership and use. A small fraction of India's rural population owns and operates more than half of India's arable land while the remainder are small holders, tenants, and agricultural laborers. On this point there is no disagreement among observers of rural India.

2. The introduction of the new technology known as the "green revolution" has accelerated the process of turning this small class into capitalist farmers, who produce for the market, evict tenants and turn them into agricultural laborers, adopt displacing machinery which forces down the wages of agricultural laborers, push small farmers out of production because they cannot afford the costly inputs of modern agriculture, and displace village artisans as the new rural rich purchase urban mass-produced consumer goods.

3. The result of the expansion of capitalist agriculture is thus greater *relative* inequalities in the countryside and among substantial sections of the rural poor, an *absolute* decline in their well being through a process of immiseration.

4. In the absence of fundamental institutional changes, that is, radical land reform, increases in agricultural productivity within this capitalist framework will still further worsen the lot of the poor and increase the concentration of land in the hands of a growing capitalist class.

Among those who share this perspective there is considerable disagreement as to what should be done about it. Some argue for arresting the process of capitalist development until the country carries out radical restructuring of the land system. Others would continue the green revolution but modify it so that it does not worsen rural inequalities—by limiting the use of machinery, and by establishing minimum wages for agricultural laborers while pressing for land reform. Still others use this analysis of agrarian change to formulate a political strategy for the left. It enables them to make predictions as to which agrarian classes are likely to be responsive to radical appeals.

Before one turns to an assessment of how capitalist agriculture has affected income distribution and well-being in India, it is important to ask how meaningful is the Marxist definition of capitalist agriculture and whether a distinction between "capitalist" farmers and "peasant" farmers is useful.[6] For Marxists, the question of what kind of classes or subclasses exist among the peasantry is important for ascertaining the contradictions or conflicts within the countryside and what the implications are for a political strategy on the part of the left. Indeed, for some Marxists the *absence* of polarization indicates that agrarian capitalism has not yet developed. "There has not yet been among the farmers of Punjab," writes Asok Rudra, "any strong polarization and I have expressed doubt whether it serves any important purpose to talk about capitalist development before polarization has reached a sufficiently high degree."[7]

Answering the question of what is a capitalist farmer has proven to be difficult in India. Rudra excludes from his definition of capitalist any farmer who gives his land out for lease and does not himself cultivate. Like other Marxists (and on this point, classical economists as well) he insists that laborers must be able to sell their labor. If laborers are bound to landlords, if they work to pay off their loans or are tied in some other fashion, then labor is not free and capitalist agriculture does not exist. Other Marxists, such as Utsa Patnaik, place greater emphasis on whether there is an "accumulation and reinvestment of surplus value in order to generate more surplus on an ever-expanding scale" so that there is an increasing "capital intensification."[8]

The question of whether wage labor is employed and how much capital intensification and investment in farm machinery there is is particularly troublesome when one considers India's middle peasantry. India is a country of small farmers. Three quarters of India's cultivators own less than two hectares (five acres). In fact only three percent of all rural households own more than eight hectares. It is the small and medium holdings (five to fifteen acres) that have gained in both numbers and area while what Indians describe as "large holdings" (fifteen acres or more) have declined. (What is considered large capitalist farming in India is elsewhere often considered small family farms.) The middle peasants no longer produce only for subsistence but also produce for the market, but they do not necessarily hire labor. Unlike the rich peasants who rely heavily upon agricultural laborers, the middle peasants often do their own manual work, though they may hire agricultural laborers during the harvest. In some areas the middle peasants may even hire out their own labor or that of family members.[9]

The question of whether the number of middle peasants is

increasing and the question of whether they employ wage laborers is significant in the debate over what is capitalist agriculture and whether it is growing in India. The notion of scale or size of land-holding as a mark of capitalist agriculture was central for Marx since he believed that peasant farming would be replaced by capitalist farming. He distinguished between "petty commodity production" characterized by the unity of labor and capital, and capitalist production "predicated on the very separation of labor and capital."[10] For Marx, capitalist agriculture is essential for capital accumulation. Thus small traders, shopkeepers, artisans, small manufacturers, and peasants would (and should) disappear; they stand in the way of accumulation and therefore are standing against History.[11] The self-employed small farmer thus is condemned.

However, in Germany, France, Japan, and in the United States small family farmers have diminished in number, but not disappeared, any more than have small businessmen. Since the Marxist conception of capitalism emphasizes scale, they do not see the small sector, including peasant agriculture, as an inherent part of the capitalist economy (which implies accumulation). And since small farmers do not employ wage laborers, they do not exploit and hence by definition are not capitalist. The Marxist definition of capitalism, by emphasizing the class division between small and large farmers suggests that the smaller farmers, who are being squeezed out, should politically ally themselves with the exploited landless laborers. Marxists thus distinguish between peasants on the one hand and exploiting landlords and capitalist farmers, money lenders and traders on the other. They see the introduction of commercialization of agriculture as facilitating the conversion of semi-feudal landlords into capitalist farmers or "kulaks." This political conception of what constitutes capitalist agriculture was articulated in the Sixth Congress of the Communist International in 1982. This conference set the framework for subsequent radical interpretations of Indian agrarian developments by emphasizing the conflict between the upper layers of the peasants and the poor peasants and the landless. The Marxist views on agrarian issues were subsequently developed in the works of several well-known Indian Marxists but, writes P. C. Joshi, all of these "drew upon the penetrating and perceptive analysis of the agrarian problems offered in the political thesis called 'The Revolutionary Movement in the Colonies and Semi Colonies by the Communist International' of 1928."[12]

The question of whether hiring agricultural laborers is an indication that a farmer is a capitalist is particularly complicated in

India since some small farmers, especially those without sons, or whose family members have left to work elsewhere, hire workers even when their holdings are small, while some larger farmers make greater use of *family* labor. The latter may accumulate more capital than the former and, in fact, be more mechanized. Which one is capitalist?

To most non-Marxists these are arcane distinctions that throw little light on the central questions of what makes agriculture more productive, whether production for the market is squeezing out smaller farms, and whether the rural landless are becoming better off. But for Marxists these distinctions are central because, in theory at least, they predict class polarization and provide the left with the basis for formulating a political strategy.

The use of the term "capitalist" to refer to agriculture is further confused by the failure to distinguish between "capitalism" as a *system* of production and the capitalist as the individual entrepreneur who operates within that system. In a developing country, capitalism as a system often operates side by side with precapitalist modes of production, and within precapitalist systems there are also individuals who behave as capitalists. Moreover, even among non-Marxists there is a tendency to define the capitalist not only by how he behaves but by the scale of his operation—to think of the large industrialists and farmers as capitalists, but not those who run small manufacturing shops or small farms.

The definition one employs is thus shaped by the questions one asks. For our purposes, we shall define capitalist agriculture as production for market and for profit without regard to whether wage labor is employed or how much mechanization there is. The definition thus excludes the rent collecting landlord, the "gentleman" farmer producing for pleasure, and the "feudal" farmer more concerned with his status and power than with profit-maximization, but it may include as a capitalist farmer the small farmers, though some employ labor, some mechanize, and some do neither.

It should be recognized that in the real world of peasant farming in India, theoretical distinctions do not readily fit: some peasants may be engaged in subsistence farming as well as in production for the market, while some farmers may be both rent-collecting landlords and cultivators. This is not to suggest that it is not useful to distinguish between small and large farmers, just as it is useful to distinguish between small and big businesses. They have different needs, and government policies may affect them differently. But it does not follow that one is capitalist and the other is not, with its implication of the withering away of the so-called non-capitalist small farmer.

Agricultural Growth and Changes in Rural Well-Being

There are a number of hypothetical reasons why capitalist agriculture might decrease the well-being of the rural poor. For one thing, farmers oriented toward producing for the market at a profit may turn to labor-displacing machinery, resulting in a decline in the use of agricultural labor and a decline in agricultural wages. While in the United States and in West Europe the demand for industrial labor absorbed those who were displaced from agriculture, most third world countries have experienced population growth rates that have made it difficult for the urban sector to absorb the annual increase in the number of people who enter the labor force. A second possible negative consequence is that capitalist agriculture tends to be capital intensive. Smaller farmers, lacking savings or adequate access to credit, may be unable to purchase the new costly inputs, with the result that they either remain subsistence farmers or will leave cultivation by selling out to larger, more efficient farmers. A third possibility is that agricultural prices increase as a result of the rising costs of inputs in agriculture to the detriment of the urban and rural poor. Still another possible negative consequence is that as the income of the richer farmers increases they purchase urban consumer goods rather than consumer goods produced in the village and they no longer need village artisans to repair traditional agricultural implements. These latter two arguments are not persuasive: an increase in agricultural output and a reduction in cost per ton of output is likely to result in a reduction in prices, and a rise in the income of the middle size and richer farmers is likely to result in an increase in demand for rural services resulting in an expansion of employment in the nonagricultural rural sector.

To these presumed inherently inequalitarian features of capitalist agriculture one should also consider the traditional agrarian system out of which capitalist agriculture emerges. Traditional agriculture is often characterized by inequalities in land ownership and use. A small fraction of the rural population may own and operate most of the land as non-cultivating landowners while the majority of the rural population consists of small holders, tenants and agricultural laborers. The introduction of new agricultural technologies and market-oriented agriculture may turn this small class of landowners into capitalists farmers, producing for the market, turning evicted tenants into agricultural laborers, adopting labor-displacing machinery to force down the wages of agricultural laborers, and buying out smaller farmers who cannot afford the costly inputs of modern agriculture. Larger landowners may no longer perform their traditional functions of maintaining irrigation channels now that they have their own tubewells and pumps, with the result that poor farmers suffer. Moreover, the larger farmers are able to use their political influence to monopolize credit, marketing and irrigation facilities.

In evaluating these arguments for India we shall focus on three major dimensions of the impact of agricultural growth on the rural poor.

1. How has capitalist agriculture affected the landless and near landless, that is, those who have holdings of less than an acre?
2. What has been the impact on the number of middle sized holdings? Is this group growing and, if so, is it because larger holdings are fragmenting, or small landowners are buying land, or is this group being squeezed out? In other words, is polarization taking place in land ownership?
3. Is the employment of agricultural labor declining as a consequence of the growing mechanization of agriculture, and are wages dropping?

Landlessness and Landownership

Has landlessness increased or not? There are two conflicting interpretations of the data. K. N. Raj, a distinguished Indian economist, has argued that capitalist agriculture in India has increased polarization by increasing the number of dispossessed landless and by turning small farmers into the near landless. He draws these conclusions by examing data collected by the National Sample Survey, India's most reliable national data source, for the years 1954–55, 1961–62, and 1971–72. But another distinguished Indian economist, V. S. Vyas, drawing from precisely the same data, concluded that the number of small owners has increased and that the middle peasantry has grown. He concludes that many of the landless have become small farmers while some of the larger farmers have sold or forfeited land.

In a study for the Population Council reviewing the arguments of both Raj and Vyas, Mead Cain[13] concludes that neither argument can be verified. One reason is that the data do not distinguish between land that is used for housing, and land used for cultivation. On one point both sides agree: 45% of India's rural population is either landless or owns less than one acre, a figure that has more or less remained constant during this period. But the percentage that owned *some* land *increased* from 14.2% to 19.2%, while those who remained completely landless *declined* from 30.8% to 25.6%. What is not known, however, is whether the land that is now owned is a houseplot of less than an acre or arable land used for productive purposes. In any event, an increase in the percentage of those who own even land for houseplots is of some significance for, as Cain writes, "the market price for a unit of land that is suitable as a houseplot is normally several times the price of the best arable land."[14]

There is no evidence that for India as a whole the percentage of landlessness has increased, or that those who have land have become near landless. To the contrary, for most of the country the number of ownership holdings below one hectare (2.5 acres) has increased.

A decline in the *percentage* of landless is not inconsistent with the finding of scholars that in some parts of the country (particularly eastern U.P. and Bihar) the *absolute* number of landless has increased. Apart from the obvious fact of regional variations, rapid population growth can lead both to a *decline* in the percentage of landless and to an absolute *increase* in their *numbers*. This simple distinction between percentages and absolute numbers is particularly important in a country where population has increased nearly 25% per decade in 1961–71 and 1971–81. For the same reason, it should be noted, the percentage of literate persons has increased in India since 1961, but the absolute number of illiterates has also increased.

There is some evidence of a decline in the inequality of land ownership throughout India. Holdings of less than one hectare constituted 5.4% of the land in 1953, 6.9% in 1961 and 9.2% in 1971. Still, there is a substantial concentration of land holdings. In 1971–72, 78% of all rural households owned either no land or less than two hectares (5 acres) and these accounted for only 25% of the area owned. At the other end three percent of all rural households owned more than eight hectares (20 acres), accounting for nearly 30% of the area owned. Cultivated holdings in excess of ten acres account for 10% of the holdings, but nearly 54% of the owned area.

In the Punjab, according to a study by Inderjit Singh of the World Bank,[15] the number and area of both the smallest and largest size farms have declined, while the number of medium size holdings has increased.[16] Singh concludes that there is no evidence that big farmers are purchasing the land of small farmers or that small farmers are becoming landless laborers, though there has been an increase in the number of agricultural laborers. Singh's arguments are supported by Sheila Bhalla's data from Haryana. She reports that 35% of cultivating households owned 15 or more acres in 1961, but this declined to only 19% of the households in 1971. Small holdings under five acres increased from 16% to 45.6% from 1961 to 1971.[17]

One likely explanation for an increase in the number of agricultural laborers is that many tenants have been evicted. In the 1960s, state governments, under pressure to carry out land reform, imposed ceilings on landholdings. The legislation was intended to end absentee landlordism and to bring about a greater distribution in land ownership. The legislation permitted noncultivating landowners to "resume" cultivation of lands that had previously been cultivated by tenants. Under this loophole many landowners evicted tenants on the pretext that they were themselves becoming cultivators, but in reality they merely converted their tenants into agricultural laborers. The result was an increase in the number of agricultural laborers and a corresponding decline in the number of tenants.

In a series of field reports conducted while he worked for the World Bank, the noted agricultural economist Wolf Ladejinsky described how land reform legislation was being evaded.[18] The legislation, he pointed out, was intended to provide tenants with security of tenure, reduce rents, confer ownership by limiting the size of holdings, and distributing the surplus. Some three million tenants and sharecroppers did become owners of seven million acres of land but there were also wholesale evasions of the ceiling provisions and widespread evictions of tenants. Ladejinsky concluded that security of tenure for tenants rather than redistribution of land would have been a more realistic legislative goal.

India continues to have a serious problem of maldistribution in land ownership with attendant effects on income distribution. Maldistribution may in itself be a constraint upon increasing productivity. In parts of Bihar, for example, the upper caste Brahmins and Takurs have converted their tenants into sharecroppers or agricultural laborers. Large landowners do not themselves personally cultivate and remain more concerned with the rent they receive and the prestige and power that comes from landownership than in increasing productivity and profit.[19] With producers subordinate to owners, tenants without secure rights, land rent acquiring more importance than profitability, and land dominance by castes that do not cultivate, it is no wonder that the green revolution has not taken hold in the semifeudal conditions that characterize portions of Bihar and eastern Uttar Pradesh. But where land ownership has shifted from the rentier class to owner-cultivator farmers, there is a greater prospect that capitalist agriculture, with its orientation toward the market and production for profit, will take hold. And where capitalist agriculture has emerged there is no evidence that it is resulting in the ouster of the small farmer by the large farmer. To the contrary the number of middle sized farmers is growing.[20]

Raj Krishna, onetime chief economist for the Indian Planning Commission, reports that, according to the Agricultural Census of 1970–71, nearly 70 per cent of rural households had operational holdings of five acres or less, and 51 percent had 2.5 acres or less. In all, 49 million holdings belonged to the category of small farmers out of a total number of 70.5 million holdings. Though 70 percent of operational holdings were small, they constituted only 21 per cent of the country's arable land. Contrary to what one might expect, the small farmers had *more* access to irrigation, fertilizers and credit than their share of land. Though their share of total cultivated area was only 21%, their share of net irrigated area was 31.4%. Their share of total fertilizer use was 32%. And their share of agricultural credit was 33%. "This means," writes Krishna, "that small farmers, as a class, command more productive assets and inputs per unit of land than large farmers. But, of course, since they constitute 70 per cent of agricultural households, assets and inputs availability per household is less in the small farm sector than in the large farm sector. As a result, income per household, and even more, income per capita, is less in the small farmer sector: . . . Poverty persists in the small farms because they support a much larger population per unit of land."[21]

Since small farmers apply more input per unit of land than large farmers, with 21 per cent of the land they produced 26 percent of the value of agricultural output.[22]

Agricultural Wages and Employment

"The weight of the evidence suggests that where agricultural growth has been rapid enough to outstrip growth in rural population, real agricultural wages and real rural incomes have increased. In particular real wages rose significantly in those areas where the impact of the green revolution has been significant—the Punjab, Haryana, Gujarat, Western U.P. and Tamil Nadu—while real wages have remained stagnant elsewhere where per capita agricultural outputs have remained stagnant. This evidence suggests that agricultural growth does benefit the poorest of the poor, and that some, though small, benefits have 'trickled down' to the poor, directly or indirectly." So concludes Inderjit Singh in his extensive review of the data and literature in his study, *Small Farmers and the Landless in South Asia*.[23]

Montek Ahluwalia, in a World Bank Study, reports that there is no evidence of either an increase or decrease in the incidence of rural poverty for India as a whole from the period 1956–1957 to 1973–74.[24] Given the growth of population this means that the *absolute* number of rural poor has grown significantly, on an average of about five million people per year. Both Ahluwalia and Singh argue that it is the slow pace of agricultural growth per capita that accounts for the failure to redress rural poverty in India but that there is no evidence that the poor have become poorer because of agricultural growth.

The real wages of agricultural workers have grown. Using an index of 100 for 1965, Singh reports[25] that the index of real wages for agricultural workers in Punjab and Haryana for 1956–1959 was in the high 70s, 100 for 1965 and 117 for 1970. There were also substantial increases in western Uttar Pradesh, Karnataka, and Gujarat, areas where agricultural growth rates were high.

There has been a marked increase in the number of agricultural laborers in India, but this indicates neither a growth in the demand for labor nor that landlessness is increasing. In part the increase reflects population growth and in part it reflects a shift of many rural people from the category of tenants to the category of agricultural workers, the consequences of loopholes and evasion of land reform legislation. While some decline in tenancy is an indication that tenants have acquired ownership rights, much of the decline reflects the resumption of land by owners from sharecroppers and tenants. The onset of the green revolution may have been a factor impelling some landowners to evict tenants, but it is worth noting that the decline in tenancy in the Punjab largely took place in the 1950s, prior to the onset of the green revolution.[26] Moreover, tenancy continues to remain high both in Punjab and Haryana.

In assessing what changes have occurred in the well-being of agricultural laborers, two factors must be kept in mind. One is that many agricultural laborers are also small farmers—about 12 million households or 15% of all rural households in India. A second consideration is that many agricultural laborers have other income sources—not only from land, but from dairying, poultry, and from nonagricultural employment. For India as a whole the landless and near landless derive only 50% of their income from agricultural labor. Agricultural wages are thus not the only measure of rural income among the poor.

Rural unemployment and underemployment remains high in India. The high population growth rate of the past fifteen years assures an annual growth in the number of people entering the rural labor force. Rural employment may increase faster than the growth in the labor force if there is a growth in demand for farm employment as a consequence of multiple cropping and more labor intensive agriculture, an increase in employment in ancilliary farming activities such as dairying, poultry, fisheries and forestry, or an increase in non-farm employment. But for the country as a whole there does not thus far appear to be any significant diversification of the rural occupational structure along these lines.

However, in areas where there have been high rates of agricultural growth over a considerable period of time there is some evidence of an increase in rural employment.[27] Increasing employment has resulted from multiple cropping and from what economists describe as "forward" and "backward" linkages. Forward linkages refers to the increased economic activity and resulting employment for marketing, processing and transporting farm outputs. Backward linkages creates labor demand as a result of a growing demand by farmers for inputs like fertilizers, fuel, machinery, pesticides and the systems to produce, transport, market and repair them. Employment is also generated by the growth in credit and extension services and power and transport infrastructures. There are also multiplier effects: the increased demand for bicycles, furniture, bricks, utensils, improved farm implements, irrigation pumps and electric motors are often met by small engineering workshops located in rural towns.

Against these positive effects on employment of agricultural growth one must also assess the possible negative consequences of increased mechanization. While some mechanization may increase agricultural employment by making multiple cropping possible, some mechanization, especially of harvesting and processing, may reduce agricultural employment. After reviewing the many studies that have been conducted on this subject, Singh concludes that the net effects on rural employment are positive, but that they can be dampened considerably by the use of capital intensive technologies.[28]

Capitalist Farming in Punjab

What have been the distributive effects of agricultural growth in Punjab? This state, with nearly 17 million people, was among the first to feel the impact of the green revolution and it has had the highest agricultural growth rate. An assessment of what has happened here may throw some light on the distributive effects of the green revolution elsewhere in the Third World.

Early reports on the distributive effects of the green revolution in Punjab were generally negative. The large farmers adopted the new technology while the smaller farmers did not. Some small farmers sold out to the larger farmers. The new technologies, especially the use of tractors, initially appeared to be labor saving. Some landowners "resumed" cultivation, forcing tenants to become agricultural laborers. Some of the early reports indicated an absolute increase in rural poverty. Two widely read studies, one by Wolf Ladejinsky, the other by Francine Frankel, provided evidence that the lot of the rural poor was deteriorating.

Recent studies suggest that the initial reports were alarmist. Smaller farmers, as we have noted earlier, have adopted the new technology. The number of agricultural laborers tripled from 1961 to 1981 and real agricultural wages rose, though only by a modest 15% from 1961 to 1981. The percentage of landless households declined from 1954–55, 1961–62 and 1971–2 from 37%, to 12% to 9%. The percentage of farmers with less than five acres rose from 32% to 58% to 60% of the rural population during this period while the larger farms with over 25 acres declined from 37% to 30% to 23%. What negative displacement of labor has resulted from the use of tractors seems to have been offset by rapid agricultural growth.

The impact of the green revolution on income distribution among cultivating households in the Punjab is the subject of a study by G. S. Bhalla and G. K. Chadha. This study is based upon a survey of 1,663 farming households in 180 villages. Bhalla and Chadha report that small and marginal farmers "compare very well with farms of larger sizes as regards output per acre."[29] They note that small farmers also derive some income from non-agricultural activities, from poultry and dairy farming and wage employment in and outside of agriculture. They find no evidence of distress land sale among small farmers. There has been some increase in the proportion of agricultural laborers, but it appears to be due to an influx of workers from other sectors of the economy or immigration of labor from outside the state, not a decline in the number of owner cultivators. They conclude that "all categories of cultivators have been able to record substantial increases in their output and income through the adoption of new technology."[30] *While there are inequalities in the distribution of gains, they report that small farmers record almost as much an increase in productivity as the bigger farmers.*

A much cited study by Montek Ahluwalia, however, though generally optimistic about the effects of agricultural growth on reducing the incidence of poverty throughout India, concludes that "the most disquieting feature of our results is the evidence from Punjab and Haryana which does not support the hypothesis that improved agricultural performance will help reduce the incidence of poverty. This region has experienced a dramatic growth in agricultural output per rural person but there is no evidence of a downtrend in the incidence of poverty. . . . the poorest 25% of the rural population experienced stagnant levels of real consumption."[31] But Ahluwalia suggests that the explanation may be that *an increasing portion of the bottom 25% consists of migrants from other states,* an argument supported by evidence of increased in-migration and increased labor demand. "This group consists increasingly of individuals whose consumption is higher than it would have been if they had not migrated. In other words, 'trickle-down' benefits have taken the form of increased employment benefiting migrants from other states, rather than increased wages benefiting the preexisting poor."[32]

Finally, a variety of reports on life in Punjab villages describe an improvement in food consumption, clothing, medical care, and improved housing for the poor. Most striking of all is the growth of urban employment which increased by 50% between 1971 and 1981. Agricultural growth has apparently been a stimulus for the entire economy, especially for the numerous small workshops that produce consumer goods.[33]

The Argument Recapitulated

Efforts to assess the impact of the growth of market-oriented capitalist agriculture in India have proved difficult for five reasons. One is that scholars often disagree as to the validity of the evidence. National surveys are sometimes at variance with intensive village investigations, with the latter generally more positive about the effects on the rural poor than the former. Moreover, some scholars question the data on changes in land ownership, while others question data on increasing impoverishment among the rural poor. Secondly, even when there is agreement on facts, there are disagreements as to causes. How, for example, does one decide whether an increase in the number of agricultural laborers is the result of land reform legislation that has led to the eviction of tenants, market agriculture that had led to the selling of land by small landowners, or a population increase among the rural poor? Agrarian changes can often alternatively be explained as a consequence of agrarian policies, demographic factors, or by the growth of capitalist agriculture. The scholar's interpretation is often determined by his theoretical orientation. Third, agricultural growth rates have been high in India by both historical and comparative standards, but the growth rates on a *per capita* basis nonetheless remain low because of high population growth. *Even in high growth areas, per capita growth rates have been modest when viewed from a twenty year perspective. Under these conditions, whatever benefits might accrue to the poorest classes are bound to be limited.* Agricultural wages are up, but only modestly. More agricultural workers are employed, but not nearly enough to provide employment for all those entering the labor force each year. Elsewhere in the world it has been the urban industrial sector and urban services that have been labor absorptive. Green revolution areas in India have made greater use of labor, but given the already intense use of labor it is hard to conceive of any agricultural strategy or agricultural growth rate that could absorb the projected increases in manpower. As we have noted, *the sharp decline in mortality rates during the past several decades, while an indication of improved well-being, also increases the absolute number of people in the lower income categories.* If population growth rates are greater among the lower- than middle- or higher-income groups, one would expect, other things being equal, a proportionate increase in the number of poor, even though a high agricultural growth rate may absorb *some* additional labor.

A fourth difficulty in assessing costs and benefits is that the effects are not limited to those who live within the areas experiencing high agricultural growth. An end to below-market procurement prices, for example, may temporarily increase food prices to the detriment of the urban poor, but increased peasants purchases for urban consumer goods, farm machinery, fertilizers, and pesticides benefits urban employment. Moreover, an increased demand for agricultural workers may provide employment opportunities for the rural poor from other regions by inducing migration. Finally, there continues to be confusion over the difference between equality as a *relational* notion, and well-being (or immiseration) as an *absolute* notion. Inequalities can be growing, but the poor may be better off in an absolute sense while in a situation of low economic growth, policies could increase equality but make the poor worse off.

Nonetheless, I am persuaded that a close examination of the evidence from areas of India where the growth of market agriculture has resulted in increased productivity leads to the conclusion that the population of these areas, including many among rural poor, are better off than in those areas that have not experienced comparable rates of agricultural growth. *There is persuasive evidence that in the high growth areas the number of middle size farmers has increased, that many who were landless now own some land (if only houseplots), that agricultural wages and employment have gone up, and that nearby towns have prospered.* At the same time India continues to have a vast impoverished population whose numbers are increasing, for even in high growth areas the number of poor has grown. But it is critical to note that in the absence of the agricultural growth that India has maintained over the past twenty years, the rural poor would be even more numerous and poorer.

One striking statistic is that India's mortality rate has declined from 23 to 14 per thousand from 1960 to 1979, a decline of 40.5%. In contrast, in the average low income countries of the Third World, mortality rates dropped by 35%. In Africa, where agricultural growth rates have been lower than that of India, mortality rates have declined at a lower rate.

A second point that needs emphasis is that *the introduction of market agriculture does not necessarily ensure an improvement in the well being of the rural poor.* The position of small farmers, for example, can improve or worsen depending upon government policies. Small farmers need assistance in acquiring technical know-how, and in gaining access to transportation, warehouses, and a variety of agricultural inputs; most of all, they need access to credit on comparable terms given to richer farmers. The market does not ensure equal access to small and large farmers alike.

Nor should one assume that allowing cultivators the right to acquire any and all forms of labor-saving machinery will necessarily lead to greater productivity on the land and more employment for all. Farmers may choose to utilize machinery because it is more profitable to do so, because it may be more reliable to use machinery than to employ agricultural workers, or for reasons of status. It is not unreasonable that policy makers permit farmers to import some machinery (e.g. diesel pumps for the tube wells, and tractors) but not other equipment, such as harvesters, which may reduce labor use without increasing productivity per acre.

Nor is it unreasonable for policy makers to impose a ceiling on the acquisition of new land, otherwise small farmers may be induced to sell before they have acquired the wherewithall to make their land more productive and more profitable. The land ceiling legislation in India may not have resulted in any massive redistribution of land, but it probably prevented an increase in the concentration of land holdings.

Finally, an increase in procurement prices paid by government can be an important incentive for the growth in investment by farmers, but it can present a cruel dilemma for policy makers. Price incentives are not only necessary for producers, but they are also necessary if agricultural wages are to rise. But high agricultural prices leave the underemployed and unemployed worse off. The alternative, of course, can be worse. Artifically maintained low food prices mean lower agricultural wages, a low rate of agricultural growth, an increase in food import, a reduction in resources available for industrial investment, and reduced demand by farmers for urban produced consumer goods. Moreover, it is critical to recognize that as productivity increases and the unit cost of producing food declines the free market price for the consumer goes down.

There is no hidden hand which ensures that any and all forms of capitalist agriculture must necessarily improve the well being of the poor. On the other hand, there is no evidence that capitalist agriculture must necessarily lead to immiseration. One can even be more positive: capitalist agriculture, at least as it has developed in India, increases the possibility that the lot of the rural and urban poor can be improved. But what kind of growth takes place and how the benefits are distributed ultimately depends upon the package of public policies adopted; an extension of irrigation to dry regions, public investments in roads and in electricity, more research and development on the improvement of agricultural technologies, a progressive agricultural income tax, and various land reform measures are all compatible with a market-oriented system of agriculture.

The Consequences of Alternative Perspectives

The belief that market-oriented policies must necessarily worsen the position of the rural poor can be an impediment to the adoption of policies that do in fact ultimately improve rural well being. A case can be made that this indeed happened in India. In the 1950s and 1960s many Indian policy makers and economists argued that agricultural growth in the context of capitalist agriculture would result in growing immiseration. This belief in the inegalitarian consequences of capitalist agriculture led many policy makers to oppose price incentives that would enable farmers to invest in the HYV seeds, fertilizers, pesticides and other agricultural inputs. The issue was sharply drawn in 1966 when neoclassical critics within the government took issue with the government's agricultural policies.[34] Their arguments were strengthened by the reality of India's growing dependence upon imported food and by pressure from the international aid community, including the World Bank, the International Monetary Fund, and the U.S. Agency for International Development. Opposed to the new agricultural policies were those who argued that higher agricultural prices would adversely affect the poor, that the use of high yielding variety seeds would benefit rich farmers and increase rural inequality, that increased imports of fertilizers, pesticides, and machinery would drain foreign exchange reserves, and that by making the larger farmers more prosperous, they would become politically more powerful and make it still more difficult to carry out land reforms.

The advocates of the new agricultural policies won. But even their strongest supporters recognized that additional measures had to be taken to improve the well being of agricultural laborers and small marginal farmers. Thus, the Janata government (1977–79) pursued policies of expanding rural works programs providing credit for small farmers, encouraging new programs, for animal husbandry, and a variety of other measures to increase employment and income for the rural poor.

Nonetheless, from time to time policies have been adopted that reflect the older point of view. At various times in the 1970s paddy prices were kept low. A 1977 study by the Asian Development Bank reported that paddy prices in India were below that of other developing countries and below the prevailing market price while procurement prices for wheat were close to the market price. [35] At other times the government, viewing the private trader as a threat to its control over procurement, issued rice-milling licenses primarily to cooperative and to public sector firms and threatened to nationalize the entire grain trade. The result, according to one analyst, is that there was little private investment in either storage or milling facilities, even though the marketing costs of private traders had been well below government agency costs.[36]

Though government officials asserted that their primary purpose was to reduce costs by eliminating the middle man, critics believed that their primary objective was the political one of increasing control over the grain market.

Government also imposed restrictions on the interstate movement of grains (known in India as "zonal" restrictions) to prevent grain moving privately from low price surplus to high price deficit areas. To prevent grain from moving out of high producing districts and states, the government would throw a cordon around the region; prices would fall when crops arrived in the market. The government would then buy wheat at the "prevailing" market price which had been arbitrarily forced down. The system, according to one analyst,[37] actually forced the smaller farmers who needed money to sell more readily than the richer farmers who could sit out the blockade.

When world foodgrain prices rose and production costs went up in 1972–73, the government of India banned the private trade in wheat and imposed zonal restrictions to secure a monopoly on procurement. Government was then able to procure wheat at less than the real market price, but some of the wheat moved into a free market underground. Subsequently, government shifted its policy to buy half of the farmers' output and permitted the remainder to be sold in the free market.

One prediction of the critics of the new agricultural policy has proven to be correct. The better off farmers have acquired more political clout and have made it increasingly difficult for government to pursue policies that hurt their interests. Wheat farmers are now able to obtain better prices from the government. As the farmers of the better irrigated paddy fields both in Punjab and in the Krishna and Kaveri deltas in South India have become more powerful, they have also successfully pressed government for more remunerative prices for rice. It has become increasingly difficult for government to adopt policies that run counter to the interests of the millions of Indian peasants now cultivating for the market. Moreover, some of the earlier critics of the green revolution have modified their position, recognizing that India's rural poverty is not the consequence of nor made worse by capitalist agricultural growth. Land reforms are advocated, but few would now argue that capitalist agriculture should be halted until land reforms are adopted. Indeed, more attention is given to how irrigation can be extended, access to credit broadened, what can be done to strengthen the position of small farmers, and what assets (e.g. milk producing cattle) can be made available to the landless and near landless.

But even many of the most ardent supporters of capitalist agriculture are prepared to put some brakes on the demands of the farmers. One issue is *how much* incentive need be provided? To what extent should inputs be subsidized and support prices raised? A second issue is the question of agricultural income taxes, currently so low as to leave the increases in income earned by the agrarian sector virtually untaxed. And the third issue is the question of what kinds of restrictions should be imposed on the import and use of farm machinery that might significantly reduce the use of farm labor in a country where the prospects of absorbing surplus labor into the urban sector remain so slim.

There is also the question of what policies can best *extend* high growth capitalist agriculture to areas that, often for many different reasons, have not yet felt its impact. In some areas the constraint is the lack of assured irrigation and dependence upon rain-fed agriculture. But in some areas where irrigation is available, land tenure systems deprive non-owning cultivators of incentives. How best to extend capitalist agriculture is, for some of the relevant ministries and for the international aid agencies, a central issue.

Capitalist Agriculture, Class Formation, and Political Behavior

The impact of the spread of capitalist agriculture on the class structure in a society characterized by social hierarchy has been a major issue in India and among scholars of India. Many Marxists (and those influenced by Marxism) take a reductionist position, inferring the emergence of certain "class" attitudes and behavior from new class formations. Indeed, as we have noted earlier, for some Marxists the *absence* of class conflict even suggests that capitalist agriculture has *not* emerged!

Some Marxists advocate agrarian policies that would squeeze out the small farmers in order to create a polarized class structure. Eager to win support from the peasants, both rich and poor, who seek better terms of trade with the city, India's communist parties have actually advocated *higher* procurement prices for grain, but their support is over the objection of many Marxists who believe that low prices, by squeezing out the smaller farmers, would intensify class struggle within the countryside. One Marxist supporter of higher prices admitted that "a better price situation would help the peasants to cling on to and cultivate their parcels of land and that this (would) retard the development of capitalism," but only, he writes, the "landlord path of capitalist transformation."[38]

One of the most interesting theoretical questions is whether the creation of capitalist agriculture in an overwhelmingly agrarian society with such a large and rapidly expanding population will set in motion forces (or in Marxist terms, "contradictions") that will ultimately lead to its own destructions. The positive answer given by Marxists rests upon the assumption that agrarian capitalism leads to class polarization which in turn leads to class conflict. Neither of these arguments hold for India ("not *yet,*" Marxists may retort.) In a country of nearly seven hundred million, India has experienced virtually every kind of political conflict imaginable. Those who want to find examples of conflicts between agricultural laborers and landowners, between tenants and landowners and money lenders and between small cultivators and large landowners can readily do so; but one can also find numerous examples of rural coalitions that cut across class lines, or sharp political cleavages based upon caste, religious, or linguistic differences that are also independent of class. In fact, some of the most articulate and influential political movements of the past few years have been more closely related to regional than to class issues: in Assam, for example, a major political movement developed to protest the infiltration of large numbers of illegal migrants from Bangladesh; in Punjab, a minority of Sikhs disrupted the state by demanding an enlarged autonomous and virtually independent state; in Goa, a "sons of the soil" movement erupted, leading to the forceful ejection of substantial numbers of Kannada-speaking workers; in Andhra, a film star organized a regional party that defeated the Congress party in state elections. In some areas, especially in the north, there have been Hindu-Muslim tensions, and conflicts between ex-untouchables and some of the lower Hindu castes.

The most significant class-oriented rural movement has been by farmers demanding higher procurement prices and subsidized inputs. Farmer agitations have assumed mass proportions in Karnataka, Tamil Nadu and especially in Maharashtra where one farmer leader articulated the slogan "Bharat versus India," using the Hindi word for India as a symbol of the rural areas, and the English word for the urban centers.

If any one feature characterizes these various forms of politics it is that *protest and demand making is advanced among the more modern and mobile sectors of Indian society:* farmers who gained from the green revolution, the urban middle class, and the more advanced, upwardly mobile sectors of the Muslim, ex-untouchable and tribal communities. There are no indications thus far that the lower social classes, especially those who are worse off, are in the forefront of political agitations. Earlier arguments that the green revolution would turn red as immiseration among the lower classes grew do not appear to be valid. The farmer movements in Andhra, Karnataka, Tamil Nadu, and Maharashtra, the regional movements in Punjab, Andhra, Assam, Goa, and elsewhere, and the workers movement in Bombay are all within the more developed regions or among the more advanced social strata.

Some scholars have argued that the erosion of traditional reciprocal obligations between landlords and their tenants, agricultural laborers and sharecroppers, and their replacement by wage relations (from "status" to "contract," in the terms of modern sociology) would liberate the lower classes for class struggle against their exploiters. The fallacy of this argument is not only its presumption that class interest will be paramount over religious, caste, regional and sectoral identity, but that any *single* form of political identity will prevail. In fact, political identity is quite contextual. Agricultural workers may support the claims of farmers for higher procurement prices, persuaded that only if farmers earn more can laborers' wages go up; at other times, agricultural workers may be mobilized along ethnic lines or as untouchables or as Muslims engaged in conflict with middle and higher caste Hindus; and at still other times, agricultural laborers may band together to demand higher wages. Much depends upon leadership, opportunities, circumstances. Small farmers may clash with larger farmers over gaining access to irrigation facilities or credit from the local banks, but they may join together in demanding high procurement prices from government; indeed, some smaller farmers, given their lower margins, may be as anxious about higher agricultural prices as larger farmers.

Moreover, in India's democratic electoral system there is virtually no limit to the kind of appeals made by party leaders. Competing political leaders belonging to the same class, caste, or religious community may pull their group in different political directions. It is well known that in democratic systems there are strong tendencies for political parties to make appeals that cut across classes. In short, given India's social complexities, the structure of its political life, and the presence of overlapping rural interests, there is no reason to expect rural politics to take a *class* form although they may take a *mass* form.

Here and there class conflicts may erupt in the Indian countryside and in some instances, especially when urban radicals take the lead, a local political movement may even call for revolutionary change, but neither past experience nor any well-founded contemporary theory should lead us to expect any mass movement for the overthrow of agrarian capitalism.

Opposition to India's emerging agrarian capitalism is more likely to surface in urban areas. Urban dwellers have an obvious interest in keeping food prices down; urban radicals look upon the rural poor as a potential revolutionary army; and westernized intellectuals have a preference for "modern" class politics rather than "traditional" politics based upon religion, caste, and tribe. Moreover, many intellectuals, as Schumpeter once wrote, have a vested interest in social unrest, while large state-run bureaucratic structures often try to undermine independent entrepreneurship and innovation. The pervasiveness of neo-Marxist perspectives is so great among Indian intellectuals that it is widely assumed that a pro-equalitarian outlook must necessarily be anti-capitalist. Equality and capitalism are assumed to be incompatible.

The Governor of the Reserve Bank of India, for example, concluded an analysis of agricultural policy by saying that "growth and equity will not be adequately harmonised" under capitalist farming and that "the only answer then—whether feasible or not—would be some form of collectivisation of agriculture not so much because it is superior to a capitalist form of agriculture in terms of efficiency or production but because it offers, if I may put it that way, better chances of disguising unemployment in a socially acceptable form. In developing countries with a slow rate of growth and considerable unemployment, socialisation of the means of production and particularly of land may thus have its primary justification not so much in the interest of growth as in the interest of equity."[39]

It is striking that many Indian intellectuals and bureaucrats refer to India's better off farmers as "kulaks," a term with its unmistakable implication of a class that is to be liquidated.[40] Agrarian capitalism in the Soviet Union, it should be recalled, was destroyed not by the uprising of poor peasants, but by the *state* when peasants refused to sell it grains at unremunerative prices. Unable to feed the urban areas, the army, and to export, and unwilling to pay higher prices to the peasants, the Communists launched their war against the peasantry in the name of repressing capitalist kulaks. No such move is possible in a country that remains democratic. For this reason the vitality of India's capitalist agriculture is closely linked to the persistence of its democratic system.

NOTES

For suggestions and comments on this paper I am grateful to Paul R. Brass, Morris David Morris, Abraham Weisblat, Pranab Badhan, Robert Lucas, the late Raj Krishna, Francine Frankel, George Rosen, Norman Uphoff, John Mellor, Joshua Cohen, Paul Streeten, Philip Oldenberg, Richard Eckaus, and Ronald Herring, none of whom, of course, have any responsibility for what is written here, and some of whom, I know, take exception to some of my views.

1. Teodor Shanin, *The Awkward Class: Political Sociology of Peasantry in a Developing Society: Russia 1910–1925*. Oxford at the Clarendon Press, 1972, p. 1.

2. According to one study, procurement prices for wheat in some years was close to the market price, while the procurement price for rice was 20% below the market price. See C. H. Hanumantha Rao, *Technological Change and the Distribution of Gains in Indian Agriculture*. Delhi: Macmillan Co. of India, 1975.

3. Francine R. Frankel, *India's Green Revolution: Economic Gains and Political Costs*. Princeton: Princeton University Press, 1971, p. 39.

4. *Ibid.*, p. 108.

5. *Ibid.*, p. 177.

6. For a review of the Marxist debate on agrarian classes and modes of production in rural India, see the three part series by Alice Thorner, "Semi Feudalism or Capitalism," *Economic and Political Weekly*, Dec. 4, 11, 18, 1982). Thorner deals with three issues in this debate: (1) Is Indian agriculture capitalist, pre-capitalist, semi-feudal or dual and if not capitalist do these modes impede agricultural growth? (2) What are the principal rural classes and to what extent do they conflict? (or in Marxist terms, what are the "contradictions" in rural India?) (3) What are the implications for political action by left parties that follow from the answers given to these questions?

7. Quoted by Thorner, *Ibid*, p. 1965.

8. *Ibid.* p. 1964.

9. The importance of the middle peasants is described by Pradhan Prasad, Pranab Bardhan, Kalpana Bardhan and John Harriss. For a review of their positions, see *ibid* p. 1996.

10. For a discussion of the Marxist view of the family farm as a noncapitalist form of agriculture see Susan A. Mann and James M. Dickinson, "Obstacles to the Development of a Capitalist Agriculture," *Journal of Peasant Studies*, July 1978, pp. 466–481. The argument is that if there is no separation of labor and capital there is no capitalism and, (by definition), no class exploitation.

11. Asok Mitra, "The Terms of Trade, Class Conflict and Classical Political Economy," *Journal of Peasant Studies*, January 1977. The impoverished peasant proprietor, writes Mitra who "tenaciously clings to his individual plot, thereby reducing the scope of higher output and larger capital formation, is to be excommunicated" according to this perspective. (p. 189).

12. P. C. Joshi, *Land Reform in India—Trends and Perspectives*. Bombay: Allied Publishers, Ltd. 1975, p. 19.

13. Mead Cain, *Landlessness in India and Bangladesh: A Critical Review of the Data Sources*. New York: Population Council, May 1981.

14. *Ibid.*, p. 8.

15. Inderjit Singh, *Small Farmers and the Landless in South Asia*. Washington, D.C.: World Bank, 1981. This massive study brings together data from an exceptionally wide variety of sources.

16. In personal letters Ronald Herring and Pranab Bardhan dispute Singh's

findings on land ownership, arguing that the reason land ownership distribution data shows a decrease in inequality is that there is an increase in the underreporting of land in the larger size class induced by the land legislation.

17. Sheila Bhalla, "Agricultural Growth: Role of Institutional and Infrastructual Factors," *Economic and Political Weekly*, November 5, 1977. p. 1901.

18. See Wolf Ladejinsky, *Agrarian Reforms as Unfinished Business*. New York: Oxford University Press, 1977. This important collection of papers contains Ladejinsky's field reports on Sihar and Punjab as well as his more general writings assessing the impact of the new agrarian policies. Written between 1968 and 1974, these essays still remain among the most valuable assessment of the green revolution. In his articles on Punjab, Ladejinsky reports that demand for casual labor had increased, wages for landless laborers were up, small farmers had begun to produce for the market, and the yields attained from the new technology, given the availability of water, were the same for small as well as for larger farmers. But Ladejinsky remained concerned over the worsening position of tenants, the greater benefits obtained by larger landowners, the failure of the credit system to adequately help small farmers and tenants, and the structural impediments to the technological changes in some areas, especially in Bihar.

19. For a description of agricultural stagnation in Bihar, see Kusum Nair, in *Defense of the Irrational Peasant: Indian Agriculture after the Green Revolution*. Chicago: University of Chicago Press, 1979. See also Ladejinsky, *Ibid.*, pp. 442–462.

While land reform in Bihar may be a precondition for rapid growth, there is, of course, no assurance that land reform in itself need make a difference. Kerala, for example, is widely regarded as having passed the most stringent land reform legislation of any state, but its rate of agricultural growth is well below that of the high growth green revolution states. Clearly other factors can be at least as critical—the availability and management of irrigation, technology, credit, etc.

20. There can be a variety of reasons for an increase in the number of middle size farms, including at least one spurious one. A farmer with 20 acres may put 10 acres in his wife's name in order to evade ceiling legislation; a multiplication of middle-size holdings has taken place, but there is no change in the concentration of land by families. The same farmer may also divide his land among his three sons. The result may again be an increase in the number of holdings (a legal concept), but not in the number of household farms (an operational concept). However, the sons may in fact partition the holdings; in this case demographic factors lead to an increasing subdivision of operational holdings in India.

21. Raj Krishna, "Small Farmers Development" *Economic and Political Weekly*, May 26, 1979. p. 913.

22. John W. Mellor, *The New Economics of Growth: A Strategy for India and the Developing World*. Ithaca: Corness University Press, 1976., p. 82.

23. Inderjit Singh. *op. cit.* Chapter 1, page 2.

24. M. S. Ahluwalia, *Rural Poverty and Agricultural Growth in India* Washington, D.C.: World Bank, Development Research Center, 1977.

25. Inderjit Singh, *op. cit.* Chapter 1, page 31.

26. *Ibid.*, chapter 2, p. 103.

27. *Ibid*, chapter 8, page 1. Singh reports that there is evidence from East and West Punjab, Taiwan, South Korea and Malaysia.

28. *Ibid*, chapter 8, p 33.

29. G. S. Bhalla and G. K. Chadha, "Green Revolution and the Small Peasant—A Study of Income Distribution in Punjab Agriculture," *Economic and Political Weekly*, May 15, 1982 (part 1) and May 22, 1982 (part 2), p. 831.

30. *Ibid* p. 876.

31. Montek S. Ahluwalia, "Rural Poverty and Agricultural Performance in India," *The Journal of Development Studies*, vol. 14, no. 3, April 1978, p. 315.

32. *Ibid*, p. 316.

33. John Westley and M. C. Gupta, *Agricultural growth in India: Policies, Performance and Impact*, USAID, India May 1982, pp 52–74. Other assessments include M. S. Randhawa, *Green Revolution: A Case Study of Punjab*, New Delhi: Vikas, 1974; Richard H. Day and Inderjit Singh, *Economic Development as an Adaptive Process; The Green Revolution in the Indian Punjab*, Cambridge University Press, 1977; Biplab Dasgupta, *Village Society and Labor Use*, Delhi: Oxford University Press, 1977; Sheila Bhalla, "Real Wage Rates of Agricultural Labourers in Punjab, 1961–1977, *Economic and Political Weekly*, Review of Agriculture, June 1979; Murray J. Leaf" The Green Revolution in a Punjab Village, 1965–1978" *Pacific Affairs*, Winter 1980–81, pp 617–625; Gilbert Etienne, "India's New Agriculture: A survey of the Evidence," *South Asian Review*, Vol 6, no. 3. April 1973. For two studies focusing on agricultural wages and employment, see Robert W. Herdt and Edward A. Baker, "Agricultural Wages, production and the High Yielding Varieties," *Economic and Political Weekly*, Review of Agriculture, March 1971, p. A 23-A 30 and D. S. Tyagi, "How Valid are the Estimates of Trends in Rural Poverty," *Economic and Political Weekly*, June 26, 1982 which challenges the view that the incidence of poverty has been increasing.

In this paper I have cited only a small portion of what is now a substantial cottage industry of literature on the green revolution and its impact. Several other books and articles, not already cited, were particularly useful to me: Biplab DasGupta, *Agrarian Change and the New Technology in India*. Geneva: UN research Institute for Social Development, 1977; T. N. Srinivasan and P. K. Bardhan, *Poverty and Income Distribution in India*, Calcutta: Statistical Publishing Society, 1974; Donald W. Attwood, "Why Some of the Poor Get Richer: Economic Change and Mobility in Rural Western India," *Current Anthropology*, vol 20, no 3, September 1979; Dharma Kumar, "Changes in Income Distribution and Poverty in India: A Review of the Literature," *World Development*, vol 2 (1974); and *Poverty and Landlessness in Rural Asia*. Geneva: International Labour Office, 1977.

A distressing (but true) comment made by Ronald Herring in a personal communication—"For every source you cite in the text, there are contradictory sources not cited"—is a reminder not only how difficult it is to assess the equity consequences of north India's modest per capita agricultural growth, but how undramatic these effects have thus far been, one way or the other.

34. For an interesting first-hand report on the opposition to the introduction of HYV seeds and price incentives in 1966 see David Hopper, "Distributions of Agricultural Development Resulting from Government Prohibitions," in Theodore W. Schultz, ed. *Distortions of Agricultural Incentives*. Bloomington: Indiana University Press, 1978, pp 69–78.

35. Schultz, *op. cit.*, p. 16.

36. Uma Lele, "Considerations related to optimum pricing and marketing strategies in rural development," in *Proceedings*, 16th International Conference of Agricultural Economists, Nairobi, Kenya, 1976.

37. Prem Shankar Jha, *India: A Political Economy of Stagnation*, Oxford: Oxford University, 1980, p. 32.

38. Dev Nathan, "On Agricultural Prices," *Economic and Political Weekly*, December 25, 1982, p. 2104.

39. Dr. I. G. Patel, "On a Policy Frame Work for Indian Agriculture," Coromandel Lecture, New Delhi, 18th December, 1980, p. 38.

Capitalist Development on Taiwan

Gustav Ranis and
John Fei

I. Introduction

THERE CAN BE LITTLE DOUBT that when the history of
the second half of this century is definitively set down, the effort
of so many overseas territories to achieve modern growth will be
one of the more momentous events to be recorded and analyzed.
Moreover, at least until the impact of the change in the international environment of the mid- and especially the late 70's made
itself felt, there is also little doubt that the overall actual performance of the developing world was generally good with respect to
growth, i.e. exceeding on the average the post-war annual targets
of 2½% per capita, but rather unsatisfactory with respect to the
elimination of unemployment and the distribution of the gains
from growth, i.e. the distribution of income and/or the elimination of poverty.

When we disaggregate a bit more we find, of course, that this
generally satisfactory growth record itself hides very substantial
differences between the upper tier, or "middle class" of developing countries, heavily concentrated in East Asia and Latin America, and the really poor countries, heavily represented in South
Asia and Africa; moreover we note that the East Asian fast

growers have generally managed to combine this with good and
improving performance on distributional equity, while the Latin
American fast growers have not. Finally, disaggregating a bit
further, there is by now growing recognition that perhaps the
single best performing developing region in the post-war era is
represented by the case of Taiwan, a medium-sized member of the
East Asian group.

While several (or even one) exceptions to any general rule
admittedly do not prove the (contrary) case, it is also true, in the
social sciences as well as in mathematics, that they do tend to
disprove the general rule. Taiwan's experience, along with other
countries in East Asia, has proved that rapid growth is indeed
possible without having to sacrifice, perhaps for several decades, if
not forever, employment and distributional objectives. It is for
this reason that the Taiwan case in particular (as well as East Asia
in general) merits our special attention. If there is no inevitability
in nature attached to the necessity of a painful trade-off, then man
and his institutions can assert themselves. How then was this
minor miracle on Taiwan, of real per capita income growth rates
averaging more than 6% annually over three decades, coupled
with the elimination of unemployment and the continuous improvement (rather than deterioration) of all measures of equity,
achieved? And how relevant, or irrelevant, transferable or non-
transferable, is this experience for the rest of the developing
world?

This chapter is devoted to an examination of these two rather
important questions but with the expectation that we will be able
to shed light on them rather than provide definitive and in-
controvertible answers. Our approach to the problem will be to
first (Section II) examine the overall notion of LDC transition
growth abstractly both in its narrowly economic and its broadly
organizational contexts. Second, this scaffolding will be used for a
thumbnail presentation of the actual historical Taiwan case and
the specific reasons for Taiwan's success. Finally (Section IV), our
conclusions will be summarized and their potential relevance to
other parts of the developing world briefly assessed.

II. Transition Growth: Economic and Organizational Dimensions

The notion of transition growth which we shall adhere to in this
chapter is based on an essentially evolutionary view of develop-

ment. This metamorphic stance envisages the existence of sub-phases in the course of a transition from agrarianism to modern growth as defined by Simon Kuznets, with each of the subphases characterized by a distinct set of structural characteristics and a distinct mode of operation of the economy. By this we don't mean to imply any sense of inevitability or movement along a fixed historical path, but only to record what seemed to have been a set of evolutionary phenomena in many of the postwar developing countries, as well as, incidentally, in such "early late-comers" as Japan. Systems clearly may undergo different sequences or sub-phases due to differences in their policy choices and behavior over time. The evolution from one subphase to another is in turn related both to cumulative changes in the fundamental economic conditions, for example the end of labor surplus, and the pres-ence or absence of accommodating economic and institutional policy changes.

The recognition of the importance of subphases in the course of transition must thus be related to typological differences in initial conditions, both economic and organizational, as well as to changes resulting from the development of the system in a meta-morphic sense, on the one hand, and the effects of accom-modative or obstructive policy changes, both economic and organizational in nature, on the other. The analysis of "ideal" and "actual" transition growth paths, in other words, is best accom-plished by emphasizing typological differences among developing countries at the outset, i.e. conditions given by nature (or history), by internal forces making for structural change, and by the role of man and his organizational and economic policy choices.

To bring this matter down to earth we may usefully distinguish between a system such as Kenya, representing a relatively land-surplus, natural-resources rich, human-resources weak, "African type"; Mexico, representing a moderately labor-surplus, relatively natural-resources and human-resources rich, "Latin American type"; and Taiwan, representing a heavily labor-surplus, natural-resources poor, human-resources rich "East Asian type." Other important dimensions of the initial conditions on the economic side would include "size," hence the potential role of trade during the transition, as well as differing colonial antecedents, reflecting the quantity and allocation of infra-structural investments, and differences in religious and cultural antecedents as well as with respect to the method of economic organization selected.

Given such historically-determined or nature-given initial con-ditions, the beginnings of the transition growth effort may be set rather arbitrarily at the point where the system begins to move from its colonial resources allocation and trade pattern, during which it has mainly exported primary products in return for the importation of manufactured consumer goods for the purpose of attracting workers into the export enclave, as well as capital goods for the purpose of expanding the productive capacity of that same enclave.

The next subphase almost invariably constitutes an effort at industrialization via import substitution, with the newly politically independent system capturing control of its foreign exchange earnings and allocating them for building up the capacity to produce domestically the previously imported non-durable consumer goods. While this so-called primary import substitution subphase is shared by virtually all developing countries, when this *modus operandi* of the system runs out of steam, as, due to the exhaustion of the domestic market for these consumer goods, it eventually must, we may note a substantial and important deviation of the societal choices made. Some, i.e. the majority of LDC's, continue with import substitution, but this time shifting to the manufacture of capital and durable consumer goods and the processing of intermediate goods. Others, a minority of which Taiwan happens to be a member, shift towards something we call primary export substitution which basically consists of exporting into international markets the same non-durable consumer goods previously supplied only to domestic markets.

The majority choice, i.e. opting for secondary import substitution, means a continued emphasis on the domestic market, requiring continuation, if not intensification, of protectionist policy packages already in place, with the economy likely to be at a still somewhat greater distance from its international comparative advantage position. While production is now more costly and capital intensive, this choice nevertheless entails a continuation of rapid industrialization while it avoids the need for any major restructuring of the policy regime.

Such continued pursuit of import substitution, usually financed by continuing ample natural resource exports in combination with foreign capital inflows, is often coupled eventually with an effort to export some of the increasingly sophisticated range of industrial goods. This can, of course, be accomplished only by way of subsidy, provided either directly or indirectly—and is often accompanied by the continuation of a policy of discrimination against food-producing agriculture and by the increased importation of foodstuffs.

The minority cases, i.e. those which select primary export substitution, on the other hand, require a substantial shift in the policy mix summarized by the gradual removal of the protective devices favoring the new industrial class so that domestic prices can be brought into somewhat closer alignment with international prices. Consequently, the regimes associated with the primary export substitution choice of subphase are substantially closer to the free market paradigm, with industrial exports expanding on the basis of a dynamically changing comparative advantage, and entrepreneurs increasingly in a position to take full advantage of the abundant domestic supplies of unskilled labor en route to full employment.

The choice of the third transition subphase follows more or less naturally from the choice of the second already discussed. It is fair to say that an objective of all developing countries in making the effort at transition is to ultimately produce, both for the domestic market and for the international market, a wide and increasingly sophisticated range of industrial products. In the case of the minority this is likely to represent a natural sequel to primary export substitution in the sense that when one's labor surplus has been successfully absorbed and exported one experiences a "natural" tendency to shift towards the more capital and technology intensive mixes both for domestic and ultimately, depending on their size, export markets for this increasingly sophisticated set of commodities. For the majority, on the other hand, the combination of secondary import substitution with the promotion of exports on a selective basis essentially continues. Particular industries or individual firms are encouraged by administrative action to "push out" exports in the absence of a general shift in policies away from the import substitution package. As a consequence, whatever increase in industrial export orientation is recorded—and it is likely to be much less than in the minority case—it is caused less by the product cycle evolution, resulting from increased entrepreneurial maturation and changing comparative advantage, and more by the working of additional incentives planted "on top of" a pre-existing policy superstructure. This choice of sequence of subphases continues to be clearly much less export oriented overall and is characterized by a much lower proportion of manufactured exports than the minority case. Nevertheless it can continue as long as the fuel for the ever more costly industrialization effort, provided by natural resources and/ or foreign capital inflows, does not dry up. This is in contrast to the minority case in which the burden of financing continued industrialization along the product cycle is gradually shifted, first to the resources generated by the exportation of non-durable consumer goods, then the more sophisticated durable consumer goods, capital goods, and intermediate goods, thus gradually getting industry to pay for its own further expansion in terms of the required foreign exchange and savings funds.

We have several times, in passing, referred to the need for substantial policy change if the minority subphasing sequence is to run its course, from primary import substitution to primary export substitution to secondary import and secondary export substitution. In contrast, the alternative majority sequence (i.e. from primary import substitution to secondary import substitution coupled with export promotion) can avoid such, sometimes painful, changes in the productive structure. The societal choices implied here are related in part to differences in initial conditions, most probably, for example, differences in natural resource endowments and size. But they are also related to differences in organizational choice in a more basic sense and in terms of the ability to adjust such choices over time. While this matter is closely related to the issue of policy choices, these clearly do not take place in a vacuum but are related to an institutional/organizational typology which must constitute part of both the initial conditions and of changing behavior patterns over time.

We are here dealing with such matters as the initial organization of the society as between elements of feudalism, capitalism and socialism, i.e. the extent to which there is feudalistic intervention in markets, a relatively free play for the market, or pure socialist intervention in the market. Just as in the case of alternative economic resource typologies and alternative sequences of subphases, there are no "pure cases" in the real world with respect to this organizational dimension. In other words, when the curtain rises on the transition growth effort, most developing societies find themselves with some ingredient of at least feudalism and capitalism, with pure socialism less likely to be present. Capitalist elements are likely to predominate in the so-called organized industrial sectors, while agricultural sectors continue to reflect the aftermath of an economy just emerging from feudalism and only gradually being penetrated by market forces. Virtually all large developing countries share this feudalistic condition in at least part of their initially predominant agricultural hinterlands. But their subsequent choice as to the respective role of government and markets is relatively wide-ranging, from a preference for heavy intervention by the government in the form of public-sector ownership of most industrial enterprises, to indirect intervention in the market, mainly via fiscal, monetary, and exchange rate policies. The first is often referred to as direct or horizontal controls, the second as indirect or vertical controls.

The initial position on the mixed economy spectrum is thus usually heavily a function of history, i.e. closely related to the country's colonial experience before independence. In the majority of cases the overseas territories had witnessed a fairly strong administrative structure focused on law and order in their organized commercialized sectors, with colonialism associated with the rule of the market under these agreed rules of the game. The effort to change this configuration then yielded a certain inherent initial bias on behalf of government intervention of a direct or horizontal kind in the early post-independence period.

A second reason for the customary strong bias in favor of more government intervention and less reliance on markets in this early stage is, of course, the nature of the primary import substitution policy package itself which translates into selecting a particular class, often drawn from among the landed aristocracy or merchant groups, to receive particular favors through a direct allocation system; such favors include import licenses, under artificially overvalued foreign exchange rates, cheap credit, tariff protection, etc., all intended to provide windfall profits during an infant industry maturation process. The required administrative selection as to who shall live and who shall prosper of course requires a heavy emphasis on discretionary decisions and relatively small reliance on the automatic adjustment mechanism of markets. Consequently, both for historical/ideological reasons and due to very practical considerations, one finds developing countries typically making horizontally interventionist organizational and policy choices during their almost universally practiced initial primary import substitution subphase.

The state of modern growth in the Kuznets sense is associated not only with an attitude that emphasizes the role of science and technology but also with the forces of egalitarianism, secularism and nationalism. Unfortunately, and perversely, in the process of transition to that same modern growth, some of these cultural values, especially when embraced by latecomers, may, in fact, adversely influence the chances for successful transition, mainly because they bias the choice along the spectrum as between market determination and government intervention. Nationalism, for example, the claim of a community to be grounded in a common historical and cultural heritage, arises in part as a natural consequence of the opposition to colonialism. It therefore often takes the form of rejecting the tools, along with the objectives, of colonialism, therefore intrinsically inheriting a bias against the market and embodying a greater faith in the power of government intervention in the economic as well as political spheres. Similarly, with respect to egalitarianism, the denial of inherited differences among individuals, the legitimate desire to break down feudalism and thus move toward greater equality of opportunity, is often interpreted as trying to achieve quickly an equality of outcomes which can only be guaranteed by continuous government intervention. And finally, with respect to secularism, this worldly approach implying free occupational choices based on economic criteria, its effects in the transition as opposed to the final state of modern growth are less clear-cut and obvious; here also the authority of the state over the church often translates into an undue faith in the state's capacity to make all those directly allocative across-the-board decisions.

In the absence of a long entrepreneurial tradition, there usually exist considerable doubts in the early transition period with respect to the availability of the requisite human resources, their ability to bear risk and to perform the vital entrepreneurial functions. This leads to a tendency either for the government to want to take over the function or, more frequently, to attempt a careful administrative selection of those, thought to be more capable than others, to whom the various required pieces of paper, commanding necessary inputs at subsidized prices, were to be dispersed. With respect to the working class, there is a tendency toward egalitarianism which often reflects itself in an emphasis on minimum wage legislation, generosity in government hiring, and wage practices with a focus on wage rates rather than wage bills. An extension of this is, of course, an early acceptance of so-called state welfare legislation in a variety of areas, shifting somewhat prematurely from the family to the state as a provider of social and old age insurance. All this is usually coupled with a strong tendency to try to exclude foreigners from the system since they are seen as having participated in its colonial version.

The intervention by a group of, often Western educated, civil servants, focusing on the provision of public goods as assistance to indigenous elements, thus seems fully justified for both ideological and pragmatic reasons. The very understandable effort to distance oneself from the heritage of the past is joined with the practical concern of implementing an infant industry protectionist regime during which entrepreneurs need temporary protection against the world of the most advanced countries, the provision of infrastructure, plus, possibly, a redistribution of assets (such as land) at the outset, together yielding a very strong bias in favor of direct government intervention.

While this is understandable, certainly during the first subphase of transition, the proof of the pudding ultimately lies in the system's performance over time. As already indicated, when primary import substitution runs out of steam the vast majority of LDCs choose to persevere with the same policy regime directed towards a new set of goods and fueled by the same combination of natural resource exports and foreign capital inflows; the regime thus continues to depend heavily on direct government intervention. The minority choice, on the other hand, which requires a shift from import to export substitution, is highly correlated, as we have also indicated, with a substantial shift in that policy regime, based on a different organizational structure which moves the system in a more market oriented direction along the organizational choice spectrum.

How do developing countries indeed perform as they make substantially different economic/organizational choices in the course of their transition growth effort? This is a subject to which we will now turn. While our emphasis will be mainly on understanding and explaining the minority case, represented by Taiwan, the contrast with the less successful majority case which tends to continue to adhere more closely to its original view of the proper role of the state will, of course, be helpful.

III. The Taiwan Case in Comparative Historical Perspective

Taiwan is a member of the so-called small labor surplus LDC type located in the population-dense, natural-resources poor region of East Asia. Its initial conditions include a relatively high level of literacy and participation, within the Japanese empire, in a typical colonial pattern, i.e. exporting traditional agricultural products, rice and sugar, and importing consumer non-durables from Japan. Moreover, given the fact that the Japanese were interested in food as the colonial import, Taiwan was particularly favored by the relatively heavy attention paid to its rural infrastructure, including irrigation, power and transport. Thus at the time when the transition effort to modern growth can be said to have started (i.e. around 1951, subsequent to both independence from Japan and separation from the Mainland) Taiwan entered the previously described primary import substitution subphase with some natural advantages. Here, as elsewhere, a good deal of government intervention was called for in order to shift the allocation of the foreign exchange proceeds from export earning towards a new industrial class, but food producing agriculture started out with a much better base than is usually encountered.

Taiwan's metamorphosis out of colonialism meant that her traditional exports, in this case rice and sugar, remained the basic fuel of the system, but that these proceeds were now utilized to import producers' goods for the industrial sector's expansion; moreover, domestic markets for the non-durable consumer goods previously imported from the mother country could now be provided by domestic entrepreneurs under the cover of a good deal of protection. In fact, the import substitution strategy is almost entirely intended, by modifying the market system, to transfer income from farmers and consumers and provide temporary windfall profits to a new urban entrepreneurial class.

The tools of this policy regime are quite well known and were applied in Taiwan: a combination of tariffs and quantitative controls; an overvaluation of the domestic currency, worsening with inflation over time; artificially low interest rates; and other direct allocations by the government in markets for such scarce commodities as steel, power, etc. While this is almost universal, systems differ in the extent of their reliance on direct or indirect controls such as the use of quantitative restrictions versus tariffs, as well as in the extent of the choice of public enterprise versus private enterprise as the beneficiaries of the protection and other favored treatment being granted.

While Taiwan clearly followed the same early pattern of primary import substitution as other developing countries, we must also note that the levels of protection of the industrial sector, the extent of discrimination against the agricultural sector and the volume of intervention in the credit, foreign exchange and other markets for scarce inputs were all consistently and substantially lower than in the majority of developing country cases, such as in Latin America, Africa and other parts of Asia. Strong views about the inequities of colonialism and the deficiencies of the market mechanism often associated with it were in evidence here as well. It is nevertheless fair to say that nationalism, to the extent it means exclusion of foreigners and full faith in one's own bureaucrats to lead the country into modern growth, though clearly present also in Taiwan, was not as pronounced as elsewhere. Important infrastructural investment decisions, especially favoring the rural areas, were made. Intervention in the distribution of assets, e.g. land reform, took place, the recent experience on the Mainland not having been lost on the Government. Planned parenthood programs were instituted and, of course, industrial entrepreneurs enjoyed the usual package of favors. Nevertheless, if one tries to distinguish along a spectrum as to the extent or "weight" of government interventions during this primary import substitution sub-phase, using effective protection and extent of market price/shadow price distortion indicators—we can clearly classify Taiwan among the few relatively "mild" cases of primary import substitution.

However, once this subphase of transition comes to its inevitable end, developing societies have an even more crucial choice to make. They either continue with the import substitution package, but now focusing on intermediate goods, capital goods, and durable consumer goods production, mainly in the first instance for the domestic market; or they shift towards what we called primary export substitution; i.e. exporting the same non-durable consumer goods which were previously supplied mainly to domestic markets. Taiwan, like the other East Asian countries (Korea, Hong Kong, Singapore), as well as Japan at a much earlier date, chose to move towards primary export substitution, clearly a minority choice within the developing world. One could think of this as a very natural evolution for a labor surplus country, i.e., once domestic markets for labor intensive goods are exhausted, to export these to the rest of the world. However, given the hot-house conditions with respect to relative prices, rationing by direct controls, etc., established earlier, this requires a substantial shift in policies, i.e. a much greater reliance on markets, for foreign exchange, for credit, as well as a reduction in the effective protection rate; usually it implies as well a shift from direct to indirect controls, e.g. from quantitative restrictions to tariffs, followed by greater uniformity and a gradual reduction in these tariffs, as well as an improvement in the agricultural sector's terms of trade. Such a change in policy clearly implies a much greater overall reliance on the market mechanism rather than continuation of the dominant role of direct government allocative decisions.

This choice did not come overnight in Taiwan. Rather, it was the subject of long and acrimonious debates in the late 1950s. As domestic markets for nondurable consumer goods began to shrink, the high rate of growth of industry, to which entrepreneurs had become accustomed, began to decline and industrialists initially approached the government asking for more protection, cartelization and other types of intervention. Only after a time was the argument resolved in favor of a shift of the policy regime towards a much greater reliance on industrial exports requiring, in turn, a greater reliance on the market.

The reasons for this crucial set of decisions reached over a three or four year period of time are complicated and extremely interesting. They include such negative reasons as the underlying limitation of natural resources which ultimately tends to preclude the alternative of being able to continue fueling an increasingly inefficient and costly import substitution path; more positively, given the somewhat lower temperatures pre-existing in the primary import substitution phase, the competence of the system's entrepreneurial and other human resources could assert itself more readily to "send out" its labor surplus in the form of internationally competitive manufactured goods. While it does not always play this role, foreign assistance was also helpful in easing the pain of the policy changes which occurred between 1958 and 1961 in Taiwan.

Most observers focus on the industrial export orientation of this primary export substitution subphase. But less fully recognized is the important complementary mobilization of the agricultural sector which permitted the rapid reallocation of so many man-hours from agriculture to nonagriculture to fuel this process and permitted industrial exports for the first time to help finance the further expansion of nonagricultural activities. One may well say that in Taiwan, the period between 1961 and approximately 1970, i.e. the period of the most rapid growth of nondurable consumer goods exports, along with growth in domestic agriculture, represents the heyday of capitalism within the mixed economy framework. This is not to say that government intervention did not continue to be an important contributor, only that it took more and more the form of vertical or indirect interventions, e.g. in the fiscal and monetary arenas, plus investment in social overheads, e.g. the construction of export processing zones as a transitional device.

The direction, at any rate, was always clear: a reduction in the gap between market prices and equilibrium prices both in factor and product markets. The exchange rate was now being maintained at fairly close to equilibrium levels; interest rates were raised even though credit rationing continued to play some role—as it does in most countries—and both nominal tariffs and effective protection rates generally declined.

Perhaps most importantly, millions of individual farmers, mainly rural households participating increasingly as well in non-agricultural activities, were able to have more and more access to scarce inputs at a price, rather than having to queue up for "favors" with the allocative authorities, either those dispensing foreign exchange or domestic credit, or steel, or cement, or whatever else had a scarcity value and was being directly tagged to a favored class during the prior import substitution regime.

As far as entrepreneurial reaction to liberalization is concerned, it is, moreover, clear that the consistency in the trend of government policy is much more important than the actual average level of intervention. In other words, Taiwan, during the 60s in particular, was able to avoid the stop-go experience of so many developing countries which typically experiment with periods of liberalization followed by renewed restrictionism and intervention, only to be followed by yet another cycle of liberalization—all increasing the uncertainty on the part of market participants. There seems to be little doubt, on the basis of comparative development experience, that a policy more or less consistently adhered to, even if on the average less favorable, is to be much preferred to one which suffers from wide oscillations even if it is superior "on the average." There can be little doubt that the new environment created by the export substitution policy package, i.e. the 19 points of reform of 1959 to 1961, plus such institutional construction as the export processing zones, permitted the system to rapidly shift its exports from a raw-material to an unskilled-labor base.

The very success of this labor based "vent for surplus" development path means that it also ultimately has to come to an end—as it did in Taiwan in the late 1960s. The rapid reallocation of the labor force, doubling from three percent to six percent annually between the 50's and the 60's, far exceeded its natural rate of increase and led to the beginnings of labor shortage, as indexed by rising unskilled real wages in both agriculture and non-agriculture, by the end of the decade. Industrial output and manufactured exports now tended to become necessarily more skilled labor, technology and capital intensive; i.e. we may say that the subphase of secondary import and export substitution had been reached. In fact, as skills and both entrepreneurial and technological capacity continued to increase, Taiwan has, since the early 70s, moved into production for the domestic market and for export of intermediate goods, capital goods and consumer durables. At the same time the agricultural sector's productivity potential in the form of sustained increases in output has been substantially exhausted and, as that sector has now become less of a leading sector and more of an appendage to the rest of the economy, the underlying need of a basically natural-resources poor system like Taiwan to import food has begun to assert itself and will continue to do so in the future, subject only to considerations of food security.

What is important for our purposes here is that once the unemployment problem had been "solved," Taiwan, by the early 1970s, began on a path of continued adjustment of her industrial struc-

ture in the well-known dynamic comparative advantage (or product cycle) context that we are familiar with in the mature economy.
In a small country like Taiwan the wings of the so-called "flying
geese" pattern which characterizes this product cycle are likely to
be shorter; i.e. there is likely to be only a short gap, if any, between
import substitution in these more sophisticated commodities and
the need to export, given the more pronounced economies of
scale dominating the technologically more sophisticated industries. While there is some tendency for public enterprise and
government intervention to reassert themselves during the beginnings of secondary import substitution, it may be noted that
Taiwan has not yet yielded substantially to those pressures and is
continuing to maintain a relatively market-oriented environment.

The performance of the Taiwan economy between 1952 and
1980 has been nothing short of remarkable. Real per capita income growth rates, though now considered somewhat old-fash-
ioned, still signify an important enhancement of choice and
capacity in any society. Growth rates on Taiwan have been on the
average in excess of six percent per year, most rapid during the
60's but very respectable during the import substituting 50's and
70's as well. What is even more interesting, however, is that the
distribution of income improved substantially during the 50's,
continued to hold at very equitable levels during the rapidly
growing 60's and improved further after the end of the labor
surplus in the late 1960's. This combination of rapid growth with a
consistent improvement in the distribution of income runs counter to overall LDC experience as summarized in the so-called
inverse U-shaped or Kuznets Curve hypothesis.

The contrast with the majority of LDCs is quite sharp. In Africa
equity seems to have been fairly well maintained—except in places
like Nigeria—to the extent that statistics are available; however,
growth has been negligible. Elsewhere in Asia we note intermediate levels of performance with respect to growth and equity but by
no means as favorable in either dimension. In Latin America the
contrast is most sharp: growth rates, somewhat lower than those
of Taiwan but quite respectable by LDC standards, have been
maintained but linked with increases in unemployment and a
worsening of the distribution of income. To cite but one example,
in 1960 in both Taiwan and Colombia the income share of the
bottom 20% of households was 5%; by 1970 it had risen to 8.8% in
Taiwan and fallen to 3.2% in Colombia.

The reason for this unusually good performance on Taiwan,
clearly rendering output growth and equity improvement complementary "goods," can be found in the way output was gener-

ated. While we can't go into details in the context of the present chapter,[1] among the more important determinants of the family distribution of income is the pattern of the distributive shares as between non-agricultural wage and property income, which is, in turn, closely related to the technological flexibility and employ- ment generating capacity of the system as a whole. The employ- ment and income inequality consequences of a developing society's growth path can thus be analyzed in relation to the share of labor income which, if high and rising, is likely to lead to more overall equity—just as the simultaneous decline in the share of property income, which is less equally distributed, usually favors overall distributional equity. Thus, one major reason for the im- provement in equity in the presence of rapid growth on Taiwan was the rapid absorption of unskilled labor hours into new rural and urban industrial and service activities leading to a high and rising relative share of labor.

A closely related important element affecting this favorable growth cum equity outcome on Taiwan was the unusual spatially decentralized pattern of the industrialization process itself. Small- scale rural industries and services provided 30% of total rural family income in 1961, at the beginning of primary export sub- stitution, in contrast to more than 50% by the end of the decade, with higher percentages for the smaller (poorer) farmers throughout. Since income from rural nonagricultural activities was more equitably distributed than income from rural agri- cultural activities, this shift was important to the improvement of the overall rural family distribution of income. It was further aided by the fact that these rural nonagricultural service and industrial activities were very labor intensive and increasingly so as witnessed by high and rising shares of labor over the decade. As government intervention in the allocation of such scarce inputs as foreign exchange, credit, fertilizer, etc. kept diminishing throughout the 60's, it became much easier to avoid the normal discrimination against rural, medium and small-scale enterprises.

Agricultural incomes themselves also showed an improvement in terms of both equity and growth during the 50's and 60's, not only due to the initially favorable effects of land reform but also because new technologies were developed which rendered small farm household activities more productive over time and permit- ted a shift from more land intensive crops, such as sugar and rice, to more labor intensive crops such as mushroom and asparagus. Land was used more intensively for double cropping and showed evidence of the green revolution or labor-using type of tech- nology change. More importantly, poor farmers were able to participate more than proportionally in these new agricultural activities.

There can be little doubt that Taiwan was favored by her pre-existing rurally oriented colonial infrastructure, as already mentioned. But it should also be remembered that the post-colonial government maintained and expanded that infrastructure, thus encouraging vigorous balanced rural growth as between agricultural and nonagricultural activities—an essential if not always a spectacular feature of the success story on Taiwan. As rural industries provided more side-line employment and income-generating activities, the transport and urbanization costs of industrialization were reduced, permitting an effective compromise between economies of scale and market area. In addition, the proximity of a modern industrial sector in the rural areas, leading to frequent and close rural-urban contacts, contributed to the modernization of agriculture both in the incentives and market interactions sense.

We have, in other words, a tendency of dispersed decision makers in both rural and urban areas choosing more appropriate output mixes and technologies as there was a substantial reduction over time in relative factor price distortions as well as, in general, an increasingly competitive overall environment. The pronounced negative impact of a prolonged regime of windfall profits via the absence of pressure to choose better output mixes and technologies and thus on industrial sector growth is often underestimated. Import licensing systems, overvalued exchange rates, officially low interest rates for favored borrowers, and all the rest of the import substitution policy package, create an environment that induces satisficing rather than maximizing behavior. If it is true, as is now believed by the profession, even by some engineers, that there exists in nature a wide range of options, both in terms of imported and, more importantly, indigenous adaptive process and output specifications, it is clear that economic actors have to feel some pressure to engage in the necessary search and R&D activities. Reducing the hot-house temperature brought the Taiwan government into more of a catalytic rather than interventionist mode and thus materially improved dispersed producers' desires to search for appropriate processes and products and consequently their ability to sell competitively abroad. Such technological flexibility makes a huge difference in terms of both the employment generating capacity of rural balanced growth and in terms of finding the appropriate niche over time in both mature and other developing country markets.

It is impossible within the scope of this chapter to attempt to compare the Taiwan case in detail with that of the majority of the LDCs during their post World War II transition growth effort. Suffice it to say that growth rates during the primary import substitution subphase were generally as high in Latin America, for example, as in East Asia, which undoubtedly can be traced to the initially higher levels of natural-resource endowments and per capita incomes there. Africa and South Asia are probably less relevant, given their relatively less favorable starting point in terms of both natural and human resources. In general, we may be able to say that the import substitution policy package deployed is generally more severe elsewhere perhaps partly because it has been of substantially longer duration, especially in such regions as Latin America. This has led to an important consequence, i.e., a much greater relative neglect of the food-producing agricultural subsector and a reinforcement instead of colonial policy antecedents, concentrating attention on raw material exploration. Most crucial, however, is the aforementioned difference in the societal choice at the end of the primary import substitution subphase, with the majority choosing to move directly into secondary import substitution coupled with some export promotion, while, as we have seen, Taiwan, along with the other East Asian countries, chose to shift into the new pattern of what we have called export substitution.

Faced with a decline in the rate of industrial growth for nondurables in their protected domestic markets, the Latin American countries, in contrast, decided to shift to the manufacture of producers' goods, the processing of intermediate goods and the production of durable consumer goods in the 1950's—a pattern which requires not only the maintenance of the prior protection and controls oriented policy structure but also its further deepening and strengthening. As this orientation takes the system further away from its international comparative advantage position, we witness a much greater tendency to move quickly into the more sophisticated industries in terms of technology, the application of skilled labor and of capital. Almost invariably, the exportation of such commodities produced under a highly protective policy regime can be affected only via subsidies. The general pattern thus is one of the encouragement of particular industries or firms through public sector tax concessions, the granting of differential interest rates, or enforced private sector cross subsidization, e.g. by ensuring firms of continued high windfall profits in protected domestic markets in exchange for meeting industrial export targets set by the public authorities. Such "prolongation" of import substitution with the eventual addition of industrial export promotion is likely to be socially costly even if it can be made privately profitable by the proper set of interventions. It can be paid for, in the Latin American context for example, by favorable natural resources and/or foreign capital inflows which continue to "pay the piper" and help maintain respectable growth rates.

As the experience of Mexico, Brazil, Indonesia, and the Philippines makes clear, this effort to "skip" the labor intensive export substitution subphase means that the labor surplus is not mopped up en route to mature growth, and that both the employment and income distribution situations deteriorate through time. As protectionism and interventionism deepen, the discrimination against agriculture deepens and more of the proceeds from cash crop exports supplemented by foreign capital inflows have to be devoted to food imports. Instead of shifting away from traditional export cash crops and towards the usually more labor intensive food crops, we can observe lower labor absorption levels within agriculture and a worsening distribution of income in the rural areas. Industry tends to be more centralized, fairly large scale and urban; as a consequence, in a place like Colombia, only 15% of farm family income (declining to 10% over time) is generated in nonagricultural activities, in contrast to the 30 to 50% figures already cited for Taiwan. Nonagricultural activity, both rural and urban, often tends to be much more capital intensive, contributing much less to favorable employment and equity outcomes, as labor shares are typically markedly lower and falling as compared to Taiwan where they are higher and rising for the entire period under discussion.

The choice of continued direct interventionism of the import substitution type also means that output and technology choices continue to be made without the benefit of any competitive pressure or discipline from outside the system. As a consequence, the typical developing country case has seen a much greater inward orientation, i.e. a smaller relative participation in the world economy and much less structural change. Natural resources, in combination with foreign capital, continue to finance a more and more "expensive" urban industrial sector while food production and rural industry continue to languish—with substantial pockets of unemployment and underemployment persisting, along with poverty and a worsening overall distribution of income.

It is, of course, difficult to generalize about so many countries in the developing world; but the essential contrast between the majority and the minority case represented by Taiwan should by now be fully clear. Even in the period since 1973, when the international environment for all LDCs deteriorated considerably, the performance differential as between the minority and majority cases with respect to both growth and equity has been maintained. In other words, while everyone has been adversely affected by global stagnation, inflation, oil price rises, protectionism, etc., Taiwan's performance has continued to be remarkably better than that of the average developing country. It has accumulated less debt, has maintained very respectable (if lower than earlier) growth rates and has been remarkably resistant to the trend towards increased interventionism and protectionism currently in vogue in both rich and poor countries.

It remains for us to ask why more countries have not followed the Taiwan example, with appropriate modifications, of course. A basic purpose of any examination of the economic and institutional choices a system makes would be to attempt not only to distill conclusions relevant to an interpretation of that particular historical event, but also to see what is relevant and transferable to other developing societies and what is so "special" that it is unlikely to be applicable elsewhere. There are those who claim that these are all a matter of culture, that Chinese-derived societies are superior, in some sense "smarter" than others, and that this is sufficient to explain the minority case and its relative success. It is indeed difficult to render judgment on matters of that kind.

The forces of secularism embedded in the Confucian philosophy of egalitarianism represented by the competitive examinations system, and of nationalism providing strong cultural glue for a relatively homogeneous society, could undoubtedly be mobilized more effectively on behalf of the transition growth effort on Taiwan than in, say, Latin America. Their particular expression on Taiwan represents a set of cultural attributes not easily remediable by protection and other hot-house interventions by government and undoubtedly facilitated the conversion of a traditional population into a society with substantial economic and class mobility. We reject the frequently heard notion that much of the difference in performance can be simplistically laid at the doorstep of some superior human intelligence or racial advantage for the developmental task. Rather, we believe that much of the gap in performance can be explained in terms of different initial conditions, given by nature, reinforced by the ability or inability to overcome the resistance of powerful vested interest groups which often find it possible quite rationally to resist changes in policy of the kind followed by Taiwan and the other minority cases. In this task Taiwan's cultural preparedness was surely a great help, most notably in ensuring that nationalism could be enlisted on behalf of the transition effort rather than constituting an obstruction to it.

IV. Summary and Conclusions

In the real world, it should be remembered, economies move along an ambiguous, uncertain and non-monotonic path, usually lurching forward in one direction, moving sideways, often partially retracing their steps. Moreover, they are much too complicated as economic and institutional organisms to be as neatly packaged into either well-defined typologies or transition subphases as we have tried to do here, largely for reasons of expositional emphasis. In the same vein, characterizing the choice along the mixed economy spectrum between the use of direct controls and the rule of the market mechanism usually requires a subtle differentiation among many shades of gray, rather than between black and white. But, given the recognition of this array of subtle real world differences, it nevertheless does make sense to attempt to locate a system at any point in time.

Initial conditions are, indeed, provided by "nature," given the fact that we cannot trace them back to Adam and Eve and must agree on a point of departure for the attempted transition to modern growth. Given those initial conditions, there are indeed no inevitable sequences or unbreakable straitjackets. Instead, we accept the notion of a "natural" transition from a colonial pre-transition era to primary import substitution and on to export substitution as an empirically demonstrated accomplishment— adhering to Kuznets' view of the associated role of organizational and policy choice, i.e. that such transitions in the realm of institutional/organizational change can either be viewed as obstructing or accommodating the underlying economic forces at work. Changes in structure and in the mode of operation over time, as one moves from one subphase to another, must be related to cumulative changes in the fundamental international conditions, plus the presence or absence of accommodating institutional change to further the objectives of the majority of the participants in a society. Taiwan undoubtedly had some initial good luck in terms of its rural-oriented Japanese colonial masters plus a relatively high level of literacy. Once it had moved through its inevitable primary import substitution subphase it, moreover, had little choice but to eventually, after some hesitation, move towards a greater role for the market required by export substitution; i.e., given its relative natural resources poverty, to shift the engine of growth from land to unskilled labor by means of an overall liberalization strategy. Then, once its labor surplus had been successfully used up, Taiwan was able to shift into a technology and capital intensive phase of secondary import substitution coupled with secondary export substitution, a phase in which foreign technology imports play an increasingly important role, culminating ultimately in the modern growth regime in which a system begins to generate its own technology in a relatively routinized fashion.

This choice of a growth path was "wise" in the sense that government intervention could be viewed as a temporary aberration from rationality and not as a permanent way of "fighting against the endowment." The choice was also "necessary," given the absence of natural resources—plus the ultimate realization by government officials that policies needed to be changed, given the system's inability to support continuation of an import substitution strategy. The very nature of capitalism itself was thus changing as part of the transition on the institutional side. Import substitution was an important element of post-independence nationalism, i.e. a special type of nationalism which, along with egalitarianism and secularism, represents a central Chinese cultural characteristic at work. The notion that nationalism required intervention in the market on a quasi permanent basis could, however, rather quickly be discarded. The tendency to liberalize various markets and abandon the relatively large early role of public enterprises during the primary export substitution subphase of the 1960's can be interpreted as a willingness to retreat from the close identification between colonialism and the market mechanism, on the one hand, and nationalism and direct controls, on the other. In fact, the willingness not to give up on political nationalism but to let it manifest itself in more and more non-economic arenas, while utilizing the market mechanism for non-colonial, i.e. national development objectives, was clearly in evidence in Taiwan and the other East Asian minority cases.

Given the lack of feasible alternatives in the form of a continued, dependable flow of natural resource exports and/or generous foreigners to keep the process going, it became relatively easy for decision makers in Taiwan to convince industrialists that the effort would have to be made to shift to large volumes with small earned profit margins in selling to the rest of the world rather than trying to maintain high profits on low volume in a restricted and rapidly diminishing domestic hot-house environment. It was similarly easy to convince workers that they would be better off with larger wage incomes from having more members of working families employed rather than higher wage rates for only the employed heads of households. It was even easier to explain to civil servants, whose power and sometimes extra incomes are severely and negatively affected by the shift towards liberalization, that the alternative was essentially not maintainable in the long run.

The majority of the LDCs represented by some of the Latin American economies start with more favorable man-land ratios, much better natural resource endowments and a more concentrated distribution of assets; they are usually somewhat larger in size, generally sport somewhat higher initial levels of per capita income and somewhat weaker human resource endowments. Faced with the decline in the rate of industrial growth and the threat of competitive price wars at the end of primary import substitution, they are more likely to make the choice of directly moving into secondary import and export substitution, usually requiring more than the mere maintenance of prior protection and controls oriented policies but rather its further strengthening and deepening. Industrial exports are often added, but these are grafted onto import substitution regimes favoring fairly high technology, high capital intensity industries such as automobile assembly, aircraft, electrical machinery etc., at a fairly early stage, i.e. related less to the march of dynamic comparative advantage and more to the government's willingness to subsidize industrial exports which have become increasingly recognized as the hallmark of successful development.

The relative luxury of "skipping" the labor intensive primary export substitution phase as well as the luxury of not feeling the need to fully mobilize domestic food-producing agriculture—and, if necessary, importing food instead—is made possible by the underlying relative abundance of exportable natural resources, frequently supplemented by foreign capital inflows. This means, first of all, that even if there are large labor surpluses left to be mopped up—especially given the often increased pressures of population growth—the underlying exchange rate remains unduly strong, thus effectively discouraging labor intensive exports. Secondly, and perhaps more important, this so-called Kuwait effect is often associated with a political "cushion effect" whereby favorable export proceeds and/or foreign aid receipts make it possible for the system to continue to "afford" the prolongation of the import substitution region and to move into more and more "expensive" areas of industrial output in which the system has less and less of a comparative advantage at this stage of development.

In much of the developing world such a pattern of continued import substitution growth, starting with primary and shifting directly into secondary, has led to entrenched habits and strong vested interests increasingly able to resist reform. Windfall profits and wage margins are channeled to rent-seeking industrial entrepreneurs and to organized workers who happen to have jobs in the protected industrial enclave. Even in the presence of substantial underemployment and unemployment real industrial wages can be raised by means of government-supported union pressure and minimum wage legislation, while the possibilities of sustained agricultural productivity increase are sacrificed with the help of ever increasing food imports.

Once again, of course, we are talking about what is essentially a gray area, with Brazil, for example, containing a good deal of export substitution in its total policy make-up, just as Korea within the East Asian contingent contains some export promotion characteristics. But the basic point is that a majority of LDC's have in the past been able to "afford" to march down a politically "easier" growth path, made possible by a combination of the bounties of nature and the cooperation of foreign capital, public and private. Such a process can continue for many decades *if* the society is willing to accept worsening unemployment plus a highly unequal and worsening distribution of income, but accompanied by respectable growth rates, as demonstrated by many of the Latin American systems. But as more recent events indicate, such societies are also much more vulnerable to the vagaries of changes in the international situation, including the possibility that foreign capitalists may become gun-shy and refuse to continue supporting a relatively inefficient and narrowly based development path. Thus, a combination of internal pressures and fluctuations in the international environment may well, in the future, put an end to what was viewed as a desirable and feasible growth path for the majority of LDC's during the golden post-war era, 1950 to 1975.

One of the unintended by-products of the present international crisis in growth, in debt, in the lack of flexibility of adjustment shown among both rich and poor countries, may well be a need on the part of the majority of LDC's to reassess the nature of their own transition growth efforts. Societies in some sense act like individuals and are prone to take the "easy road" of less resistance if they can "get away with it." In theory, of course, a system should be better, not worse off, if it has access to a combination of natural

resources and/or additional foreign capital for the asking, since
this makes it able to better buffer the always difficult problems of
policy adjustment involved in liberalization. But it is not difficult
to see that such a situation is more frequently used to put off or
even entirely avoid making such decisions. In this case this means
trying to "skip" the labor intensive export substitution subphase
altogether, thus avoiding the necessity of having to offend vested
interest groups or having to mobilize an always stubborn agricultural sector at the same time. One only has to look at the
performance of Indonesia or Nigeria or Venezuela or Mexico
before and after the quadrupling of oil prices to demonstrate the
point. There is a certain seductiveness attached to using one's own
natural resources to embark on an independent development
path, with governments not only dominating the "heights" of the
economy in terms of public sector enterprise but also intervening
directly throughout its valleys; that is, if one can afford it, politically and materially.

In a Toynbeean sense the problem facing Taiwan was indeed
"easier." There was no real alternative but to mobilize her large
human resources, first unskilled then skilled, on behalf of the
transition growth effort. Such mobilization was first achieved by
utilizing an impersonal market system to the fullest extent possible, reserving to government intervention those things which the
government is best capable of handling effectively, i.e. the provision of infrastructure and its equitable allocation between urban
and rural areas; the creation of special facilities such as export
processing zones and rural credit institutions to facilitate the transition from one subphase to the next; the gradual shift of policies
from higher direct to lower indirect interventions in the various
markets for key inputs; the increasing assistance in areas of information diffusion on appropriate technologies, markets, etc. with
respect to both processes and goods; and, possibly on a time
limited basis, special time-constrained help in areas where economies of scale or externalities can be demonstrated to be truly
important. When governments proceed beyond that point in the
name of nationalism they are prone to intervene in all kinds of
horizontal decisions which are beyond their capacity for all types
of reasons. Whether they basically intend only to enhance growth
or as well to redistribute income, the results are, in fact, likely to
be counter-productive on both counts.

These conclusions are not merely based on the force of simple
logic as much as on the reality of the many observed actual cases
of development performance over time which are really now
available for study for the first time. It is increasingly clear that the

mobilization, in a more or less coordinated and efficient fashion, of large numbers of economic actors cannot be undertaken, either in rich or poor countries, and certainly not in areas where administrative capacities are substantially lacking, by government bureaucracies. While the answer is not a textbook laissez-faire market system, a strong government's ability to exercise self-negation in selecting its various activities along the mixed economy spectrum is of very large importance for the achievement of societal objectives. If coalitions can be formed to effect the necessary policy changes, all parts of the society can benefit over the longer term. In the absence of successful reform initiated by a relatively enlightened set of indigenous decision makers, possibly abetted and aided from abroad, the task of successful transition to modern growth becomes much more difficult and much more painful for the vast majority of the population.

NOTE

1. See, however, the authors' (with S. Y. Kuo) *Growth With Equity: The Taiwan Case*, Oxford University Press, 1979.

Capitalist Development and Income Distribution

Gustav F. Papanek

The work underlying this paper was supported in part by the U.S Agency for International Development (AID/OTR-G1872) who is in no way responsible for the views expressed.

IT IS WIDELY ACCEPTED that a capitalist strategy of economic development for poor countries promotes a high rate of growth, but at the cost of an unequal distribution of income. Moreover, it is argued that income distribution will tend to become less equal in the early stages of development. One consequence of inequality is political tensions. These tensions are generally dealt with by repression. Therefore authoritarian regimes and capitalist development go together, according to some analysts. The socialist alternative has equally serious defects, it is argued—although generally not by the same analysts. Widespread government intervention is needed to counteract the natural tendency for unequal income distribution. Such intervention, in the form of government ownership and operation of the "commanding heights" of the economy and control of the rest, inevitably is accompanied by inefficiency, waste and corruption. The result is either slow economic growth or authoritarian measures to extract enough resources from a poor population to achieve a reasonable rate of growth, despite inefficient use of these resources. Authoritarian measures then are needed as well by socialist regimes, either to extract resources or to deal with dissatisfaction which results from slow growth.

Poor countries therefore face a grim alternative: either slow growth or inequality, and an authoritarian regime in either case. Yet there is good evidence that a few countries have achieved both a high rate of growth and an egalitarian distribution of income. A few others have maintained democratic regimes. The crucial questions then are what strategy can achieve both growth and equity, and what their effect is on political events. This paper ignores the political consequences of development strategy and concentrates on the relationship between development strategy and income distribution.

A. Factors in Income Distribution—A Survey and Critique of Conventional Wisdom

First, however, a brief digression on nomenclature. The economic system dominated by private ownership and management of enterprises, with prices and quantities determined largely by the interaction of firms in a market, has been given various names. Advocates generally like to call it "free enterprise"—because freedom is prized by most of us—while critics prefer "capitalist," which has become a pejorative in some circles. "Private enterprise" is perhaps the most neutral term. It will here be used interchangably with "capitalism" and "market system." Similarly countries that have relatively low income per capita, with much of that income derived from agriculture and other primary sectors, are given various names. "Developing" is widely used, although some are not, and the rich countries are also developing. "Poor" is frowned upon, perhaps as implying poverty in non-material aspects as well. "Less developed countries" or LDC will be used here because it is probably the best description. Finally "improving income distribution" is taken as synonymous with more equal income distribution, although the former clearly implies a value judgment.

1. The Conflict Between Growth and Equality

With that out of the way it is desirable to examine first of all what factors are assumed to affect income distribution, in order to understand why growth and equity might conflict under different strategies of economic development.

a) *Development and Inequality—The Kuznets Curve*

The most widely accepted rationale for the conflict is the well known "Kuznets Curve" hypothesis. Propounded by Simon Kuznets, the hypothesis has been supported by an array of empirical studies. Few economic propositions advanced in the last 50 years have gained as much support. It holds that the process of development which has, over the last century, doubled per capita income over 3 to 7 decades in different countries, is accompanied by less equal income distribution until a per capita income of $400–600 is reached. As per capita income rises thereafter income distribution tends to become more equal.

The analytical underpinnings of the Kuznets Curve have focused on several notions:

a) in the early stages of development, physical and human capital (machines and training) are scarce and command a high premium. The few who have accumulated savings or obtained education realize high incomes.

b) development begins in some areas and in some industries. Individuals associated with the rapidly growing regions or activities receive more rapidly rising incomes than others.

c) income is less equally distributed in the urban areas which expand more rapidly with development.

A satisfactory foundation could have been provided for the Kuznets Curve by the theory of surplus labor economies first advanced by W. Arthur Lewis and elaborated by John Fei and Gustav Ranis. All workers are employed in the Lewis, Fei/Ranis model. There are redundant workers in agriculture in the sense that some can be withdrawn with no decrease in output. Landlords employ redundant workers and pay them a wage which is excessive on purely economic grounds because of a traditional relationship. The modern or industrial sector pays a wage slightly above the agricultural wage. At that wage it can attract an unlimited supply of labor as long as any surplus workers remain in agriculture. (That is, until the marginal product rises to the institutionally set wage.) With (unskilled) workers' wages remaining constant and per capita income rising with development, income distribution must become less equal, as all the gains accrue to owners of physical or human capital. When the surplus labor in agriculture is exhausted, the wages of unskilled workers throughout the economy begin to rise and for that reason alone the deterioration in income distribution will slow and can eventually be reversed, explaining the U-shape of the Kuznets curve.

The near-universal statistical confirmation of the Kuznets Curve's existence has been used to justify the need for extensive government intervention in the economies of LDC. The argument is straightforward: without intervention income distribution will deteriorate at a level of income which is so low that inequality means acute deprivation and misery for the poor. Only govenment can counteract the near-inevitable, structural tendency for worsening income distribution with development at low levels of income. The low incomes provide a moral imperative as well as political need for such government action.

Despite the wealth of statistical data in its support there are good reasons for doubting the importance of the Kuznets phenomenon (Papanek, 1975; 1978) seeing that the statistical support for it is part artifact. A number of other factors are simultaneously correlated with per capita income and with income distribution. If these factors are not controlled for, the impact of the Kuznets Curve on income distribution is exaggerated. Inequality is associated with both a high proportion of primary (raw material) exports and a dualistic socio-political system, one where the elite is of different ethnic origin than the majority of the population (eg: South Africa). At the same time, primary exporters and dualistic societies are mostly middle-income countries. In other words the middle part of the empirically established Kuznets curve is substantially populated by countries whose high inequality and middle level income are both the result of heavy reliance on primary exports and a dualistic socio-political structure. Clearly, to the extent that the Kuznets correlation is explained by these other variables, cross section analysis can not be used to predict what is likely to happen in a particular country over time. That is, just because dualistic countries, heavily dependent on primary exports, like (then) Rhodesia, South Africa, Jamaica and Gabon had a very unequal income distribution and a per capita income of $200–500 (in 1964 prices) does not mean that when countries with different characteristics, like Pakistan, India or the Sudan develop and reach that middle level of income, their income distribution will necessarily deteriorate.

When other variables correlated with income distribution are taken into account, the Kuznets Curve is still found to exist in cross-section analysis, but its effect is relatively weak. In 1964 prices, $400 is the level of per capita income where inequality is greatest. As a country moves from $100 to $400 per capita the share of the poorest 40% of the population decreases by only 1.3%—from 13.7% of total income to 12.4% (for the evidence supporting statements in this section see Papanek and Kyn). While this decline is of some significance, it explains only a small part of the variation in income distribution among countries, since the share of the poorest 40% can range from 7–9% to about 20%.

Moreover there is some slight evidence from the same analysis that the effect of development on income distribution has declined over time. If confirmed, this trend could by now have eliminated the Kuzents Curve effect as a significant influence on income distribution.

Finally, time series analysis of the same data does not support the existence of a Kuznets Curve. That is, when one looks at changes over time for the same country the evidence from 36 countries does not support the notion that income distribution first becomes less equal and then more equal as per capita income rises.

In short, the evidence is rather weak for the contention that income distribution becomes less equal as development first raises per capita income. There is therefore little support for the argument that government intervention is needed to avoid a deterioration in income distribution that otherwise is a natural consequence of development in its early stages.

b) *Inequality and the Rate of Growth*

Another closely related factor, which is also believed to make for inequality is the set of policies required to achieve a high rate of growth in a capitalist or mixed system. While the Kuznets hypothesis has to do with the structural change that accompanies development over several decades, the second argument relates to the rate of economic growth in a year or a few years. Again the argument seems plausible: in a private enterprise system the economic actors respond to economic incentives. To achieve a high rate of growth requires massive rewards to those who control assets to get them to change their customary behavior. Landlords have to be induced to adopt new seeds, to use fertilizer, to invest in irrigation. Those with discretionary income have to be enticed to save a large part. Potential entrepreneurs need incentives to take the risks of innovating. But all those for whom incentives must be provided are well off. The poor whose economic contribution is labor require no special incentives: unlike the owners of assets they command no scare resource, and they have to work hard just to survive. In a market system where the significant reward is greater income, steps to increase growth inevitably mean greater incentives and therefore greater income to groups that are already better off.

While the argument is logical, the evidence is quite equivocal on the relationship between rates of growth and income distribution. Various earlier studies (Chenery et al; Cline; Papanek, 1975; 1976) show no relationship between growth rates and equality for the few countries where income distribution data are available for several years. Income distribution became more equal about as often in high growth rate countries as vice versa. But limited data availability did not permit any strong conclusions.

The study previously cited (Papanek and Kyn) analysed the same question across a number of countries and came up with the same answer: when one correlates the growth rate with income distribution in a later year one finds no support for the contention that a high rate of growth can be achieved only at the cost of equality. Using cross country comparison for conclusions on what happens over time is a notoriously risky procedure, and the underlying data are poor, so the results can not be taken as conclusive, but together with equally limited time series data they cast doubt on the hypothesis at least. Beyond statistical evidence one needs to provide a model, that is a rational hypothesis, for how high growth rates can be achieved without worsening income distribution. This is done below.

c) *Government Intervention, Private Enterprise and Equality*

The third sense in which growth and equality are sometimes assumed to be in conflict is that private enterprise is believed to speed growth, while government intervention improves equality. It is argued that both theory and experience provide evidence that private enterprise, that is reliance on market forces, is efficient in allocating and managing resources. Decentralized decisions in response to market incentives provide the best assurance of efficient decisions and of the elimination from major economic influence of those who make wrong decisions. It is true there are "market failures," instances where private decisions are not efficient from the point of view of society. But, it is argued, there is ample evidence that government intervention, more often than not, far from improving the functioning of the market leads to further distortions and loss of efficiency. In fact the market system is more efficient than alternative forms of organization. That is widely accepted, but so is the proposition that it inevitably is accompanied by a skewed income distribution. Government intervention is needed to redress inequality, even if it is at some cost in efficiency. It is particularly needed in LDCs where inequality means acute misery for the poor and indeed often results in malnutrition, illness and death.

The evidence on this aspect of the growth/equality conflict is also murky. There are, of course, no purely private enterprise economies, nor any wholly public enterprise ones. Indeed the "capitalist" or "socialist" label is often quite misleading. Self-proclaimed socialist India has a public sector no larger than self-identified capitalist Korea (Jones and Papanek). Nevertheless, there clearly is a great deal of difference between the public/private mix in, say, North and South Korea, Nicaragua and Costa Rica or even Bangladesh and the Philippines. The best index on where an economy is located on the spectrum would be one which measures the share of the economy where decisions are made primarily by private, as against public, units. It is, however, difficult to determine which ostensibly private decisions are influenced by government. If private investments require government permission, the extent to which discretion is exercised by the private investor, as against the government controller, determines whether the decision is largely a private or largely a public one. However, there is considerable correlation between the extent of government control and the degree of government ownership and management of enterprises. Where much of industry is nationalized, the rest is usually quite tightly controlled. The share of government investment in total investment is probably an even better proxy for the extent of government intervention in the ecocomy than the share of government ownership. When policies change, the latter usually changes only slowly. However, the share of new government investment in total investment can change quite quickly, so it is a good index of how "interventionist" or "socialist" a government is.

Using this proxy, one could test the belief that private enterprise tends to be favorable to the rate of growth, at the cost of a more unequal income distribution. One comparison indeed showed a 50% higher rate of growth in the more capitalist economies than in those where government played a larger role (Papanek, 1975; 1978). But this was a rather superficial analysis since no other factors were taken into account and it did not even address the question of whether government intervention seems to have caused low rates of growth or vice versa.

The analysis of the effect of intervention on income distribution is almost equally unsatisfactory. Earlier cross section studies concluded that economies are more egalitarian if government intervenes more extensively. (Adelman and Morris, 1973, Papanek, 1975). But the more extensive cross country analysis referred to earlier (Papanek and Kyn) found no statistically significant relationship between the degree of government intervention, measured by the share of public investment, and income distribution in LDCs.

One caveat: these conclusions (as those reached earlier) are from an analysis that excludes Communist LDCs where asset redistribution has been quite radical and could have led to a dramatic increase in equality. But no good studies exist of income distribution in these countries and some aspects are almost impossible to measure with any degree of accuracy. A substantial but unknown part of resources flow through the "second economy," various barter transactions, black market arrangements, and income in kind. These also bedevil mixed economies, but not to the same degree: the tighter and more rigid the controls, and the more egalitarian the official measured income, the greater the need and incentive for unofficial or semi-official transactions not captured in the statistics. The Communist LDCs are therefore also ignored in this analysis. It is obvious, however, that ignoring them probably also means ignoring the most conclusive evidence that following a capitalist strategy implies a less egalitarian income distribution. Until data and careful studies of income distribution are available for countries such as North Korea, Vietnam and Cuba, little can be done about this.

2) Education, Trade, Transfers and Assets as Factors in Income Distribution

Before turning to an attempt to explain why the conflict between growth and equality in LDCs is not nearly as serious a problem as widely contended, it is worthwhile to analyze other factors that seem to influence income distribution. Most of these are well recognized.

a) *Education*
The more widely distributed education is, the larger the proportion of the population that has access to the higher incomes which accrue to the educated. Various studies have found that the spread of education is associated with equality (Adelman and Morris, 1973; Ahluwalia; 1976). The extensive recent study (Papanek and Kyn) confirmed these results, but also found that the

spread of primary and secondary education benefits particularly the poorest 40% of the population, since middle class children were already in school in most countries.

The relationship of education and income distribution provides part of the explanation for the weakness of the Kuzents Curve effect. Even if other factors make for a worsening income distribution in the early stages of development, the spread of education will counteract their effect. The impact of education may also help explain why there is little relationship between the extent of government intervention and equality: most interventionist governments accelerate the spread of primary and secondary education, and in the statistical analysis their effect on education can be picked up by that variable rather than by the intervention variable. To the extent that populist or socialist governments improve income distribution through greater expenditure on education, the impact of that factor needs to be added to that of the variable measuring their greater intervention in the economy to evaluate their true effect on equality.

b) *Trade Patterns—Open vs. Closed Economies*

There are two conflicting views of the effect on equality of an open as against a more autarchic economy. Many critics of capitalism argue that the more closely a country is tied to the capitalist world trading system, the greater the inequality within the country. The "comprador bourgeoisie" of the country is the only group benefitting from these ties, while the mass of workers, exploited by multinationals or their national allies, only loses. Advocates, on the other hand, argue that the world trading system allows LDCs to take advantage of their abundant labor by exporting manufactured goods. (See Chenery and Syrquin; Papanek, 1978.) With labor in demand, wages will rise. Moreover, economies able to compete on world markets are likely to have fewer distortions and to operate more efficiently. Finally they will generate fewer of the windfall gains which distortions produce and which accrue mainly to the upper income groups. This group often cites the experience of the Asian "Gang of Four" (Korea, Taiwan, Hong Kong, Singapore), where rapid growth and continuing equality accompanied a strategy stressing manufactured exports.

The evidence on these arguments is mixed. Heavy reliance on primary exports is accompanied by unequal income distribution (Papanek and Kyn). The major reason is that exports of oil, minerals and plantation crops tend to generate concentrated incomes. Those who exercise control over these economic resources derive political power from them, which they use to assure that their own incomes are high. Whether an oil company, mine or plantation is in private or public hands seems to make relatively little difference to the income of those involved. These are economies closely tied to the world trading system and they do have unequal incomes, but since this is true even where the exporting firms are government owned, it is doubtful that it is largely because of exploitation by multinationals or "comprador" bourgeoisie. Rather, it appears to be related to the concentration of economic and political power.

The opposite argument is not well supported either: a strategy emphasizing manufactured exports is not accompanied by an egalitarian income distribution, according to the study previously cited. Casual observers seem to have been misled by the experience in the four Asian LDCs that followed this strategy. Their income distribution was indeed egalitarian and became more equal during the 1960's. Other countries that also emphasize manufactured exports particularly in Latin America, have an unequal income distribution. Why the same strategy should have different outcomes is another issue addressed later.

c. *The Role of Fiscal Transfers: Taxing the Rich and Subsidizing the Poor?*

A major element in the assumed relationship between a greater government role and greater equality is the impact of government fiscal transfers: a progressive tax system that collects more from the rich and spends the resulting resources on social services and subsidies that differentially benefit the poor. It is argued that the reversal of the Kuznets Curve, the improvement in income distribution in the developed countries, is due to the increasing role of such transfers in the wealthy Western democracies.

But a series of studies of LDCs have concluded that the impact of such government transfers in several countries is quite small and not always in the intended direction (Meerman; Husain). There are other countries where subsidies are massive, but do not transfer resources from rich to poor. Egypt is an outstanding example. One estimate is that the income of the poor would have to be raised by over 50% if subsidies were eliminated. But the wealthier groups receive subsidies that are almost as large. Subsidies for both are financed by aid, oil and Suez Canal revenues—that is, levies on foreigners. Oil rich countries, like Egypt, generally have subsidies, but they appear not to contradict the conclusion that fiscal transfers generally do not change income distribution.

In a few countries a significant share of income derived from aid or oil is used for a labor intensive works program which benefits the poor. For a few years in the early 1960's Bangladesh (then East Pakistan) used food aid to finance such work. Only the poor participated, given the low wage rate (Thomas). A similar program was launched in Indonesia in the 1970's (see Falcon, Patten and Dapice for similar conclusions). But there are only a few such programs and even in the countries which implement them on a massive scale the fiscal system also provides subsidies for the rich—eg: via free university education—so its impact on income distribution may be negligible.

Sri Lanka seems to be the only mixed economy LDC that successfully transferred substantial resources from wealthier to poorer residents. Several characteristics of Sri Lanka may account for this unusual performance: (i) a democratic system of long standing, in which two major parties compete for popular support and votes by providing economic benefits; (ii) some of the cost of the transfers was borne by foreign plantation owners and some probably by plantation labor from India, neither of whom voted; (iii) a long tradition of egalitarianism.

Fiscal transfers therefore have not been an important factor in income distribution. The Sri Lankan case is sufficiently unusual that it is unlikely to be emulated by other countries.

d) *Asset ownership*

A crucial element in current income distribution is the historically given distribution of physical assets. In many LDCs the principal such asset is land. Whether land is held primarily in small units, and cultivated by its owners, or in large tracts cultivated by hired labor is partly the result of how the land was originally settled, of population pressure and of the systems of government and taxation that prevailed over centuries. Another important factor is whether there has recently been a far reaching land reform. The distribution of other assets is similarly influenced by historical accident. Equality in Korea and Taiwan in the 1960's, for instance, was in large part the result of historical factors. The principal owners of assets had been Japanese colonists. With the end of the colonial regime, it was relatively easy and in part automatic to bring about widespread land-reform and a relatively egalitarian distribution of other assets. On the other hand, the pattern of Spanish conquest and settlement in parts of western Latin America guaranteed an unequal income distribution.

The importance of asset ownership is difficult to measure, because there is little or no information on the distribution of assets in LDCs. But an examination of the countries whose income distribution is not well explained by regression analysis suggests that about one-third had an unusually skewed or equal asset distribution, especially with respect to land (eg: Iran, Kenya, Rhodesia for the former and Israel, Korea and Taiwan for the latter. See Papanek and Kyn).

B. Determinants of Labor Income and their Effect on Income Distribution

To explain why income distribution is little affected by the process of development, that is, by change in per capita income, or by the rate of growth, or by greater government intervention in the economy, one needs to examine the factors that determine the income of unskilled workers. Most of the poor in LDCs have few, if any, physical assets. Nor do they possess much "human capital," the education or skills which can also enhance income. Most of the poor essentially derive their income from selling their unskilled labor, whether as wage earners or self-employed. Their income and changes in their income then depend on the income earned from unskilled work.

Some of the poorest 60% of the population, even some of the poorest 40% do possess some capital. Small holder-cultivators have some land, urban peddlers possess some inventory, for instance. Their income is the joint product of their labor and returns on their asset. But the income of peddlers, in at least one study, is not all that different from that of workers without assets (Papanek and Kontjorojakti). The implication is that labor is the dominant factor in income for at least some of these groups of poor asset owners. Income distribution at the bottom of the scale therefore depends primarily on whether the income of unskilled workers changes more or less rapidly than per capita income.

The income of the poor could rise more rapidly than "earned income" derived from their labor, if there were income or asset transfers to them. But it has been argued earlier that such transfers are very rare.

Nationalization, the transfer of assets from private to public hands, is more frequent. But its impact on the income of the poor is either via an increase in wages or via fiscal transfers. So nationalization is not a separate category, but can usually be traced through its effect on labor income. The crucial determinants of income distribution, at least at the lower end of distribution, then are the factors which influence the change in the real (adjusted for price changes) labor income.

1) Differences and Similarities in Labor Income

It is quite well known that wages vary widely among regions, occupations and personal characteristics in all economics. In LDCs these variations may be even greater than in countries where movement is easier because transport costs and social barriers are less of an obstacle. There clearly is no single labor market, but a series of segmented markets and one can question whether it is meaningful to talk of changes in labor income.

a) *The "Protected Sector"*
In most LDCs there is a "protected sector" where wages are set by government, unions or a management which values labor peace more than saving labor costs because unskilled workers are a small fraction of total costs. Wages in this sector are higher than elsewhere in the economy and changes are determined largely by non-economic factors. The bulk of this sector usually is large scale, publicly owned enterprises or a few large, capital intensive industrial firms.

It generally employs fewer than 5% of the labor force, often less than 1%. As a labor elite they are not among the poorest 40%. For purposes of this discussion the "protected sector" can largely be ignored. Not only are its workers middle class, their wages are only tenuously related to other wages.

b) *Changes in Labor Incomes Outside the Protected Sector*
Outside the protected sector the income of workers tends to move together, even if the level differs among groups. There are several, often related, reasons for differences in wage or labor income levels: (i) the characteristics of workers differ (eg: some activities require reliable, highly motivated workers); (ii) differences in cost of living, so different nominal wages can be equal in purchasing power (real wages); (iii) temporary, functional differences that will decline with time, only to be followed by temporary differences elsewhere (e.g.: when demand for labor in a region or industry rises, wages will temporarily rise to attract workers); (iv) barriers to entry.

These barriers exist for a variety of reasons and are generally more important in LDCs. Ethnic, family, tribal, caste and regional ties are important in gaining access to many occupations. They are important in part because trust is needed and social sanctions must be available against those who violate that trust, in part because groups deliberately exclude others to derive rents from the "social assets" thus created (Papanek and Kontjorojakti). Peddlers, for instance, develop an informal organization to allocate territories. Caste barriers are even stronger, as are family ties in working on family-owned land or a family-owned business.

So for all these reasons differences in unskilled workers wages up to 50% are not unusual (Papanek and Dey; Papanek, 1981). But at the same time wage movements are generally quite closely correlated: they move up and down together, albeit sometimes with a lag of a few months or a year, and by somewhat similar orders of magnitude (Ibid). The exceptions are countries like India and Indonesia where differential movements may take place in distant regions, especially if differences in language make migration extremely difficult. In these countries wages in a region whose growth is slow may lag by years behind those where it is rapid. But even in India, which is more comparable to the European Economic Community than to a smaller country, wages in a North Western and a North Eastern state move together in the same year, because language is similar, but not among states with completely different languages (Ibid).

In other words, there seems to be a single labor market for each country, segmented by barriers of different height. Labor migration tends to keep labor income moving together in different activities and different regions, although sometimes with a lag. If the difference between labor income becomes too great the barriers are scaled. These conclusions are based on analysis of some 20 wage series from six countries (Egypt, Pakistan, India, Bangladesh, Sri Lanka, and Indonesia), including series on agricultural wages. Although they deal with wages, not with the labor income of the self employed, there is further discussion below of reasons why the incomes of self employed unskilled workers may be roughly parallel to those of wage workers.

Wage movements are also considerable. As mentioned, one of the most influential theories of development (Lewis; Fei and Ranis) postulates that real wages in labor surplus economies remain constant for considerable periods. But the experience of southern Asia is otherwise. In addition to annual changes of 5% to 15%, wages have changed substantially over five to ten years. In Indonesia, for instance, real wages declined by 50% between the mid 1950's and the mid-60's and doubled to the early 1970's (all in real terms, after taking account of price changes). In Bangladesh the increase from the late 1950's, to the mid-60's was 35–50%, and the decline to the mid-1970's 45–65%. Changes in India, Sri Lanka, and Pakistan (and Egypt) was in general were less dramatic, but their wages too were far from stable.

In short, one can trace major changes in wages. These changes are quite similar in different activities and regions although absolute wages can be quite different. When real wages fell by 50%, while per capita income remained unchanged, as they did in Indonesia during the Sokarno regime, income distribution became less equal. Conversely, when wages rose 100% while per capita income rose less than 25% in the same period, income distribution improved, if wages reflect labor income in general as argued earlier.

2) The Work and Income Sharing Model of Labor Income Determination

An alternate model to standard neo-classical doctrine provides one explanation of changes in real wages.

a) Work and Income Sharing

In the poorer LDCs a widespread phenomenon is the sharing of work and income from particular activities. (See Papanek, 1981; Dey.) The small, family operated farm or business is an obvious example of such "work and income sharing" (sometimes referred to here as work sharing or income sharing). Family members who work in the farm or enterprise share the income it produces, so that their income changes with the average product. The compensation is not related to the output lost if a worker were to be withdrawn (marginal product), which may be quite low. In fact in some of these enterprises so many family members may be working that one could leave and output would not drop at all (the marginal product is zero). But they leave to accept work outside the family enterprise only if the pay they are offered compensates them for the income lost for leaving the family farm or business (their "reservation wage"). Similar work and income sharing can prevail in informal or casual sector occupations outside family businesses. There may be more shoe-shiners, lottery ticket sellers, or construction workers than can be employed at the current rate of pay. They would like to work more hours or days or serve more customers at that pay, but all refuse to lower the rate they accept in order to obtain more work. Instead they prefer to share the work and income available in that occupation at a rate per hour/day/trip etc. which they regard as appropriate. Others whose income is less in other occupations cannot enter because they do not have the right connections, or "social assets," in terms of region, caste, class, or friendship. But if the gap in wages becomes too high, the barriers to entry begin to break down until the gap in wages again reflects "exclusion costs," the ability of the in-group to keep outsiders out or the strength of other barriers to entry into the activity. An economy may also have some activities where there are no barriers to entry and where income is correspondingly low.

Enterprises and activities to which work and income sharing do not apply but whose wages are set competitively (not "protected"), can attract labor only if they offer a wage which compensates workers for forgoing the average product in the work and income sharing sector. Labor compensation in the work-sharing sector, which consists primarily of the self-employed, then determines wages and wage changes throughout the economy (except for the protected sector). Differences in absolute levels there will be, but movements will be comparable. If the average product increases in much of the work and income-sharing sector, then the reservation wage of workers in the sector will rise and with it wages throughout the economy.

An example may clarify the mechanism. As a result of the new seed-fertilizer-irrigation technology, output in most of agriculture rises. Families that own land will have higher real incomes. With higher incomes from their own land, they will be less willing to work elsewhere, unless wages in alternative occupations also rise. Some of the artisans and laborers those landlords hired were also paid in shares of the harvest. Their income also rises with output. Fewer landowners, artisans and harvest workers will now be available for alternative occupations at the existing wage and migration to towns will slow. If demand for workers outside agriculture keeps expanding, then wages there will have to rise to attract the necessary labor.

b) *The Implications of Work and Income Sharing for Income Distribution*

In the labor surplus countries, if real wages change with the average product in the work-sharing and income-sharing sector, and the average product is simply total output in the sector divided by the number of its workers, income distribution then depends on the number of productive jobs created for unskilled workers in relation to the increase in their numbers. In the short or medium term—say 15 years—the labor supply is largely fixed. People who will enter the working population have been born already. Number of hours worked can vary, but in this model that depends on the same factors that determine compensation.

Compensation for unskilled labor in the work and income-sharing sector then depends on: (i) the value of output in the sector which, together with the number of workers, determines average product; (ii) demand for labor outside the sector, which helps determine how many workers remain in it to share its output; (iii) whether the income-sharing sector is shrinking, growing or remaining unchanged. Each of these points warrants some elaboration.

i) The *value of output in the work-sharing and income-sharing sector* in turn is primarily a function of the increase in agricultural output and of demand for the services of the whole sector. Where labor is abundant, workers who derive much of their income from agriculture are by far the largest component of the work-sharing sector. Therefore the rate of growth in agricultural output is a direct and crucial factor in real wages. Indirectly it also influences the demand for the services provided by the rest of the work-sharing sector. The greater the demand with a given supply the greater the value of total and of average output (i.e.: average value product).

ii) *The spread and pattern of growth* of the commercial sector, where work-sharing is absent, directly determines the demand for labor drawn from the work sharing sector. Indirectly it also affects the demand for the output of the work sharing sector. The strength of the commercial sectors' demand for labor explains much of the difference in real wage trends in many LDCs, and therefore their income distribution. This demand in turn depends on:

—how fast the commercial sector is growing

—how labor intensive is the technology used in the sector. For instance, if growth is primarily in the textile industry it makes a great deal of difference whether the predominant technology is handlooms, with lots of labor per unit of capital and output, or simple power looms, or semi-automatic power looms, or fully automatic power looms, with very little labor per unit of investment and output.

—whether the pattern of development stresses labor or capital intensive industries. This appears to be the crucial difference among countries. Investment in an oil tanker or a steel mill may create only one to ten jobs for each million dollars invested, while in some parts of the electronics industry one million dollars is enough for several thousand jobs. Whether the strategy emphasizes petrochemicals, steel and airlines or electronics, garments, furniture, textiles and agriculture can make a great deal of difference to the number of jobs created, with the same rate of investment.

iii) the *strength of forces supporting work sharing and income sharing*. If the social and political sanctions which support work and income sharing break down in a large part of the sector, then workers who no longer have access to incomes in one part of the sector will crowd into those activities where the system still works. Average product there will drop. For instance, it has been argued that work and income sharing were widespread in harvesting in Java until a decade ago. Since then some land-owners have drastically reduced the number of workers allowed to participate. The excluded workers crowd into the remaining work-sharing activities open to them. The average product in these activities will be less than it would have been without this influx and this will be reflected in wages throughout the economy.

Commercialization tends to break down the social sanctions on work sharing. So the extension of commercial or capitalist agriculture will, other things remaining equal, reduce real wages in economies where work and income sharing remains important. In a private enterprise economy the political forces making for work sharing are also likely to be weaker than under populist or socialist governments.

In short, under the assumptions of this model labor income depends on the rate of growth in agricultural output and the increase in labor demand from the commercial sector which primarily affect labor income, with the speed of any breakdown in work-sharing another influence.

3) Other Models of Labor Income Determination and Some Evidence

While there are clear implications for an analysis of income distribution of the work and income-sharing model, the model itself is new and not widely accepted. The neo-classical and Lewis, Fei-Ranis models have far greater currency.

a) *The Neo Classical Model*

In the standard neo-classical model there is a single labor market, where labor is paid its marginal product, the equivalent of the output added by the least productive worker. The price of labor is determined like any other price, by the supply of and the demand for labor. As development proceeds investment takes place. This raises the marginal product of labor, and with it the wage.

For the more developed, more commercialized of the LDCs this may be a reasonable first approximation of the situation for many workers, since work sharing is much less of an influence. Under the neo-classical model, in LDCs the wage also responds primarily to the demand for labor. The supply of unskilled labor is relatively fixed and their income is too low to permit the luxury of unemployment or a shorter work week. The change in the demand for labor in turn is almost wholly a function of the speed of growth and of its labor intensity in the commercial sector, since the work sharing sector is small.

If standard neo-classical economics describes the situation in LDCs, then one can readily conceive of circumstances in which income distribution will become less equal with development. Even if the *shares* of unskilled labor and of physical and human capital in total output remain unchanged with development, but the number of poor increases more rapidly than of the wealthy, income distribution would become less equal. With modern public health measures the death rate of the poor is closer to the death rate of the rich than is the birth rate, which declines with income and education, so the number of poor rises more rapidly and their relative income would fall. If the share of unskilled labor in total income declines with development that would further reduce their relative income (share).

b) *The Lewis, Fei-Ranis Model*

Since the neo-classical model did not seem to fit too well the realities of the poor, labor-surplus LDC, alternative models have been sought. The implications of the Lewis, Fei-Ranis model for income distribution have already been sketched. If workers in traditional agriculture are paid a wage above the marginal product and determined by tradition or subsistence needs, and if other wages are set to equal the agricultural wage, then wages will not rise until the marginal product in agriculture equals that wage. If the marginal product in agriculture is very low, then it can take decades of development before enough workers have been drawn from agriculture so the marginal output of those remaining equals the wage. The wage throughout the economy then will not rise until this "inflection point" is reached. Development will not "trickle down" to the poor. Their wage and income will remain unchanged, all benefits of development accrue to those who have assets and income distribution will inevitably become less equal in a private enterprise system.

c) *Evidence on the Three Models*

The Lewis, Fei-Ranis model is consistent, its implications for growth are considerable and positive, but its implications for income distribution are dismal. But fortunately the empirical evidence does not bear it out. The model can accomodate fluctuations in real wages, but not longer term trends. In labor surplus countries real wages are supposed to remain constant over extended periods. But wages in the countries of southern Asia that are labor surplus, if such a category exists, show substantial changes of up to 50% over a 5 to 10 year period.

The support for the neo-classical model is not much stronger if one examines wages in Southern Asia. The differences in compensation for casual unskilled labor is so great in the same activities in different areas, and within the same area but in different activities, that it is clear that the labor market is highly segmented, at least in the five countries of Southern Asia (Indonesia, Bangladesh, India, Pakistan, Sri Lanka) which are included in a separate study (Papanek and Dey). For instance, in Dhaka Bangladesh, unskilled construction workers in 1979 were paid at Tk 12–15 a day, while the same workers received Tk 5–6 a day on days when they could not find construction work and served as porters in the market (Farashuddin).

There is also some statistical evidence, necessarily rough and subject to dispute, that the marginal product in Java rice agriculture approaches zero and that the wage substantially exceeds the marginal product (Handoko), circumstances inconsistent with the neo-classical model, but perfectly consistent with that sketched earlier. Casual empiricism and interviews with workers confirm that in many LDC cities there are more shoe shiners, bicycle rickshaw pullers, lottery ticket sellers, construction workers, peddlers and other informal sector sales and service workers than are
. needed. There is competition for customers, not in terms of prices but of pressure to use a particular individual. Most of these workers are actually performing their function for only a fraction of the time they are at work. They express a willingness to work many more hours, or service many more customers, at the same rate (Farashuddin; Dey). In India landless workers report many hours spent "looking for work" at the prevailing wage (Sharif). All

of this evidence suggests that the labor market, at least in Southern Asia, is far from the textbook version of a single market where marginal product and wage are more or less equated.

Conversely there is evidence that in the countries of Southern Asia wages are related to the average product in agriculture, the largest element in the work and income-sharing sector (Papanek, 1981; Dey). That model is consistent with substantial changes in wages over time, since the average product can change substantially. It is also consistent with substantial involuntary unemployment. The essence of the work and income-sharing sector is that there is not full time work for everyone in it. So workers will be idle part of the time, willing to work more but unwilling to engage in price cutting and competition that would reduce the number of people in the activity sufficiently so everyone is fully employed.

What seems most likely is that there is a continuum of economies, with those dominated by work sharing at one end and those where the commercial sector is overwhelming at the other, and a whole range of mixes in-between. The average product of labor largely determines the labor income in the former, the marginal product in the latter. But in both, demand for labor is an important determinant of labor income.

4) Other factors in labor income.

Three other factors which affect the real income of workers bear mention: migration abroad, the external terms of trade and, in the short-term, the rate of inflation. Nominal wages tend to lag behind prices when inflation is high or accelerating by a year or two, so real wages drop when inflation increases. When inflation slows, real wages tend to rise again. There is solid statistical evidence for this relationship (Papanek and Dey; Dey). But the effect of inflation tends to be short-lived (unless it continues to accelerate over a long period, which has happened in only a few countries) so it is not significant for this longer-term analysis.

The external terms of trade can have a significant effect on real wages in countries where trade is a major element in the National Income. If the price of commodities exported drops, value of output will decline and with it the average value product—that is, the purchasing power which a producer actually receives. In a country like Indonesia, where plantation crops are important, the smallholder producer families will see their real average income decline if world commodity prices fall. The income of those working on plantations may also decline. The reservation wage of both will drop, and that could affect wages throughout the economy, if they are an important group. The terms of trade are only one of the exogeneous factors influencing wages and therefore income distribution, but they are an important one in many countries. For instance, in Bangladesh a major factor in the decline and stagnation of real wages over a decade has been a tragic deterioration in the country's terms of trade. The weather is even more important in the short term in most LDCs, but it affects fluctuations, not trends. It is therefore of little importance to an analysis of the effect of a private enterprise strategy on income distribution.

Migration to other countries has been an important factor in reducing the supply of labor in some countries in the last decade. In Egypt and Pakistan enough workers have left to affect the number remaining in the work-sharing sector and therefore the wage throughout the economy. A tie to the—essentially capitalist—world trading system has been an asset in raising wages in this respect.

C. Capitalism, Labor Intensity and Strategy

With this model of wage determination in mind one can analyze four alternative strategies and their impact on income distribution. There are, as already mentioned, no pure cases of either public or private enterprise economies. One can, however identify three reasonably distinct strategies that have actually been pursued and a fourth which exists only in part. They are: the classical capitalist or market oriented; market oriented, but with government intervention that distorts prices; populist, which adds substantial government ownership; a proposed synthetic strategy.

1) The Private Enterprise Strategy

While the empirical evidence in this connection is poor, it is probably fair to say that reasonably pure strategies have done better on growth than the truly mixed economies. Many Communist countries, excluded from this paper (see above), have had a high rate of economic growth and so have most countries that come close to pure private enterprise. The former usually do so by government extracting a high proportion of total resources from the society to be used for investment. The private enterprise economies, in contrast, provide strong incentives for private savings and the efficient use of resources. Consequently, their rate of growth is quite high. Income may be unequally distributed, but distribution may not worsen over time. As a result there can be rapid growth in the absolute income of the poor.

The best example of such an economy is Hong Kong, where there is probably less government intervention than in any other country (Chow and Papanek). Several other countries in East/ Southeast Asia, including Taiwan, Singapore and Thailand, also come reasonably close to the private enterprise end of the spectrum, although the government's role is considerably greater than in Hong Kong.

A second group of economies is in a capitalist phase after a period of extensive nationalization, controls or other shocks. In many cases the introduction of private enterprise was regarded by the policy makers as akin to drug withdrawal: "cold turkey" was the only suitable approach. When there are severe distortions in an economy such a drastic approach has proved difficult and costly. It is very difficult, for instance, for enterprises to face overnight the competition of imports, if for a decade they have become used to being overstaffed and overcapitalized, producing low quality goods in a highly protected market. As a result these countries have often not done well and it is difficult to distinguish the effect of the dual shocks—first tight controls and nationalization, then exposure to the market and de-nationlization—from the effect of the private enterprise strategy (eg: Lebanon, Chile, a brief period in Argentina).

Finally, there are countries that have shifted less radically, or over a longer period of time between a more controlled and more market oriented economy. In many ways their experience is the most useful, since it enables one to examine the consequences of somewhat different strategies, while the level of development, the resource endowment, the nature of the economy and society, and other factors are held constant.

a) *Rapid economic growth* is one characteristic of most of the capitalist economies except for the countries suffering from rapid change. With strong and appropriate incentives, input (factor) prices that reflect their scarcity and an open economy able to benefit from comparative advantage and economies of scale, capitalism is an efficient and effective engine of growth, as both Adam Smith and Karl Marx recognized. The usual problems do crop up, but have turned out to be less serious than many analysts of LDCs supposed 30 years ago.

Small markets and monopoly are not too serious a problem if the economy is relatively open. Competition from imports then keeps within bounds the inefficiency and monopoly profits that might otherwise result. Other market failures, extensively discussed, turn out not to be too serious in actual fact. Natural monopolies not subject to import competition (eg: railroads) are universally publicly owned. A combination of public investment with planning and "administrative guidance" has been used in most of these countries to deal with activities which cannot be developed in isolation, because they depend on simultaneous investment in other fields or because they have a large positive or negative effect on other investors (eg: a steel mill that requires a port which is economic only if other industries locate there, and if there are fabricating plants nearby). Large units that require resources beyond those which private investors can command have been supported by public loans.

Another problem prominent in early writings was the achievement of an adequate rate of savings. The "demonstration effect" was supposed to promote a developed country standard of consumption among the wealthier in countries that still had LDC levels of production. As a result they saved little, while the mass of the poor had nothing to save. Indeed, in some private enterprise LDCs savings have been low, especially where growth has been slow, because it is more difficult to save when income is increasing little and returns on investment are moderate. The savings problem has been serious in some Latin American and African countries, in part because of political and other uncertainties, in part for historical and social reasons. In some Asian countries a high rate of growth, at first financed in substantial part by foreign resources quite quickly facilitated high savings. By the late 1970's rates of saving around 30% were achieved not only in countries such as Korea, Taiwan and Singapore, but also in Thailand, Malaysia and a few African and Latin countries. High returns for domestic savers, and even more for foreign investors, can create serious political problems, but private enterprise economies did not face unusual economic difficulties in achieving a high rate of savings and investment.

In short, a number of such economies achieved a high and efficient rate of growth, generally with close ties to the world market.

b) *Instability*

These ties added a further element of instability to private enterprise economies. Most LDCs, heavily dependant on agriculture, are severely affected by the vagaries of the weather. In addition private enterprise economies are subject to shifts in attitudes of domestic business and to changes in the world market. Indonesia in the mid-1970's went through a painful re-adjustment period when foreign bankers stopped debt roll-overs to its oil company, although a year earlier they had been delighted to extend loans almost without limit. Hong Kong has suffered sharp fluctuations in its economy, including the income of its workers, because it is affected to an extreme degree by fluctuations in world demand for its goods (Chow and Papanek).

To the extent that LDCs are often marginal suppliers of marginal goods, they experience the vagaries of the world market in extreme form when they are well integrated with that market, whether fluctuations are caused by the business cycle or changes in tastes or technology. The problem is compounded because, almost by definition, LDCs do not have diversified economies and export patterns. Some export a single primary product or a group of closely related ones whose prices often move together (eg: cocoa, coffee and palm oil). If they export manufactures they are usually heavily dependent on such good as textiles, garments and shoes. Uncertainty and fluctuations in the economy thus frequently accompany rapid rates of growth for market-oriented LDCs.

c) *Distribution of Income and Levels of Poverty*

But the central question in this essay is not growth or stability, but income distribution. Among market-oriented LDCs there is a very wide range in the pattern of income distribution and an equally wide range in the extent of absolute poverty. The share of the poorest 40% ranges from as little as 5–7% for such countries as Ecuador, Gabon, 1956 Iraq and Peru, to as much as 17–20% in Barbados, Cyprus, 1957 Israel, (South) Korea, Taiwan, Pakistan and Trinidad. The degree of inequality depends largely on the historically determined distribution of assets.

The absolute income of the poor also depends very much on the average per capita income. Although Indian income is quite equally divided, with the poorest 40% having about 17% of total income, when per capita income was only $85 (in 1964 prices) that meant a per capita income of $35 or so. For the poorest 20% in the really poor LDC, a per capita income equivalent to $20–25 is quite typical. In wealthier countries with a per capita income of

$300, but a share of only 2% for the poorest 20%—by no means unusual—the absolute income of the poorest is only slightly higher.

For a family of 5 to live on $100–150 a year means bare subsistence at best, with malnutrition, hunger and even slow starvation during bad periods. It is morally impossible to justify an economic system where society takes no specific action to transfer resources to the poor when this is needed to assure survival. The moral justification usually given for a private enterprise system which does not redistribute income or assets is that redistributive measures are damaging to economic growth on which poverty alleviation ultimately depends.

d) *Changes in Income Distribution under Capitalism*

Since a private enterprise economy can achieve a rapid rate of growth, its ability to alleviate poverty depends very much on what happens to income distribution with this rapid growth. That the cost of labor and capital are not distorted in such economies is a crucial factor in avoiding a worsening of equality. Without distortion the cost of labor is low, compared to scarce capital in labor abundant LDCs. Businessmen in pursuit of profit will therefore invest in activities and technologies that are intensive in labor.

Rapid, labor intensive growth in the commercial sector, by drawing workers out of work and income sharing will raise the average product, therefore the reservation wage and with it unskilled workers wages throughout the economy, in terms of the model sketched earlier. The absolute income of workers will rise, and it will rise quite rapidly, if the demand for labor expands greatly. Under these circumstances capitalist development can be quite consistent with greater equality. The absolute income of workers would also have to rise under the standard assumptions of neo-classical economics. The only model under which income distribution would definitely become less equal and the absolute income of the poor might actually decline is the Lewis, Fei and Ranis description of labor surplus private enterprise economies. The absolute income would decline only if there is a weakening of the institutional/social forces that maintain the uneconomically high real wages in agriculture. But since the empirical evidence does not support the notion of constant real wages, the assumption underlying subsequent discussion is that labor income will change with average or marginal product, with the former more important in the poorer LDCs.

Three characteristics of the capitalist system then affect changes in income distribution with development: rapid growth, a labor intensive pattern, and the political as well as economic power of the rich. These interact with historically given aspects of the economy to affect several factors that directly determine changes in equality:

(i)*Increasing ownership of assets* by the poor is clearly one factor in their income. Rapid growth in a private enterprise system exerts strong pressures on government to spread education. Learning by doing will also be accelerated. Both will speed the process of providing the poor with human capital. Moreover a labor intensive pattern of growth means that a large number of workers will be acquiring training and experience—human capital—in modern activities.

On the other hand, a private enterprise system will not deliberately transfer assets to the poor, either directly (eg: land reform) or indirectly (eg: by expanding education more rapidly than required for economic reasons). On the contrary, the rich may use their power to restrict access, for instance by charging fees for a good education.

(ii) *Return on assets owned by the poor.* It is clearly an abstraction to assume that the poor own no physical assets. The self-employment income of smallholders in agriculture, peddlers, craftsmen and service workers of various kinds is some combination of labor and property income. Without special help from government some of these groups may actually lose with development. Their larger competitors may be able to lower costs more, prices will drop as a result and the owners of smaller units will lose in the competition. The differential impact on smaller units can be the result of economies of scale (i.e. larger units are inherently more efficient), or because larger units have readier access to the new technology, bear its risk more readily, or can obtain finance more easily. In addition to their real economic advantages, larger units can also use their greater political and economic power to gain an unfair competitive edge over smaller units (eg: the largest landlord in a village is often also the only available source of credit).

(iii) *Demand for unskilled labor* is the crucial determinant of changes in labor income in the model driven by average product and is important in the neo-classical model. Demand for labor will increase quite rapidly in a capitalist system because of its high rate of growth and the labor intensive pattern assured by relative labor/capital prices. But how rapidly it increases depends in part on such exogenous factors as demand in the world market for labor intensive goods, the location of a country and other factors influencing its access, and its natural resource endowment for producing labor intensive goods (eg: rubber and rice production require much more unskilled labor than oil, mining or wheat production).

(iv) *The proportion of unemployed or underemployed labor* influences the rate of increase in labor income in response to increased labor demand. In a neo-classical world, as demand for labor increases wages will not rise until the unemployed are absorbed. Labor income will rise since some workers previously without job or income, and supported by their families, now receive a wage. When the unemployed are absorbed wages will rise and labor income will increase more rapidly.

In the alternative model sketched in this paper there are no unemployed unskilled workers. The poor cannot afford to be without income. But there is "underemployment" in the work and income-sharing sector. These workers are active for fewer hours, or days, or have fewer customers than they would be willing to serve at the prevailing rate of compensation. If the work sharing sector is large in relation to the increase in demand for labor from the commercial sector, then the average product and the wage will rise more slowly than if it is small, with a given increase in labor demand.

v) *The effectiveness of work and income sharing* matters in societies where average product in that sector is a determinant of the real wage. If the sector shrinks as workers are pushed out of some activities, and have to seek work in other activities where they are still allowed to share the work, the result will be a lower average product and lower labor income. A private enterprise system, with its emphasis on individual rewards, competition and commercial relations is likely to speed the weakening of the social sanctions which make work and income sharing possible. Moreover, government in that kind of society may also reduce the effectiveness of political sanctions, for instance by weakening the political parties or other organizations that support landless laborers. Both commercialization and political change are, it is argued, responsible for the gradual breakdown of work sharing in Indonesian agriculture (Collier et al; Hart).

e) *Empirical Evidence: Capitalism and Income Distribution*
In sum, there are forces in a capitalist system making for higher absolute incomes for unskilled labor, that is the poor, and tending towards greater equality and there are negative forces as well. *A priori* either a worsening or improvement in income distribution is possible. What has actually happened is therefore an important question.

Earlier it has been mentioned that in a large-scale, cross section analysis of income distribution data no statistically significant relationship was found between income distribution and the proxy for government intervention in the economy, nor between the rate of growth and income distribution. At least this study provides no empirical support for the notion that greater reliance on the market in a mixed economy results in a worsening of income distribution (Papanek and Kyn).

Another piece of evidence is the experience of Hong Kong, probably the best example of untrameled private enterprise in the post-War world. Income distribution at first may possibly have become less equal, as the pool of underemployed was large and was rapidly being augmented. However, income distribution very soon became somewhat more equal. Growth was extremely labor intensive and rapid, averaging 9% a year (Chow and Papanek). As a result, wages of unskilled workers actually rose more rapidly than those of skilled labor and somewhat more rapidly than average per capita income. This experience runs counter to the argument that in a capitalist system the high rewards to asset owners inevitably lead to worsening income distribution until the pressure of the electorate in a democratic system produces government redistributive measures. As one of the few old-style colonies left in the world, electoral pressures are minimal. It is often argued that Hong Kong is atypical. So it surely is, although perhaps no more so than India, on which so many conclusions in the development literature are based. The Hong Kong experience supports the conclusions of the cross country study.

So does an analysis of five countries in Southern Asia. During a period of rapid growth in Pakistan and Bangladesh in the decade after 1959, measured income distribution became more equal. Wages of unskilled workers rose quite rapidly as well. This was a period of greater reliance on market forces, of a move away from government controls (Papanek, 1979 and 1986). No good income distribution data exist for Indonesia, but real wages of unskilled workers rose much more rapidly than per capita income between the mid 60's and the early 70's, so income distribution most probably became more equal. This was also a period of rapid growth (7-8%) and a strong move away from a highly controlled economy to one closely tied to the world economic system, with no control over foreign exchange transactions and a substantial decline in other controls (Papanek, 1980). In all three of these countries there was rapid growth in agricultural output (the average product in agriculture increased) and in a variety of labor intensive activities: notably public works projects in Bangladesh and Indonesia, and industry in Pakistan.

The experience of Korea for much of the 1960's, provides additional support. Wages rose rapidly and income distribution improved during a period when the rate of growth was high (Lee). The engine of growth was labor intensive exports. In 1970, Korean manufactured goods exports were about equal as a percent of National Income those of Japan only two years earlier.

Malaysia provides evidence of a different sort. Rapid growth was accompanied by unequal and worsening income distribution for the early 1960's through the late 70's, although labor and capital costs were not severely distorted and Malaysia was a market-oriented economy. The principal reason was barriers to labor movement, principally due to ethnic cleavages (Othman).

In short, both cross section data for many countries and time series for a few in Asia support the contention that rapid growth in a mixed, largely private enterprise economy is quite consistent with unchanging, even slightly improving income distribution. In all cases the commercial sector was labor intensive and in most cases there was comparatively rapid growth of output for small holder agriculture. In several cases the absolute income of the poor increased more rapidly with a move towards greater market orientation.

2) Modified Capitalism—Cheap Capital, Better Wages

A number of countries have modified the private enterprise system by substantial intervention in the economy to raise the cost of labor and lower the cost of capital. This is usually justified as improving the well-being of workers and preventing their exploitation, by raising their real wages, while encouraging growth by stimulating investment through cheaper capital.

a) *Distorting Input Prices*
Wages are raised by legislating minimum wages, by requiring the provision of various fringe benefits at the cost of the employing firm—health care, leaves, housing, pensions—and by protective legislation—overtime pay, restrictions on women working at night. In some countries the most costly step makes it difficult or virtually impossible to dismiss workers, which turns labor into a fixed cost and can lower labor productivity. The consequence is indeed a higher real income for workers who are effectively covered by the rules, and protection from some dangerous, ex-

ploitative practices. The price of capital is lowered by fixing rates of interest below market levels. Another, often even more important, method is to have an overvalued currency, which makes all imports relatively cheap. On most imported goods there are high tariffs and/or they are subject to import licensing, but machinery is exempt from tariffs and import licenses for it are freely granted. Therefore, imported machinery is cheap. Finally there may be generous depreciation allowances or other tax concessions on machinery. As a result, the cost of machinery going into investment is substantially below what it would be without government intervention.

As a consequence, the ratio of labor to capital costs can be severely distorted. The minimum wage can be 30 to 60% above the market wage. Fringe benefits can add another 30%. The real cost of inability to fire workers is difficult to compute, but even measurable costs may double the wage as a result of government intervention. The distortions in machinery prices can be almost as large. Tariffs, or the tariff equivalent of import licenses, often average 30 to 60% on imports other than capital goods. The interest rate has been 5 to 40% below what might be a reasonable market rate. As a result, the ratio of labor costs to capital costs can be three times what it would have been without distortions. (Papanek and Schydlowsy).

In addition, tariff protection and sometimes export subsidies, are often greatest for the least efficient activities. They receive the highest implicit subsidies because they could not survive otherwise and they are inefficient most often because they are capital intensive. The high subsidy encourages further investment in these industries.

The effect on labor use is difficult to quantify, because empirical studies on this subject are notoriously of dubious reliability. But even the most conservative analyses suggest that a tripling of the wage/capital cost ratio could reduce employment by about a third, as a result of a change in technology alone (Morawetz). Even more important is the consequent discouraging of labor intensive industries.

A study of Bangladesh has confirmed (Farid et al.) what other studies have shown: a perverse incentive pattern. The greatest incentives are generally provided to industries where Bangladesh's comparative advantage is least. The high cost of labor/low cost of capital and the implicit subsidies to inefficient industries are the principal reasons for such a pattern of investment. The results are low efficiency, inability to compete in the world market and a waste of resources. Another result is less employment. Finally, low capital costs and high labor costs, especially for the night shift, discourage full capacity use of installed equipment. If existing machinery in industry alone were used to capacity, one study of 6 Latin American countries suggests the employment created could absorb the equivalent of all the increase in the labor force for several years (Schydlowsky).

b) *The Consequence for Income Distribution*

The first effect of such distortions is slower growth because of the inefficiencies introduced. That in itself reduces the number of jobs created. Second, the capital intensive pattern of the investments and the technology chosen further reduces labor demand in the commercial sector. The real wage falls and with it the income of the poor.

There are workers who benefit, it is true. They are essentially a labor elite in the protected sector. Labor legislation in the really poor countries does not help most workers in agriculture, trade, services, handicrafts, or small and medium sized industry who constitute 60–90% of the unskilled. The gains of the labor elite are at the cost of slower growth and of the great mass of poorly paid workers, including the self-employed, outside the protected sector.

The other beneficiaries, of course, are those investors who receive the subsidized capital. These again tend to be a small group, sufficiently powerful and usually quite wealthy, who gain access to cheap credit, cheap machinery and various tax exemptions.

Cheap capital and credit do encourage investment. But they encourage investment that will be inefficient. At the same time the problem in most LDCs is not an inadequate willingness to invest but an inadequate rate of savings. When capital is subsidized the demand for it often exceeds the supply that savers are willing to make available. The result is the need to ration credit. It usually is the rich and powerful who obtain it. They are better risks, they have greater influence and, when it comes right down to the realities, they can afford to pay higher bribes. It takes an unusual government—or one staffed by saints—to resist the pressures to allocate scarce resources to the elite.

c) *Some Empirical Evidence*

There are many examples of basically private enterprise economies which adopted policies that distorted these prices. But the consequences of the policies for growth and equity have been studied in only a few instances.

Korea in the 1970's is one example. In the 1960's it carried out a labor intensive development program, which achieved one of the highest growth rates on record, with improvement in the income of the poor. The government decided to shift the mix of industry and exports from overwhelming reliance on such labor intensive activities as textiles, garments, toys and simple electrical goods to more skill and capital intensive steel, chemicals, ship building, automobiles, and engineering goods. To encourage investment in these activities, government provided cheap capital to the largest conglomerates, who were responsive to its "administrative guidance" in moving into these industries. Singapore also decided to move away from industries dependent on cheap, unskilled labor, because rapidly rising wages made that an infeasible long-term strategy. But Singapore emphasized skill intensive industries. Korean investment, in contrast, went into industries that were also capital and energy intensive. They were hard hit by the rise in energy prices and the world recession. The distortions introduced by encouraging capital intensity also had consequences for income distribution. The full capital subsidy was available only to a handful of the largest firms in the country and therefore benefitted the richest families. Simultaneously it slowed the demand for labor, particularly unskilled labor. Income distribution deteriorated in the 1970's (Lee).

In Indonesia, as far as one can tell from the sketchy data available, wages for unskilled workers increased little, if at all, between 1970/71 and 1978/9. In rice agriculture on Java (where 60% of the population live) wages rose little and the share of wage labor in the value of total output declined (Handoko et al.). During the 1970's the growth rate per capita continued at a very high 5–6% per year. Income distribution therefore almost certainly became far less equal (Papanek, 1986). The basic reason was the capital intensive nature of investment (see Dapice).

There is an instructive contrast for Indonesia between probable improvement in income distribution in the late 1960's and deterioration in the 1970's. Government ideology and reliance on the market were the same. But in the 1960's, substantial resources went into a labor intensive rehabilitation of infrastructure and an imaginative, locally organized publics works program. Moreover, after the failed coup of 1965 over one million deaths, detentions and dismissals reduced the labor force. Finally, output increased, including in small holder agriculture and in other parts of the work-sharing sector. The average product in that sector rose, because output was increasing, labor was moving out into various commercial activities, primarily construction, and the labor force had declined. As a result wages rose rapidly (Papanek, 1980).

In the 1970's the situation was different, at least until 1978. Rehabilitation had been completed, the works program was not expanding rapidly, the labor force was increasing rapidly and, above all, the bulk of the increased output came from such capital intensive activities as mining, logging, oil and gas production, and the chemical, steel and artificial fiber industries. The textile industry also expanded. While it is labor intensive, it also drove out many small textile firms which were even more labor intensive. Competition from imports also affected some labor intensive, well established, industries. Indonesia suffered from the "Dutch disease" exports dominated by natural resources (gas for the Dutch and oil, gas, timber and minerals for Indonesia) which produced an exchange rate at which more labor intensive production was just not competitive, unless subsidized. Indirect subsidies were provided for industry through cheap credit, protection against imports, government investment and so on. These almost invariably went to large, modern, capital intensive firms. Distortions also made labor expensive (i.e. fringe benefits, legal difficulties in dismissing workers) plus the fact that wages were higher than the marginal product because they related to the average product. No wonder that few jobs were created in the commercial sector. The natural increase in the labor force (plus released detainees) largely crowded into the work-sharing sector. On top of that was the tendency (Hart; Collier et al.) for work and income sharing to be less effective in agriculture. Finally there was the rapid mechanization of some activities (rice mills instead of hand pounding, motorized vehicles instead of bicycles and bicycle rickshaws, markets instead of peddlers). This was caused by changing tastes and increased income for the middle class and the ready availability of imported machines and vehicles and was abetted by government policy. All these factors counteracted the job-creating aspects of rapid growth and led to stagnation in real wages and worsening income distribution.

d) Modified Capitalism—The Economic and Political Costs

On the whole, therefore, policies to help workers by raising their wages and to stimulate investment by lowering its costs, end up slowing growth and worsening income distribution. Governments do not face a trade-off between growth and equity: these policies worsen both. Then why do governments adopt such policies? Governments want to remain in power. In terms of this objective perverse economic policies can be quite rational. The groups that benefit from raised wages and lower capital costs tend to be well organized and politically powerful. Workers in the protected sector are often the only ones organized into unions. The businessmen who receive cheap capital are the more powerful. Moreover, the allocation of capital that is scarce because it is cheap gives the bureaucracy considerable powers and perks and the bureaucracy is an important interest group in its own right. Allocating any scarce commodity or service is also a crucial source of political patronage. These distortions have the incidental advantage that they help the privileged in the guise of benefitting poor workers and speeding the rate of growth.

So there are good short-term political reasons for policies that have substantial economic costs. In the slightly longer term there are political costs to those policies that are often not fully recognised. There is good evidence that when real labor income (or real wages) drops, as a result of cheap capital and expensive labor, this quickly causes political difficulties for governments (Papenek, 1986). So the political benefits can be quite short-lived of policies which distort the price of labor and of capital.

3) Populist Strategies—Nationalization, Price Distortions, Controls and Social Services

The label "socialism" has been appropriated by such a variety of governments and societies that have little in common that it is not a useful analytical concept unless carefully defined and circumscribed. Moreover it carries such emotional baggage, both positive and negative, that its use can make communication difficult, unless its meaning to a particular author is carefully explained. So the term "populist" will be used here, to characterize governments whose stated objectives give high priority to equality. These are governments that intervene extensively in the economy with the objective of curbing the capitalists and of providing benefits to the poor.

a) *Distortions in Labor and Capital Costs*
In fact, governments with a populist strategy very often have distorted prices for labor and capital in ways, and for reasons, that are similar to those in the modified capitalist strategy. The results are similarly anti-poor. Organized labor is often one of their

major political constituencies, so they have raised minimum wages, and expanded fringe benefits and protective legislation. The consequence is the same as under the modified capitalist strategy: benefits to a labor elite at the cost of the underemployed and poorly paid majority of the labor force.

The rhetoric of the populist regimes, and the fear they engendered among the wealthier groups, discouraged investment. Nationalization and attempts at land reform further frightened investors. In attempts to prevent a decline in investment as a result, the populist regimes often went further than those pursuing a modified capitalist strategy in lowering the cost of borrowing and of investment goods to private firms.

Publicly owned firms often have an effective cost of capital close to zero. If they are financed by government through the budget, the only cost to the managers is that of persuading the relevant authorities to include their project in the budget. Even if nationalized enterprises borrow their capital, the cost to a manager is close to zero if repayment is not required during the term of a manager and if the interest rate about equals the rate of inflation. If capital is free, then using it lavishly will mean a high rate of profit, usually seen as a sign of efficiency. Capital intensive enterprises can also afford to pay high wages, since they have few workers. High wages and few workers minimize labor strife. Populist regimes frown on managers with unhappy workers, afraid that this is undermining labor support for the government. So both to generate high profits and to avoid labor trouble, managers will use lavish amounts of capital and few workers.

Populist governments are often also strongly nationalistic. For this and other reasons capital and skill intensive showcase projects—conspicuous investment—are emphasized: international airlines, steel mills, oil refineries, petrochemical complexes, superhighways.

The result is a pattern of investment and operation which employs very few unskilled workers. The consequences for the income of the poor is predictable from the previous analysis: lower real labor income and therefore a worsening income distribution. In this respect populist regimes are not all that different from the modified capitalist ones although their rhetoric may be quite different.

b) *Nationalization and Controls—Their Effect on Growth and Poverty*

They do assign a larger role to the public sector, often nationalizing all the banks, much of large-scale industry and some aspects of trade, and tightly controlling decisions by the private sector. The consequences of nationalization in effectively reducing the cost of capital have already been discussed. But there are also consequences for efficiency.

The reasons advanced for both nationalization and controls are quite similar, are well known and are believed to be stronger in LDCs than in developed countries. They center on the need (i) to avoid faulty decisions by private businessmen, industrialists and farmers which stem partly from their ignorance of the decisions of others and from distorted prices, such as those which result when labor has to be paid its average product, not its marginal product; (ii) to generate the savings and investment which society as a whole considers appropriate; and (iii) to help and protect the poor and weak against the rich and powerful.

These standard arguments for intervention are widely accepted, with only their importance in dispute. The arguments for the efficiency of private enterprise are equally well developed in the literature. They emphasize the importance of decentralization of decisions which the market makes possible, combined with strong economic incentives, to assure decisions which are efficient in economic terms. These arguments are also considered particularly powerful in LDCs because: (i) information required for centralized decision is less readily available; (ii) correct information is more important because the essence of development is rapid change; (iii) incentives need to be stronger in societies where radically changed behavior is essential for development.

The evidence in South and Southeast Asia supports the arguments that intervention, by reducing incentives, and by centralizing and bureaucratizing decisions, reduced efficiency and therefore growth. Dramatic changes in economic strategy towards greater market orientation occurred in Indonesia in 1966/67, in Pakistan and Bangladesh (East Pakistan until 1971) in 1959 and again in the mid 70's. The rate of growth accelerated dramatically after these changes in every instance. India, better endowed in a variety of ways at independence (more industrial capital, a well functioning civil service, a higher level of education and training, better infrastructure etc.) changed its policies less dramatically, had a steadier growth rate, but was consistently outperformed when the other areas moved toward greater reliance on the market (Papenek, 1979; 1986). The same relationship can be traced by contrasting agricultural development in two sets of regions that are quite similar in most characteristics: the two Punjabs and the two Bengals. Output in the Pakistani Punjab and Bangladesh (East Bengal) increased more rapidly than in the corresponding Indian Provinces when the former relied more heavily on market forces (1960–66/7; 1974/5–1980). Growth was generally slower in these areas when they, as well as India, used controls extensively (Papanek and Mujahid).

Similar comparisons can be made between more market-oriented East and Southeast Asia, and more command-economy-oriented South Asia. The former consistently outperformed the latter in terms of growth over the last decade or two. However, this evidence is less persuasive than that from changes in strategy in a particular country, because there are obviously differences other than the extent of intervention which may be the principal reasons for differences in growth rates.

If the rate of growth does not affect income distribution, as suggested earlier, then the higher the rate, the more rapidly absolute income of all groups, including the poor, will increase. A slower rate of growth therefore affects the extent to which poverty is alleviated, which may be even more important to most poor people than their relative share in incomes.

c) *The Provision of Services and Transfers of Resources to the Poor*

While populist regimes seem to have done less well in terms of the rate of growth, they seem to have been more successful in providing social services to the poor. Government-supported health facilities, housing, transport and, above all, education are particularly important for poorer groups. Not only do they raise real well-being, even if not reflected in income distribution statistics, they also increase equality of opportunity. The populist regimes on the whole provided more resources for services that effectively benefitted the poor. Democratic regimes tended to do more than authoritarian governments. When a government and party have to face the electorate every few years they are likely to respond more to the demand of the majority for better schooling, better health facilities and so on. India and Sri Lanka, democracies largely ruled by populist regimes since independence, have had a higher proportion of children in school, for instance, than other Asian countries with comparable per capita incomes.

Most populist regimes in South and Southeast Asia were not notably successful, however, in transferring either assets or income from rich to poor. Nationalization did take assets from a business/industrial elite, but the beneficiaries were largely a political, bureaucratic and labor elite, not the poor. Those who benefitted were a handful of workers in the enterprises, the managers who ran them and the civil servants who controlled them and the consumers of their products, the great majority of them from the wealthier groups (Jones). There was also a "dead-weight" loss, as a result of lowered efficiency. That is, former owners lost more than the gains to other groups.

Subsidies and price controls for urban consumer goods are widespread in poor countries, regardless of regime, but they tended to be somewhat larger under populist regimes. The extent to which this actually benefitted the poor depended on the extent to which: (i) lower prices discouraged production and therefore raised prices subsequently, (ii) price controlled goods flowed into the grey or black market serving primarily the wealthier groups, and (iii) lower prices affected goods consumed by the poor, as against the urban middle class.

Various partial studies and income distribution data all support the tentative conclusion that there are few governments, populist or market-oriented, that have succeeded in transferring a significant share of income from rich to poor. The net effect of food subsidies tends to be progressive, but that is compensated for by the heavy subsidy on education, transport, communications, water supply and other services for the wealthier (Husain). A major exception is Sri Lanka, at least until 1977, where populist policies of free and highly subsidized rice achieved a significant transfer. But in most countries the net effect of fiscal policy was rather small, as already noted, but may have been greater for populist regimes.

There was another offsetting factor: the windfall gains of the wealthier groups from the control system. When investment, inputs and "luxury" goods are tightly controlled and competition is not effective, someone benefits from the resulting scarcity. Usually it is those with political or social connections, or the resources to bribe officials, in short, the wealthy and powerful. For instance, when imports are controlled and scarce they sell at a premium. It is difficult to keep the person receiving the import license from benefitting from this premium or to keep the officials awarding the license from sharing the windfall gain (Papanek, 1967).

In short, with the exception of Sri Lanka, the populist regimes studied in Asia did not seem to have improved income distribution. The impact on the poor was probably less favorable than in the modified capitalist strategy.

4) Capitalist Production, Socialist Consumption - An Alternative Strategy

Both strategies therefore have costs in terms of lower growth and less equity and, in the longer run, political disaffection. Pure capitalism can achieve higher growth and greater equity in the longer run, but exposes the poor to sharp shocks and visible evidence of their povery in contrast to conspicuous consumption of the rich. This too can lead to political problems with pressure for government to intervene to avoid them. Moreover, in a really poor society there are compelling arguments for government intervention to improve the situation of the poor. Finally, there are good arguments for government intervention to correct or compensate for well-known market failures. There are special reasons for intervention to deal with inherent distortions in LDCs, especially in labor abundant economies.

a) *"Capitalist Production" - Ownership and Management*
But that intervention needs to take a form which does not undermine the economic efficiency of the system. Governments that are populist or that call themselves socialist often take on functions that a government is least well equipped to perform: managing hundreds of individual enterprises, setting thousands and tens of thousands of prices, determining thousands of investment decisions. If most firms and farms are left in private hands, the economy will benefit from decentralized decisions and the strong incentives which capitalism provides to hard work, savings, risk taking and enterprise.

To the extent that public enterprises already exist, or need to be established for a variety of reasons—often political—they can operate as much as possible like private firms. If the principal objective set for managers is to maximize profits and they are rewarded for their performance in terms of this objective, then public firms can function as well as private firms. They may even function better if private firms appoint incompetent managers because they are family members, while public firms look to a manager's competence. On the other hand it is practically impossible to give public firm managers the same incentives as private ones, and it is usally difficult to give them the same freedom from political interference.

b) *Intervention to Improve the Efficiency of the Market - Labor Subsidies*
There are well known arguments applicable in any economy, which will not be repeated here, for government intervention to improve the functioning of the market. They center on government's role in providing information about the planned actions of other private firms and of the government itself, which is the essence of "French Planning"; on government provision of in-

frastructure and other investments which benefit several firms or which are natural monopolies. Governments also set the rules of the game and regulate monopolies which are in private hands. Some of these functions are more important in LDCs. For instance, agricultural research is universally subsidized by governments because of its externalities, but is more important in societies where less is known about agriculture, where agriculture is more important and where there is no tradition of private firm research in agriculture. But there is little controversy about these forms of intervention, and they do not directly affect income distribution, so they are not discussed further.

Three other reasons for intervention are often significantly stronger in LDCs than in developed economies and have been neglected: (i) the importance of risk and uncertainty; (ii) a wage which is inevitably distorted; and (iii) discrimination against exports.

The reasons are obvious for greater risk and uncertainty in LDCs: the rate of change in economy, polity and society is greater and information is less readily available. As a result private decision-makers are often unwilling to invest for the long term and in activities that are especially subject to changes in government policies. Agricultural producers are reluctant to shift from subsistence food crops to higher value cash crops. The latter are more risky since food can always be eaten if prices drop. So government needs to guarantee minimum cash crop prices, and may have to absorb some of the risk of particular investments.

More closely related to income distribution is the distortion in unskilled labor costs. If such labor is paid its average product (total output divided by the number of workers) while an additional worker, of course, produces only the marginal product (the output of one more worker) which will usually be less, then too few workers will be hired by the commercial sector. The commercial sector will hire only enough workers to equate their marginal product with the average product in work and income sharing. Output in a country will then increase if the government subsidises employment by the commercial sector until marginal product of its labor falls to the marginal product in work sharing. The increase in output, equal to the difference between average and marginal product, can be considerable if the marginal product is low.

The most efficient way to subsidize unskilled labor is directly, by government in effect covering part of the wage in the commercial sector. Alternatively, it can be subsidized indirectly by government subsidizing part of the cost of food, housing, health care, transport or other expenses of such workers. The latter approach may be administratively simple, but is also quite costly since it is impossible to restrict the subsidy with spillover to benefit skilled workers, workers in the income sharing sector and even the middle class. These "leakages" are a cost, as is the need to raise the resources necessary for the subsidy. Those need to be offset against the benefits of the subsidy, benefits which are only large if the difference between marginal and average product of labor is large. As long as there is such a gap, a labor subsidy can be justified purely on efficiency grounds. It can be one form of government intervention that does not distort prices and incentives, but that corrects distortions that inevitably exist in some LDC economies.

Another widespread distortion is that infant industries are subsidized (through tariffs) or other measures if they produce for the domestic market, but not if they are exporters. Exports should not be discriminated against, so they may need a subsidy unless the problem can be met with a (compensated) devaluation or similar measure.

c) *"Socialist Consumption"—Increasing the Consumption of the Poor, Restricting that of the Rich*

It was argued at length earlier that the crucial variable in income distribution is the demand for unskilled labor. Subsidies for the use of labor in the commercial sector obviously increase demand from the sector for labor, and with it the real wages throughout the economy. So this is one step which can both increase the rate of growth and improve income distribution. There is no conflict here between the two goals. If the subsidy is provided indirectly via cheaper food, health services, education and training it can also help meet the "basic needs" of one group of the poor. Subsidies to education for unskilled workers also increase their human capital and therefore their income in the future.

The best way to finance those subsidies, and the labor intensive works program discussed later, is by taxing consumption of the rich. The consumption patterns of different income groups are obviously not the same, so excise taxes can be imposed which are paid in the first instance only by the rich: on automobiles, other consumer durables, high quality cloth, commercially produced housing above a certain size, first class travel and travel abroad, electricity use above a bare minimum, certain foods, gasoline for private cars, etc. Many of these taxes are relatively easy to collect. Unlike income taxes they need not reduce savings. While they reduce purchasing power, and therefore have an "income effect" on savings which is negative, they also make consumption more expensive and less attractive and this "price effect" can offset the income effect and leave savings unchanged or even increase it.

At the same time, by discouraging luxury consumption such taxes create an atmosphere of austerity which can make a major contribution to social peace. The poor are not much concerned about income distribution in any society. Almost no one knows what income distribution is, unless they carefully analyze the relevant statistics, which few people do. But conspicuous consumption is painfully evident to many people: the big cars and houses, and the lavish parties of the rich are very visible and are particularly resented in a poor society. High taxes, up to several hundred percent, can discourage such conspicuous consumption.

Such taxes can yield quite a bit of revenue if they are collected from the wealthiest 20–40% of the population. In a really poor country even the richest 20% may have incomes of only $400 a year and would not be considered at all wealthy in an international comparison. If the taxes are limited to the consumption of those who are wealthy by international standards, they may affect only the top 1 or 2%. So "rich" has to be defined in terms of the average for that society, if enough is to be collected to finance the subsidies of labor which are needed.

It could be argued that such taxes will destroy the very incentives on which a capitalist system rests. If the rich find consumer goods very expensive they will no longer have the incentive to take risks, to work hard, to save and invest. But that is not necessarily the case. For one, since it now takes more money to live luxuriously, people may work all the harder. More important, it is quite possible that in an atmosphere of austerity, competition among businessmen will take the form of competing to see who can most rapidly expand their empire, not who buys the biggest car or the biggest house. If that is the form of competition among the rich, it will reinforce the tendency to put much of their income into savings and investment, a tendency already encouraged by the high rate of taxation on luxuries. This is what seems to have happened in Pakistan in the 1950's and early 1960's, when quite astonishing rates of savings, up to 90% of profits, were achieved by many wealthy industrialists (Papanek, 1967).

d) *A Labor Intensive Works Program to Increase Labor Demand and Growth*

The revenue from these taxes can also be used to finance a

major, labor intensive, locally organized, public works program. Alternatively, such a program has been financed by surplus food provided as aid by developed countries. If most of the expenditures under the program are on unskilled labor, then much of the additional demand will be for food. If that is offset by aided food imports, then most of the funds to finance the program can be generated by additional food aid, with little effect on other prices.

Such a program can develop crucial infrastructure, such as irrigation and drainage works, rural schools and local roads to lower transport costs. As a result it will increase output and the rate of growth as well as the demand for unskilled labor, with wages rising as a consequence. The effect will be especially great if the work is concentrated in the agricultural slack season, when underemployment is a particularly serious problem. Successful programs of this kind have been carried out in a few countries (Cf. Thomas; Falcon, Patton and Dapice).

e) *Increasing Equality of Opportunity and Stabilizing the Income of the Poor*

The importance of improving equality of opportunity for the poor has been mentioned several times as have some steps to achieve this (eg: subsidized education for workers in the commercial sector). The feeling that government is trying to open opportunities for the future is important to provide hope and to defuse political tensions. Greater access to education (and health services) for the poor is also important to speed growth. An educated work force is clearly important for labor productivity and also contributes to an equitable income distribution.

The poor also suffer especially from the instability under capitalism. They can least afford any further reduction, even if short-term, of their already low incomes, as a result of rapid inflation or other shocks. In really poor countries the stabilization of wage goods prices is important to avoid sharp short term declines in the income of the poor and the unrest which frequently accompanies them.

f) *The Politics and Practicality of a Mixed Strategy—Socialism or Capitalism?*

One cannot point to any country which has adopted such a strategy, using the market and capitalist incentives to guide production decisions, but with a heavy dose of government intervention to compensate for distortions and other market imperfections and to improve equity. But elements have been used in different countries. In Asia, Sri Lanka has gone furthest with respect to Socialist consumption. Pakistan in the early 1960's had elements of both aspects of the strategy, but lacked deliberate equity measures.

One major factor in the appeal of the modified capitalist and populist strategies is that they provide immediate and tangible rewards to politically important groups, including workers in the protected sector, those who manage private or public enterprises, and civil servants who control the economy. But both strategies have economic costs, which can quite quickly turn into significant political costs (see above and Papanek and Dey). On the other hand, the proposed mixed strategy involves policies that would offend politically important groups. That may be the principal reason it has not been more widely adopted. But its economic benefits, in growth and in raising the income of the poor majority, could over a somewhat longer period, bring political returns as well.

It may seem a peculiar use of terminology to call the proposed mixed system "Socialist Consumption." Socialism has been widely identified, at least until recently, with government intervention in the economy and especially with public ownership. But surely that is a means. The objective has been greater equality of consumption and opportunity, and a floor to poverty, even if achieved at the cost of less power, wealth and income for the elite. At one time the only effective device for reaching these objectives may have been direct public ownership. With the development of the fiscal system, taxes and subsidies can achieve the same objectives more efficiently. The proposed mixed system would take advantage of the recognized efficiency of capitalism in generating output, but mitigate its consequences for inequality and poverty, and its inherent distortions in labor abundant, poor economies, by taxes, transfers and subsidies. By achieving Socialist objectives more efficiently—objectives which are widely shared—it could lay more claim to the term than those who use it to cloak exploitation by a government/political elite instead of a business/industrial elite.

D. *Summing Up*

It is widely accepted that poor countries, and especially those that are labor abundant, face a dismal trade-off between rapid economic growth in a predominantly capitalist system with great and rising inequality, and slower growth with government intervening to improve equality. It appears that there is some conflict between growth and equality, but that it is not very serious. When one excludes Eastern Europe and Communist LDCs from the analysis there is little evidence in cross country analysis that the

choice of economic system affects the tradeoff, that greater reliance on the market is more favorable for growth and less favorable for equality. There also appears to be no conflict between
equality and a high rate of growth in a mixed or private enterprise
system.

The higher the rate of growth the more rapid the passage from
very low incomes, where income distribution is egalitarian,
through middle incomes where it tends to be unequally distributed, to the level of a developed country which again tends to
be egalitarian. This tendency for per capita income and income
distribution to be related, known as the Kuznets Curve, however,
seems to explain only a small part of the large differences in
equality among nations. If one examines particular countries over
time there is even less evidence that it exists at all. A comparison of
countries therefore does not provide much support for the argument that governments need to intervene in the economy to
prevent a worsening of income distribution in the early stages of
development.

In addition, income distribution as widely expected is:
—more equal, the more widespread education
—related to concentration of asset ownership, which in turn is
influenced by various historical developments, and by land redistribution
—less equal in countries heavily reliant on primary exports.

But, contrary to the assumptions of some analysts, it is:
—not significantly affected by the importance of manufactured
exports

But the basic determinant of income distribution in the poorer,
labor abundant, Asian LDC is the income of unskilled labor, the
principal source of income for the poor. If labor income rises
more rapidly than average income in the country, then equality
has increased. In labor abundant economies labor income depends on the output and the number of workers (that is the
average product) in activities where work and income are shared,
where workers are not hired and paid in terms of their contribution to output (marginal product). Their average product becomes the "reservation wage," which the more capitalist
"commercial sector" has to pay to attract labor, and therefore
affects labor income in the rest of the economy. The crucial
determinants of real labor income then are the rate of growth in
agricultural output, which affects the average product in agriculture, and the rate and labor intensity of growth in the commercial sector which affect its demand for labor. Any tendency for
work and income sharing to break down can have a negative

effect on the income of the unskilled in economies where this relationship is significant.

Given this model, the forces in a capitalist system making for higher absolute incomes for unskilled labor, that is the poor, are a rapid, labor intensive pattern of growth. Since labor is cheap, capital expensive, in labor abundant LDCs, profit seeking capitalists will naturally invest in labor intensive activities and technologies. How quickly labor income rises depends in part on the pool of underemployed labor and the extent to which the poor gain some command of assets. The weakening of sanctions for work-sharing operates in the opposite direction. Other negative elements are: the decline of employment in traditional industries; the high incentives and rewards offered to scarce assets in the hands of the wealthier; and barriers to movement of labor to the more lucrative modern sector occupations. A priori either a worsening or improvement in income distribution is possible. Cross section data for many countries and time series for 8 Asian countries support the notion that, in fact, rapid growth in predominantly private enterprise economies is consistent with unchanged, greater or less equality. The "purer" the capitalism, the more rapid the growth on the whole and the more labor intensive the commercial sector. In Hong Kong the capital/labor cost ratio was not distorted, employment grew rapidly, and income distribution tended to remain unchanged or even to improve slightly. The same was true where commercial sector employment grew less rapidly, but the per capita output of small-holder agriculture increased (Pakistan 1960's, Indonesia late 1960's). The result of rapid growth and unchanged income distribution was, of course, a rapid increase in the absolute income of the poor.

The outcome was less favorable for growth, income distribution, and poverty when capitalism was modified, ostensibly to benefit workers by raising wages and to step up investment by reducing the cost of capital. The result was inefficient, high cost, capital intensive development that created little employment. Further distortions were then introduced by giving implicit subsidies to inefficient industries that otherwise could not survive.

"Populist" regimes distorted labor and capital prices even more, because widespread nationalization increased the role of decision makers for whom the price of capital was close to zero, while labor was potentially very costly. The result was lower demand for unskilled labor, highly unfavorable for the poor. Nationalization and controls also slowed growth, reducing the rate of growth of the absolute income of the poor—as of other groups. Controls also produced windfall profits for civil servants and those rich and powerful enough to obtain allocations of scarce resources. Nationalisation and controls transferred power over assets, and therefore income, from an industrial/business elite to a civil service/labor/political/managerial elite, not to the poor.

Taxes and subsidies provided somewhat greater benefits to the poor under populist regimes, particularly subsidized food and such services as education. But this was not enough to compensate for the slow growth of the economy and for the capital intensive nature of that growth. The effect of the latter on income distribution probably explains the lack of any relationship between income distribution and government intervention found in the cross country analysis. In five countries of Southern Asia income distribution often became less equitable during the periods when populist regimes were in power, as wages of unskilled workers rose more slowly or declined more rapidly than per capita income. Sri Lanka is an exception (Papanek, 1986; Jayasundera), because it succeeded in taxing the rich and subsidizing the poor. Despite their rhetoric and success in curbing the business class, these governments so distorted the economy that the poor suffered somewhat in relative and substantially in absolute terms, compared to several periods under growth-oriented regimes.

All three strategies have considerable long-term political costs. Populist governments can find their natural constituency, the urban workers, turning against them as their incomes stagnate and promised equality remains elusive. If the capitalist strategy is sufficiently modified, rising inequality, if obvious in the conspicuous consumption of the wealthier groups, inevitably leads to tension. With both of these strategies growth is slow if real returns to investment are low, because prices are distorted and competition is restricted. Slow growth further worsens the situation. The less distorted the prices, that is, the purer the capitalism, the less serious are most of these problems. But even a pure capitalist system has serious political problems. In poor countries any setback to the economy is difficult for the poor to bear, yet such setbacks are inevitable, and are more frequent in economies tied to the world capitalist system. In a private enterprise system there is then little help for the poor, little attempt to curb the consumption of the rich. The poor are painfully aware of their suffering when their income drops while conspicuous consumption continues unabated. Hong Kong is not typical in this respect. With a colonial government and the bulk of the population refugees, happy to be there, these tensions may have been tolerable, but other societies can have more serious problems.

Economists have criticized distortions in labor, capital and goods prices in LDCs as contributing to inefficiency and therefore slower growth. To this criticism one can add: they worsen income distribution and quite soon contribute to political difficulties. The political attraction of the two strategies which result in such distortions—modified capitalist and populist—has been based on the assumption that most of the politically significant elite would benefit from them. They also assume that most of the urban working class would be insulated from their undesirable consequences. But the latter assumption is not tenable if one accepts the average product model. Workers in the protected sector still benefit, but they are a small group. The great majority of urban workers, however, lose because their income is tied to labor income throughout the economy, including in agriculture. If labor income in the work-sharing sector of agriculture declines, increased migration to the city will put pressure on all urban wages, except for the protected sector. So even if the rural poor are not a political factor, governments that wish to stay in power cannot ignore rural poverty, because of the link via labor income to the urban population.

To get "prices right" has been the slogan of neo-classical economists. Their arguments have been couched in terms of efficiency and growth. The analysis here has suggested that in private or mixed economies, it is also the appropriate slogan for those concerned with an equitable distribution of income. While distortions in prices can bring immediate political benefits, these are outweighed by the political costs for any government that expects to be in office beyond a short time.

There are thus compelling political reasons to consider an alternative strategy. It relies on market incentives, private ownership and management of individual enterprises—"capitalist production." But it calls for government intervention through taxes and subsidies to compensate for market imperfections, especially the high risk and uncertainty of LDC and distorted labor costs. If labor is compensated according to its average product, too little will be used and a labor subsidy can be justified on both efficiency and equity grounds. Labor and other subsidies, including a labor intensive works program and greater access for the poor to education and other social services, can be financed by taxing the consumption of the rich. This will also reduce the tensions of a poor society and encourage savings rather than consumption. This strategy is in some ways the mirror image of the modified capitalist and populist ones: it has short term political costs because the elite bears taxes rather than gaining benefits, but longer term political gains because of a higher rate of growth and greater equity.

BIBLIOGRAPHY

Adelman, Irma and C. T. Morris (1973) *Economic Growth and Social Equity in Developing Countries,* Stanford: Stanford University Press.

Ahluwalia, Montek (1976) "Inequality, Poverty and Development," *Journal of Development Economics* 3 (4).

Chenery, Hollis and Moises Syrquin (1975) *Patterns of Development, 1950–1970,* London: Oxford University Press.

——, M. S. Ahluwalia, C. G. Bell et al. (1974) *Redistribution with Growth,* Oxford University Press.

Chow, Stephen and Gustav F. Papanek (1981) "Laissez-Faire, Growth and Equity—Hong Kong," *Economic Journal,* June.

Cline, W. (1975) "Distribution and Development: A Survey of the Literature," *Journal of Development Economics,* 1 (4).

Colfier, W. L., G. Wiradi and Soentoro (1973) "Recent Changes in Rice Harvesting Methods," *Bulletin of Indonesian Economic Studies,* 10 (2).

Dapice, David O. (1980) "An Overview of the Indonesian Economy," in *The Indonesian Economy,* Gustav F. Papanek (ed), New York: Praeger Publishers.

——, (1980) "Trends in Income Distribution and Levels of Living, 1970–75," in *The Indonesian Economy,* Gustav F. Papanek (ed), New York: Praeger Publishers.

De Wulf, Luc (1976) "Fiscal Incidence Studies in Developing Countries: Survey and Critique," *Staff Papers,* International Monetary Fund, March.

Dey, Harendra (1984) "Changes in Real Wages: The Effect of Growth, the Consequences for Income Distribution," unpublished Ph.D. dissertation, Boston University.

Falcon, Walter P., Richard Patten and Belinda Dapice (1980) "An Experiment in Rural Employment Creation: The Early History of Indonesia's Kabupaten Development Program," in *The Indonesian Economy,* Gustav F. Papanek (ed), New York: Praeger Publishers.

Farashuddin, Mohammad (1980) "Shadow Price of Labor, Investment, Foreign Exchange and Fiscal Resources: A Second Best Disequilibrium Approach for Bangladesh," unpublished Ph.D. dissertation, Boston University.

Farid, Shah M. *et al.* (1980) "The Industrial Comparative Advantage of Bangladesh," unpublished report prepared for The World Bank, Boston University.

Fei, John C. H. and Gustav Ranis (1964) *Development of the Labor Surplus Economy,* Homewood, Illinois: Irwin.

Handoko, Budiono Sri (1982) "Productivity, Size of Land and Labor Use in Rice Production in Java and Bali," unpublished Ph.D. dissertation, Boston University.

———, G. Hart, G. F. Papanek and A. Partadiredja (1982) "Technological Change, Productivity and Employment in Indonesian Agriculture," unpublished report, Boston University.

Hart, Gillian (1978) "Labor Allocation Strategies in Rural Javanese Households," unpublished Ph.D. dissertation, Cornell University.

Husain, Ishrat (1981) "Impact of Government Expenditure on Income Distribution: An Empirical Study," unpublished Ph.D. dissertation, Boston University.

Jayasundera, Punchi Bandara (1986) "Economic Growth, Income Distribution and Welfare Expenditure: The Case of Sri Lanka," unpublished Ph.D. dissertation, Boston University.

Jones, Leroy P. (1984) "Public Enterprise for Whom?: Some Perverse Distributional Consequences of Public Decisions," *Economic Development and Cultural Change*. January.

———, and Gustav Papanek (1983) "The Efficiency of Public Enterprise in Less Developed Countries," in *Government and Public Enterprise: Essays in Honour of Professor V. V. Ramanadham*, G. Ram Reddy (ed.) London: Frank Cass & Co.

Lee, Suk-Chae (1982) "Growth Strategy and Income Distribution: Analysis of the Korean Experience," unpublished Ph.D. dissertation, Boston University.

Lewis, W. A. (1954) "Economic Development with Unlimited Supplies of Labour," *The Manchester School*. May.

———, (1972) "Reflections on Unlimited Labor," in *International Economics and Development Essays in Honor of Raul Prebisch*, Luis Eugenio Di Marco (ed.) New York.

———, (1979) "The Dual Economy Re-visited," *The Manchester School*.

Meerman, Jacob P. (1974) "Budget Incidence and Income Distribution," *Review of Income and Wealth*, Series 20, No. 4.

Morawetz, David (1977) *Twenty-five Years of Economic Development 1950–75*, Washington, D.C.: World Bank.

Othman, Aris Bin (1984) "Growth, Equality and Poverty in Malaysia, 1957–80," unpublished Ph.D. dissertation, Boston University.

Papanek, Gustav F. (1967) *Pakistan's Development: Social Goals and Private Incentives*, Cambridge: Harvard University Press.

———, (1975) "Distribution of Income, Wealth and Power," in *Economic Growth in Developing Countries*, Y. Ramati (ed.), New York: Praeger.

———, (1978) "Economic Growth, Income Distribution and the Political Process in Less Developed Countries," in *Income Distribution and Economic Inequality*, Z. Grilliches, W. Krelle, H. Krupp and O. Kyn (eds.), Frankfurt: Campus Verlag.

———, (1979) "Real Wages, Growth, Inflation, Income Distribution and Politics in Pakistan, India, Bangladesh, Indonesia," *Discussion Paper* Number 29. Department of Economics, Boston University.

———, (1980) "The Effects of Economic Growth and Inflation on Workers' Income," in *The Indonesian Economy*, G. F. Papanek (ed.) New York: Praeger.

———, (1981) "Planning Against Poverty: Wage Data as a Tool," *Economic Bulletin for Asia and the Pacific*, Vol. XXXII, No. 2. December.

———, (1985) "Agricultural Income Distribution and Employment in the 1970s," *Bulletin of Indonesian Economic Studies,* xxi (2).

———, (1986) *Lectures on Development Strategy, Growth, Equity and the Political Process in Southern Asia,* Islamabad: Pakistan Institute of Development Economics.

——— and Harendra K. Dey (1982) "Income Distribution, Labor Income and Political Unrest in Southern Asia," Paper presented at the annual meetings of the American Economic Association and the Association for Comparative Economics, December 28–30, unpublished, Boston University.

——— and Oldrich Kyn (1986) "The Effect on Income Distribution of Development, the Growth Rate, and Economic Strategy," *Journal of Development Economics.* June.

——— and Dorojatun Kontjorojakti (1975) "The Poor of Jakarta," *Economic Development and Cultural Change.* October.

——— and Eshya Mujahid (1983) "Effect of Policies on Agricultural Development: A Comparison of the Bengals and Punjabs," *American Journal of Agricultural Economics,* Vol 65, No. 1. May.

——— and Daniel Schydlowsky (1980) "Shadow Prices, Comparative Advantage and Trade Policy for Bangladesh Industry: Executive Summary," unpublished report. Boston University.

Sharif, Mohammad (1981) "Labor Supply Behavior of the Poor in Labor Abundant LDCs," unpublished Ph.D. dissertation, Boston University.

Thomas, John W. (1971) "Rural Public Works and East Pakistan's Development," in *Development Policy II: The Pakistan Experience,* Walter P. Falcon and Gustav F. Papanek (eds.), Cambridge: Harvard University Press.

Variables of Success and Failure in Third World Development

Brian and Rachel J. Griffiths

ONE OF THE MOST REMARKABLE facts about Third World development over the past three decades is its diversity. The countries of East Asia (Hong Kong, Taiwan, South Korea, Singapore) have grown far more rapidly than those of South Asia (Bangladesh, India, Pakistan, Sri Lanka, Burma, Nepal, Bhutan). Asia as a whole has grown more rapidly than sub-Saharan Africa. Individual countries of sub-Saharan Africa, such as Ivory Coast, Kenya and Malawi, have developed much more rapidly than the region as a whole. In some countries (Taiwan, Sri Lanka) high rates of economic growth have led to decreasing poverty and decreasing inequality, while in others (Brazil, Mexico) high growth has produced a reduction in absolute poverty despite increasing inequality. Low growth has been variously accompanied by increasing poverty (India), decreasing poverty (Sri Lanka), increasing inequality (Bangladesh) and decreasing inequality (Costa Rica). In some countries economic development has been temporary, ended by an overthrow of government and a retreat to economic stagnation (Iran). In other countries, rapid economic development and the accompanying social change has acquired a legitimacy and appears to have become a permanent feature of those societies (the newly industrializing countries of East Asia).

..he interesting question is why Third World development ex-
..ts such diversity. Although the subject is an enormous one,
..s chapter is a first attempt to examine some variables which may
..ccount for the success and failure experienced by individual
countries and regions. Before doing so, it is necessary to say
something about the criteria which we might use for "success" and
"failure" and to outline more systematically the wide diversity of
Third World performance over the past few decades.

Criteria of Success and Failure

No set of criteria used to distinguish between success and failure in Third World development can be concerned only with
increased material prosperity,but must also include an assessment
of other features of society necessary for a country to be regarded
as "successful." The four criteria used in this paper have been
widely discussed in the development literature. They are, *firstly,*
and most obviously, an increase in prosperity as measured by GNP
per capita; *secondly,* a concern for equity, so that the increasing
prosperity reaches the whole and not just part of society; *third,* a
respect for human rights; and *fourthly,* evidence of sustainability,
so that if prosperity and equity are both achieved, the development process would be likely to continue.

During the post-war period increasing GNP per capita has been
the expressed objective of the majority of LDCs. No Third World
Country which in which GNP per capita has been falling for a
decade or more could be considered successful. But by itself per
capita GNP is a narrow measurement of economic welfare. It tells
us nothing about how the increased income has been distributed
throughout the population nor about how it has affected conditions for the very poor. Therefore the measure of growth per se
must be supplemented by measures of economic equity relating to
changes in the distribution of income, the attainment of a minimum level of income by the very poor, the creation of employment and the fulfilment of basic needs.

A number of different methods have been used to determine
whether or not income has been distributed more equitably. One
approach has been to measure relative income inequality by assessing the way in which the income of particular groups has
changed relative to others. This evidence can be summarized by
the Lorenz curve and relative inequality expressed either by a

Gini coefficient or by taking the income share of, say, the poorest 40% or the richest 10% of the population, or by some transformation of the data shown on the Lorenz curve, for example the coefficient of variation, the Atkinson index or the Theil index. An alternative measure of changing income distribution is obtained by examining the absolute level of income of various groups, in particular the poor, and how this has changed over time. The most common approaches to determining this figure are first to define for a particular country an income level equal to the poverty line, calculate the proportion of the population below that line and then observe how this proportion has changed through time; and secondly to measure the increase over time in the real income of very poor families. These two approaches—relative inequality and absolute poverty—can give conflicting measure of the change in equity over time.

A very good example of this is the Brazilian economy in the 1960s. Over the decade, per capita income increased by 3.2% per annum but various studies showed that relative income inequality also increased. The obvious conclusion was that the poor had failed to benefit from the rapid economic growth. However, the absolute income approach gave quite different results: the average income of those below a widely accepted poverty line (minimum wage) rose by 60%—which was substantially greater than for the rest of the labor force—and the proportion of families living below the poverty line fell from 37% in 1960 to 35.5% in 1970.

Another measure used to assess changing economic equity and the reduction of real poverty in developing countries has been the attempt to assess the fulfillment of basic needs, such as food, health care, housing and education. The advantage of this kind of index is that it would provide a very specific (and direct) measure of economic well-being and at first sight it would appear relatively straightforward to define the essentials of life and measure the extent to which they are being provided. In practice, however, the measurement of needs is fraught with difficulties in every area. In the area of health, the number of medical personnel per thousand people may hide great differences in training and regional distribution; in housing, needs are clearly relative to climate; in education, quantity is no guarantee of quality; and as far as nutrition is concerned, there is great ignorance of current, let alone past, consumption patterns. It is tempting to give up measuring fulfillment of needs directly and to rely on income as an indication of their fulfillment. However, the relationship between the level of GNP per capita in various countries and the provision of basic needs is weak—rising GNP per capita only leads to increased provision of specific basic needs (improved nutrition, reductions in infant mortality, more dwellings with access to electricity); it is no guarantee of a general improvement in the provision of all the basic needs of the population.

"Success" in Third World development, then, must include assessment of economic welfare in addition to a straightforward measure of increasing GNP. However, economic factors by themselves are not enough. If prosperity were increasing, absolute poverty being eliminated and basic needs being met, but at the same time human rights were being flagrantly violated, such development could hardly be labeled 'successful'. The definition of requirements in this category is again difficult and value judgments inevitably play a major part. Cases such as China under the Red Guards, Cuba under Castro, Uganda under Amin and the Central African Republic under Bokassa are clear-cut and well-documented instances of the systematic violation of human rights. Less easily categorized are India under Mrs. Gandhi, Chile post Allende, Argentina in the '70s and Iran under the Shah.

The final criterion for success in Third World development is the sustainability of that development. Too many countries over the past thirty years have experienced periods of economic glory—crudely measured in terms of rising GNP per capita—but have been unable to maintain the momentum of what was originally assumed to be economic "take-off." The development literature is littered with analyses of Third World countries judged at the time to be successful but now relegated to the class of failure. Often, such short-term expansion is the effect of changes exogenous to the society—the excitement of political independence (Zimbabwe), the introduction of a particular economic plan which catches the imagination of the people and causes a short-lived boom throughout the country (Tanzania), investment of foreign capital for political rather than sound economic reasons (South Korea), an unprecedented rise in the world price for a particular commodity (such as the price of oil for Iran and Nigeria). The success of a country's development therefore cannot be judged wholly in terms of GNP per capita. There has also to be some assessment of the basic values and institutions of the society, because if these are not compatible with the requirements of the modern industrial state, nor are they changing to meet these requirements, economic growth is unlikely to be sustained. The effects of political independence, economic planning, foreign investment and rises in commodity prices are not in themselves bad, but if there is no underlying structure to maintain and exploit the economic explosion, its effect will be only temporary.

II. Varieties of Third World Experience

South and East Asia

The experience of various countries *within* the continents of Asia and Africa is striking evidence of the diversity of Third World development. In East Asia between 1960 and 1977, Hong Kong, Singapore, South Korea and Taiwan averaged national product growth rates per person in excess of 7 percent. Between 1960 and 1980, South Korea's growth rate was 7.0% and Taiwan's 6.6%. Over the same period the countries of South Asia fared less well—India had a growth rate of 1.4%, Sri Lanka 2.4%, Pakistan 2.8%, Bangladesh 0% (zero), Burma 1.2%, Nepal 0.2% and Bhutan 0.1%. Other basic indicators served to reinforce this record. In 1976 the adult literacy rate in South Korea was 93% and in Hong Kong 90%. Yet in Bangladesh it was 26% and in India 36%. Sri Lanka with an adult literacy rate of 78% was an outstanding exception to the remainder of South Asia. Life expectancy was lower generally in South Asia (Bangladesh 46 years, India 52 years, Sri Lanka 66 years, Pakistan 50 years) than East Asia (Singapore 72 years, Hong Kong 74 years, South Korea 65 years). Urbanization increased much more rapidly in Taiwan (from 58% in 1960 to 77% in 1980) and South Korea (28% to 55%) than in South Asia (Bangladesh 5% to 11%, India 18% to 22%, Sri Lanka 18% to 27% and Pakistan 22% to 28%). The same also holds true of industrialization. Although South Asian countries have made a priority of industrialization, the results have been disappointing compared with countries such as South Korea in which between 1960 and 1977, manufacturing value added grew at a greater rate than that of Brazil (Table 1). The contrast between the countries of South and East Asia is not confined to economic growth and industrialization. It also applies to poverty and the distribution of income. Using as a standard of poverty the income per head accruing to the 46th percentile of the population of India, and then applying this to other countries in order to compare poverty, the evidence for 1976 was that the population in poverty in Taiwan was 5%, in South Korea 8%, but in Pakistan 43%, in India 46% and Bangladesh 64%. Sri Lanka was the exception for South Asia with a figure of 14%. A similar picture emerges from the figures of income distribution. During the early and mid-70s, the highest 10% of households had an income share of 24.7% in

Taiwan, 27.5% in South Korea, just over 28% in Sri Lanka and 33.6% in India. The income share of the lowest 20% of households however did not easily fall into geographically distinct patterns (Taiwan 8.7%, Sri Lanka 7.5%, India 6.7% and South Korea 5.7%).

Sub-Saharan Africa

Another region which exhibits remarkable diversity is sub-Saharan Africa. Although there are differences in size, natural endowments, colonial heritage and prevailing ideology between the 45 countries of this area, nevertheless they have many features in common: many are small, most are open to foreign trade and heavily dependent on the export of a few primary products, the majority of the population works in agriculture and lives outside an urban environment. All are newly emerging states with a labor force lacking education and a multiplicity of ethnic backgrounds. Yet economic performance over the past two decades presents great contrasts. Between 1960 and 1979 the growth of GNP per capita *fell* in eight countries (Chad, Somalia, Niger, Madagascar, Uganda, Ghana, Senegal and Angola), averaged less than 1% in 11 countries (Upper Volta, Benin, Mozambique, Sierra Leone, Zaire, Guinea, Central African Republic, Sudan, Zimbabwe, Zambia, Congo) and yet grew in Lesotho by 6% per year, in Swaziland by 7.2%, Botswana 9.1%, Gabon 6.1%, and in Malawi by 2.9%, Kenya 2.7%, Cameroon 2.5%, Tanzania 2.3%, Ivory Coast 2.4% and Nigeria 3.7%. The contrast between neighboring countries such as Ivory Coast and Ghana, Kenya and Tanzania, and Malawi and Mozambique is particularly acute. In the 1970s per capita income *fell* on average each year in 15 countries and rose by less than 1% per annum is no less than 19 countries. Between 1960 and 1979, the growth of GNP per capita was less in sub-Saharan Africa than in any other part of the world including South Asia. (See Table 3.)

The position in agriculture in this region is particularly serious. Throughout the region the growth of agricultural production began to decline in the 1970s compared to the 1960s, and food production per capita actually fell in the 1970s. Throughout the latter decade the growth of exports was negative. Yet there still exists a diversity. In the 1970s agricultural output *grew* by over 3% a year in six countries (Cameroon, Ivory Coast, Kenya, Malawi, Rwanda, Swaziland), yet *declined* or remained stagnant in seven others (Angola, Congo, Ghana, Mauritania, Mozambique, Togo and Uganda). As a result of poor performance, food imports grew rapidly, as did food aid.

The experience of sub-Saharan Africa is also interesting in that it is possible to distinguish two general types of development strategy which have been pursued by these countries. Countries such as Guinea, Ghana, Senegal, Sudan, Tanzania and Zambia have pursued etatist policies consisting of:

a) a high degree of state ownership with the state as the driving force of development;

b) direct economic controls, lack of faith in the market mechanism and public sector monopolies in trading;

c) rapid Africanization of jobs in public administration and commerce;

d) a big push for industrialization fostered by government;

e) a resistance to international market forces, severe controls over trade and foreign investment linked to import substitution.

These policies of African "socialism" have usually been linked to the strong leadership and personal philosophy of men such as Sekou-Toure, Nkrumah, Senghor, Nyrere and Kuanda.

The alternative strategy, pursued by countries such as Ivory Coast, Kenya and Malawi has been "market-oriented" and made up of the following elements:

a) state ownership mainly confined to public utilities and infrastructure;

b) greater reliance on markets, especially international factors, to allocate resources;

c) slower Africanization of key jobs;

d) a tendency to allow the balance between agriculture and industrialization to be determined by market forces;

e) encouragement of trade and foreign investment.

Poverty and Inequality

The empirical evidence on the extent of poverty and inequality in Third World countries during the development process shows a variety of outcomes. As can be seen from Tables 4 and 5, a reduction in absolute poverty has taken place in a number of Third World countries over the past two to three decades— Bangladesh, Brazil, Costa Rica, Pakistan, Puerto Rico, Singapore, Sri Lanka, Taiwan, Thailand and Mexico. This has happened under conditions of rapid, moderate and slow rates of growth. At the same time poverty has increased in Argentina, India and the Philippines, two of which were countries of high growth and one of which (India) was a country experiencing slow glowth. Exactly the same array of outcomes holds true with respect to inequality and growth. Inequality fell in Costa Rica and in four countries in Asia—Pakistan, Singapore, Sra Lanka and Taiwan. For India the evidence is not clear. But for four countries in Latin America (Argentina, Brazil, El Salvador and Mexico) inequality increased, as it did in the Philippines, Bangladesh and Puerto Rico.

In certain cases the two welfare measures, poverty and inequality, show the same trend, while in others they give differing results. In the cases of Argentina and the Philippines, absolute poverty and inequality both increased over the period, while in the cases of Costa Rica, Pakistan, Singapore, Sri Lanka and Taiwan, they both declined. In the case of Bangladesh, Brazil, Mexico and Puerto Rico, absolute poverty declined although relative inequality increased, while in the case of India the opposite occurred, namely absolute poverty rose despite a fall in relative inequality. The other major conclusion which emerges from these tables is that while there is no necessary connection between growth and the alleviation of poverty, nevertheless poverty does seem to have been alleviated more in countries with higher rather than lower growth. Both the Philippines and Argentina experienced rapid rates of growth yet poverty increased at the same time. Bangladesh and Sri Lanka experienced slow growth and yet poverty was reduced in both cases. A similar result holds for inequality. Once again, Bangladesh and Sri Lanka with low growth show a reduction in relative inequality but in the Philippines, Brazil, Mexico, Puerto Rico and Argentina high growth was accompanied by rising relative inequality.

III. Economic Factors

It is commonly assumed that economic development is directly related to the natural resources of a country. Rich countries are those with plentiful natural resources, poor countries those without. However, evidence from both Asia and sub-Saharan Africa indicate that natural resources are not a crucial factor determining success in development. Looking first at Asia, it has already been shown that, taking as measures of success either GNP per capita or more generalized indicators of economic welfare, the countries of the Indian sub-continent are grouped together low on the scale of success. Bangladesh and Sri Lanka are poorly endowed, having little in the way of mineral wealth and few natural resources other than land. Pakistan however does have some mineral wealth—coal, chromite and iron ore, as well as oil and natural gas fields. India itself has an abundance of minerals—coal, iron ore, manganese, mica, bauxite, copper and other minerals used in alloys, in addition to building stones of first-class quality, natural gas, gold and minerals suitable for atomic fission.

By contrast, the countries of East Asia are generally high on the scale of success, yet their natural resources are not as great as those of some South Asian countries. Taiwan has useful but not abundant resources of coal, oil and natural gas and small deposits of gold, silver and copper. South Korea has substantial coal and tungstan and small reserves of lead, zinc and copper but is not as rich as North Korea. But Singapore and Hong Kong have hardly any mineral wealth. Again it has been argued that lack of success is due to the pressure of population growth relative to land—what might be termed a negative resource—but the effects of this can also be exaggerated. In 1975 the number of people per hundred hectares of arable land was 244 in India and 204 in Pakistan, but 660 in Bangladesh and 641 in South Korea. In addition, the four major countries of South Asia have more educated manpower and a legacy of administrative experience uncommor in the Third World. Similarly, in sub-Saharan Africa there is little evidence to support the idea that success in development is closely linked to natural resources. Countries such as Bostwana, Gabon, Guinea, Nigeria, Zaire, Zambia and Zimbabwe are all rich in minerals and oil, yet they have very different per capita levels of GNP and growth rates of GNP.

From the variety of Third World experience it is, however, possible to make certain important generalizations regarding economic development. Growth has been more rapid in countries with market oriented development strategies than in countries which have made the state the driving force of development. The second is that those countries which have pursued discriminatory policies against ethnic minorities, including expatriates, have fared less well than those which have permitted a slower pace of

change and less discrimination. The third is that high growth
Third World countries tend to have low tax structures while low
growth countries tend to have high tax structures.

What then is the evidence for the greater success of market-
oriented economies? It has already been stated that in sub-Saharan Africa it is possible to distinguish two general types of
development strategy—etatist policies and market-oriented policies. In the market-oriented countries (Ivory Coast, Kenya, Malawi) the average rate of growth of GNP between 1960 and 1975
was 6.9%, whereas the etatist nations (Ghana, Guinea, Tanzania)
averaged only 3.8%. A similar pattern is found in Asia: Hong
Kong, Singapore, South Korea, Taiwan and Japan, which have
encouraged the private sector and private markets, have grown
more rapidly than countries such as India and in the past Sri
Lanka, which have emphasized state ownership and state planning.

One particular area in which the contrast between the two
approaches is particularly acute is agriculture. In sub-Saharan
Africa during the 1960s and 1970s, a number of countries invested heavily in large-scale, publicly-run estates involving heavy
capital investment in mechanization and irrigation; for example,
Nigeria (irrigation), Ivory Coast (sugar scheme) and Ghana,
Congo, Ethiopia and Zambia (state farms). Most of these schemes
were not successful because of poor management, overmanning
and lack of technical expertise for maintenance of equipment.
This is in marked contrast to the productivity of private smallholders in Kenya, which in no small measure accounts for its
growth rate of agricultural production of over 4% between 1955
and 1979. From the mid-fifties, smallholders were permitted to
grow products such as coffee and livestock which previously had
not been possible and, following independence, land reforms
meant an increase in smallholder agriculture. Not only did smallholders expand production rapidly in new areas (such as maize
and tea) but, according to a 1974 rural survey, both output and
employment per hectare for land of equal quality tended to be
higher in small farms than in large. For example, for smallholdings of less than one-half hectare output was 19 times greater per
hectare and employment 30 times greater than on smallholdings
whose size was over eight hectares.

In addition, the acceptance of etatist policies for development
has led to further economic regulations—price controls, foreign
exchange controls and production subsidies, with disastrous
effects. Exports are crucial to the prosperity of LDCs but protectionist policies raise the cost of exports, directly through higher

input prices resulting from higher tariffs, and indirectly by having to compete for scarce resources against the protected industries, which once more means higher cost and less profit. As a result, the evidence shows that exports have grown most rapidly in those countries which have pursued the least protectionist policies, such as Hong Kong, Taiwan, South Korea and Singapore. By contrast, India, Pakistan and Sri Lanka (before Jayewandene)—countries which have pursued highly protectionist policies—have performed far less well, as is clear from Table 6.

Government legislation has discouraged exports of LDCs in other ways. In many African countries, producer prices for agricultural products are legally controlled and exports are marketed by state trading organizations. Exporters face not only prices which are frequently below world market levels, but marketing boards which charge levies, excessive marketing costs, governments which impose export taxes, and overvalued exchange rates. One measure of the extent of this taxation is the "Nominal Protection Coefficient," defined as the price paid to the producer, divided by the world price less transport, marketing and processing costs. An NPC of more than one means that the crop is being subsidized, while an NPC of less than one means it is being taxed, with the size of the subsidy and the tax varying with the deviation of the coefficient from 1. Table 7 shows the nominal protection coefficients of various export crops in selected sub-Saharan African countries. On the basis of these figures, it is hardly surprising that agricultural export performance in Africa has been so poor.

The most dramatic examples of the effects of such "taxation" are in Tanzania and Ghana. Between 1966 and 1980 the major exports of Tanzania (cotton, coffee, cloves, sisal, cashews, tobacco and tea) fell by 28% and export earnings as a percentage of GNP fell from 25% to 11%. Cotton and tobacco exports fell because of the increase in domestic consumption. But for other crops exports fell because of substantial cutbacks in production resulting from low prices paid to farmers. The fall in prices was not the result of a fall in world market prices but the size of the domestic 'taxes' imposed on farmers due to export duties, marketing and administrative costs. In Ghana between 1965 and 1979, cocoa production fell by one-half and Ghana has fallen from first place in world production to third behind Ivory Coast and Brazil. Again this was the result of farmers being taxed through low prices. Between 1963 and 1979 the consumer price index in Ghana rose 22 times, the price of cocoa in neighboring countries rose 36 times, while cocoa prices to Ghanaian farmers rose only 6 times.

A second generalization is that those countries which have pursued discriminatory policies against ethnic minorities, including expatriates, have fared less well than those which have permitted a slower pace of change and less discrimination. At the time of independence most African countries were extremely short of indigenous administrators, technicians and entrepreneurs. They faced the choice of whether to Africanize as rapidly as possible by specifying that certain jobs could only be undertaken by Africans and hope that they would learn by doing, or else to allow expatriates and ethnic minorities considerable freedom of employment. Countries such as Tanzania, Zambia and Ghana opted for the former. In Tanzania, for example, the policy of 'citizenization' meant that the percentage of citizen officers in the middle and senior grades of the civil service increased from 62% in 1961 to 90% in 1971, at the same time as the number of posts in these categories increased by 140%. The weakness of this policy was that because the educational system was geared to producing clerks and teachers, the management skills of the public administration in terms of running public utilities was quite weak. The weakness was even more exposed by discrimination against Indian entrepreneurs in construction, transportation and particular kinds of repair and maintenance activities. These problems were far less evident in Kenya, Malawi and Ivory Coast. In Kenya the government did not attempt to force a rapid pace of Africanization and did not discriminate against other ethnic minorities. In Ivory Coast the European population, which has been involved in public administration, has remained important: in fact absolute numbers have increased from 30,000 in 1965 to 50,000 in 1975. Once again, Ivory Coast has pursued a slow policy to achieve Africanization.

A third generalisation is that high growth Third World countries tend to have low tax structures while low growth countries tend to have high tax structures.

Third World governments have adopted two entirely different approaches to the financing of public expenditure: some have promoted high growth on the basis of low tax rates, while others have fixed high tax rates on a stagnant or slowly growing economic base. Looking first at South and East Asia, the newly industrializing economies of East Asia—Hong Kong, Singapore, Taiwan and South Korea—have opted for the low tax rate/high growth alternative with positive results not only for the private economy but also for public sector consumption. By contrast, India has pursued the high tax/low growth path with depressed rates of public consumption.

Hong Kong is the prime example of low tax policies: the top

marginal rate for personal income tax in Hong Kong is 15% of gross income (reached at approximately $15,000 for a single person and $20,00 for a married person). This is remarkably low even by comparison with other East Asian countries. Yet this low level of personal taxation has financed an expansion in public expenditure—on education, health, transport, housing, etc.—of 8.6% per annum between 1960 and 1970 and 9.3% per annum between 1970 and 1979. If we compare these rates of growth in public sector spending with those of Sweden (which has the largest public sector of any Western economy), public consumption increased by only 5.4% per annum between 1960 and 1970 and fell to 3.18% between 1970 and 1979. Growth in public spending in Sweden has been constrained by lower rates of economic growth: while economic growth (measured by GDP) rose by 10% in Hong Kong between 1960 and 1970, the Swedish economy grew at only 4.4% during the same period; between 1970 and 1979, Hong Kong grew at a rate of 9.4% whereas Sweden's growth fell to only 2%.

In Singapore—another low tax rate economy—the average annual growth rate of 8.6% between 1960 and 1977 has generated more public revenue than the most optimistic forecasts had anticipated. Because the low tax/high growth system has proved so effective in generating funds for all the government's public spending requirements, Singapore has cut personal income tax rates between 6.8% and 19.9%. Here, low tax rates have led to high rates of growth, which in turn have made possible lower tax rates with the expectation of still further economic growth.

The second alternative—of high tax structures and low economic growth—has been followed in India. Here, in spite of high tax rates, public consumption *fell* by an average of −0.67% per annum between 1960 and 1977. The reason lies in India's low growth rate of 1.3% during this period. Turning to Africa, the contrasting experience of neighboring Ivory Coast and Ghana confirms the picture that high growth/low tax countries tend to be better able to provide for the social needs of their people, including the poor, than those that adopt high tax rates which curtail the growth of the economic base on which the welfare of all sectors of society depends. Ivory Coast has opted for free trade and low tax policies (its top marginal rate of tax is 37½% at $20,922). Ghana has adopted a protectionist and high tax policy (with a top marginal tax rate of 75% at $12,522). The different results of these two policies is dramatic. The average annual growth rate of GDP in Ivory Coast was 8% between 1960 and 1969 and 6.7% between 1970 and 1979. As a result of this high rate of economic growth,

Ivory Coast could afford to raise public expenditure by an average of 11.8% during the 1960s and to maintain an average annual increase of 11.8% during the 1960s and to maintain an average annual increase of 10% during the 1970s. In Ghana, however, growth was only 2.1% during the 1960 to 1969 period and fell to −0.1% from 1970 to 1979. This low level of growth necessitated a reduction in public expenditure increases from 8.5% per annum between 1960 and 1970 to −2% from 1970 to 1979.

IV. Political Factors

The political experience of the countries of sub-Saharan Africa and South and East Asia has been extremely varied. Most of them have come to independence following colonization, except Liberia and Ethiopia. Many have experienced considerable political instability in the form of coups, plots or even civil wars. Nearly all of them are pluralistic in culture, language and religion. In many, ethnicity has emerged as an important force. In most of them the commitment to democracy is weak and the more typical form of government has been either a one-party state or an authoritarian regime. Any generalizations on the basis of such a welter of evidence must of necessity be tentative and exploratory. Yet certain patterns do seem to emerge.

Statehood and Development

One is that the Weberian concept of the empirical state would seem to be a necessary condition for development.

An important difference exists in the concept of statehood as developed by Max Weber and used by many political scientists and that which is used by international legal theorists. Weber's definition of a state is a corporate group which has compulsory jurisdiction, exercises continuous organization and claims a monopoly of force over a territory and its population. The emphasis here is on the de facto rather than the de jure characteristics, on means rather than ends, even though he recognizes the legal aspects. What he ignores is the extent to which the state as a legal entity is recognized in international law. The heart of Weber's definition is the exclusive use of force in a given territory. Using this definition, the situation in Nigeria with Biafra would have required the recognition of two separate states. Both Biafra and Nigeria were able to exercise effective force over given territories and populations for substantial periods of time. If, on the other hand, no one group or groups are able to establish dominance, then anarchy or statelessness prevails. This has been the case at one time or another in Chad, Angola, Ethiopia, Nigeria, Sudan, Uganda and Zaire.

The alternative definition as developed by Brownless, a legal theorist, is that the state is a legal person, recognised by international law and having (a) a defined territory, (b) a permanent population which subsumes a stable community (c) an effective government with centralized administrative and legislative organs and (d) independence in terms of foreign policy. The weakness of this approach is the inclusion of permanent population and effective government in a definition of statehood without their having specific content, alongside legal concepts which are very precise. For example, in the states of sub-Saharan Africa the empirical properties of the state, namely the permanence of population and effective government, have varied greatly over time, while the juridical elements have remained fixed. Hence, following Jackson and Rosberg and using the Weberian and Brownless concepts, it becomes possible to conceive of two different kinds of state, the empirical and the juridical. The empirical state depends in a narrow sense on the monopoly of force and in a broader one on a stable community and effective government. The juridical state depends on its being recognised by other states and international organizations as a sovereign territory which can claim protection by international society from intervention by other states. It can also be argued that economic development depends on the empirical state as much as on the juridical state. The efficient working of the market economy requires a certain degree of certainty. The fact that the state is protected from external aggression is important. But so too is internal stability and respect for law. Internal instability can be just as damaging to direct investment and job creation as the threat of war.

By empirical standards, many of the states of black Africa are weak and derive their statehood more from international society than internal stability. They are arbitrary units resulting from colonial times and owe their boundaries to the late nineteenth century struggle for Africa. By contrast, the countries of East Asia can be characterised as both juridical and empirical states. Most of the states of black Africa could not be considered stable communities. With the possible exception of Somalia, all are made up of distinctive ethnic groups. In numerous cases basic ethnic differences are reinforced by regionalism, language and religion. Ethnicity when politicized can be a powerful source of conflict and internal instability, leading ultimately to doubts over the ability of the state itself to survive. Ethnic factors have been major causes of civil war and uprisings in the Sudan (1956–64), Zaire (1960–65, 1977–78), Ethiopia (1962–82), Zanzibar (1964), Burundi (1966–72), Chad (1966–82), Uganda (1966; 1977–82), Nigeria (1967–70), Angola (1975–82), and Zimbabwe (1982–82). The potential disrupting effects of ethnic conflicts has also been a major factor leading to the rejection of parliamentary democracy and the development of the one-party state.

It would be difficult to describe most black African governments as having effective administrative and legislative institutions in the Western sense. The creation of political institutions, such as parties, parliaments and elections, which continue independently of the authority of strong leaders is not something which generally speaking has developed in black Africa. The cases in which African governments could be characterized as having compulsory jurisdiction are usually associated with strong personal leadership, whether it is autocratic as in Ivory Coast (Houphouet-Poigny), Malawi (Panda), Gabon (Eongo), Cameroon (Ahidgo), Togo (Eyodema), oligarchic as in Kenya (Kenyatta), Sudan (Numeiri), Senegal (Senghor), or ideological as in Tanzania (Nyrere) and Guinea (Torre). Administrative efficiency, with the possible exception of Ivory Coast, Kenya and Malawi, is also generally lacking. On both criteria for the empirical state therefore, it would be difficult for many black African states to qualify as such.

By contrast, the more successful countries of South and East Asia tend to be empirical states as well as juridical ones. Like sub-Saharan Africa, these countries have a plurality of religion, culture and language, and also have political systems which tend to be monolithic and single party states. By Western standards they tend to have authoritarian governments with a limited regard for opposition political parties (the exception being Japan), freedom of the press and the rights of dissenters. Nevertheless by comparison with sub-Saharan Africa, their communities could be described as more stable and better governed.

The political stability of East Asian states and the contrasting political instability of many states in sub-Saharan Africa can readily be seen from Charts 1 and 2.

Poverty, Inequality and Public Policy

A second generalization which emerges from examining political factors is that Third World governments cannot simply rely on higher rates of economic growth to achieve a reduction in the level of absolute poverty. Typically governments must be committed to policies which will reduce poverty. Generally, the trickle-down effect will occur, but it cannot be guaranteed to be of help to the poorest of all. Sri Lanka is a country which has reduced the level of absolute poverty in spite of its being poor and having a slow rate of economic growth. Between 1953 and 1973 the income share of the poorest decile of the population rose from 1.9% to 2.8% and the proportion of income recipients with incomes below a poverty line of PS 100 (in constant 1963 prices) fell from 63 in 1953 to 41 in 1973. This was achieved through deliberate policies of income redistribution such as price guarantees for rice growers, land reform, subsidized rural credit, progressive taxation and a free rice ration. The case of Taiwan is more interesting because it is one of the very few Third World countries in which rapid growth has been accompanied by the alleviation of poverty and a reduction in inequality. Its success in achieving both growth and equity has resulted from: (i) an initial redistribution of assets in the early stages of growth, through land reform and the privatization of public enterprises in the early 1950s, so that assets were not distributed too unequally; (ii) a willingness to remove protectionist policies and controls and to allow prices for commodities and labor to be market-determined in order for resources to be allocated efficiently—something which resulted in a broad-based economic growth across all sectors of the economy; (iii) a policy of decentralization which helped develop small industries in agricultural areas and reduce rural-urban migration.

One country which has experienced rapid economic growth— 6% a year in real output and 3% in real output per capita between 1950 and 1973—is the Philippines. Yet, despite this, absolute poverty has increased. Between 1961 and 1971 average absolute income among the poorest 20% of the country actually fell. The burden of this was borne by the rural rather than the urban section of the community and resulted from government policies which subsidized the manufacturing sector through over-valued exchange rates, low interest rates and investments subsidies by taxing the agricultural sector. Compared with Taiwan, rural development in the Philippines suffered from lack of credit facilities for farmers, inadequate marketing and transport systems and poor irrigation.

V. Culture and Economic Development

The final section of this paper is concerned with the values and attitudes of the peoples of sub-Saharan Africa and South and East Asia, the religions which inspired these beliefs, the behavior patterns which result from them and the effect these have on economic life and economic development. Few social scientists have confronted the question of the relationship between value systems and economic achievement. A good deal of the analysis of success and failure in less developed countries has been conducted by economists. Economics is a powerful science, but it derives its predictive ability from holding preferences, tastes and values unchanged and then considering the effect of changing constraints; for example, the effect of a rise in real income on the demand for cars, a reduction in money supply growth on the rate of inflation, a change in the real effective exchange rate on the structure of production, a change in unemployment compensation on the total numbers of unemployed. It is able to do this only because values are impounded *in ceteris paribus*. Even when dealing with the matter of economic organization, the typical experiment suggested by Milton Friedman is the comparison of two societies, alike in almost all respects except their economic systems (East and West Germany, Taiwan and mainland China, Japan and India). Differences in performance are then ascribed to differences between market and non-market forms of economic organization. The strength of economics is its ability to predict by changing constraints. The weakness of economics is its inability to handle differences in values, changes in values or even to consider those values which are necessary and/or sufficient either for a market economy to exist or for there to be a sustained increase in the wealth of nations. Similarly many sociologists, in particular those in the tradition of Marx and Durkheim, see values and beliefs as a reflection of social or economic status—an effect rather than a cause; whilst the behavioral sciences are concerned with changes in behavior that result from changing external stimuli rather than internal beliefs. Values are difficult to define and impossible to quantify, hence the inevitably speculative nature of much of the existing work on the relationship between values and economic growth and its relative inaccessibility to rigorous scientific testing. Where large-scale surveys have been undertaken, problems in formulating standard questions across cultures have frequently led to apparently conflicting results. Perhaps as a result of this lack of "hard" evidence, perhaps because any attempt to rank value systems is inimical to the moral relativism of the late twentieth century, it seems that the majority of those concerned with international aid and development would endorse the view expressed in the Brandt Report—that "all cultures deserve equal respect, protection and promotion."

It is our contention that while all cultures deserve equal respect, nevertheless if economic development and material prosperity are taken to be a goal, then all cultures do *not* provide an equally effective means to that end and therefore are not equally deserving of promotion. Our reasons for arguing this are twofold. Firstly, there is the prima facie evidence of differences in economic performance between otherwise comparable societies and secondly, we have the evidence derived from detailed examinations of certain cultures by Weber, Banfield, Nye and others.

There exists prima facie evidence to suggest that different groups of people in Third World situations faced with a similar environment, a similar opportunity and a similar form of economic organization, but with different cultural values tend to perform differently in economic terms. Within Nigeria the performance of the Ibos has been noticeably superior to that of other tribes; in Malaysia the Chinese have tended to be far more enterprising than the Malays, in East Africa the Indian population has shown more resourcefulness than the indigenous African population, and in India the Sikhs in the Punjab have experienced something of an economic miracle which is in marked contrast to the Muslim Bengalis. The last of these is particularly interesting. The Sikhs were moved to the Punjab after partition in 1947. Farm production increased rapidly, major new initiatives were taken in irrigation and infrastructure, and then in the 1960s there was an enormous surge in agricultural output—wheat production trebled between 1966/7 and 1970/1, the rice crop increased from 280,000 tons in 1965/6 to 1.9 million tons in 1973/4. This is in marked contrast to the stagnation associated with the caste system in other areas of India.

The starting point for the modern discussion of the effect of culture on economic development is Max Weber's *The Protestant Ethic and the Spirit of Capitalism*. In it, the ethos of capitalism is related to the notion of predestination and the concept of work as a calling in the theology of biblical Protestantism. This work needs to be read in conjunction with his other two major works in this field, *The Religion of India* and *The Religion of China,* which contrasts Calvinistic values with those of Hinduism in India and Confucianism and Taoism in China. Cultural factors are also emphasized in Edward Banfield's *The Moral Basis of a Backward Society,* which attempts to explain the backwardness of a South Italian village in terms of the average family's exclusive concern with the short-term interests of its own members and of its perception of the outside world as a hostile environment in which other nuclear families will behave in a similar fashion. In a study of the Mexican village of Tzintzuntan, G. M. Foster, an American anthropologist, shows how the perception of wealth as something fixed discourages self-improvement and progress and fails to provide a sound basis for economic development. In another study, *Politics, Personality and Nation-building,* Lucien Pye attempts to explain the failure of development in Burma in terms of the absence of certain values such as security, trust and decisiveness, which are crucial to development.

It has been argued earlier in this chapter that economic growth tends to be more rapid in market rather than state-oriented economies. However, as Hayek has pointed out, the creation of a free market economy assumes the acceptance of certain basic premises—most importantly, personal responsibility and a non-egalitarian distribution of income, which may or may not be acceptable to a particular culture. If it were possible to show that certain cultures eschewed the market-oriented approach to development because of certain cultural values, that in itself would be important in determining success or failure in economic development. Given that the idea of a free market is acceptable to a society, three questions still remain to be asked about the influence of cultural factors on economic development. Firstly, which cultural factors are necessary to initiate development? Secondly, what kind of cultures find it easiest to initiate economic success? And finally, which cultures are most likely to sustain economic development?

In answering these three questions, the contrast between South/East Asia and sub-Saharan Africa is of particular interest. Neither region initiated economic change; both set out to copy the economic success of other regions, particularly the West. Furthermore, a strong indigenous merchant class did not emerge in the early stages of development in either South/East Asia or sub-Saharan Africa; rather, both regions have been dependent on state capital at least during the initial period of development. Yet while East Asia and some countries of South Asia have achieved distinctive free-market economies with consistently high levels of economic growth, the countries of sub-Saharan Africa have generally failed to do so.

In analyzing the cultural factors crucial to economic development we return to Weber's thesis outlined earlier—that certain Judaeo-Christian values, freed from the confines of the medieval Church and applied to the world, were particularly compatible with modern capitalism. It is not without significance that the branch of Protestant theology analyzed by Weber is Calvinism, which takes as its starting point not the Crucifixion but the Creation. The following analysis focuses therefore on six sets of values crucial to economic development, all found in embryonic form in the Hebrew creation story and developed in later Judaeo-Christian literature, but with parallels in other teachings and cultures. These are: attitudes to the physical world, to time, to individual/personal responsibility, to other members of the group (individuality and trust), and to work.

The Physical World

Development depends on transforming and improving the physical environment. Prosperity depends on minerals being extracted, land being cultivated, dams being built and trees being cut down. The feasibility of these activities depends critically on the view of the physical world, which is derived from cultural and especially religious norms. There are three elements in the Christian attitude to the physical world, as expressed in the Creation story, which are crucial to economic development. First, the physical world is seen as altogether separate from God. Secondly it is seen as different and separate from man. Thirdly, it is seen as something essentially good.

In many cultures, however, God is not seen as a separate being, apart from the created world. Instead of belief in one God, there is belief in "spirit," "life", "vital force," which exists not in a separate heaven but in every aspect of the physical world. Animate and inanimate objects are possessed of a spirit which may be neutral, harmful or beneficial. The continuing power of the medicine man or witch doctor in even urbanized Africa today consists in his being able to divine and manipulate these spirits. A development of this view moves from spirit worship to the worship of nature (sun, moon, stars, seed time and harvest) in which visible gods replace the invisible idols. If the Spirit of Life is to be found in all things, it follows that the physical world is not to be tampered with. The African Bishop of Pururi, Mgr. Bernard Pududira, in an article in an African magazine in 1981, on "Fundamental Causes of Underdevelopment," speaks with remarkable candor on the traditional African view of nature:

"Our African people endure the vicissitudes of nature without resisting them. Improving nature is tantamount to rebellion against its hidden powers. African stories are proof of this attitude."

At its best such a view of the physical world logically prevents any attempt at improving material conditions. At its worst it creates the kind of paralyzing fear described by Warneck in his account of the Battak tribesmen of Indonesia:

"Animism seems devised for the purpose of tormenting men, and hindering them from enjoying life. To that must be added fear of the dead, of demons, of the thousand spirits of earth, air, water, mountain and trees. The Battak is like a man driven in frenzied pursuit round and round. Ghosts of the most diverse kind lurk in house and village; in the field they endanger the produce of labour; in the forest they terrify the woodcutter. From them come diseases, madness, death of cattle and famine. Malicious demons surround women during pregnancy and at confinement: they lie in wait for the child from the day of its birth; they swarm round the houses at night; they spy through the chinks of the walls for their helpless victims. Gigantic spirits stride through the villages, scattering epidemics around them; they lurk in the sea and rivers with the view of dragging travellers into the depths . . . the dead friend and brother becomes an enemy, and his coffin and grave are the abode of terrors. It is fear that occasions the worship of the departed, and the observance of their mourning usages in its smallest details; fear decides that host of prohibitions which surrounds every movement of their daily life. Fear is the moving power of animistic religion, in Asia as well as in Africa."

Remnants of animistic folk religion may be found in Eastern religions in the secondary spirits of Confucianism and the ancestor worship of Shintoism. However, the teachings of the mystical religions—Buddhism and Taoism—are that gods or spirits are not to be found in the physical world. To the extent that a God is recognized, he is the First Cause, the supreme Reality of Mahayana Buddhism from which the universe emanated, the "first of the first . . . without a name . . . the beginning of heaven and earth" in Taoism. Truth is to be found not in relating to that initial source of life but in merging with that one indivisible life. Thus in Taoism everything is accomplished by not striving for anything, by "perpetual accommodation of self to one's surroundings with the minimum of effort." In Buddhism, the doctrine of impermanence teaches that life is one, its many forms must all pass through a cycle to birth, growth, decay and death, as one form of life gives place to another. Individual existence and the physical world are alike illusions, the temporary form of an everchanging, eternal entity. The effect of this doctrine on the economic and social life of Burma has been summed up by Stackhouse:

"The overwhelming cultural influence among the Burmans who dominate the other peoples of Burma is a particular style of Theravada Buddhism . . . . in Burmese Theravada there can be no crime against humanity, no sin against God, *no violation of nature*. All ethical teachings are essentially instrumental means for getting good fortune on earth or gaining spiritual status in karmic rebirth—both being connected with the realization that all other persons and material things are nothing but the rise and fall of substanceless temporal agglomerations."

Finally, we come to Confucianism, recognized by Weber as having a rational world view. In its view of the physical world, Confucianism, in contrast with the mystical religions of South-East Asia, accepts the external, material world as reality and the First Cause as not being the initiator of life but the creator of the material world. The words with which the Chinese Emperor greeted Huang T'ien Shong Ti (the Supreme Ruler of Imperial Heaven) at the annual Imperial Sacrifice can be closely compared with the first three verses of the biblical account of creation in Genesis:

"Of old, in the beginning, there was the great chaos, without form and dark. The five elements had not begun to revolve, nor the sun and moon to shine. In the midst thereof there presented itself neither form nor sound. Thou, O Spiritual Sovereign, camest forth in Thy presidency, and first didst divide the gross from the pure. Thou madest heaven; Thou madest earth; Thou madest man. All things got their being, with their reproducing power."

"In the beginning God created the heavens and the earth. The earth was without form and void, and darkness was upon the face of the deep; and the Spirit of God was moving over the face of the waters."

There follows the creation of every form of life and finally man. Both accounts see the physical world as real, and man as a distinctive part of that reality. Both place God outside the physical world, so that the natural world, free of spirits, may be developed through science and technology. Derived as they are from patterns of thought found in earlier religions, the secular humanism of the West and the modern religions of Japan share this view of the natural world as a reality separate from God and distinguishable from man.

One further point needs to be made before leaving the subject of the Confucian view of the physical world. Weber distinguished between Puritan rationalism, which attempted to exercise rational control over the world, and Confucian rationalism, which was an attempt to accommodate oneself to the world in a rational manner. Certainly the pattern of modern capitalism in East Asia, and particularly in Japan, is very different from the pattern found in the West.

We return to the third element in the Judeao-Christian creation story mentioned at the beginning of this section—that the physical world is seen as the creation of God and not unworthy or neutral but positively good. The phrase "and God saw that it was good" recurs seven times in the Genesis account of the creation. As Christianity moved out of the church and into the world in the wake of the Reformation, it was to be expected therefore that the forms of thought would switch from the sterile scholasticism of the previous centuries to an interest in the world God created, which was good and reflected his goodness. That this application of rational thought to the discovery of the physical world has led to a scientific world view independent of any concept of God, is not in itself a refutation of the proposition that the Enlightenment (as much as modern capitalism) is the product of the Reformation, nor that the Western interest in pure science has its roots in Judaeo-Christian thought. And here there is an important contrast to be made between the development of the West and the development of East Asia. Interest in the West has always been in scientific truth of which the development of technology is a byproduct. This is reflected even in the current economic crisis in the demand for university places in pure sciences while university departments of applied science (engineering, etc.) are closing down through lack of demand. The reverse is true in Japan. From the time of the Meiji Restoration, the Japanese slogan was "Japanese spirit with Western technology." Today the most popular university subject in Japan is engineering, while there is little interest in pure science. According to Morishima, in 1974 only 3%

of all undergraduate students in Japanese universities were in science faculties compared with 24% in the UK; at the universities of Kyoto and Tokyo, however, 40% of students were studying engineering.

Time

An understanding of time is fundamental to economic development. Not only is time crucial in the sense of dividing the day accurately into hours and minutes, which makes possible the kind of corporate activity implied by industrialization, but at a deeper level development cannot take place without an understanding of the passing of time, of the making of history. Ideas such as growth, progress, expectations and reform are futuristic in character; the development process, in an economic sense, is dependent on foresight, planning, investment and saving. Implicit in all of these ideas is a concept of time which can be divided into past, present and future, and the idea not just of change but of development.

This linear concept of time can be seen very clearly in Hebrew thought. The first act of creation undertaken by Yahweh is the creation of time itself: first there is light, then the separation of light from darkness and with it the appearance of "day" and "night", "morning" and "evening." The six days of creation are followed by a sabbath rest, which in turn becomes the token of the "Day of the Lord." From this follows a conception of history in terms of Israel's destiny, which is ultimately realized with the coming of the Messiah and the judgement of peoples and nations. Old Testament events, even visions, are invariably placed in historical time, genealogies are recorded in detail, the ages of key characters are given with accuracy, all contributing to a sense of time passing—time which had, in the story of creation, a beginning and which will have, in the coming of the Messiah, an end to which the nations of today make a contribution.

If not for this concept of time already there and already part of Western thought at all levels of the population, the Industrial Revolution could not have taken place. Capitalism implies saving. Saving in the present will not occur where there is no hope of spending more in the future.

By contrast, the traditional African concept of time is static rather than dynamic and circular rather than linear. Past and future are not distinguished but are understood only in terms of the present. Ancestors live, unseen, in the present and death has no more significance than the transition from childhood to adolescence or from youth to old age. This concept of time is explained by Adda Bozeman:

"Non-literate African thought is radically different from that which has ruled life in the West . . . the actual functioning of the social and cosmological order, with all its interpenetrating forms, models and norms, is perceived as perfect and unchangeable. The awesome dynamic that keeps it going may cause contractions here, expansions there, but its movement is essentially circular, not linear. To distinguish between past, present and future dimensions in such a closed universe would be nonsensical . . . Ideas such as aspiration, progress, development, reform—all futuristic in tone, content and purport—could not thus have been generated . . ."

She quotes Richard Wright making a similar point in his book *Black Power:*

"It bothered me that I couldn't find among educated Africans any presentiment of what the future of their continent was to be . . . The African did not strain to feel that which was not yet in existence: he exerted his will to make what happened happen again. His was a circular kind of time: the present had to be made up like the past. Dissatisfaction was not the mainspring of his emotional life, enjoyment of that which he had once enjoyed was the compulsion."

As the African has no sense of the future, he has no sense of the past. Explanation of history is in terms of a cycle of myths, which may absorb known events and known civilization, but is not an attempt to relate these accurately or to explain their place in historical—as opposed to mythical—time. This view of the past is again illustrated by Bozeman with reference to the cycle of stories, telling of the loss and rediscovery of Wagadu, a mythical city of West Africa:

". . . Wagadu, in its later incarnations, may well have been identical at one time with what is Agadu today, at another with ancient Ghana . . . , then with Silla, to be subsumed, thereafter, by the next contender for supremacy over the region, the empire of Mali. But its historicity is finally irrelevant; for in the African consciousness Wagadu is primarily a city of the mind: a potent word or name, capable of evoking differing but related memories of glory; an image summarizing centuries of human movement and encounter; a symbol of the flux of power and shift of cultural strength from one centre of gravity to the next."

Such an understanding of time leads quite logically to attitudes and motivations which are basically anti-development. If there is no sense of the reality of the past and no sense of expectancy about the future, then saving becomes meaningless and investment purposeless. This applies as much to settled agriculture as to industrialization—crop rotation, allowing land to lie fallow, making compost (in Upper Volta, for example, compost is almost unknown) investing in fertilizer, developing and maintaining irrigation schemes all depend on a concept of progress, of development and of improvement. Saving or investment depends on creating a surplus of work or goods in the present in order to enjoy a greater consumption in the future. In a society in which there is no sense of the future as apart from the present, no value will be placed on work, except that which is required to supply the needs of the immediate present. Leisure, not work, gives status. A surplus of either work or goods is not produced, nor are those assets already in existence maintained for use in the future. An example of this can be seen in the attempt in the 1950s to irrigate the Wawa bush area in Upper Volta. Before 1919 the area had been occupied by settled Fulani farmers using shallow wells and ponds for their water supply, which were maintained by their slaves. With the arrival of the British in 1919 this system broke down. Then in the early 1950s an attempt was made to improve irrigation in the area to help those farmers already settled there and to encourage semi-settled Fulanis to make permanent settlements. At a cost of £250,000, 31 ponds were excavated in 1956. Twelve years later, only three still held water. Among the most important reasons for this failure were the lack of maintenance of the ponds and the continuing damage done by cattle which were not prevented from trampling in the sides of the wells.

In his study of the Tzintzuntzan peasants of Mexico, G. M. Foster finds that while they are concerned about the future, they take few steps which could be thought of as influencing the future. "Foresight is shown primarily in traditional activities alone."

How does this view of historical time compare with the view of history found in East Asia? As in Africa, time in East Asia is not seen as a series of unique, non-recurring events, causally connected. In the mystical religions of the East, such as Hinduism, Buddhism and Taoism, time and space are both illusory. Reality is spiritual and all-embracing, defined neither in terms of space nor time and inwardly perceived. By contrast to this sense of the mystical wholeness of all things, the detailed chronology of actual events in time, a mere device for coping with the day-to-day demands of living, is of little significance. The East Asian view of history is not of a sequence of events causally and chronologically related but of a picture, the details of which are well-known, since Asians are characterized by well-developed powers of memory, and which is given perspective not by the passing of time but by the significance of the event (in terms of this unseen spiritual reality), so that in the same plane are placed not those events which occurred at the same time, but those events which have a comparable significance.

The effect of this cyclical view of time is seen in Mulder's description of the way Buddhism affects the economy of Thailand. Long-term planning, Mulder claims, is ruled out:

"In an Animist world view, the small and continuous communal group knows itself to be surrounded by a vast amount of diffuse, amoral power with which it makes short-term contracts to ensure safety and protection. . . . The Animistic perception of short-term order in a sea of uncertainty seems to be the most pregnant of their time perspectives."

In the case of Japan, however, this mystical sense of time which is characteristic of the Eastern religions, has been tempered by a strong sense of national purpose. Morishima argues that Buddhism, Taoism and Confucianism, in their transfer from China to Japan, were all deliberately modified to be in tune with the Japanese national spirit and to suit the purposes of the Japanese nation. All three religions came from China during the sixth century. Taoism, a magical and mystical religion affecting only the fringes of Chinese society, became Shintoism in Japan and provided divine sanction for the Imperial system, the Imperial family being the only family able to claim direct descent from the Sun Goddess, Amaterasu. The story of this relationship is recorded in a series of myths found in both the Kojiki and the Nihongi, which are today taught in all Japanese primary schools. Similarly, Buddhism was modified in Japan. As Shintoism has accepted the Emperor as the Manifest God, so Buddhism was utilized to uphold the doctrine of the Divine Land, which holds that Japan is the country of the "Divine Land" in which the Manifest God reigns and which should therefore be eternal as heaven and earth. Thus from the very introduction of Buddhism and Taoism, Japan had superimposed on the mystical view of time and space common to all the East Asian religions, a sense of national origin and national purpose in external chronological time, which had divine sanction.

Within this framework, it seems unlikely that a spontaneous bourgeois revolution of the Western variety could have occurred. Certainly, Confucianism, the religion of the ruling class which provided an ethical framework for society as a whole, stressed some of those values necessary for capitalist development. Confucianism taught that frugality was noble and towards the end of the Tokugawa period, commercial activity—albeit within the confines of Japan—was considered acceptable; indeed, during the eighteenth century efforts had been made to encourage the merchants in saving and money lending. However, since the only concept of past and future in Japan belonged not to the merchants but to the "Land of the Gods" as a whole, it is not surprising that when the confrontation with Western technology finally came, it was not the merchants who spearheaded the Meiji Restoration, but the low-ranking samurai and the intelligentsia. Similarly, in the drive for industrial development which followed, it was again not the merchant class which set up the first industries and found the necessary capital (through land tax), but the new government. Even when in 1880, the Meiji government was no longer able to maintain these enterprises and was obliged to sell them off to private entrepreneurs, they were not sold to the merchants of the Tokugawa period but to the new "political merchants" who had come from the old samurai class.

Trust

Development depends on enterprising individuals being able to operate within the framework of community. An emphasis on individualism to the exclusion of the community or equally an emphasis on the community which destroys individuality are both harmful to development. In a study of a village in Southern Italy, Banfield found that the fundamental impediment to its development was an inability by families to act either in concert or for the common good. Their behavior could be treated as if they followed the rule: "Maximize the material short-run advantage of the nuclear family; assume that all the others will do likewise." As a result no-one would further the interests of the group unless it were to his advantage, and deliberately concerted action would be very difficult to achieve, as this requires people to behave in a reasonably unselfish manner. Another example of precisely the same attitude was found by Foster in his study of Mexican peasants.

The people were remarkably individualistic in attitude and behavior and saw themselves as competing with others for control over scarce resources. They saw themselves facing a hostile world and the only area of trust as being within the nuclear family. Taking up the same theme and contrasting this attitude with that which makes for successful capitalism, Weber observes that:

"The universal reign of absolute unscrupulousness in the pursuit of the making of money has been a specific characteristic of precisely those countries whose bourgeois-capitalistic development, measured according to Occidental standards, has remained backwards."

Trust is essential to cooperation in enterprises involving more than one individual, and an essential foundation on which to build a free market. If a market is to work there must be rules— tacit or explicit—and these must be accepted and obeyed by all those involved in market transactions. In other words, there must be a commitment to and trust in a group beyond the immediate family or kin group.

Such a situation is not found in traditional African societies. The identity of the tribe or kinship group is found in the myths which have accumulated concerning its nomadic history. The present experience is expressed through an oral language and through the symbolism of masks, drums and stools. Its purpose is the continuance of the family tree and its accompanying ideology. To quote Bozeman:

"A tribal 'constitution' is thus imbedded in the sum total of myths by which the entire metaphysical community is maintained; credentials of rule are mystical and tribal 'laws' are not just to regulate human behaviour, but also—indeed primarily—to assure the proper workings of superior powers, to keep evil away and to prevent untoward things from happening. What counts on the strictly human level is the continued existence of the group in conditions of strict conformity with all traditional arrangements and beliefs, for the core of the indigenous culture is kinship, real or imaginary."

In such a society the perspective is by necessity inward looking, concerned only with the workings of the tribe. Cooperation with other groupings is not seen as desirable, nor indeed is it possible. As Bozeman has argued, one key feature of traditional African society is that it is non-literate. Oral language is only meaningful in the moment; it does not allow of comparison either through time or through space. Thus moral principles, which are in essence an abstraction from material reality, cannot be developed. Within the group this means that there can be no rules which transcend the immediate experience. Morality consists in re-enacting the same behavior pattern when the same situation arises. Across groups, the development of a common morality is inconceivable.

In such a situation, both tribal expansion and trading involved not cooperation but war. The Berbers, the Arabs, the Tuaregs and the Negroes were all successful traders who organized regional markets and trade routes. But their style of trading did not rely on cooperation or the acceptance of a rule of law.

"Commerce was very much a matter of large and petty forays that had the effect of reducing to waste what had been prosperous and promising in neighbouring societies."

The most important trade item was slaves—members of other tribes sold into slavery—a trade which reached its peak with the trans-Atlantic slave trade but which had been established long before that.

Trust is central to the whole spirit of Japanese and Chinese capitalism. For example, the Chinese religion which is practised in such South East Asian countries as Indonesia, Malaysia and Singapore is an amalgam of Confucianism, Taoism and Buddhism, sometimes known as Han San Wei Yi (three faiths which are one). It rests on the three major pillars of filial devotion, materialism and organism. Central to Confucianism is the pursuit of human perfection, the culmination of which is a special filial relationship between father and son. Materialism is not concerned simply to improve one's standard of living through hard work and saving but to benefit one's family in the process. Cooperation therefore is fundamental to evaluating Chinese business enterprise, and this covers relationships with the head of the extended family, the clan and others originating from the same district as themselves and speaking the same dialect. More than this, in Chinese business life there is the concept of the "kongsi"—a term used for cooperation among Chinese businessmen. It is too informal to be described as an organization and is more aptly termed an organism. It is at heart a mutual trust between businessmen, which means that as a consequence business can be conducted in a purely informal manner.

A similar emphasis is to be found in Japanese Confucianism which stresses: (i) duty to the state; (ii) respect for one's elders; (iii) love and obedience to one's parents; and (iv) goodwill towards friends. From this it is not surprising that relationships within companies resemble those within families. Trust is important therefore even if individualism suffers.

The individual and personal responsibility

Development implies change and improvement. People move from a lower to a higher standard of living. People accept new ways of doing things. But this requires a certain mental attitude and an involvement by people. It implies a view of man as understanding his environment, exercising at least some control over it and using it for his own ends. Such a view of the world is implied by the Hebrew account of creation in which man is created as a unique, distinct part of the creation with a specific mandate to subdue the world. Man is, as in the Confucian view, a separate creation, and God is seen to be external to the physical creation; as a result, nature can be understood and mastered.

Such a view of the world and of the individual within it stands in stark contrast to the traditional African view. Believing himself to be surrounded by spirits which inhabit the physical world, the traditional African does not see himself as controlling the physical world but being controlled by it; he sees his role to be that of pacifying rather than understanding this world. Thus the Bishop of Bururi, whom we quoted earlier on the African view of nature, concludes by noting that:

"It therefore follows that the concept of people having to accept responsibility themselves for making the necessary changes to outmoded economic structures is not being taken over. This fatalistic belief in 'providence' manifests itself in all the underdeveloped societies of Asia, Africa and South America. It is without doubt one of the most serious causes for slowness or even socio-economic stagnation [inherent in the fabric] of these countries. The tendency to expect everything from God, to be passive towards life and accept poverty as fate-ordained acts as a check on human willpower and prevents a person from attaining his full potential and facing up to the problems of life."

This same tendency Foster observed in his study of Mexican peasants. Because the world is so capricious and uncertain, it becomes presumptuous and futile to plan ahead. Fate and chance are more powerful influences than foresight and planning.

"Something happens, not because of preordained regularities in the universe and in the world, but because God—or whoever the ultimate authority in this particular instance may be—willed it. A child dies, it was part of God's plan. The highway comes to town: General Iazaro Cardena willed it. Since chance and accident are the mainsprings of the universe, systematic expectations and consistent behaviour are seen as valueless. Western-style foresight is a positive value only within a predictable system."

How does the attitude of Eastern religions compare with the attitude of traditional African thought to the significance and effectiveness of the individual? The Buddhist views the material world as ephemeral and consequently sees the purpose of life as being to lose all individual identity and to merge with the universal unconscious and also the maintenance of complete harmony with others. In contrast to Buddhism and Taoism, Confucianism accepts the reality of the external physical world and man as a distinct part of it. The teaching of manners implies that the individual has a significance. Nevertheless, the emphasis of that teaching is on good relationships, on benevolence, harmony and, in the case of Japan above all, on loyalty. It is for this reason that Morishima argues that Japanese society could not have produced the kind of individualism which led to the development of modern capitalism in the West. The ethic of Confucianism gives negative value to originality and to differentiating oneself from the group.

For successful economic development man must feel his actions to be effective in terms of his environment. It has already been shown that the predominant value of Japanese Confucianism is loyalty and that one of the distinctive features of development in East Asia is the "shared values" of the company, which dominate every area of life for the employee. It may be concluded that the form of modern capitalism found in East Asia, and particularly in

Japan, leaves little room for the individual. The reverse is in fact true. Nakane has shown how the Japanese company, like other Japanese institutions, is structured not from a set of strata identified by role—managers, clerks, accountants, assembly line workers, etc.—as is the case in the West, but from a series of vertical relationships between a particular worker and his immediate superior and inferiors. These relationships extend beyond the place of work. As Nakane points out, it is normal for a department head to attend an employee's wedding ceremony as a go-between. If there is a funeral in the director's family, his secretary and subordinates help with arrangements for the ceremony while his wife and friends are received as guests. At New Year, visits to the superior at the place of work receive priority over all but parents. Thus the relationship between a leader and his followers or a manager and his men in Japanese society depends on this emotional relationship. To quote Nakane: "if a man is unable to capture his followers emotionally and glue them to him in vertical relationships, he cannot become a leader." This vertical organization held together by emotional ties rather than respect for the superior's attributes in terms of wealth, knowledge or power, results in each individual member of a company having a personal value greater than the role he plays. Nakane recounts how American executives are surprised to find their Japanese counterparts unable to explain the details of their own enterprise and continues:

"Japanese directors. . . . rely cheerfully on their beloved and trusted subordinates to run the business; of much greater concern to them is the maintenance of happy relations among the men. . . . One would have to search widely in Japan to find the company, so common in the West, run by only one or two men at the top while the employees act as simple tools. In such a pattern, employees are easily replaceable, and the lines of responsibility between manager and employee are clearly drawn. In the Japanese pattern there are no clear-cut spheres or divisions of responsibility between the manager and his subordinates, and the entire group becomes one functional body in which all individuals, including the manager, are amalgamated into a single entity."

It may be concluded perhaps that a sense of individual effectiveness is required at two levels for the success of modern capitalism. In the first place, the initiation of industrialization required risk-taking on the part of certain individuals not afraid to differentiate themselves from the group. It is possible that this was lacking in Tokagawa Japan. However, if capitalism is to continue successfully, a sense of individual effectiveness is required at another level—that of the average worker in a large company. At this level it is possible that the West has much to learn.

So far we have argued that there are grounds for thinking that culture matters, and we have examined cultural values which are conducive to development. One interesting contemporary application of this view is the case of sub-Saharan Africa. Despite colonialism and modernization, there exists in Africa today—whether it is expressed as negritude, the African Personality, Pan Africanism, African Socialism or the Organization of African Unity—an African cultural consciousness which transcends individual states. The cultural revolutions which took place in the seventies in such countries as Chad, Zaire, Kenya, Ethiopia and Uganda were an attempt to strengthen Africanism against trends from outside, such as education, Christianity and European influences. Traditional customs and structures remain powerful therefore despite the arrival of modernity. The reason sub-Saharan Africa is important in this respect is that this region is facing an economic crisis. A World Bank report on the region summarizes the position as follows:

". . . . for most African countries and for a majority of the African population, the record is grim and it is no exaggeration to talk of a crisis. Slow overall economic growth, sluggish agricultural performance coupled with rapid rates of population increase and balance of payments and fiscal crises—these are dramatic indicators of economic trouble."

However, as we have examined values conducive to growth, it was also interesting to observe that whether in its view of the physical world, time, fatalism, individuality or trust, traditional African culture embodied values which are fundamentally opposed to development. It is not simply that they are neutral or even marginally opposed but, as the Bishop of Bururi has said with great courage as well as great insight, they embody concepts which are incompatible with progress unless they are changed.

VI. Conclusion

If success is defined in terms of prosperity and economic growth, then this profile of a successful Third World nation is one which fosters the market economy, has strong government and whose culture contains norms and values conducive to enterprise. At a general level the contrast between sub-Saharan Africa and East Asia in these respects is quite marked. For a successful economy, so defined, to achieve equity, however, requires active government involvement: it cannot be left to the market. One of the most successful examples is Taiwan which succeeded in redistributing assets at the beginning of sustained growth. Nevertheless, even in those economies which have not pursued markedly redistributionist policies such as Brazil and Mexico, the poor have benefitted from the growth process.

East Asia has succeeded in developing along lines parallel but not identical to the development in the West. Whether such development will be sustained depends on two factors:

(i) whether the new religions of Japan offer an alternative provision for affective need making the shared values of the zaibatsu redundant;

(ii) whether the kind of Christianity being spread in countries like Singapore supports the values which are a necessary underpinning of modern capitalism or whether its emphasis on personal pietism precludes the kind of commitment to the economy implicit in the Calvinist view of "calling."

TABLE 1
FAST AND SLOW GROWING COUNTRIES OF SUB-SAHARAN AFRICA 1970–1979

Country	Average annual growth rate of GDP 1970–1979
HIGH GROWTH COUNTRIES	6.6
Mauritius*	8.2
Ivory Coast	6.7
Kenya	6.5
Malawi	6.3
Cameroon	5.4
LOW GROWTH COUNTRIES	1.2
Senegal	2.5
Liberia	1.8
Sierra Leone	1.6
Zambia	1.5
Ghana	−0.1
Upper Volta	−0.1

Source: The World Bank, *The World Development Report 1982*, Washington, D.C., 1981.
*from: The World Bank, *Accelerated Development in Sub-Saharan Africa: An Agenda for Action*, Washington, D.C., 1981, p 36.

TABLE 2
FAST AND SLOW GROWING COUNTRIES OF SOUTH AND EAST ASIA 1970–1979

Country	Average annual growth rate of GDP 1970–1979
HIGH GROWTH COUNTRIES	9.5
South Korea	10.3
Taiwan*	9.9
Hong Kong	9.4
Singapore	8.4
LOW GROWTH COUNTRIES	3.7
Pakistan	4.5
Burma	4.3
Sri Lanka	3.8
India	3.4
Bangladesh	3.3
Nepal	2.7

Source: The World Bank, *The World Development Report 1982*, Washington, D.C., 1982.
*from: John C. Fei, Gustav Ranis, and S. W. Y. Kuo, *Growth with Equity: The Taiwan Case*, Oxford University Press, 1979, p 36.

TABLE 3

GROWTH RATES OF AGRICULTURAL PRODUCTION 1969–71 TO 1977–79
(Average annual growth rate in volume as a percentage)

4+	3–4	2–3	1–2	0–1	<0
Kenya	Cameroon	Benin	Botswana	Ethiopia	Angola
Malawi	Ivory Coast	Burundi	Chad	Gabon	Congo
Swaziland	Rwanda	Central African Republic	Guinea-Bissau	Gambia	Ghana
		Liberia	Lesotho	Guinea	Mauritania
		Upper Volta	Madagascar	Somalia	Mozambique
		Zambia	Mali		Togo
		Zimbabwe	Mauritius		Uganda
			Niger		
			Nigeria		
			Senegal		
			Sierra Leone		
			Sudan		
			Tanzania		
			Zaire		

Source: FAO *Production Yearbook* tapes, reproduced in The World Bank, *Accelerated Development in Sub-Saharan Africa: An Agenda for Action*, Washington, D.C., 1981, p 50.

TABLE 4
GROWTH AND POVERTY IN THIRD WORLD COUNTRIES

	HIGH GROWTH	LOW GROWTH
INCREASING POVERTY	Philippines (1967–71) Argentina (1953–61)	India (1960–68/9)
DECREASING POVERTY	Taiwan (1964–72) Brazil (1960–70) Puerto Rico (1953–63) Pakistan (1963–69/70) Singapore (1966–75) Thailand (1962/3–78/9) Costa Rica (1961–71) Mexico (1963–9)	Sri Lanka (1953–73) Bangladesh (1963/4–73/4)

Source: Gary S Fields, *Poverty, Inequality and Development*, Cambridge University Press, 1980, pp. 171ff.

TABLE 5
GROWTH AND INEQUALITY IN THIRD WORLD COUNTRIES

	HIGH GROWTH	LOW GROWTH
INCREASING INEQUALITY	Philippines (1961–71) Brazil (1960–70) Mexico (1963–75) Puerto Rico (1953–63) Argentina (1953–61) El Salvador (1945–61)	Bangladesh (1963/4–73/4)
DECREASING INEQUALITY	Costa Rica (1961–71) Taiwan (1950s–70s) Singapore (1966–75) Pakistan (1963/4–69/70)	Sri Lanka (1953–73) India (1960/1–68/9)

Source: Gary S Fields, *Poverty, Inequality and Development,* Cambridge University Press, 1980, pp. 88–93.

TABLE 6
EXPORTS AS A SHARE OF MANUFACTURED OUTPUTS (%)

	1960	1966	1973
South Korea	1	14	41
Singapore	11	20	43
Taiwan	9	19	50

Source: Bela Balassa, *The Process of Industrial Development and Alternative Development Strategies,* International Finance Section, Princeton, 1980.

TABLE 7
NOMINAL PROTECTION COEFFICIENTS OF SELECTED EXPORT CROPS

Crop	1971–75	1976–80	Crop	1971–75	1976–80
COCOA			**GROUNDNUTS**		
Cameroon	0.37 (2)[a]	0.45 (2)	Malawi	0.70 (5)	0.59 (2)
Ghana	0.47 (5)	0.40 (4)	Mali	0.57 (2)	0.43 (4)
Ivory Coast	0.56 (2)	0.38 (1)	Senegal	0.48 (4)	0.66 (4)
Togo	0.50 (5)	0.25 (4)	Sudan	0.85 (3)	0.67 (1)
			Zambia	0.70 (5)	0.71 (4)
COFFEE					
Cameroon (Arabica)	0.72 (2)	0.60 (2)	**MAIZE**[b]		
Cameroon (Robusta)	N.A.	0.36 (1)	Kenya	0.96 (1)	1.33 (1)
Ivory Coast	0.68 (1)	0.36 (1)	Malawi	1.68 (5)	1.34 (2)
Kenya	0.94 (1)	N.A.	Zambia	0.72 (5)	0.78 (4)
Tanzania	0.80 (5)	0.59 (4)			
Togo	0.42 (5)	0.23 (4)	**SESAME**		
			Sudan	0.83 (1)	0.59 (1)
COTTON			Upper Volta	N.A.	0.88 (1)
Cameroon	N.A.	0.79 (1)			
Ivory Coast	0.79 (1)	1.05 (1)	**TEA**		
Kenya	1.07 (1)	N.A.	Kenya	0.89 (1)	N.A.
Malawi	0.68 (5)	0.75 (2)			
Mali	0.55 (2)	0.44 (4)	**TOBACCO**		
Senegal	0.65 (2)	N.A.	Malawi	0.42 (5)	0.28 (2)
Sudan	0.78 (2)	0.60 (1)	Zambia	1.09 (5)	0.88 (4)
Togo	0.62 (5)	0.79 (4)			
Upper Volta	N.A.	0.79 (1)	**WHEAT**[b]		
			Kenya	N.A.	1.43 (1)

Source: World Bank data.

N.A. - not available.

a. figure in brackets indicates number of observations (years).
b. maize and wheat have been alternately exported and imported in these countries.

341

Memories of Development

John O'Sullivan

IN A MODEST TECHNOLOGICAL SENSE, we already live in a post-capitalist world. For the thirty years after 1945, economists were so dazzled by the Keynesian revolution that they tended to look upon labor less as an active agent than as a passive factor of production that would find employment only if there were a high enough rate of investment. As Mary Jean Bowman put it in 1966, ". . . out of Keynes's great but ambiguous polemic. . . . came some quite remarkable progeny—long-term 'growth' theories in which virtually everything was explained by the amount of physical capital and its rate of increase."

Development economists were especially infatuated by this theory. They increasingly looked upon the supply of capital, either free or at artificially low rates of interest, as a necessary and perhaps almost a sufficient requirement for economic growth. This stress on external capital arose from a widespead belief that the poorer countries were trapped in a "vicious circle of poverty." They were poor because they were poor. Or in Professor Paul Samuelson's crisp formulation:

They cannot get their heads above water because their production is so low that they can spare nothing for capital formation by which their standard of living could be raised.

It naturally seemed to follow that cheap external capital would be essential for the economic development of these countries.

342

But, as Professor P.T. Bauer pointed out, this theory was plainly at variance with both fact and logic. In the first place, if it had been true, then innumerable individuals, groups and communities could never have risen from poverty to wealth as they have in fact done. Secondly, all developed countries had originally started as poor and undeveloped. Their later prosperity was achieved without external aid as such, and generally without large supplies of external capital. And, finally, in the decades before aid, there was remarkable economic advance in a large number of LDCs. According to the Economic Commission for Latin America, the gross national product in Latin American countries increased over the period 1935 through 1953 at an annual rate of 4.2 per cent, and output per head by 2 per cent.

The fallacy embedded in the vicious circle theory did not, of course, invalidate the importance of cheap external capital altogether. It was still seen as a major contributory factor to growth. But the evidence on this more modest point was also doubtful. As David Morawetz points out, since 1955 the total contribution of all external capital—foreign private investment, official government aid, and public and private debt—has generally averaged no more than about 10 per cent of total investment expenditure of the developing market economies. The percentage for all developing countries is even lower. But the widespread demand for debt cancellation or rescheduling suggests that much of this investment, including presumably "soft" loans, has not been productively employed. And when statisticians have attempted to estimate whether there is a correlation between foreign aid and economic growth, they have produced conflicting results.

Chastened by this experience, economists have been skeptically reexamining their enthusiasm for capital inputs. As early as 1966, Simon Kuznets estimated that increases in capital and labor accounted for less than 10 per cent of the growth of industrialised countries over the last two centuries. And within developing countries in recent years, domestic capital accumulation has apparently risen in line with the opportunities for its profitable employment. It might indeed make sense to regard capital investment as a symptom of economic development rather than its cause. If other factors that favor development are present, then capital will be attracted. If not, capital will be wasted.

What are the other, presumably more vital, factors? Natural resources are of only minor importance. Two of the most successful developing countries are the almost resource-less Hong Kong and Singapore. And Middle-East oil was of no practical value to the Arabs living above it until foreign companies exploited it and made them wealthy. As the 19th-century South American sociologist, Juan Bautiste Alberdi put it:

"South America is occupied by a poor people who inhabit a rich land, just the opposite of Europe, which is occupied mainly by a rich people who inhabit a poor land."

Professor Kuznets argues that growth is mainly attributable to the "residual" factor—namely, human capital, technological change, organization skills, enterprise, innovation, etc. Since all of these are either human attributes or the result of human effort, they are often grouped under the general heading of the "human factor." But it is a truism that human beings produce economic development. Why do some groups produce more than others? Why do some nations exhibit a high level of prosperity while others remain mired in the poverty that was once universal? The answer seems to lie in two sets of factors: cultural or social influences, and official government policies.

The influence of the cultural or social environment is, of course, an extremely broad, elusive, even deceptive concept. When asked what should be included under the heading "culture" for the English, T.S. Eliot listed ". . . Derby Day, Henley Regatta, Cowes, the twelfth of August, a cup final, the dog races, the pin table, the dart board, Wensleydale Cheese, boiled cabbage cut into sections, beetroot in vinegar, nineteenth-century Gothic churches and the music of Elgar." This list is overly restrictive in two respects. First, it confines itself to a surface "Englishness" of English culture as opposed to the broad modernity which unites the industrialized West European countries, including England, and which includes railways, newspapers, trade unions, piped water, popular education, and universal suffrage. Secondly, the list limits itself to the physical expressions of Englishness. Yet the intangible attitudes—chapel morality, class deference, concern for privacy, and physical gentleness—which infuse English life (or did so at the period when Eliot was writing) are surely more important. Certainly, they are stronger influences on behavior, which is what concerns us here. For our purposes, then, culture covers institutional and ideological influences on a group of people—everything from family stability, the status of women, the influence of religion, and the value of group identity, to the stress on achievement in children's stories. If such factors have the overall effect of encouraging hard work, economic foresight, the acquisition of skills, and the propensity to save and invest, then members of that group will tend to prosper over time.

This implies, however, that the cultural environment can also function as an obstacle to development. Writing on Latin America, Jeffrey Barrett has detailed the cultural values and attitudes that have helped to keep that continent "occupied by a poor people who inhabit a rich land." He noted, significantly, that laziness is *not* a characteristically Latin vice. Indeed, academic research has found the Latin Americans to be "thrifty, frugal and hard-working." The problem is that cultural biases ensure that their hard work is generally directed along unprofitable lines. Those biases include: a reluctance to work for others; an "envy reflex" that deters the Latin poor from accumulating a modest surplus for fear of being thought socially ambitious; an unwillingness to do profitable work if it denotes an inferior status; a pervasive lack of trust which encourages nepotism and obstructs the decentralization of business decisions; the low status of business compared to the professions; an aversion to economic risk once a modest fortune has been achieved; and pressures for conspicuous consumption and conspicuous idleness by the rich that misdirect funds away from investment and effort away from economic activity.

Against such a background it is hardly surprising that entrepreneurs in Brazil are drawn disproportionally from foreign immigrants. Or that, in 1939 not a single native Latin American manufacturer in Sao Paulo could trace his origins to the Brazilian lower or middle class. Or that, in the early sixties, less than 0.5 per cent of Brazilian companies employed more than 500 workers. Or that, in 1961, only 4 per cent of Peruvian students expressed an interest in entering business after graduation.

Two caveats about the influence of culture should be entered at this point. The first is that, as Thomas Sowell points out:

"It is . . . pointless to grade cultures in any absolute sense, for some cultural features that produce success and prosperity within an industrial and commercial economy and society might well prove futile and embittering in a peasant economy or in a fishing and hunting community."

As an example, he cites the various failed attempts by Jews, the most successful of America's ethnic minorities in an urban setting, to establish agricultural communities in Oregon, New York and Louisiana. Although subsidized by leading Jewish organizations, such colonies failed because the colonists made such basic errors as purchasing the wrong kind of land. Secondly, it is just as pointless to condemn a culture for failing to encourage economic development. If people place a higher value on a religion of contemplation, or on the absolute sanctity of life, or on a prohibition on women working outside the home than upon material enrichment, that is their affair. People have the right to remain poor but authentic.

So much for the influence of culture. The link between economic development and official policies, on the other hand, is almost tautological. If such policies promote saving, investment, entrepreneurship and the prudent use of scarce resources, then they are likely to promote development. Contrariwise, if governments pursue such policies as "the penal taxation of small farmers by state export monopolies, extensive official support of uneconomic activities, large-scale spending on show projects, suppression of private economic activity especially trade, forcible collectivization of farming, restriction on the inflow of capital, and persecution of both rich and poor members of unpopular groups such as Tamils in Sri Lanka, Asians in East Africa and Ibo in Nigeria," then they are likely to obstruct development. But more of this later.

A strict distinction between cultural and official factors is not possible, however, because each influences the other. Mr. Barrett points out, for instance, that the Latin American middle classes, acutely conscious of status and dignity, have traditionally avoided socially useful jobs in favor of prestigious but parasitic ones. A visitor to nineteenth-century Brazil commented that the number of civil and military officers was enormous: "inspectors innumerable, colonels without end, devoid of any object to inspect, without any regiment to command." In 1901, no less than three quarters of the Venezuelan army was composed of officers. It is reasonable to infer that this status-consciousness has helped to shape the bureaucratic parasitism that is so marked a feature of modern Latin American society. Not only are government departments grossly overstaffed, but many of the bureaucrats perform only a minimal service for their pay and perquisites. A survey taken in Uruguay in the fifties, for instance, revealed that eight per cent of government employees were working at second jobs during their bureau's office hours.

But official policies also shape cultural attitudes. P.T. Bauer argues that such policies as the expulsion of Asian traders from East Africa and restrictions on the inflow of capital, in addition to their directly damaging effects, also reduce the number and variety of commercial contacts in the society. Since such contacts spread new wants, crops and methods of production to the local population, they contribute to molding attitudes, mores and modes of conduct that are congenial to material advance. Official policies obstruct this transformation. Similarly, when state subsidies to unproductive enterprises waste scarce resources, this instills in people wasteful and prestige-oriented attitudes to economic questions.

If official policies influence cultural factors and vice versa, it would seem well-nigh impossible to disentangle their separate influence on development. In fact, we can establish the presence and importance of each one by two simple criteria. First, do members of the same national or cultural group, who obviously labor under the influence of the same cultural background, perform differently under different economic regimes? If so, it must follow that official policies are in themselves an important factor in development. And when we examine the evidence, we do indeed discover that the Taiwanese (and the overseas Chinese in general) are substantially more productive and prosperous than their fellows in mainland China. Similarly, the West Germans are much more successful economically than the East Germans.

The second question is: do different groups, equipped with distinctive cultural traits, attain different levels of economic achievement when living under the same economic regime? If so, then cultural factors are an important determinant of development. Once again, the evidence is clear. The overseas Chinese, despite discriminatory government measures against them in some instances (e.g. Malaysia), generally outperform their neighbors in South-East Asia. Similarly, the Asians prospered in comparison with their African neighbors in East Africa. And the Greeks were economically more successful than the Turks under British rule in Cyprus.

But some of the most interesting evidence on differential group achievement is provided by the varying performances of West Indian, Pakistani and East African Asian immigrants to the United Kingdom in the last 30 years. Insofar as differences in group achievement reflected obvious advantages, we might expect the West Indians to attain greater success than other groups. They have been in England since the early fifties and they speak a dialect of English as their native tongue. Most Asians have arrived only since 1962, and African Asians since the late sixties. As recently as 1974, 42 per cent of Asians spoke English slightly or not at all.

But an analysis of the job levels reached by different groups in 1975 shows unexpected patterns. African Asians had advanced remarkably. Although they were recent arrivals, many of them penniless following their expropriation and expulsion, they most resembled the native British population in their occupational pattern. Thirty per cent were in management and white collar jobs, and 44 percent were doing skilled manual work. There were actually fewer African Asians than whites (2 per cent as against 6 percent) doing unskilled manual labor. West Indians were under-represented in both white collar jobs and in the rank of unskilled workers. Almost 60 percent of them were in skilled blue-collar jobs, perhaps as a result of their longer sojourn in the United Kingdom. It was the Pakistanis who were disproportionately found (58 per cent of them) in unskilled and semi-skilled occupations. Yet they were far from being an apathetic underclass. No less than 85 per cent of unskilled manual Pakistani workers owned their own homes, compared to a mere 20 per cent of the same occupational groups among whites and 39 per cent among West Indians. Indeed, the figures for home ownership among Asians were, by British standards, socially perverse. The poorer and less skilled an Asian was, the more likely he was to own his own home.

Various explanations can be hazarded to account for these different economic patterns. Private housing, for instance, especially served the needs of immigrants because unlike subsidized local authority accommodation, it was immediately available with no waiting period required. But the most striking anomalies seem to be related to cultural patterns. Thus, the remarkable advance of the African Asians is surely related to their previous experience of operating within a hostile society. They then developed not merely business and commercial skills, but also the skills and aptitudes of circumventing discriminatory prejudice.

In short, both appropriate cultural attitudes and sensible official policies are necessary for economic advance. On its own, however, neither one is a sufficient condition. Accordingly, political strategies for development must be two-pronged. They must promote development directly with incentives for saving, hard work, investment, etc.; and they must seek to foster the cultural values that in the long term are conducive to development—what is sometimes called the "modernization of mind."

These tasks are difficult enough. But they perhaps become more difficult if we set ourselves the further problem of combining development with equity. But what is equity in the context of development? Most observers would agree that, in societies where poverty means an extremely low standard of living, equity requires improving the lot of the poorest. But does it require, further, a more egalitarian distribution of income, as some other contributors to this volume argue? If greater equality arrives in the course of development, as seems to have happened in Taiwan, clearly few would object to it. Equally, no one would welcome greater equality if it were to be brought about by a rising death rate among the poor. The desirability of equality is inseparable from the desirability of the means necessary to its establishment.

Thus, the first point to be made is that official policies aimed at promoting equality will almost certainly restrict liberty. But is not liberty itself an important element in equity? A peasant who is deprived of his right to sell his goods on the open market, but is instead instructed to dispose of it to a state export monopoly at a fixed price, will interpret this as arbitrary and unjust action by the state. Secondly, the attempt to achieve a more egalitarian distribution of income necessitates the imposition of various bureaucratic controls. It brings about, in fact, a *less* egalitarian distribution of power. Such a result is likely to be especially inequitable in a society where official corruption and extortion are rife. Many, if not most, LDCs fit this description. Insofar as the poor are made better-off as a result of redistribution, therefore, they are also more likely to be the prey of corrupt officials. Greater equality, like so much else in LDCs, would then be a fiction of the official statistics. Finally, economic controls may be granted for egalitarian purposes but employed by the government to enhance its political power. During the Indian "emergency" Mrs. Gandhi used price controls as a means of curbing opposition newspapers. P.T. Bauer makes the point that the concentration of political power required for egalitarian redistribution actually provokes severe political tensions and conflict in multi-racial and multi-tribal societies since it becomes a vital matter for each group to control the government that controls its economic prospects.

It must be admitted that some of these objections apply to the more modest redistribution necessary to improve conditions for the poorest in LDCs. But degree is important here. Taxation for such a limited purpose will be lighter, the incentive for evasion less strong, and the methods of enforcement correspondingly less intrusive. This is one of those instances in which Marx is correct: a change in quantity becomes a change in quality, governing becomes extensive social control. In short, we cannot identify equity with the movement towards equality. When that movement is state-enforced, moreover, it will almost certainly lead to greater inequality. So, except when otherwise stated, equity is used here to denote improving the lot of the poorest.

Official Policies and their Consequences

In his masterly essay, "Capitalist Development and Income Distribution," Prof. Gustav Papanek outlines three types of economic

regime, classical free market capitalism (e.g. Hong Kong), modified capitalism (e.g. Indonesia) and the populist model (e.g. Algeria) and examines their records in achieving growth and equity.
He concludes that classical capitalism, which combines low taxes,
reliance on markets, limited government and free trade, has
broadly succeeded in obtaining rapid economic growth, rising
incomes for the unskilled and even a modest movement in the
direction of equality. Modified capitalism, in which the modifications are the minimum wage, fixed interest rates, price control,
tariffs, import licenses, tax concessions, a prohibition on dismissals, etc., has been much less successful. It produces, in his view,
higher unemployment, over-capacity, low growth rates, a *less*
egalitarian income distribution and lower incomes outside the
protected sector which, after all, is where the poor are. And
populism consisting of nationalization, price distortions, import
controls and generous social services, has results similar to modified capitalism, except that the more generous social service provision seems to effect some improvements in health and education.
It is plain from this survey, supported as it is by a vast array of
empirical evidence, that if we are seeking official policies to bring
about growth with equity *and* if we are confined to these three
systems (for Professor Papanek subsequently suggests a hypothetical fourth), then classical capitalism most suits our purposes.

Within this overall conclusion, however, some more specific
observations can be made about the effects of official policies
towards the public sector, agriculture and trade policies in LDCs.
These are three areas, after all, in which policies have been pursued which were justified as likely to improve on the performance
of classical capitalism in promoting growth with equity. After
sustained experiments, what conclusions can we reach? The first is
that high public spending on housing, health, education, the social
services and public sector investment, though often designed to
assist the poor, will not necessarily do so and may worsen their
position. The reason is that such spending places heavy fixed costs
on the productive sector of the economy and thus retards overall
growth. As a result, though the *level* of spending may be high, its
rate of growth will be low and even negative. Melvyn Krauss
estimates that private-sector oriented LDCs tend to have higher
growth rates of public consumption (because they enjoy higher
rates of economic growth) than non-communist public-sector oriented LDCs. Thus, the growth rate of public sector consumption
in Hong Kong, South Korea and the Ivory Coast in the period
1970–79 ranged from 9.3 per cent to 10 per cent. India, Ghana
and Zaire, however, had rates ranging from 4.5 per cent to a

negative 2.2 per cent. These differential trends can be traced back
at least twenty years and, though there are obviously variations
(India, for instance, has improved its performance from a 1960's
public sector growth rate of a negative 1.5 per cent on average),
they seem to be accelerating. Over time, therefore, the absolute
levels of public provision enjoyed by the inhabitants of private
sector LDCs will tend to be higher than those available in public-
sector oriented LDCs.

Once governments are "locked into" high public spending on
either social entitlements or major public investment projects,
moreover, they find it extremely difficult to withdraw. This heavy
burden of spending then hinders, perhaps even prevents, LDCs
from adjusting to changed economic conditions. Two examples of
this are Uruguay and Costa Rica. Uruguay has been a welfare
state since 1914 with an eight-hour working day, restrictions on
female employment, free medical care and generous state pensions. In Mr. Barrett's words:

The most damaging case of abundant magnanimity is found in Uruguay where members of the military, if they have put in 15 years of
service, can retire as early as 32, where women with children can claim a
pension after only ten years service. . . . By 1972, 350,000 pensioners
had to be supported by a working population of less than a million.

In the 1960's, however, the world price of the country's leading
export, meat, fell sharply. With its income greatly reduced, the
government was able to finance this entrenched level of welfare
spending only by money creation. As a result, the Uruguayan peso
fell from 11 to the dollar in 1960 to 250 to the dollar in 1968.
Similarly, in the 1970's the Costa Rican welfare state saw the price
of its principal export commodity, coffee, fall sharply on the
world market. And, similarly, the Costa Ricans financed a continuing high rate of spending by a mixture of international loans
and money inflation. Indeed, inflation reached over 40 percent a
year in 1981. Yet inflation is particularly damaging to equity,
however defined. Not only does it enrich some groups and im-
poverish others on a largely arbitrary and often socially harmful
basis—borrowers benefit, lenders are penalized; householders
gain, home-buyers lose; purchasers of gold and antiques prosper
in comparison with industrial investors—but the poor and unorganized workers, which means most workers in LDCs, are especially vulnerable to rising prices and the unemployment which
follows in inflation's wake.

The usual justification for policies of high public spending and high taxation, of course, is that they are necessary to offset and correct the inegalitarian distribution of income attendant upon capitalist forms of development. But the case of Brazil, though often cited as an example of growth plus inequality, does not in fact provide unambiguous support for this argument. Admittedly, it is true that Brazilian economic growth in the 1960's increased relative income unequally as measured by the Gini coefficient and Lorenz curve. But Gary S. Fields has demonstrated that in fact such measurements are misleading. Their findings of greater inequality reflect an increased inequality *within the middle income range*, with incomes becoming more equal at the upper and lower ends of the scale. When he turned to examine how Brazil's growth had affected the *absolute* incomes of poor people, Professor Fields discovered that the income of every income class rose; that there was a small decline in the fraction of the economically active population classified as below the poverty line; that the percentage increase in income for those below the poverty line was greater than the increase for those not in poverty and may have been twice as high (68 per cent to 28 per cent); and that the poverty gap (i.e. the amount the incomes of the poor would have to rise in order to reach the poverty line) decreased by 40 per cent over the decade.

A similar picture emerges from the Chilean experiment with free markets. According to the Chilean economist Joacquin Lavin Infante, all income groups have benefitted in absolute terms from the economic growth in Chile since 1973. The percentage of families in extreme poverty rose initially from 20 per cent in 1973 to a peak of 35.5 per cent in 1976, reflecting the monetary squeeze that brought inflation under control, and then declined to 13.6 per cent in 1979. Families that are still below the poverty line, moreover, have seen their income increase by 48 per cent since 1973. It should be said here that the incomes of the non-poor increased by a still larger amount, namely 53 per cent, over the period so that, unlike Brazil, the distribution of income did become more unequal in an unambiguous way. However, the comparison suggests that this is by no means an inevitable feature of capitalist development. And since the lot of the poorest was improved in absolute terms, equity was served in both cases.

To sum up, then, public spending that is high as a percentage of GNP is usually an attempt to compensate for a non-existent problem (i.e. the worsening lot of the poor under capitalist development), tends to obstruct growth and thus over time to reduce absolute real resources available for social welfare, and creates a fixed financial burden which, at times of falling revenue, can only be paid for by inflation which, in turn, worsens the lot of the poor.

The second area worthy of particular consideration is agricultural policy. Until recently, LDC policies towards agriculture might best be characterized as "active neglect." Agricultural prices were held down and producers heavily taxed. A disguised but important form of agricultural taxation was the establishment of state export monopolies. Ostensibly set up to stabilize producer prices, they acted in fact as instruments of taxation by paying the producers far below world market prices. This broad approach was justified on the grounds that farmers did not respond readily to prices and income incentives so that little production would be lost and, secondly, it was said to be necessary to provide cheap food for urban areas, to combat inflation and to raise revenue for industrialization. None of these arguments were valid and the policies that flowed from them were generally harmful.

To begin with, as the distinguished agricultural economist T. W. Schultz has argued:

. . . .there is a long shelf of empirical evidence which shows that in Africa, when the export price of cocoa, coffee, cotton, peanuts or palm fruit become profitable, the supply response of farmers is highly elastic.

The reason for the widespread belief in the opposite was that many of the best opportunities in agriculture were concealed by deliberate price distortions. The first effect of this was that production fell, often sharply. Examples of this include: Nigeria in the 1950's and 1960's where palm fruit farmers received about half the world price, causing a drastic decline in production, Argentina from 1935 to 1965 when agricultural prices in the Pampas were held down with the result that agricultural output there rose only 6 per cent compared to 38 per cent outside, Ghana where price control of cocoa has caused production to fall so far that the country, the leading cocoa producer for 67 years, has now fallen behind Brazil and the Ivory Coast, and Uruguay where agriculture was taxed so heavily that it stagnated for a quarter of a century and, after 1950, began to decline in absolute terms. Not all the examples are negative, however. Shortly after coming to power, the Jayewardene government in Sri Lanka increased the price of rice and guaranteed farmers a minimum return. As a result, paddy output rose from an estimated 65 million bushels in 1976–77 to over 90 million bushels in 1979.

Secondly, such policies have been manifestly inequitable. In the case of the West African marketing boards covering cocoa, palm oil and groundnuts, levies on the producers represented an average of between one-third and one-half of the commercial value of the product from 1940 to 1962. As a proportion of the producers' incomes, this represented a very high rate of taxation, even though most of the producers were small-scale farmers with extremely low incomes. As noted in the above paragraph, moreover, the independent regimes in Ghana and Nigeria continued the same policies of heavy taxation via the export monopolies with even more disastrous results in terms of falling production and lost exports. (Ghana's cocoa exports today are about 60 percent of their 1962 level.) If the small-scale producers penalized by export monopolies were generally people of modest incomes, the beneficiaries were politicians, administrators and some middlemen who were prosperous by local standards. And similarly perverse effects were often produced by the control of food prices which is superficially an effective form of redistribution. In Chile in the mid-sixties, the artificially low price for meat led to scarcity and rationing, and in Egypt subsidized bread is fed to animals.

Nor did this policy fund industrial diversification according to theory. The large export surpluses and proceeds of agricultural taxation went to politicians, and their expenditure was generally influenced by political rather than economic considerations. All too often, they were wasted on prestige projects, expensive government buildings, subsidized industrial ventures and loss-making projects. Moreover, high agricultural taxation inhibited the spread of cash crops, the accumulation of private capital and the development of a prosperous peasantry and an independent middle-class, all of which would have provided the foundation for economic development of a different kind. And falls in agricultural production and exports (sometimes so severe that food, once exported, now had to be imported) caused a shortage of foreign exchange which further obstructed industrial development. In short, taxing agriculture to fund industrialization with no regard for farmers' incentives caused production to fall, had perverse effects on equity, did not produce sustainable industrial development and altogether represented jejeune economic snobbery of the most self-defeating kind.

Let us examine, finally, the policies of import substitution and tariff protection adopted by many LDCs in order to limit imports, accumulate foreign currency, and promote domestic industry. The long-term aim of such policies is, of course, to boost exports, but there are good reasons in economic theory to suggest that they will in fact cripple export industries. First, if the protected good is itself used in export goods, then a tariff will indirectly either raise export prices or lower export profits. In either event, exports will tend to fall. Secondly, even if the protected good is not used in exports, import substitution policies will nonetheless render the protected industry artificially profitable. It will thus attract resources away from export industries, again increasing their costs and reducing their profits. Finally, protection invites retaliation by other countries and thus closes off export markets.

There is also a considerable amount of empirical evidence which enables us to test this theory and to make comparisons between this protectionist approach and an outward-looking trade liberalization strategy. To begin with, countries like Taiwan, Chile and South Korea, which switched from protection to trade liberalization, have enjoyed remarkable increases in economic and export growth. Between 1962 and 1970, for instance, Taiwan's exports rose from 13.2 per cent of GNP to a striking 31.1 per cent. Over the same period, Korea's exports as a percentage of GNP went from 5.2 per cent to 15 per cent. The reason, according to Professor Krauss, was that import substitution had placed substantial implicit tax on exports. When import substitution was discontinued, this had the effect of removing the tax and exports expanded accordingly.

We reach a similar conclusion if we examine a cross-section of LDCs pursuing these two contrasting strategies. In a study of ten LDCs, Bela Balassa of the World Bank points out that South Korea, Singapore and Taiwan had remarkable growth rates both in exports of manufactured goods and, despite being poorly endowed with natural resources, in primary exports too. The share of exports in manufactured output, for instance, rose from 1 per cent in 1960 to 41 per cent in 1973 in South Korea; from 11 percent to 43 percent in Singapore over the same period; and from 9 percent to 50 percent in Taiwan for those years. But India, Chile and Uruguay, which followed a protectionist approach, saw their exports decline over the period.

To ensure that like is being compared with like, however, we should look at two similarly-placed countries pursuing these different strategies. In the study cited, Professor Balassa does indeed compare the Ivory Coast, which pursued a trade liberalisation approach, with its neighbor Ghana which adopted protection. He concludes:

. . . .differences in the policies applied may largely explain why, between 1960 and 1978, per capita incomes fell from $430 to $390 in Ghana, compared with an increase from $540 to $840 in the Ivory Coast in terms of 1978 prices.

The choice between these two trade approaches also has some interesting—and unexpected—consequences for equity. Anne Krueger, the vice-President elect of the World Bank, made a study of 12 LDCs in an attempt to discover the effects of different trade strategies on employment. Three findings were especially significant. First, export goods were considerably more labor-intensive then import-competing goods. In some cases—for instance, Columbia, Indonesia, Thailand and Uruguay—there was a two-to-one difference in labor requirements. Secondly, exports to developed countries were more labor-intensive than exports to other LDCs. Thus, Chile's exports to developed countries required about 40 per cent more labor per unit of domestic value-added than did her total exports. And, thirdly, export goods require less skilled labor than do import-competing goods. Here the figures ranged from 62 per cent (of skill units in exports compared to import-competing goods) in Tunisia to 99 per cent in the Ivory Coast. The fact that most countries are likely to increase the demand for unskilled workers is one that encourages exports to the developed world over import substitution. The poor thus benefit in employment terms from trade liberalization (as well, of course, as a gaining from the lower prices of imported goods.)

Who then benefits from import substitution policies? Workers and investors in the protected industries naturally gain. So do those who possess import licenses which, when imports generally are controlled, become a valuable property. If such licenses are allocated by officials, the likelihood is that they will be paid for by bribery or given as reward for political loyalty. Or, as Professor Krauss points out, they are sometimes distributed in accordance with some economic regulation as in India where import licenses were in effect granted to companies which increased investment. The net effect was to encourage additional excess capacity. In all these cases, the benefits of import substitution are notably inequitable. They are shared between politicians, administrators and businessmen who have close links with them. Since Professor Krueger estimates that such "rents" account for 15 per cent of Turkey's GNP, import substitution must be regarded as seriously inequitable quite apart from its obstructive effect on development.

The balance sheet for these policies—a large public sector, a policy of robbing agricultural Peter to pay industrial Paul, and import substitution and protectionism—must therefore be a critical one. They have not fulfilled the objectives laid down; they have generally obstructed rather than promoted development; and they have worsened the lot of the poor in society, while distributing benefits to other groups often on the most arbitrary basis. In line with Professor Papanek's findings, the alternative "capitalist" policies have a far more impressive record of economic and social improvement.

Influencing Cultural Influence

When we turn to the influence of customs and culture on development, we must at once acknowledge that there is comparatively little that government can directly and consciously control. For instance, it is often asserted that one cause of the British disease is the low esteem in which engineers are held in British society. Suppose that this is true. What can be done about it? It is not within the power of the British government to make people admire engineers. Cultural attitudes are shaped by processes that are much more profound, subtle, and slow-moving, and consequently unamenable to the ad hoc manipulation of government policy. Nonetheless, since the Industrial Revolution, numerous groups, tribes, nations and peoples have either adopted—or, under the stress of changed circumstances, discovered that they fortuitously possessed—customs, attitudes, aptitudes and social institutions that were conducive to development. So it is reasonable to speculate whether people's habits of thinking, feeling and acting are transformed over time in ways that promote economic development by one sort of economic system more profoundly and effectively than by another. For this purpose we can identify three types of economic systems, similar to the classification developed by Professor Papanek but also exhibiting certain important differences; the socialist, the mercantilist and the liberal.

In the socialist system, the government controls and directs all economic activity and attempts to plan in detail the future development of the economy. It claims to be restructuring society in the direction of equality with the ultimate aim of creating a new man, lacking in selfishness and willing to labor for the common good. Accordingly, it nationalizes major industries, directs investment, sets prices, controls imports and exports and levies high rates of taxation. In theory, the market is abolished and replaced by the national plan; and in practice, markets are restricted, marginal and unofficial ("black markets"). Because material incentives are either frowned upon or inadequate, the state has to resort to other forms of inducement: compulsory direction of

labor (both occupationally and geographically), work quotas or
"Stakhanovism"; moral incentives ("Hero of Labor" awards, etc.),
national campaigns to arouse enthusiasm for "building socialism,"
and punishment for "sabotage." The theory behind the sustained
compulsion to industrialize is perhaps most crisply expressed by
the fictional character Gletkin in Koestler's *Darkness at Noon:*

> In all other coutnries, the peasants had one or two hundred years to
> develop the habit of industrial precision and of the handling of ma-
> chines. Here they had only ten years. If we didn't sack them and shoot
> them for every trifle, the whole country would come to a standstill, and
> the peasants would lie down to sleep in the factory yards until grass grew
> out of the chimneys, and everything became as it was before.

The mercantilist state shares some features with socialism. It is
interventionist; it imposes tariffs; it directs investment; it selects
certain industries as the industrial leaders of the future; and it
uses inspirational methods to arouse popular support for economic objectives. Three differences mark it out from the socialist
model. First, it is not opposed to markets on principle. Indeed,
the mercantilist state is quite market-oriented and regards market
success as the test of the enterprises it sponsors. Secondly, it is not
egalitarian in intention. Some mercantilist societies have considerable disparities of wealth and income; and most have low-to-
moderate taxation. Finally, the mercantilist state arouses collective
national enthusiasm not for some revolutionary transformation of
man, but for the decidely prosaic objective of economic growth.
In pursuit of these goals, mercantilist societies energize their
citizens with both material incentives and national campaigns like
South Korea's "new community" (Saemaul) movement which is a
mixture of propaganda, "pep rallies" and state agricultural subsidies. Mercantilism, in short, is an attempt to organize the nation
for economic life like a football team and looks upon international
trade as a competition in which victory goes to those with the
largest balance of payments surplus, or the largest percentage rise
in exports.

It is this national goal which more than anything else distinguishes mercantilism from the liberal model. For the government of a liberal society confines itself to the traditional tasks of
governing, such as justice and policing, and leaves goals and
aspirations to the realm of individual life. The most typical economic "goal" of a liberal government is in fact a rather static one:

the maintenance of a stable currency. Otherwise, it is very market-oriented; it raises taxes sufficient to provide revenue for its limited interpretation of government; it eschews egalitarianism, redistribution, or any economic interventions that would distort the market; it maintains modest social services to relieve absolute poverty; and it allows completely free trade and capital movements.

Of course no state in the real world conforms wholly to any of these models. Reality, like cheerfulness, will keep breaking through. Even Hong Kong, often regarded as the model of liberal non-interventionism, has always subsidized low-income public housing and, more recently, it has expanded its social services to the point where the representative of the People's Republic of China has warned that this threatens its attractiveness to foreign investors. Cuba, the socialist paradigm, materially modified its "moral incentives" program in the early seventies. And mercantilist South Korea where the government controlled two-thirds of investible resources in its period of rapid acceleration of growth and guided investment through differential interest rates and credit availabilities, nonetheless adopted a liberal trade policy in the early sixties, as we have already seen. If countries are difficult to classify, so sometimes are policies. Are free trade zones liberal or mercantilist? The answer surely is that they can be both, depending on what went before and what is likely to come after. Thus the free trade zone in Sri Lanka represents a liberal breach of previous all-encompassing economic restrictions. In South Korea, on the other hand, such zones have been used to restrict the benefits of free trade to certain industries favored by the government.

Let us first examine the success of socialism in producing cultural attitudes favorable to development. Since the transformation of attitudes is a slow and uncertain process, this means examining the Soviet Union which has had almost seventy years for the process to work itself out. A second reason for insisting upon a longer time-scale is that, as Grace Goodell points out in "The Importance of Political Participation for Sustained Capitalist Development," uprooting traditional institutions and forcibly converting the peasantry into an industrial proletariat may produce economic growth which is initially spectacular but unable to sustain itself. Indeed, even the spectacular economic growth may be illusory. First, because Russian society was industrializing very rapidly in the last 30 years of Czarism, the industrialization after 1920 may well have represented "catch-up" growth after wartime destruction similar to the 1950's recovery of Western Europe. Secondly, official Soviet statistics cannot be relied upon even by the Politbureau. Robert Conquest points out in *We and They* that

a study actually published in Communist Poland . . . shows with great thoroughness that even the production of steel, the Soviet favourite item, did not increase significantly faster under Stalin than in Russia's pre-World-War I industrialization.

If this is true of the Soviet Union, it would suggest that the underlying social and attitudinal changes have not taken root and that, as soon as coercion is lessened, the populace sinks back into apathy and inertia.

The overall picture of the Soviet economy today would tend to support this gloomy thesis. After all the sacrifices and massive forced savings of the Soviet people, it is a primitive, low-wage, low-productivity economy, plagued by shortages and gluts of essential goods, and reliant on the capitalist world for innovation in everything from advanced computers to management science which, when acquired, it cannot adapt fully to its own uses. But the effect of the socialist system on people's initiative and enterprise is a rather more complicated matter.

To begin with, initiative and enterprise in the Soviet Union are simultaneously punishable offenses and absolutely necessary to the working of the economy. As Solzenhitsyn pointed out recently, in some cases socialism becomes a sort of Potemkin village. Robert Conquest tells the story of the Georgian economy in the 1970's, where a sort of underground capitalism operated on a major scale under the official facade. Enterprises fulfilled or over-fulfilled their plans because the director would obtain raw materials on the black market, sell part of the surplus likewise, and use the excess profits to pay illegally high wages. But when the Georgian Party First Secretary was ousted in a power struggle, an anti-corruption drive was instituted and such directors were arrested or dismissed. Georgia was accordingly reduced to the general level of Soviet inefficiency.

Such a system offers high rewards for risk-taking but also imposes severe penalties. There seem to be three attitudes to risk-taking elicited by this schizophrenic policy. First, those who find the idea of illegality exciting (and who in the West might be stimulated to enter the drug trade) will actually find their enterprising instincts elicited by the system. It is well-established that "spivs" and "fixers" play an irreplaceable role in the Societ economy. It could not survive without them.

Secondly, the mass of people seem to be deterred from showing any initiative at all. This is not a naturally strong instinct in most people—and the prospect of a spell in the Gulag would root it out quite effectively. In fact, the loss of morale of the Soviet people goes far beyond a reluctance to take economic initiatives. There is a chronic absenteeism from the factory (so severe that the police have recently been routinely questioning people in cinema and restaurants in mid-afternoon about their reasons for not being at work), laziness and low standards of work ("they pretend to pay us and we pretend to work"), widespread stealing from the government, severe alcoholism, a falling birth rate, a rising death rate and shorter life expectancy. Sunk in apathy, listlessness and cynicism, the bulk of the Russian people seem to be reverting to a pre-industrial pattern rather than advancing to a new social identity, falling into the stagnation associated with traditionalism without obtaining its warmth and comfort. In this context, the revival of Russian Orthodox Christianity may represent the nearest thing to initiative, a popular response to the feelings of hopelessness engendered by the Soviet Union, "the cry of a soul in a soulless world."

Finally, what of those calculating and cautious risk-takers who, in Western society, would be investors, successful managers and entrepreneurs? It seems that the system both stimulates and represses their entrepreneurial instincts. They see the various opportunities for profit and cost-saving within the economic system but are unwilling to risk the penalties attached to the really profitable opportunities. They suffer from what might be called entrepreneurial tease.

This is borne out by two studies. Mark Beissinger studied the reactions of three groups of experienced Soviet managers in their late thirties (representing industrial enterprises, supply organization and planning groups respectively) to a case study, "the Shchekino experiment" at the Plekhanov Institute in Moscow. This dealt with the use of material incentives to save labor, rationalize management structures and stimulate technological innovation. When the scheme was explained and briefly discussed, the managers in each group rated on a show of hands almost unanimously in favor of the project. Dr. Beissinger draws from this the moral that the Soviet manager is not opposed to innovation and change "when the decisions are taken out of their political and economic context." But when it emerged in further discussions that the adoption of such a scheme would increase the factory's dependence on the planning bureaucracy, or reduce surplus manpower available to perform unexpected demands from the planning bureaucracy, and in general complicate the manager's relationship with the political and economic system the managers overwhelmingly voted "no." Managerial reluctance to innovate seems to be due to a rational calculation of the costs and benefits. And the case study "taught" them not to eliminate excess labor or introduce greater efficiency, even though they could see that this was economically sensible in a wider context.

Secondly, Zvi Gitelman has carried out a comparative study of how Soviet and American Jews adapted to life as emigrants to Israel. The Soviet Jews in the sample were urban and well-educated, generally in the natural sciences, and of course Jewish, which perhaps limits their usefulness as a guide to Soviet society more generally. Nonetheless, there are some results which seem both significant and difficult to interpret. The Soviet Jews felt that the Israeli government should provide them with more generous welfare services, whereas the American Jews were inclined to be critical of the level of welfare. The Soviet Jews generally entered the public sector; the Americans chose private enterprise. The Soviet Jews rose quickly in their jobs, partly because they had technical skills which transferred easily to Israeli society; the Americans were initially less successful because they tended to be in such professions as the law and could not immediately obtain the same income and status as in the United States. Finally, after three years, American Jews were earning higher incomes than Soviet Jews, but *both* were earning more than the general Israeli average. Both groups, then, adapted successfully to Israeli society. But the American Jews showed attitudes of greater self-reliance and initiative than the Soviet Jews whose risk-taking ability had not been eradicated by Soviet society but who had learnt to expect a high degree of economic security from the state.

A short postscript on the fate and significance of Cuba's moral incentives is perhaps justified while we are on the topic of socialism. These included: public praise by Cuba's leaders, medals, buttons, diplomas, honorable mentions in factory bulletins, Heroes of Moncada and Heroic Guerilla awards, election to the Communist Party, and an appearance with Fidel Castro in the local Plaza de la Revolucion. Che Guevara propounded moral incentives as likely to lead to a higher consciousness that would in turn lead to economic development, maintaining that "the development of consciousness does more for the development of production in a relatively short time than material incentives do."

In fact, the use of "voluntary" labor actually inculcated attitudes harmful to development. Rene Dumont pointed out that, since volunteer coffee harvestors picked only one-twelfth of what a good harvester picks, they did not even cover the cost of their food, lodging and transportation. Thus, moral incentives confused production and consumption—something recognized by the regular workers who made "uncomplimentary remarks." Secondly, the workers responded to moral incentives by paying themselves in the coinage of leisure. Absenteeism became chronic (especially since there were no goods to buy with whatever money one did earn). The result was that the sugar harvest of 1970 failed to meet its goal of ten million tons and the moral incentives program was abandoned. Wages were tied to productivity; more consumer goods made available; and legal penalties introduced against loafing and absenteeism.

To sum up, then, the effect of socialism on cultural attitudes that affect development has been clearly harmful. The socialist theory of altruistic incentives has proved utopian and perverse. And socialism in practice has either deadened initiative, diligence, risk-taking and self-reliance, or made it prudent to avoid exercising such virtues which are thus confined to the shadow world of corruption, black markets and petty criminality. The consequences for equity hardly need spelling out.

When we compare the liberal and mercantilist models, a complicating factor intrudes. As we have already seen, a tribe or nation may already possess, quite fortuitously, the cultural attitudes that promote development. Japan is an interesting example. It has greatly prospered in its post-war mercantilist phase. But it first embarked on economic development, and rapidly entered the modern world in the late 1860's after the Meiji restoration under liberal policies of free enterprise and low tariffs. If so, the question becomes not whether a given system will promote such virtues, but whether it will *erode* them. That socialism erodes developmental qualities is clear from the above account. We therefore have to compare liberalism and mercantilism in two sets of circumstances: when the qualities conducive to economic development are present and when they are not.

It was under liberal governments, of course, that the modern economic development first occurred in most Western industrialized countries—notably Britain where the Industrial Revolution first "took off." Large areas of the developing world also made substantial economic progress, beginning from often primitive poverty, under liberal regimes in the 19th and early 20th centuries. Argentina had achieved a European standard of living by the 1920's and parts of the British Empire where *laissez-faire* policies were pursued, for instance Malaya, were transformed economically. And today countries like the Ivory Coast in Africa have gone from backward conditions to relative wealth in a generation under broadly liberal policies.

The process of development under liberalism is, however, difficult to trace and describe. It is slow-moving, piecemeal, local, and—to an outsider—often mysterious or undetectable. Compared to the dramatic and trumpeted policies of mercantilism (with its "White Revolutions" and "Saemaul" programs), the role of a liberal government is decidedly humble. As Grace Goodell points out in her essay, the government must provide a climate of stability and predictability in which people can make long-term investment and work decisions because they know that their property will not be expropriated or their enterprises ruined by some arbitrary change in official policy. Because governments can rarely be trusted to restrain themselves, this implies that a liberal government will tend to exist only when a society already possesses institutions strong enough to place limits on government power. Perhaps, indeed, the essence of liberalism is that it is a regime of rules applicable to all—including the government.

The second essential contribution that liberalism makes to development is that it maintains an open economy—free trade, free capital movement and free immigration. These are powerful agents in gradual social and cultural transformation. Free trade means new goods, new services, and new incentives to economic effort. Immigration means that different skills and aptitudes are suddenly present in the society. Since immigrants tend to be the sort of people who possess attitudes, habits and skills favorable to development, their presence in the society itself suggests that there are possibilities different from traditional ways of living. Peddlers, small traders and middlemen, like the Asians in East Africa, are especially important in spreading new attitudes and, furthermore, in forging economic links between different groups in primitive society. Finally, foreign investment means training in new skills, a larger market for local products and increased demand for local labor.

Such new influences are naturally disturbing. But the disturbance wrought by commercial contacts (since they attempt to elicit voluntary cooperation and must be geared to local conditions, conduct and resources if they are to succeed) is partial, gradual and tentative. Traditional attitudes are not suddenly disrupted by imposed change. On the contrary, a traditional people are drawn slowly but surely into economic development. Their attitudes, responding to new incentives and new opportunities, change in line with economic development like infrastructure. Indeed, a sort of mental infrastructure is gradually constructed.

The corollary to this is that liberalism cannot promise quick results. As I argued above, a people may prefer to remain poor but authentic or, more likely, while desiring material advance, may nonetheless cling to attitudes which obstruct it. India, in the period between the Mutiny and 1914, is an example. Governed by a colonial power which pursued strict *laissez-faire*, India nonetheless failed to develop in this period. Indian society remained economically inert compared to the extensive development of other parts of the British Empire like West Africa and Malaya. One possible explanation is that the caste system, with its rigid specifications of permissible activities for particular castes, was an obstacle to development—but one to which the Indians were strongly attached. And, secondly, the resistance it offered to change was strengthened by British concern not to offend Indian religious or cultural sensibilities (except where, like suttee and thugee, they were themselves an affront to *British* religious feeling). Missionaries were not admitted to the country until 1816. The liberal model therefore can be summed up as offering a successful transformation of cultural attitudes in favor of development, but not a quick one.

This is the exact opposite of what mercantilism achieves. Countries like Iran under the Shah, Czarist Russia and Turkey, which have at various times pursued a "forced march" policy of industrialization, all show a surprisingly similar pattern. This is one of initial dramatic advances, at least in terms of statistical growth in GNP, followed by profound discontent, upheaval, and revolutionary violence, after which the economic performance declines and the populace becomes a listless apathetic mass capable of being aroused only by force and threats. This rake's progress has some resemblances to socialist industrialization—not altogether unfittingly since, although it has most often been followed by rightwing regimes, it is based upon a set of ideas very similar to Marxism. Essentially, it assumes that once modern economic life is forced upon a people and they are compelled to live in modern institutions, they will develop appropriate cultural attitudes and become modern. Consciousness will be determined by the stage of production. This is, of course, the central fallacy of mercantilism.

Let us look at the example of Iran under the Shah. He set out to use Iran's vast oil revenues to turn the country into a modern industrialized state. As Melvyn Krauss demonstrates, this industrialization was overwhelmingly statist in character. Over the period 1959–75, total consumption increased by a factor of 6, but public consumption by a factor of 12. Similarly public investment grew by a factor of 14 compared to an increase in total investment of a factor of 9. In addition, the Shah embarked on land reform, established a network of model villages, nationalized industry, and carried out ambitious welfare state measures such as free education and national health insurance. The scope of these measures can be judged from the fact that government expenditures on social welfare per member of the active population rose from $150 in 1972 to $700 in 1976.

The initial results of this program were apparently excellent. The rate of growth of real GNP, which ran at an average of 7.5 per cent in the period 1959–68, increased to an average 17.6 per cent for the period 1968–75. Similar figures for growth in real consumption were 7.6 per cent and 13.8,per cent respectively. Professor Krauss argues that, even from the standpoint of pure economic policy, this policy was profoundly erroneous underneath its facade of GNP growth. It created a large capital intensive sector dependent upon high tariff barriers and it penalized the competitive traditional sector which used simple technologies, cheap labor and re-cycled goods. It was still more disastrous in social and cultural terms. In the first place, unlike socialism, mercantilism mercifully does not eliminate the social groups it dispossesses and demotes. In Iran, the clergy and landowners lost their estates in land reform; the small business class was subjected to burdensome restrictions; and even some very wealthy people had been forced at some time to surrender their property to the Pahlavi family at a "favorable" price. Such groups were thus a permanent threat to the Throne and, when trouble came, made common cause with the mullahs.

More importantly, as Grace Goodell points out in her important essay "How the Shah Destabilized Himself", the Shah's policies of insustrialization and bureaucratic control undermined all the traditional institutions of Iranian society, including the family, religion and the authority of village elders. This sometimes reached almost unbelievable heights of bureaucratic *hubris*, as when officials refused to allow sons to accompany their parents when the latter were instructed to move home to new model villages. Moreover, the new bureaucratic institutions, that were intended to replace traditional bodies, fulfilled almost none of their functions. They did not represent the peasants' interests to the state or the world outside the village; they did not enable the villagers to reach agreed collective decisions—indeed they obstructed any decisions the villagers made; they only served to *control* the villagers in the interests of the Shah. So traditional customs had been undermined and exposed to contempt, but nothing had replaced them. People had been subjected to total and abrupt change (often being forced to move from the land into a modern factory), but not gradually initiated into new ways of thinking and feeling by the influence of voluntary commercial contacts. Modernity was experienced simply as an assault. The London *Financial Times* described a very understandable reaction:

For the new urban dweller, especially the industrial worker, whose memories of tranquil, slow-moving village life are still fresh, the pace of change has been upsetting and alarming. Thus the anti-Shah rampage in Tabriz a few weeks ago rapidly took on an anti-secular character. Eyewitnesses spoke of villagers pouring into town with their 'martyrs' shirts' on, ready to die, furious at examples of Western permissiveness.

There are examples of other responses to mercantilist development. But mercantilism has yet to transform attitudes in a direction favorable to development as liberalism has done in numerous cases.

We now turn to the second question: is a liberal or a mercantilist model more likely to *erode* cultural attitudes favorable to development? Difficulties at once arise. For countries which have suffered economic decline over a long period, notably England, have generally moved in a mercantilist direction during the course of the decline. England, for instance, introduced tariffs, agricultural managed markets and some cartelization in 1916 and intensified the process in the nineteen thirties. But was this a cause of the decline or a response to it? And if it was a response, did it arrest or accelerate the decline? Similarly on attitudes. There seems little doubt that British cultural attitudes towards development have become less favorable in this century. Over-manning and restrictive labor practices have grown. But is this a continuous response to the harshness of the nineteen thirties slump? Or a rational exploitation of the readiness of governments to subsidize and bail out inefficient industries? (Or, as they say, both?)

When we turn to comparisons of the liberal and mercantilist states in Asia which have the benefits of a "neo-Confucianism" apparently conducive to growth, a different problem awaits. In the relatively short time since their birth, they all seem to be doing well. Hong Kong has developed as remarkably as South Korea and *vice versa*. There do not seem to be, as yet, any signs of the cultural advantages eroding in either case.

But there is a third factor, sometimes attributable to cultural factors, sometimes to official policies, which might upset this apparent balance of virtues. This is what Mancur Olson, in an important book, calls the rise of distributional coalitions. There are all manner of groups which seek to raise their joint income by monopolizing some activity, raising its price, curtailing entry into the market and blocking alternative sources of supply—lobbies, guilds, labor unions, chambers of commerce, aristocracies, castes, national industries, etc. Such coalitions can be kept in being by official policies—tariffs, subsidies, and internal tolls, as had existed in Japan before its Meiji restoration. Or they may be the result of cultural factors like the religious caste system in India. But they will tend to have certain consequences. Professor Olson draws out nine implications for society of such coalitions, of which three are especially relevant to this discussion:

1) Stable societies with unchanged boundaries tend to accumulate more collusions and organizations for collective action over time.
2) On balance, special-interest organizations and collusions reduce efficiency and aggregate income in the societies in which they operate and make political life more divisive.
3) Distributional coalitions slow down a society's capacity to adopt new technologies and to reallocate resources in response to changing conditions, and thereby reduce the rate of economic growth.

England's decline is, according to this argument, an effect of its long political stability, which has encouraged the development of a network of distributional coalitions with damaging consequences for growth. Contrariwise, the growth of West Germany since 1945 is the result, first, of the destruction of such institutions in war and, second, of the wider economic boundaries achieved by the formation of the EEC in 1956, within which purely West German coalitions no longer enjoyed monopoly power.

This ingenious theory is relevant to liberalism and mercantilism in two ways. First, it offers significantly different accounts of the success of Hong Kong and South Korea. South Korea's rise can be put down to its severe civil war which cleared the ground of distributional coalitions—or, to what is a historical accident, since nations will not engage in destructive wars simply to avoid the rise of lobbies. But Hong Kong has enjoyed what is, by Asian standards, the long stability of British colonial rule. Its continued dynamism is the result of the policies—namely, free trade and massive immigration which would have jointly overwhelmed any conceivable distributional coalition. It follows that Hong Kong's success is much easier to emulate than South Korea's. Indeed, by liberalizing its trade policy in the sixties, South Korea has partly emulated it.

The implications of Professor Olson's theory are self-evidently hostile to mercantilism. In the first place, it condemns tariffs which he regards as "the mother of all manner of combinations and collusions." Secondly, mercantilism is a system under which the government allocates large sums to industry for such purposes as the promotion of exports. Yet the theory warns that coalitions are certain to organize in order to capture such largesse for themsleves. Mercantilist policies are, so to speak, an incentive to such combinations. But especially relevant to our present discussion is the fact that mercantilism promotes cultural values and attitudes which look favorably on economic collusion, organization and cartelization. While cartels exist at the government's behest, to promote exports etc., that may not matter much. But it will be a real obstacle to development when such organizations begin to "reduce efficiency. . . . and make political life more divisive." Even when mercantilism is assisted by cultural attitudes initially favorable to development, therefore, there is still a worm in the apple.

In relation to cultural transformation, equity raises very different considerations to those encountered previously. Opposition to the gradual transformation wrought by liberalism comes from two-ill-matched groups—those socialists and mercantilists who hanker after a more dramatic and controlled transformation, and those anthropological romantics who regret any cultural influences on backward societies as harmful contamination. Both groups, moreover, have one feeling in common. They look upon the nation's or tribe's habits of thinking, feeling and acting as something to be controlled by the government or ruling group, whether for protective or transforming purposes. Government is to be, according to both views, the moral tutor of the nation's soul, engaged in a sort of national character building. The anthropological romantics certainly—and the mercantilists and socialists probably—take this view in part because they consider that the impact of liberal commercialism is so powerful that no people can choose to resist it. It would be simply overwhelmed.

But there are several reasons for doubting this. There is the example of India, already mentioned, which suggests that when people are firmly attached to religious or cultural institutions, they cling onto them successfully. Caste remains an important influence in Indian life even today. And so, despite its self-evident incompatibility with modern economic logic, does Hindu reverence for the cow. People can pick and choose, moreover, which aspects of modernization they wish to adopt. We are familiar in advanced societies with the scientist who on Sunday in church assents without embarrassment to "creation science." Such compartmentalization is common in developing countries also. An observer of Asian religious life points out that "in the Christian case the young people with whom I had the most sustained discussions were overwhelmingly Bible-believing evangelicals with a nearly equal fascination with mechanics, computers and engineering." Finally, we know that groups differ in their acclimatization to modernity. This suggests a degree of voluntary choice as well as of adaptive capacity. Equity would therefore seem to be best served by leaving the choice of cultural adaptation to the peoples involved rather than allowing governments, whether socialist or mercantilist, to exercise the intrusive coercion required to impose on people a new cultural identity.

Implications for Policy

In terms of both official policies and cultural factors, taking both development and equity into account, the broad conclusion seems to be that a liberal economic system offers the best results. It would be nice to end at that point with a sigh of relief at the absence of contradictions. Unfortunately, there is one general problem still left to solve. In accordance with his criticism of India's failure to develop under laissez-faire, Professor Olson's theory points to a regime of active liberalism that would break up and scatter the distributional coalitions that ultimately inhibit growth. But this prescription conflicts with the stability and predictability which, as Dr.Goodell points out in her chapter in this volume, are necessary for sustained capitalist development. It also sits unhappily alongside the fact that such groups are the building blocks of development, indeed that the forging of links between them is the process of development. Professor Olson acknowledges this himself, stating:

The dense network of distributional coalitions that eventually emerges in stable societies is harmful to economic efficiency and growth, but so is instability. . . . instability diverts resources that would otherwise have gone into productive long-term investments into forms of wealth that are more easily protected, or even into capital flights to more stable environments. On the whole, stable countries are more prosperous than unstable ones. . . . but . . . the most rapid growth will occur in societies that have lately experienced upheaval but are expected nonetheless to be stable for the forseeable future.

Squaring this circle involves two sets of policies. The first is the maintenance of free trade, free movement of capital and, if possible, free immigration. Should this be done, organizations and linkages in between them may be established with useful results in spreading economic knowledge and political participation. But any attempt they make to monopolize some activity will be curtailed, indeed swamped, by the effects of a liberal trade regime. Secondly, since a fully liberal trading system increases the climate of short-term economic instability for companies, unions, investors and entrepreneurs, and prevents them organizing to restrain that uncertainty, there should be a regime of rules, embodied in legislation, which would limit politically-inspired instability. This would, for instance, provide security for savers and investors against political expropriation, rule out subsidies for particular companies and industries, since these undermine their competitors, place restraints on the government's powers of money creation to forestall inflation and the numerous secondary instabilities it produces, and strictly enforce contracts, including those to which the government is itself a party. Such a regime must also include provisions to reinforce the effects of trade liberalization, described above, with strong anti-trust laws and restraints on the ability of professions to restrict entry.

In the real Third World of import controls and economic favoritism, such proposals sound utopian. Governments do not readily renounce powers to benefit themselves and their political allies. We should therefore be prepared to consider such second-best solutions as free trade zones, entrepreneurial education and encouragement for the small business informal sector. To give some encouragement to governments to follow the path of economic virtue, we should examine ways of re-directing aid so that it becomes an incentive to policies promoting productive growth.

Free trade zones are already a part of the development strategy in several LDCs, notably Sri Lanka, and the Newly Industrialising Countries (NICs). In 1975, for instance, there were three free trade zones in Taiwan, containing more than 260 factories and employing over 160,000 workers. Total capitalization came to about $160 million, of which $105 million was outright foreign investment, $16 million Overseas Chinese investment and about $29 million from joint ventures. The total value of exports from these zones came to over $500 million and was equivalent to 10 per cent of all Taiwanese exports. Although such zones represent a departure from ideal liberalism and cannot threaten distributional coalitions because they produce exclusively for exports, they nonetheless might lead otherwise skeptical governments to experiment with trade liberalism.

It is often argued that education is a good investment for LDCs because it pays in economic terms and helps to modernize attitudes. The evidence does indeed suggest that primary education benefits LDCs in these ways. But the higher one goes up the education scale, the more doubtful the proposition seems. First, does secondary or vocational education actually fit people for the world of work? Lisa Peattie quotes several studies which show that the graduates of technical institutions are not thought by employers to be more competent than others who have never had the schooling, but have merely had a number of years of working experience and, secondly, that most technical graduates are not working in jobs that utilize their expensive training. Secondly, the training also gives them an exaggerated idea of their status, an unrealistic expectation of immediate or early promotion, and a reluctance to engage in necessary but "demeaning" manual work. Education of this kind is a form of consumption rather than an aid to greater production. "On the job training" would almost certainly be both better work experience and likely to inculcate more realistic attitudes. A possible reform, therefore, is to redirect some educational spending to the private business sector in the form of training vouchers which a young person could exchange for an apprenticeship or similar scheme.

Finally, the small business "informal sector" both makes economic opportunities available to those who might otherwise lack them, in particular women and the unemployed, and helps to diffuse enterprising attitudes and skills throughout the community. Small loans at favorable rates to this sector, while technically a breach of liberal non-discrimination, would be a miniscule cost in comparison with overall state spending programs. But the best assistance that would be given to this sector would be a sensible macro-economic policy.

How, finally, can Western industrialized countries encourage the broad liberal policies here discussed and recommended? Opening Western markets to Third World products (i.e. reducing tariffs, abandoning the pressure for "voluntary quotas" on imports, and ceasing to subsidize Western industries threatened by

Third World competition) would be very considerable incentive. Not only would it greatly increase the market for their goods, but it would also reduce prices to Western consumers. A secondary policy might be re-directing aid along liberal lines. Thus a USAID grant might be made to pay for the temporary deficit following a tax reduction, or to finance transitional subsidies to agriculture to compensate for allowing agricultural interest rates to increase, or to pay for income maintenance programs that mitigated the impact of withdrawing food subsidies on the urban poor, or to finance the re-training of workers displaced by the reduction of import substitution policies.

In various ways, therefore, development with equity can be stimulated and encouraged by "the magic of the marketplace." But a final cautionary note is perhaps called for. Magical though it be, the marketplace cannot transform every Chad into a Hong Kong. It can only make the distinctly limited promise of a better Chad. Indeed, if all the Chads were to pursue the liberal vision, then Hong Kong would itself suffer some relative deprivation. After all, the paradox at present is that Hong Kong enjoys something of a monopoly profit in competition.

Notes on Contributors

Peter Berger is University Professor at Boston University and author of *The Capitalist Revolution* (Basic Books, 1986).

James O'Leary is Associate Professor and Chairman of the Department of Politics at Catholic University.

Nicholas Eberstadt is a Visiting Fellow at Harvard University's Center for Population Studies and a Visiting Scholar at the American Enterprise Institute for Public Policy Research.

Grace Goodell is Associate Professor and Director of the Department of Anthropology at the Johns Hopkins University School of Advanced International Studies.

Laura L. Nash is a project director on public/private partnerships at Harvard University's Center for Business and Government.

Alan M. Kantrow is Senior Editor of the *Harvard Business Review* and a Director of the Winthrop Group, business history consultants.

Jason Brown is a Private Enterprise Officer with the United States Agency for International Development in Barbados.

Myron Weiner is the Ford International Professor of Political Science at M.I.T.

Gustav Renis is Frank Altschul Professor of International Economics at Yale University.

John Fei is Professor of Economics at Yale University.

Gustav F. Papanek is Professor of Economics and Director of the Center for Asian Development Studies at Boston University.

Brian Griffiths is Head of the Policy Unit, Office of the Prime Minister, England.

Rachel J. Griffiths is a sociologist.

John O'Sullivan is Associate Editor of the London Times and was formerly a Fellow of the Institute for Politics at Harvard University.